rn this book

DEVOLUTION
IN
CONTEXT

DEVOLUTION IN CONTEXT:

Regional, Federal & Devolved Government in the Member States of the European Union

W John Hopkins, BA (Hons), PhD

Lecturer in Law, University of Hull

Cavendish
Publishing
Limited

London • Sydney

First published in Great Britain 2002 by Cavendish Publishing Limited,
The Glass House, Wharton Street, London WC1X 9PX, United Kingdom
Telephone: + 44 (0) 20 7278 8000   Facsimile: + 44 (0) 20 7278 8080
Email: info@cavendishpublishing.com
Website: www.cavendishpublishing.com

© Hopkins, J   2002

British Library Cataloguing in Publication Data

Hopkins, John
Devolution in context: regional, federal and devolved government in the EU
1 Decentralisation in government – European Union countries 2 Local
government – European Union Countries 3 Federal government – European
Union Countries 4 Constitutional law – European Union Countries
5 Administrative law – European Union Countries
I Title
342.4

ISBN 1 85941 637 3

Printed and bound in Great Britain

To Karen

ACKNOWLEDGMENTS

There have been so many individuals involved with the development of this project over a number of years that I could not possibly mention them all here. Nevertheless, there are a few who deserve special mention. In particular I owe a great deal to my former supervisor at the University of Sheffield, Professor Ian Harden, for all his support and help in developing the research which became the basis of this volume.

Thanks also go to my 'Devolution and Federalism' final year students (in particular Jessica Northey and Mike Varney) at the University of Hull Law School, who have given me much salient comment and inspiration.

Thanks also to Dr Steven Brown for his consistently useful comments on my work and Dr Karen Grant, my wife, for her help and advice in reading the final version and for keeping me sane throughout the process.

And thanks, finally, to my parents, without whom none of this would have been possible!

CONTENTS

TABLE OF CASES

TABLE OF LEGISLATION

Netherlands

Portugal

Spain

Sweden

United Kingdom

United States

Treaties and Conventions

International Treaties

INTRODUCTION

The past half century has seen two inextricably linked constitutional revolutions in Western Europe. The first, the development of a *sui generis* European level of government, has progressed in fits and starts over the past 50 years. This revolution has witnessed the creation of pan-European institutions, to the extent that European Community legislation and decisions of the European Court of Justice are supreme within the functional parameters of the Community. Notwithstanding the protestations of some constitutional theorists, in a practical European context national sovereignty is dead.

In tandem with these developments at the supranational level, a second revolution, little noticed in the UK, has occurred at the sub-national level. This regional revolution is the subject of this volume. In 1939, Europe was a patchwork of unitary states. In the 20 year interlude between the collapse of the old order in 1919 and the resumption of hostilities, only three states had experimented with federal or regional structures. The ill-fated Weimar and Austrian federal republics lasted less than 14 years, while the Spanish republic lasted a mere three. In contrast, the period since 1945 has seen a burgeoning of the federal principle and the decline of the classical unitary model in Western Europe. The regional state, with a democratic level of governance in the space between the national and the local, is no longer the exception; it is the norm.

By the 1990s, only the UK had bucked this trend amongst the large Member States of the EU. Aloof in its defence of the unitary model despite the clamouring of its periphery, it finally succumbed in 1998, with the passing of the devolution Acts (the Scotland Act 1998, the Government of Wales Act 1998 and the Northern Ireland Act 1998). Despite the apocalyptic warnings of those who opposed such change, the sky did not fall on our heads. If these prophets of doom had spared a moment to glance across the channel, they would have realised the ridiculous nature of their warnings (although in many cases they reflected an emotional opposition to the ideals of devolution rather than any rational criticism of it). The failure of the UK to notice the shift from unitary to federal and regional forms of government that has slowly and rather erratically swept across Western Europe was the starting point of the research that has developed into this volume.

The UK general election of 1992 was marked in Scotland by a constitutional debate. Unusually for a UK election, the Scottish electorate appeared genuinely concerned about the constitutional question. Although opinion polls consistently placed constitutional reform way down the list of priorities, this created a false impression. Few people would give constitutional change as their reason for voting, but discussions on most issues would at some point return to the question of devolution or the status quo. Education may have been important for the Scottish people, but part of that issue was who should run it.

During this period, I was struck by the arguments of those who opposed constitutional change, many of which revolved around the charge that any change would inexorably lead to the disintegration of the UK. Had I not stood in the *Landtag* of Hamburg only a few months before? Germany seemed to be doing rather well, despite its federal system. Nearly a decade on, devolution has happened and the UK is no longer a unitary state, yet knowledge of the systems and operation of European regional governments remains limited. This is at least partly evidenced by the term 'devolution', which no other federal or regionalised system uses or recognises. The impression given is that the UK is different.

This volume aims to challenge this idea. The UK's system of devolution is certainly distinct, but it is not isolated. Instead, it takes its place amongst the regional and federal systems of the European Union. The devolved institutions fit into an already constructed regional tier. For a true understanding of how the devolved institutions of Wales, Scotland and Northern Ireland (and possibly those of England) will operate, and what they can learn from the more mature regions of the European Union, we must place devolution in context.

As a result of the devolution debate, interest in regional systems beyond the shores of the United Kingdom has been stirred. Even in England, politicians, policy makers, academics and their students are beginning to take an interest in a subject that had been something of a specialism both in the policy field and in academia. On the back of this renewed interest, a number of worthy volumes examining the regional level in Europe and beyond have emerged. Notable amongst these have been the works of Keating (1998) and several collected works, particularly those edited by Keating and Jones (1995), Jeffrey (1997) and Sharpe (1993). These works are of a high standard, and significant reference will be made to them in the following pages; however, none has undertaken such a study from the constitutional viewpoint, and all assume a degree of knowledge which most readers lack. This book does not attempt to supplant these volumes. Instead it intends to give readers a comparative introduction, from a constitutional viewpoint, to the various types of regional, federal and devolved systems that operate in the European Union.

To achieve this, the volume attempts to map out the regional level of government across the 15 Member States of the European Union. To some extent this distinction is arbitrary, as these 15 will soon be joined by a number of new states. Those new members that endured 50 years of communist rule represent a different tradition. Although the end of dictatorship in the west (in the 1940s and the 1970s) generally led to regional decentralisation in the name of democracy, the regional level in the east has remained weak, where it exists at all. Although this may prove a significant challenge to the European Union in the future, at present these states add little to a discussion of devolution in Europe. It is beyond the scope of this volume to examine the impact of these states on the regional revolution.

Although this text approaches the subject from a constitutional standpoint, and has emerged from courses taught within the University of Hull Law School, it is not a legal textbook in the traditional mould. If one wishes to understand the operation of government, one must travel far beyond the traditional limits of legal study. The parliament of the United Kingdom may have the constitutional authority to make law for China, but its practical ability to do so must be questioned. The same principle is true when examining the operation and impact of the regional tier. For this reason, the work draws upon history, politics and economics amongst other disciplines in its attempt to map out the complex regional systems of the 15 Member States as accurately as possible. Given the limits of space, there is a degree of personal discretion involved in this analysis. Emphasis is placed on the factors that, in the opinion of this author, constitute the key features in the respective systems.

The volume itself is divided into three distinct parts. The first three chapters introduce the theoretical and historical concepts which underpin regional government and its growth in Western Europe. Chapter 1 focuses on theoretical issues that surround the sovereign nation-state itself. Prime amongst these is the question of why we automatically assume that the national level is the natural unit of territorial governance. This chapter also examines the difficulties that face the traditional unitary state, and asks whether regions offer a way of saving the state or an alternative to it. Where does the regional or federal level fit within this nationally dominated view of territorial governance?

Chapter 2 leads on from this critique of the status quo to examine the federal and regional alternatives. The first question to be addressed is what we mean by the region and regional government. This chapter also briefly examines the key arguments in favour of regional government from the 18th century up to the subsidiarity debates of the 1990s. Chapter 3 takes these theoretical arguments for regional and federal government and puts them in a more practical context. The regional revolution may be a Europe-wide phenomenon, but the reasons behind it vary significantly between individual Member States. This chapter examines the indirect drivers behind this regional revolution. These do much to explain the systems and institutions that comprise the regional level even when the original purposes of the regional governments no longer define their primary role.

The second part of the book maps out the institutions and structures that comprise the regional tier in the European Union. The intention is to give the reader an understanding of the basic structures that frame the regional level in each of the Member States of the EU that possess this tier. For the purposes of analysis, these structures are examined within three broad constitutional types of regional and federal structure. Chapter 4 looks at the three formally federal structures (Belgium, Austria and Germany). Chapter 5 examines regions which are founded in the constitutions of the Member State (those of Italy and

Spain, the autonomous regions of Portugal, and the Åland islands of Finland), while Chapter 6 deals with those regions which form part of the local government structure (in France, Scandinavia and the Netherlands). Chapter 7 concludes this section by placing the United Kingdom's system of devolution within the context of existing European examples. The analysis presented in this section of the book allows particular aspects of regional autonomy to be explored in the remainder of the work.

The concluding part of this volume focuses on particular aspects of regional autonomy across the European Community as a whole. The focus in this part is comparative, and explicitly examines the formal autonomy that the various regions possess in the light of political, social and economic realities. In some cases, this can show regions such as those with local government responsibilities extending their influence beyond that of their formal role. In the majority, though, these elements are restrictions upon the formal autonomy that may be assumed to exist at the regional level on the basis of their constitutional or statutory provisions.

The key issue here is autonomy. By focusing on this rather slippery concept the volume follows a very different path from those whose authors have relegated the question of autonomy to the sidelines (Keating, 1998). In their analysis, regional autonomy is not the key to understanding the regional tier. This argument is explicitly challenged by this author. To understand the role of the regional tier in the European Union it is important to understand the complex interrelationships between regions and other levels of government. Nevertheless, the development of co-operative federalism that the increase in intergovernmental relationships entails brings with it consequences for regional autonomy that are very relevant to any discussion about the regional tier.

If the decisions taken at the regional level are undertaken collaboratively with other regions, on a nationwide basis for example, are these decisions truly regional? What rationale is there for a region if it cannot undertake policy independently? A policy taken nationally by regional leaders is not a regional policy; it is a national policy undertaken by a forum not constituted for the purpose, and often lacking transparency, accountability and legitimacy. This phenomenon is one which has been observed increasingly in Canada (Simeon, 2000) as well as in the regional systems of the European Union and at the European level itself. Although the extent of co-operation is a significant element in an understanding of the regional level, the degree of autonomy remains important in assessing the effectiveness of the region in achieving its democratic rationale.

The final chapter aims to draw together what has gone before, and offers some thoughts on the future of the regional tier in Europe as a whole and the United Kingdom in particular. In the scheme of constitutional history, half a century is but the blink of an eye. For the regions to move in this time from non-existence to a position of prominence in the majority of Member States, with the resulting degree of influence at the European level, is remarkable. Whether the pace of change will be maintained in the 21st century is another question, however. In many cases, the drivers that created them continue to exist. Regionalist or micro-nationalist political movements continue to make a significant electoral impact, while the regions themselves have become institutionalised, creating loyalties within both regional political élites and the electorate. On the other hand the governments of some regions, particularly those at the centre of existing Member States, continue to attract little interest. Although their achievements may be significant, their political profile is minimal.

Given the patchy response to the regional revolution, the future for the regional tier is difficult to predict. It is clear that the most powerful regions within the EU will need to be accommodated into the European decision making mechanism if a second democratic deficit is not be created, but it is difficult to see how this can take place when the regions themselves are so unequal.

It is into this complex situation that the UK's fledgling devolved institutions now step. What can the British Isles learn from experiences across *la Manche*? The lessons are many and varied, but three thoughts raised here will be repeated throughout the book. First, the key to the successful operation of European regional systems is co-operation. Secondly, the ability of regions to operate at the European level is dependent primarily upon their strength within the domestic system. Thirdly, the constitutional framework of European regions is not sufficient to deliver domestic power, but it is a necessary prerequisite for it. Lacking such formal constitutional power, will the UK's devolved structure deliver the regional autonomy expected of it?

Part 1

The Theory of Regional Governance

CHAPTER 1

THE REGION IN A NATION-STATE WORLD

The principal unit of territorial government for the last two centuries has been the sovereign nation-state. This is the paradigm within which all debates on the territorial organisation of government are conducted. We describe legal systems and their institutions in reference to the national level. For example, legal structures and law can be described as 'national' or 'international'. The assumption is that legal systems can be organised either on a national or on an international basis, but always with reference to the national unit. Any other method of organisation has to be explained in relation to the dominant nation-state paradigm and is regarded as an exception to it.

It is the contention of this volume that such nation-centric concepts of territorial government are not only unhelpful for academic discussion of the subject, but are a significant barrier to the development of systems of governance more suited to the realities of a modern Europe. In essence, people do not live in the neat boxes prescribed by the national paradigm, and new systems of governance (of which the region is one) reflect attempts to realise this. To examine the development of the region fully, one must therefore first examine and challenge the dominant concept of the national sovereign state.

The concept of the sovereign nation-state contains at its heart the idea of hard borders. This imagines the nation-state as a finite policy area whose borders are permanent and absolute. The nation-state boundary is the point at which one policy area ends and a new policy area begins.

The dominance of this paradigm in academic discussion of territorial governance reflects the concept's universal acceptance in practice. The entire globe is divided into nation-states of varying sizes and populations. From Luxembourg to China, under international law, all, as nation-states, possess broadly the same rights. This bundle of rights, implying equality in relations with other states and the right to organise and run domestic affairs without interference, is usually referred to as 'sovereignty'. Such rights are accorded only to nation-states, no matter their size, and never to constituent parts of these nation-states. A representative from the state of Andorra can therefore sit at the United Nations, but one from Kurdistan cannot. In the world of the nation-state, national sovereignty is everything.

In the context of the European Union, the nation-state (or Member State) enjoys a number of important privileges. Most significant of these is the right to sit and vote in the Council of Ministers, the principal legislative institution of the EU. This leads to the situation where Luxembourg has a seat on the Council of Ministers while other territories of much greater population and area are not directly represented. In those policy areas where unanimity is required, even the smallest Member State can protect its national interests through a veto. Other territories have their interests subsumed within the national interests of their Member State. The interests of 'national' territories (and in practice the dominant regions within them) are thus represented at the expense of other territories which will have specific demands and requirements but lack the status of nation-states. The 'national' voice of Denmark must be heard at the Council, while the regional voice of Catalonia will be silent.

The dominance of the nation-state paradigm in the study of territorial methods of government means that other modes of governance are generally examined in the nation-state context. This begs the question as to why nation-states should have this privileged position in the study of territorial government. In an effort to examine the development of regional government this chapter questions the adequacy of the nation-state paradigm.

1.1 THE LEGITIMACY OF THE NATION-STATE

Two pillars support the legitimacy of the nation-state. First, the traditional organic view portrays the nation-state as the political manifestation of 'nations' or 'peoples'. This is an idea tacitly accepted by most people, although few will ever have considered why. Secondly, whatever their genesis, nation-states are presented as a satisfactory method of fulfilling the interests of their populations. These methods of legitimation are not mutually dependent. Although the normative legitimacy of nation-states has become increasingly questioned, this in itself is not a reason to discard the concept. If the nation-states that exist operated successfully there would be no reason to challenge their practical manifestation. The fact that the nation-state paradigm has encountered a practical crisis (as described in section 1.1.2 below) as well as a theoretical one gives room for alternatives to the concept of hard-bordered sovereignty to be explored.

The organic view of the nation-state enlarges upon Hegel's theory of the state as an 'ethical community'. The existence of this community was grounded in the concept of *Geist* (or spirit). Hegel argued that only through participation in the ethical community of the state could the individual become free, possessed of purpose, reason and will. The neo-Hegelian view took these ideas and replaced the idea of ethical community with that of nation. The practical manifestation of this was the state. The mystical spirit upon which Hegel based his theory of the state was equated with the late 18th century notion of 'nationalism', and a legitimation for nation-states was born (Dyson, 1980, p 129). The nation-state, by representing the *Geist*, was an

4

historical and normative concept. It was consequently the 'natural' unit in which people should live.

1.1.1 The myth of nations

The basic legitimacy of the current global delineation of borders is therefore based upon the idea of the 'nation' as an organic concept. Each nation-state is the territorial representation of such a nation. Without the concept of nationhood, the present territorial configuration loses normative legitimacy. It follows that, if the concept of the nation is not a given, then the division of the globe into nation-states should enjoy no primacy in the study of territorial government. Unless it can be given the status of a natural norm, the nation-state system must be assessed rationally against other models of territorial government.

Those who defend a nationalist approach to the division of the globe often expose the contradictions within it. In the United Kingdom, for instance, the existence of the Scottish, Welsh and English nations is accepted, yet those in Scotland or Wales who wish to establish separate nation-states are described as nationalists, and are denigrated by British parties for being such. These same British parties then claim that the UK Government has authority over the British 'nation'. How can British nationalism be positive and Scottish nationalism negative? If the basis of the territorial boundaries of the British government is the existence of a nation, then surely if a part of that 'nation' wishes to form its own nation-state, the British government would oblige?

Equally, those who oppose European unity generally do so on the grounds of national self-determination. These same anti-Europeans are generally those most vociferous in their defence of current nation-state borders against those 'nations' within their borders which wish self-determination. This is clearly a contradictory position. If one supports the right of 'nations' then surely this must apply equally to those within nation-state boundaries, as well as those possessing nation-states themselves? On this evidence, 'nation-statism' is a convenient political tool rather than a coherent concept.

It is a common misconception that the idea of states, and the nations they claim to represent, dates back to early history. Today this concept seems permanent, and indeed it is in the interests of nation-states and would-be nationalists to perpetuate the myth. Implicit in this perception is the premise that the nation preceded the nation-state. For the territorial legitimacy of the nation-state to rest on the idea of nations, each nation must predate the state that represents it.

The first problem with this argument is finding a satisfactory definition of what exactly a 'nation' is. There are several competing normative definitions, none of which can explain the national divisions of the globe. The origin of the term 'nation' itself is from the Latin *natio*, birth. This represents an ethnic definition of the nation, based upon common racial links. In the modern world such a definition is impossible, and indeed the intermixing of populations that has occurred throughout history makes it very unlikely that such a definition was ever plausible. The tragedy of Bosnia is evidence both of the ridiculous nature of this notion and of the danger in believing it. Finding it impossible to draw lines on a map which would divide the various ethnic groups, extremists resorted to murder and persecution to create such ethnically pure areas. In fact, the various communities in Bosnia-Herzegovina, particularly Muslims, were in effect persecuted for their surnames. Many had the same ethnic background as their 'Serbian' neighbours, and most had ceased to practise the religion with which they were associated (Malcolm, 1996).

A cultural definition of a nation looks more promising, at least at first glance. Unfortunately, upon reflection, it proves equally problematic. There are over 8,000 languages in the world, but a maximum of 800 peoples who could be termed 'nations' and fewer than 200 nation-states. If indicators other than language are used, questions arise of where a culture begins and ends, and when it becomes 'national', making the definition entirely unworkable.

The final method of attempting a definition, and one that enjoys limited acceptance in the jurisprudence of international law (in particular under Art 1, International Covenant on Civil and Political Rights 1966), involves 'membership' or self-determination. Under this concept, a nation exists when a population believes that it does. There is, however, a significant problem with this definition too. At what point does popular affinity for a 'nation' cause it to exist? 51% of the population? 100%? Where should the boundaries of such a territory be drawn? The answer to this question will profoundly affect any test of national consciousness. The majority of Northern Irish people may regard themselves as British, but if the referendum were held on an all-Ireland basis, the result would most likely be very different.

The various problems that plague attempts to define the 'nation' through normative means suggest that this approach to understanding the nation is misguided. We must therefore look elsewhere for our legitimation of the national unit. One explanation which has enjoyed rather more success in explaining the genesis of nations and nation-states is that put forward by Ernest Gellner. His method has been to eschew attempts to find a normative method of defining the nation, instead searching for an empirical definition of the nation-state (Gellner, 1983). The reason for the existence of nation-states lies in how they were formed, not in what they represent.

The birth of nationalism and nations continues to be a controversial subject amongst academics. One camp includes a number of historians who date the genesis of nations to a period as early as the 14th century (Tipton, 1972). Another camp includes political scientists such as Keldourie (1961), Gellner (1983) and Breuilly (1993), who place the birth of nationalist movements and the concept of 'nationhood' at the end of the 18th and beginning of the 19th centuries. The two sides of the argument are not incompatible, however, and both Orridge and later Breuilly achieved a plausible synthesis of these contrasting views. Orridge argued that although there may have existed something that could loosely be termed nationalism in some territories prior to the late 18th century, the concept only achieved its modern genesis in the later period (Orridge, 1981). It was this that the Jesuit Abbé Barruel recognised in the earliest known use of the term 'nationalism' in 1798 (Gildea, 1987, p 54).

This revolutionary period saw the development of the 'nation' as the only identity worthy of recognition in government. In the words of Abbé Sieyes, 'it recognised no interest on earth above its own – neither that of humanity at large nor that of other nations' (Hobsbawm, 1962, p 54). This idea that 'nations were the natural and only true political units' (Tivey, 1981, p 4) was crucially lacking from the ideas of nationalism that preceded this period. It is this intolerance which distinguishes the modern concept of nationalism from its antecedents. The acceptance of this ideology as the basis for territorial units of government did not come about by chance, however. It owed its birth to the specific circumstances of the time.

Territorial legitimacy of government before the late 18th century was not a serious problem for the governing regimes. Theories of accountable government were in their infancy, and ruling élites largely owed their territorial legitimacy to a complex combination of divine authority, conquest and marriage. The concept of the king representing the nation was rare. Power flowed from the king to his subjects, not vice versa. In consequence, allegiance was owed to the king and his nobility, not to any idea of a nation (Rudé, 1964). The rise of republicanism and limited forms of democracy altered the position markedly. By denying the existence of divine authority, the governments replacing it were faced with a lack of legitimacy. As can be seen from the examples of the United States Constitution (1787) and the French Rights of Man (1789), this legitimacy was based upon representation of the people, but which 'people'? The people were conveniently defined as those within the borders of the existing state. These were the 'nation', of which the government and parliament claimed to be the legitimate representatives. National myths are created to legitimate such boundaries of territorial government. The eminently quotable Eric Hobsbawm summed it up; 'getting history wrong is an essential part of being a nation'.

In all but two cases (Italy and Germany), the 'nations' of Western Europe continue to reflect the boundaries of the states which preceded the fall of the *ancien régime*. The 'nations' of Europe are, therefore, reflections of territorial divisions created by political realities at the time that absolutist government fell. They do not reflect a normative division of peoples.

France is the classic example of this process within Europe. In France the successful dynasty developed from a territory around the Ile de France. These families, by conquest, marriage and diplomacy, enlarged the territory they controlled until by 1589, and the accession of Henri of Navarre to the French throne, the French kings exercised varying degrees of control over much of modern France, an area of diverse cultures and language (Knecht, 1991, pp 72–83). Breton, Catalan, Basque and the Occitan languages (among others) were all spoken in the area under French rule, and even by 1795, it is estimated that less than 50% of the population of 'France' spoke French (Beer, 1980). A few areas such as Savoy and Lorraine were added in subsequent centuries. Again, their addition was nothing to do with their being part of the French 'nation' but rather as a consequence of military actions on the part of the French state.

The formation of Germany and Italy are the exception to the above rule and appear to contradict it. German and Italian nationalists argued for the creation of nation-states to represent the 'nations' that existed prior to the unification process. Is this not evidence that the German nation predated the German state? This evidence is rather less convincing than may at first appear. In fact the process was again driven by the expansionist policies of individual states rather than by romantic notions of national unity. It is impossible for us in the 21st century to put ourselves into the shoes of the population of 19th century Germany, but it is a large leap of faith to argue that just because they spoke broadly the same language, they saw themselves as a German people. Even if they did share an identity based upon this language, this was not necessarily an allegiance to the German 'nation'. Although romantic nationalists in Germany and Italy wished to unite the peoples speaking their respective languages within one state, it was the expansionist policies of Prussia in Germany and Piedmont in Italy that completed the task. The final outcome was a Prussian takeover of the German speaking areas and a Piedmontese takeover in the Italian peninsula. If the true intent had been linguistic unity, why did the fledgling Italian state lay claim to French and German speaking areas? Similarly, if language had been the basis for Prussian expansionism, why did Bismarck engineer the defeat of his fellow German speakers from Austria, and exclude them from his bid for German unity? Once again, territorial expansion was the force that defined the boundaries of the modern state, legitimated by the rhetoric of national unification and romantic myth. The task of the new states was to build these German and Italian nations. As Massimo d'Azeglio is famously credited with announcing to the Italian Parliament, 'We have made Italy, now we have to make Italians'.

Gellner's work has gone a long way towards debunking the idea that nations and nationalism are normative phenomena. Instead, they emerged as a consequence of new systems of governance and the huge changes in society which were taking shape in the late 18th and early 19th centuries. The creation of nations thus reflected the state boundaries already in existence. The evolution of what we term a 'nation' requires a nation-state to create it and an industrial society to aid its development (Gellner, 1983).

The development of a national culture, and thus a 'nation', is caused by the replacement of distinct cultures and religions with a unifying state (or 'national') culture. The two prerequisites for this occurrence are a state, to develop or impose the 'national' culture, and an industrial society, which creates the conditions for its successful acceptance. Industrial society loosens ties between the populace and the locality, creating a mobile and culturally heterogeneous society. It was in the interests of the state that only one language existed within it. This makes communications and mobility of the populace easier and enhances the industrial economy. It is natural that the culture of the dominant élite will be the one imposed.

This imposition of one culture over another is not a new phenomenon, nor is it unique to the world of nation-states. The dominant élites of one territory have often attempted to impose their culture upon the élites of a conquered territory. In France, successive monarchs worked hard to impose their French speaking, Roman Catholic culture throughout the nobility and church of their territory (Richard, 1992). In general, however, the imposition of cultural changes on a society by the dominant élite was restricted to the ruling nobility. If changes occurred at a lower level it was by accident rather then design. Only if the lower culture was a threat to the hegemony of the ruling élites, as differences in religion were often perceived to be, were attempts made to alter the cultural affinities of the lower classes.

In the post-monarchist states, the imposition of the 'national' culture was directed at the entire population, as it had to be in the new industrial age. As the dominant post-absolutist élite was generally from the same cultural background as that prior to the change of regime, the dominant culture would remain unchanged. This meant that Castilian Spanish, French and English (to take a few examples) became the languages of the whole nation-state. This 'nationalisation' of culture required the existence of a state to develop it. The imposition of a single culture over a territory needs a monolithic educational system, which only a state can provide. It is not an organic process, and in extreme cases the minority cultural affinities may even be outlawed as a threat to national unity. Here again, there must already be a state apparatus to implement such policies and indeed to perceive the minorities as a threat to the 'national' culture.

The mass of the population neither cared about nor understood the national unification going on around them. Southern Italians, for example, are reputed to have thought L'Italia was King Victor Emmanuel's wife. The unification referendum was something of a charade, and the 99% yes vote is to be treated with some scepticism given that huge sections of the Italian population were illiterate (Keating, 1988, p 43). If such widespread support for unification really did exist, one doubts the need for the 250,000 troops used to subdue the South, resulting in the deaths of 7,000 people in battle, 2,000 executions and 20,000 imprisonments (M Salvadori, from Keating, 1988, p 44). If this was support, one wonders what rebellion would have been like.

The existence of 'organic' nations is not the criterion by which the territorial divisions of the globe are arranged. In fact, the partition of the globe does not reflect cultural, ethnic, religious, linguistic or any other normative divisions. Nation-states exist where little or no homogeneity is evident (Sudan and Iraq are typical examples) while areas with a high degree of cultural affinity may be divided into several nation-states (such as Scandinavia). The current territorial division of the globe occurred as a result of power struggles between élites for control over territory, largely in the period before the foundation of the nation-state. In Europe, the majority of divisions, with a few exceptions, reflect the process of dynastic expansion and warfare between ruling families in the late medieval period. In the rest of the globe, the divisions are due to further factors, including colonial wars between European nation-states, political compromises between those same states (the divisions of Borneo, for example) or, more unusually, indigenous dynastic expansion on a model similar to that witnessed in Europe (such as in Ethiopia).

The fact that Europe's boundaries have come to be drawn through dynastic conflict and political intrigue should come as no surprise. As Smith points out, all decisions over territorial division of power, however couched in administrative and constitutional rhetoric, are political (Smith, 1985). However, in the case of the nation-state, the boundaries that divide us, as well as the concept itself, have assumed an air of permanence. They have achieved the status of a norm that is not only undeserved but irrational. They cross cultural, religious, ethnic and linguistic boundaries that are not themselves permanent. They do not reflect climatic, natural or geographical differences, which in turn has the consequence that the nation-state packages do not address economic or political realities. The desires of one territorial area may be at variance with those of its neighbour yet both may be under the jurisdiction of the same nation-state.

Nations are not 're-awakened'. They are created as a consequence of political events (Gellner, 1983). Rather than being a rationale for the nation-state, they are a consequence of it. Without the existence of the nation-state there could be no nationalism, yet the moral authority for the existence of the nation-state is that it represents the territorial embodiment of a nationality. Without this authority, the nation-state's claim to 'organic' legitimacy is defunct. This raises a huge question. If the borders of nation-states do not reflect the existence of any normative divisions, how effective is the hard-bordered nation-state as a method of territorial government?

Although the neo-Hegelian thesis has looked increasingly vulnerable, this is not an argument in itself for reassessing the paradigm of territorial government. Whatever the weakness of its theoretical legitimation, the pragmatic defence of the nation-state concept argues that if it isn't broken, why fix it? Why look to alternative methods of territorial government, such as the non-sovereign region, if the current paradigm of the hard-bordered nation-state continues to function effectively? Even if the idea of historical 'nations' is a myth, and there was no national *Geist*, there can be little argument that something akin to it now exists within most nation-states. The nationalist defence argues that the normative basis of the nation is immaterial. What matters is that nation-states exist today and the vast majority of the global population identify with one of them. The question then arises as to whether the current structure of nation-states represents the best interests of their populations. Is there a need to look for an alternative?

1.1.2 The crisis of the nation-state

The removal of the mythical quality of the nation-state allows a rational assessment of the concept. There can be little doubt that the traditional nation-state is in crisis (Ivonen, 1993). The problems encountered by nation-states in addressing the economic, social and cultural desires of the population are not merely a consequence of the current division of the globe, but rather a consequence of the concept itself. It is therefore rational to examine alternatives. Within the European Union we are uniquely placed to reassess methods of territorial governance without the threat of national weakness, which has dogged any such discussions in the past. The protective umbrella of the EU allows reorganisation without chaos.

The boundaries of nation-states do not reflect economic realities. This is as true in Europe as anywhere else. Few, if any, European nation-states can be said to be one economic region. European Member States consist of several regions with economic needs that can differ enormously. This divergence of economic needs is not confined to areas within nation-states. Economic factors do not recognise national boundaries. Throughout Europe, economic regions transcend national borders. The rural economy of Ireland, for example, does not stop at the UK border. The county of Fermanagh in the UK province of Northern Ireland has much more in common with neighbouring Donegal in the Irish Republic than it has with London, Dublin or Belfast.

Theories of fiscal federalism put forward a similar argument in fiscal terms (Von Hagen, 1992). Nation-states do not reflect optimum economic areas, therefore fiscal policies need to vary, not only from nation-state to nation-state but from region to region, irrespective of where the national boundary lies. Moves towards European Monetary Union, through the creation of a single currency, although perhaps desirable for other reasons, will merely intensify the need for regional fiscal policy. Regional variations will continue to require fiscal policies to address the requirements of the particular region. In a currency area the size of Europe, this will become even more important.

The concept of the hard-bordered nation-state is further undermined by the increasing impact of national policy decisions beyond the nation-state border. The hard-bordered nation-state was premised on the fact that policy decisions could be segregated on national grounds. This is no longer the case as many policies now have significant spillover effects beyond the borders of the nation-state. Pollution created in one nation-state may cause environmental damage to nation-states far from the source. One nation-state cannot protect the environment within its borders by acting unilaterally (the acceptance of which is reflected in the Title XIX of the EC Treaty). Within nation-states, environmental interests are not necessarily best dealt with at the state level either. What may be regarded as an acceptable environmental risk by nation-state governments may be seen somewhat differently by those living close to the problem.

Under the principle of national sovereignty, the economic problems of the region must be addressed within the context of the nation-state rather than in an economic forum covering the region. The economic interests of one region will differ from those of another. If economic policy is undertaken at a national level, the policy requests of the more powerful regions will outweigh those of the less influential areas. In consequence, some economic regions will suffer, whichever decisions are undertaken by the nation-state. An economic region may also have much more economic common ground with other regions, beyond the borders of the nation-state, than with its counterparts within it. The 'hard border' philosophy erects barriers against co-operation between regions of similar interests.

The practical effect of these contradictory forces on the nation-state has been twofold. On the one hand, the failure of the nation-state to cope with the increasingly global nature of many sectors of society has led to the creation of supranational organisations. Primary amongst these, and most relevant to this volume, have been the institutions of the European Community and now the European Union. In tandem with the transfer of power to the European Union, there has occurred a process of disintegration within the nation-state itself. The inability of nation-state governments to cope with regional disparity has led to the formation of regional institutions.

The formation of regional authorities to reflect economic reality is part of the same process that has led to the genesis of supranational structures such as the European Union, referred to in the political science literature as 'glocalisation'. We are not witnessing a process of decentralisation or centralisation, but rather a disintegration of the nation-state as the territorial paradigm of government and an end to the concept of hard borders.

1.1.3 The micro-nationalist challenge

A vital part of the nation-state ethos was the existence of a single national culture within the boundaries of a state. Cultural affinities other than those of the nation were not supported, and could be forcibly eradicated. Failure to adhere to the 'national' culture could even result in exclusion from the 'nation'. Gellner argued that cultures that differed from the central regime had two options: assimilation or formation of their own nationalism. The original response of most minorities was assimilation, but increasingly some began to use the same rhetoric of nationalism that was used to legitimise the nation-state itself. If the nation-state of which they were part claimed to be a single 'nation', and a minority culture or ethnic group did not agree, then surely they themselves must be a 'nation' and thus deserving of a separate state. If no separate state has existed previously (as in the case of the Basques, in contrast with Scotland or Catalonia), the legitimacy of the claim must be based on ethnic, cultural or linguistic differences that distinguish this group as a separate 'nation' from the parent nation-state.

Such claims, though valid, cannot be solved by creating a plethora of new nation-states to reflect the 'real' ethnic or cultural divisions of the globe. The drawing of permanent, all-purpose boundaries will never be a solution to the problem of territorial government. Unlike nation-state boundaries, society's divisions fluctuate. Culture and language are not static. They develop both in content and in territorial coverage. If cultural, linguistic and religious affinities are fluid whilst the borders of the nation-state are not, even the most accurate reflection of these differences in territorial terms will become obsolete over time.

Even if such cultural boundaries were static, these divisions would prove impossible to reproduce in a constitutional context. People do not live in neat ethnic, linguistic, cultural or religious units that are territorially definable. No division of the world can ever reflect the variations of belief, culture and identity that exist. Any attempt will always leave an unhappy minority. If the Basque territories were granted independence, the large numbers of French and Spanish speakers living in these areas would most likely be dissatisfied.

The tragic consequences of the 'hard border' philosophy can be seen most clearly in the violence of the former Yugoslavia. Extremists laid claim to their own nation-state or 'homeland'. The reality is that such clear divisions do not exist on the ground. Wherever the divisions are placed, there will be some 'foreign' individuals within it. The rational solution (in the context of the nation-state paradigm) is therefore to evict them. No nation-state solution will ever be a solution unless the racists are successful in dividing the 'ethnically pure' from the 'enemy'. This is the logical consequence of the 'hard border' concept. To create a true nation one must drive out those opposed to it. The fact that in the Balkans people were killed and driven from their homes because of their surnames is the terrible consequence of the nation-state obsession.

The former Yugoslavia is by no means alone. In Euskadi (the Basque country), ETA still wages its war against the Spanish state, in pursuit of a Basque homeland. In Northern Ireland, two cultures fight over which nation-state the territory should belong to. In Corsica and Brittany, separatist groups have fought the French state for the past 30 years (Savigear, 1980, p 116; Fortier, 1980, p 149).

The sanctity of nation-state boundaries goes much of the way towards explaining these conflicts. A nation-state will go to enormous lengths to prevent the erosion of its borders, even to the point of spilling blood (Birch, 1978, p 340). This seems to be the case even when the people it wishes to contain within its boundaries do not wish to remain. This in turn encourages the population of those areas which see themselves as different from the dominant ruling group to strive to achieve nation-state status themselves. After all, the message of the nation-states themselves is that they are the primary unit of government. If nation-state status can be achieved, then the culture which was formerly part of another state can have its own seat at the international table. If nation-state status is not achieved then it will have nothing, unless the dominant nation-state deigns to give up some of its power.

In the world of the nation-state, the possession of a state for your culture, and thus the recognition of your 'nation', is everything. Anything less than a nation-state is nothing. The borders of the present day do not reflect the variety of peoples that populate the globe, but no combination of nation-states can ever accomplish this. It therefore follows that to resolve the cultural and ethnic conflicts that dot the globe, there must be a reassessment of methods of territorial government.

1.2 SOFT BORDERS AND THE REGIONAL ALTERNATIVE

The brief discussion presented above clearly demonstrates that the nation-state enjoys no normative status. It is an artificial unit of territorial governance which enjoys no special claim to represent the interests of its population in either the economic or the cultural spheres. Moreover, there is no configuration of nation-states that will ever fulfil the demands of the global population. It is not the current boundaries of the globe that have led to the nation-state's current crisis; rather, the concept of the hard-bordered nation-state is itself flawed.

The nation-state concept, as already discussed, is based upon the principle that the interests of a 'national' population can be served by a single territorial unit of governance. In fact, this is impossible. The areas within which a population's interests are satisfactorily represented will vary, depending on the specific interest in question. The interests of the population therefore need several overlapping and non-sovereign tiers of authority, not a single hard-bordered unit as provided by the nation-state. This concept of non-sovereign and overlapping units of governance can be termed 'soft borders'. This does not deny the need for nation-states, but merely denies that they should be the only source of territorial authority and legitimacy, from which all else springs. There is a need for the separation of various cultural, economic and social aspects of governance to reflect the interests of the population more closely. This can be provided by local, supranational, and, most importantly for this discussion, regional tiers.

The limitations of the hard-bordered nation-state concept have resulted in the *de facto* weakening of the concept and the development of new forms of territorial government. The new units have been both supranational and sub-national, though defining them in terms of the nation-state is somewhat misleading. These new methods of governance are evolving away from dependence on nation-states for their existence, and no longer justify themselves in terms of the nation-state. Instead, new methods of justification and legitimation are needed to cope with the eroding of the previous world order.

It is into this space that the principle of regional and federal government fits. This non-sovereign concept of governance has developed most recently and extensively under the protective umbrella of the European Union. Relying less upon the nation for its legitimacy, this form of government has seen the stretching of sovereignty away from the national unit. To understand it fully, we must discard the nation-state paradigm, which fails to recognise the possibility of alternative sources of legitimacy or the division of sovereignty.

The continued dominance of the nation-state concept in theoretical and political discussion, despite its disintegration on the ground, presents us with a particular problem. The institutions of governance remain based around the myth that the nation-state is still the paradigm within the European Union. At the European level, this means that the Member States retain the key decision making role in the Council of Ministers while the regions look on. Within national systems, the institutions continue to reflect traditional models of governance, with the assemblies (both regional and national) focused on the scrutiny and approval of statutes. This is despite the fact that the stretching of national sovereignty means that the actions of government happen less through statutory enactment at a single level, but rather through co-operation between several levels. Scrutiny of such decision making will remain particularly poor as long as we persist in operating as if the sovereign state remained totally intact.

As long as we continue to regard the hard-bordered nation-state as the touchstone of territorial governance in the EU, problems of democratic legitimacy and inefficient decision making will grow. The regional context of this failure to recognise the death of the traditional nation-state model is explored in the chapters that follow, but before we embark on this task let us first turn back to the question of legitimation. The above discussion has argued for the discarding of the national myth to legitimise our territorial organisation of government. This is all well and good, but this then presents us with a new problem; with what can we replace it? Perhaps more importantly, does the soft-bordered regional model really offer an alternative to the problems of the hard-bordered nation-state?

CHAPTER 2

RATIONALISING REGIONALISM

2.1 DEFINITIONS AND DIFFICULTIES

'Devolution' is the word adopted in the United Kingdom to describe what has been, until recently, a distinctly European phenomenon, namely the decentralisation of power to a regional level of government. It describes the process of creating a tier of government between the national level and the local, responsible for a number of policies that have traditionally been controlled by central government institutions. Such proposals, which had surfaced intermittently since the Anglo-Scottish Union of 1707 (indeed they were discussed in the debates surrounding this Act), had until the 1960s been referred to as 'home rule' in the United Kingdom (Kendle, 1997). Gradually, however, the term 'devolution' became shorthand for any proposal to create a democratically elected tier of government in the Celtic periphery of the United Kingdom (Northern Ireland had already experienced a form of devolution between 1921 and 1972). This change of terminology accompanied a step change in support for such reforms, reflected in the increased strength of nationalist parties in both Scotland and Wales (Marr, 1992). The practical manifestation of today's devolution settlement has seen the creation of an assembly in Wales, a legislative assembly in Northern Ireland and a parliament in Scotland. The establishment of a Greater London Authority (although purely administrative in nature) and the possibility of English regions are also part of this devolution process.

These new and proposed institutions vary considerably in their structures and powers. Only the Northern Ireland Assembly and the Scottish Parliament have primary legislative powers (and there is even some debate over this, as discussed in Chapter 7). Even between these two institutions there are significant variations in their legislative authority. Despite this, the common aim of all these institutions is the democratisation of regional decision making, and thus we class all these institutions under one heading, 'devolved'.

Use of the term 'devolution' means little beyond the shores of the UK (although recently the French have used the term *dévoulé* to describe reforms in Corsica). Amongst students in continental Europe, it raises blank stares or confusion. Yet when one describes the system that has developed in the United Kingdom there are flashes of recognition and mention of 'federal government' or 'regions'. In the European context what the UK has experienced, and is continuing to experience, is the development of asymmetrical regional government, with distinct federal overtones.

One can find many differences between the United Kingdom's constitutional reforms and those that have been experienced across *la Manche*. In particular, the term 'devolution' implies that power has been devolved from the top down. This is in contrast to the situation in many European states. The UK's constitutional system continues to rest upon the sovereignty of the UK Parliament, and the regional level only obtains constitutional legitimacy from the largesse of this institution. In theory, therefore, the generosity of the UK Parliament could be rescinded at any time, while in Europe most systems of federal or regional government are enshrined in the national constitution. In practice, however, the various methods by which these governments are given constitutional legitimacy do not distinguish them from the UK model. Together, these 'regional' units comprise a level of government with a distinct but limited policy role in most Member States of the EU. They comprise a 'third level', recognisable if difficult to define, at which policy in the European Union is developed.

2.1.1 Defining the region

Having established the region as the frame of reference of this study, we are faced with a seemingly straightforward problem that has plagued the study of regional governance. Put simply, what exactly is a region? In an effort to deal with this question, some authors have avoided the term altogether. Sharpe, for example, in his collective work of 1993, created the term *meso* (middle) to describe the level of government he recognised between the nation-state and local levels (Sharpe, 1993). He explicitly invented this term to avoid the baggage that accompanied existing terms such as region, but in doing so created his own problems. These were encountered in a more recent work which used a similar 'intermediate' definition (Larsson, 1999). In both cases such definition of the 'third level' leads to complications when more than one *meso* level of government exists. In Sharpe's edited collection, for example, authors of different nationalities interpret the term differently. Delmartino in particular has difficulties with Belgian provinces, Communities and regions (Delmartino, 1993), but similar problems would emerge from any system which has more than one level of government between the Member State and the local level. Works examining *meso* or intermediate levels of government in Germany can variously lead to discussions of the *Länder* (the constituent federal states) or the organisation of intermediate local government within them (contrast the report on Germany compiled by the Council of Europe, 1993, with Haibach and Serong, 1999, for example).

Creating a new term such as 'intermediate' or *meso* and then placing the units of governance which one wishes to study within it does not take the debate on the third level forward. There is also another, more fundamental problem with using such definitions of intermediate government. Although they clearly encompass part of the essence of the regional tier, they define the region subjectively in terms of the nation-state. It does not give a normative definition of the region itself.

Recognisable geographical regions, some of which do not correspond to political units, exist throughout the EU. Does this offer us a normative definition of the region? A typology of these geographical units is given in Table 2.1 (p 21), but it is difficult to define these territorial divisions in strict terms, such are the variations between them. Nevertheless, what most observers would regard as the 'regional' level can be broadly defined as having a population of over one million (but less than 15 million) and a territory of at least 10,000 km^2. Under this somewhat arbitrary definition, several territories which have the political status of nation-states are included while some political 'regions' are excluded.

The third level described above cannot therefore be classified in terms of geographical definitions. A third level institution is a form of government, distinct from local and national, which may (or may not) cover a geographical area commensurate with a geographical region. It is a non-sovereign unit of territorial government, existing between the local and national tiers (but not necessarily relying upon either for its legitimacy), with final responsibility for areas of policy traditionally held centrally. Importantly, it has the theoretical ability to create policy that differs from the national norm and gives the opportunity for regional variation within the nation-state. It thus exhibits constitutional characteristics closer to that of the national level than to local government. Whatever its formal constitutional status, the region is more than a level of mere administration. The region is expected to develop policy in answer to economic and social problems far beyond those expected of the local units. When the establishment of regional government for England is discussed in the UK, this is what is being referred to, not the establishment of a large local authority (although this may be what happens in practice). For such units of governance to be worth establishing, they must have a strategic role beyond that of local administration. By using such an admittedly broad definition, it is possible to identify a third level of government in the European Union. An attempt at such a typology of the regional tier is presented in Table 2.2 (p 22). To some extent, these reflect the nomenclature of territorial units for statistics (NUTS) used by the European Commission. It is obvious from these divisions that constitutional and geographical units do not always coincide. Thus, a city like Hamburg, which would come under the geographical definition of a province or district, may be afforded the constitutional status of a region.

The subject of this volume is the form of autonomous intermediate government that has developed in the political space between local government and the Member State in the European Union. This level of government is termed 'regional'. On the face of it, this term may appear too broad, particularly for a constitutional analysis. Within this broad family there are both federal and unitary systems of government. Can these be examined collectively? To answer this question we must consider the concept of federalism and its relationship to the regional concept.

Table 2.1: Geographical definitions of territorial divisions in Europe

European level	National level	Regional level	Provincial level	District level	Local level
European Union	Belgium	Régions or Communities	Provinces	Arrondissements	Communes
	-	Denmark	Amter	-	Kommuner
	France	Régions	Départements	Arrondissements	Communes
	Germany	Länder	Kreis	Bezirke	Municipalities
	Greece	Regions	Nomos	-	Communes
	Italy	Regioni	Provinces-		Municipalities
	-	Ireland	Provinces	Counties	-
	-	-	Luxembourg	Districts	Communes
	Netherlands	Euro-regions (proposed)	Provinces	Regions	Municipalities
	Portugal	CCRs and Island regions	-	Districts	Municipalities
	Spain	Autonomías	Provinces	Various	Municipalities | *Mancomunidades*
	United Kingdom	English regions	Counties	Districts	Parishes
		Scotland	Regions	Districts	Communities
		Northern Ireland	-	Districts	-
		Wales	Counties	Districts	Communities

Table 2.2: Political definitions of territorial divisions in Europe

European government	National government	Regional government	Regional administration	Local government	Local administration
European Union	Belgium	*Régions* or Communities	-	Provinces and *communes*	*Arrondissements*
	Denmark	*Amter*	-	*Kommuner*	-
	France	*Régions*	Regional Prefect and various others	*Départements* and *communes*	*Arrondissements*
	Germany	*Länder*	Regions	*Kreis* and municipalities	*Bezirke*
	Greece	-	Regions	*Nomos* and communes	-
	Italy	*Regioni*	-	Provinces and municipalities	-
	Ireland	-	-	Counties	-
	Luxembourg	-	-	*Communes*	Districts
	Netherlands	Provinces	Various	Municipalities and regions	-
	Portugal	Island regions	CCRs	Municipalities and parishes	Districts
	Spain	*Autonomías*	*Delegado del Gobierno*	Provinces, municipalities and *mancomunidades*, with regional variations	-
	United Kingdom	-	English regional offices	Counties, districts and parishes	-
		Scottish Parliament	Scotland Office	Local authorities and communities	-
		Northern Ireland Assembly	Northern Ireland Office	Districts	-
		Welsh Assembly	Welsh Office	Local authorities and communities	-

2.1.2 Federalism, regionalism and asymmetry

Defining the term 'federalism' has taxed the minds of academics for centuries. Since the earliest examples of non-sovereign collections of states (the earliest known example being perhaps the Mitanni federation of the 15th century BCE), scholars have attempted to define this form of government. The modern federalist debate can be dated to a much later event, however. The American Revolution and the explicit acceptance of the federal concept in the United States Constitution marks a watershed in the discussion of federal government. It is from this date that the modern discussion of federalism can be traced, and its impact on the study of federalism is still evident today.

The formalists of the Anglo-American school have used the US system as the epitome of a federal structure. Indeed, Watts goes as far as giving the founding fathers of the United States credit for its invention (Watts, 1994). This view is exemplified by the work of Wheare, whose classic studies of federalism were heavily influenced by the United States model. His definition of the federal model originally excluded many systems which defined themselves as federal, including Austria and Germany (Wheare, 1953). More recent definitions of federal government have broadened Wheare's original concept, but the Anglo-centric nature of the definition is still evident. Broadly speaking, the classic definition of federalism encompasses the following:

(a) two orders of autonomous government, with a formal distribution of legislative powers, executive authority and revenue resources;

(b) a provision for the representation of regional views within the central state policy making body;

(c) a supreme constitution which defines the federal system and requires the agreement of the constituent states to be amended;

(d) a constitutional adjudication system;

(e) a formal process of intergovernmental relations (Watts, 1981).

This formal definition of federalism in effect uses a description of the United States model as its basis for defining all other federal forms. It is thus limited in application and fails to address the normative concept of federalism itself. By reducing the number of federal states to a handful, it is also of limited comparative use. In more recent times, a wider definition of the federal concept has been advocated by a number of academics including Elazar (1991) and Watts (1994). This encompasses a broader concept of the federal idea, which includes some but not all of the defining characteristics of federalism listed above. Watts uses the term 'federal political systems' to distinguish these varieties of political autonomy from the 'classic' US style of federalism.

Although not explicitly mentioned in the key characteristics of federalism listed above, a further aspect is implicit in the formal federal model. Federal systems comprise a regional tier that covers the entire territory of the state. Although differences between the regional structures may be evident, broadly speaking the regional units are equal. This is the principle of symmetry and is evident, broadly speaking, in all formally federal states. Symmetry eases the inclusion of the regional tier into the national structure and allows common systems to exist throughout the state (for example, in relation to finance). Relations and intergovernmental structures are, broadly speaking, established on a 'one size fits all' basis and are not tailored to the specific needs of individual regions. The tailoring of such institutions to fit the individual needs of particular regions is a feature of regional systems, which fall outside the formal federal classification.

Non-federal regions are in the main structured around an asymmetrical model. Although some administrative regions do exhibit symmetry throughout the territory of the state (in Denmark, for example), this is the exception. Spain, Italy, Portugal and France all exhibit various degrees of asymmetry within their regional structures. Within these systems, the powers and role of the regions within the Member State vary significantly, and in some cases the existence of regional government applies only to parts of the Member State territory (as in Portugal and the United Kingdom). In both cases, such asymmetry was a response to demands by peripheral regions with high micro-nationalist or regionalist identities demanding increased autonomy. By definition, these regions will have individual relationships with the central tier, in contrast with the common institutions of a federal state.

The traditional definition of federalism given above applies to the formal European federations that have developed in Austria, Belgium and Germany. This places them in a distinct group within the regional definition. Nevertheless, the distinction between this group of formal federations and the other regional governments is not sustained in practice. In Spain, for example, although formally the constitution of the regional state can be altered unilaterally, politically this is extremely unlikely. There are more similarities binding the regional tier together than differences dividing it. The fact that the year 2000 saw the establishment of a conference of 'Presidents of Regions with Legislative Power' which includes both federal and non-federal regions (an Assembly of Regions has been in existence for several decades) is testament to this assertion.

Although the language of federalism can be applied far beyond formally federal systems, in the rest of this volume the term 'regional' will be used to describe the intermediate level of autonomous government. Regional governments, whether federal or not, exhibit some but rarely all of the aspects of the federal ideal type described above. This makes over-reliance upon the formal federal distinction unhelpful. Watts would possibly describe the wider group, which encompasses both formally federal and regional governments, as 'federal political systems'. Nevertheless, given the practical similarities that overlap these formal distinctions, the differences between systems within the same formal definition, and the fluid nature of the subject, there seems no need to complicate matters any further by introducing a new term.

2.2 REGIONALISM, DECENTRALISATION AND DEMOCRACY

The definitional problems discussed above have come about primarily because the region does not rely upon the 'national' myth for its legitimation. In contrast to the nation-state model, there is rarely a mythical 'nation' to represent. Regions have been created or developed as a response to particular strains on the classic sovereign model and do not lay claim to sovereignty themselves. In the European example, it has usually been stresses placed upon the nation-state that have led to the creation of the regional tier. If there is no national myth to sustain it, what can be used to legitimate the regional tier?

2.2.1 Subsidiarity and regional government

Despite the scepticism shown towards the use of new terminology in the previous section, 'subsidiarity' is a term that deserves some discussion in the regional context. Much trumpeted in the mid-1990s, this idea has become an accepted principle of European jurisprudence through its inclusion in the EC Treaty (Art 5(2)) and the Treaty on European Union (Art 1, Title I). Although limited in its practical application, it introduces a new concept of legitimacy into constitutional debate. The concept is based upon the idea that government should take place at the lowest possible level. This means that the Member State should only involve itself where it is necessary for it to do so, and any intervention should be under the auspices of the lowest level of governmental organisation. By implication, such institutions must be accountable to their populations.

Although simple and not apparently contentious, this idea has the potential to challenge orthodox views of national government. Through the use of this concept, sovereignty is held by the individual, and governments acquire their legitimacy through the passing up of such sovereignty from the individual to higher levels of government. Such transfers should only occur to the extent that is required, and to the lowest level capable of performing the task efficiently. Legitimacy is not granted to local or regional government through a process of decentralisation *per se* but is acquired by the higher level when it can justify such a transfer. By this concept the legitimacy of the national unit as the paradigm of territorial government is challenged. Under subsidiarity, the national level enjoys no legitimacy, and certainly no primacy, in the discussion of territorial governance. Like every other unit of governance, it achieves legitimacy only from the inability of citizens and lower levels to undertake the required task. Under this concept, the nation-state is no longer sovereign, only its citizens.

2.2.1.1 Definitions of subsidiarity

The classic definition of subsidiarity is generally regarded as that contained in the 1931 encyclical of Pope Pius XI. He defined the concept in the following terms:

> Just as it is wrong to withdraw from the individual and commit to a group what private enterprise and industry can accomplish, so too it is an injustice, a grave evil and a disturbance of right order, for a larger and higher association to arrogate to itself functions which can be performed effectively by smaller and lower societies. This is a fundamental principle of social philosophy, unshaken and unchangeable. [*Quadragesima anno*, paras 79–80, 1931; translation from Wallace and Wilke, 1990, p 12.]

This concept was used by the Papacy as a defence against fascist centralisation, especially in areas traditionally controlled by the Catholic church. This was not the first mention of the concept but this statement has become its accepted definition. Although this definition exposes the dual nature of the concept, a state versus society aspect and a territorial government aspect, only the latter context is discussed below.

Since the 1931 encyclical, the use of the concept in reference to appropriate levels of government has increased. If the subsidiarity principle favours individuals against the state then it also favours smaller groups against larger ones. In other words, the division of tasks within government should work on the premise that the lowest authority possible should exercise the relevant task. Due to the fact that most government in the Western World is organised on a territorial basis, it is unsurprising that the term has mainly been invoked to defend smaller territorial units against larger ones. Regionalist and nationalist movements in particular have used the concept to argue for the greater territorial autonomy of regions within existing nation-states. Although use of the term in this context has achieved recent prominence, this variant of the concept dates back to at least the 18th century. As early as the 1790s, Adam Smith advanced such an idea as part of his economic and political theory:

> Even those public works which are of such a nature that they cannot afford any revenue for maintaining themselves, but of which the conveniency is nearly confined to some particular place or district, are always better maintained by a local or provincial revenue, under the management of a local or provincial administration ... [Smith, 1812, p 37.]

Across the Atlantic a practical example of this concept was incorporated into the United States Constitution, in response to worries concerning the new Federal Government's ability to assume powers over the States and individuals (Sunquist, 1987, p 706):

> The Powers not delegated to the United States by the Constitution or prohibited by it to the States, are reserved to the States respectively, or to the people. [10th Amendment, United States Constitution.]

This 'negative' use of subsidiarity's territorial context, as Kliemt describes it, has a positive antithesis (Kliemt, 1993). Although power should lie at the lowest level of government possible for the satisfactory completion of a task, responsibility may equally be exercised at a higher level which can execute the task better than the lower level could. The concept does not give an assumption that lower levels of government, or indeed any level of government, will benefit from it. Nevertheless, this negative use of subsidiarity has become the dominant one in the debates surrounding the territorial application of the principle.

Practical applications of this principle (with special reference to the regional level) have been incorporated into the federal constitutions of both Germany (Basic Law, Art 30) and Austria (Art 15(1), Austrian Constitution). More generally, the acceptance of the principle is evidenced by its presence in the European Charter of Local Self Government finally signed by the UK in 1996. Arts 4(2) and 4(3) state that:

> Local authorities shall, within the limits of the law, have full discretion to exercise their initiative with regard to any matter which is not excluded from their competence nor assigned to any other authority.

> Public responsibilities shall generally be exercised, in preference, by those authorities which are closest to the citizen. Allocation of responsibility to another authority should weigh up the extent and nature of the task and requirements of efficiency and economy. (Council of Europe, 1985.)

The incorporation of the subsidiarity principle into the Treaty on European Union (TEU) at Maastricht brought the principle to wider attention and also marked its general acceptance as a principle of European governance. Within the EC Treaty, subsidiarity is specifically mentioned by name only once. Under Art 5(2) (originally 3b), the principle is mentioned in reference to the actions of the Community:

> In areas which do not fall within its exclusive competence, the Community shall take action, in accordance with the principle of subsidiarity, only if and in so far as the objectives of the proposed action cannot be sufficiently achieved by the Member States and can therefore by reason of the scale or effects of the proposed action be better achieved by the Community.

> Any action by the Community shall not go beyond what is necessary to achieve the objectives of the Treaty. [EC Treaty, Art 5(2).]

Article 5(2) of the EC Treaty is not the only use of the concept. In the TEU, Art 1 uses the general principle, without mentioning the term explicitly:

> This Treaty marks a new stage in the process of creating an ever closer union among the peoples of Europe, in which decisions are taken as closely as possible to the citizen. [TEU, Art 1, Title I, para 2.]

The specific use of the term 'subsidiarity' in Art 5(2) refers primarily to relations exclusively between the Member States and the Community. Only in Belgium, Germany and Austria was the principle accepted as applying to the constituent regions (Declaration by Germany, Austria and Belgium on Subsidiarity, incorporated as Protocol 30 into the Treaty of Amsterdam 1997). As such, the principle would seem to confirm the status of the Union as a nation-state club, rather than a truly European body. Article 1, on the other hand, seems to give a different view of the new Union, emphasising the idea that decisions should be taken 'as closely as possible to the citizen'. In this context, no mention is made of the method by which such decisions should be taken, and certainly no specific mention is made of the nation-state as the conduit through which decisions should be undertaken.

Despite its general acceptance across Western democracies, the territorial context of subsidiarity runs into difficulties when one actually attempts to define how the tasks of government should be allocated. Debates surrounding subsidiarity place much emphasis on the balancing of efficiency with liberty or accountability. Jacques Delors, during his time as Commission President, particularly emphasised the efficiency criteria of the concept, while others have argued that any intervention by higher authority must be reasonable or proportionate (Heilbronner, 1993). Such attempts are fraught with difficulties. The problem is one of definition. What is 'efficient', 'reasonable' or 'proportionate'? Even if this problem can be overcome, there seems little prospect of constructing a meaningful frame of comparison between these concepts. How many units of efficiency are needed to nullify a unit of accountability?

The introduction of the concept of subsidiarity into debates on territorial government does not answer the questions surrounding the optimal division of powers in a divided system. The concept should not be discarded, however, as subsidiarity is still useful in discussions surrounding territorial government. Although the precise definition of the optimum level of government continues to be somewhat contentious, agreement that government should be located at the lowest possible level is a major shift in Western political thinking. The concept gives a rational basis on which to argue for the optimal level of government, thus removing the nation-state's privileged position. If government is to be based at the optimal level for efficiency and democracy, the national level becomes merely another tier that must be rationally assessed according to these criteria. In essence, subsidiarity gives a new framework in which the debate surrounding territorial government can be conducted without relying on the paradigm of the nation-state for its legitimacy.

2.2.1.2 Subsidiarity and the new constitutional debate

Subsidiarity provides a post-nation-state framework in which to discuss territorial government. It offers us a rational basis upon which to debate the governance of Europe, free from the baggage of the 19th century nation-state system. It therefore gives the opportunity to discuss a more effective system of European governance, without relying on the legitimacy of the nation-state as a theoretical anchor. This offers a substantial ideological platform for regions (and other levels of governance) to claim validity in their own right, without being perceived as merely subdivisions of the national state. Although the specific criteria for the division of power may still be extremely contentious, the concept of subsidiarity removes the need to legitimate all forms of government in relation to the nation-state. Instead, legitimation is based on the interests of the population, however vague this concept may be. This applies to supranational bodies, such as the Union itself, and, of more relevance to this volume, sub-national authorities and specifically regions.

The acceptance of subsidiarity as a constitutional principle of the European Union gave a degree of theoretical impetus to decentralisation claims in Europe. Moderate nationalist parties have used to the language of subsidiarity to argue for national status in new terms. Both the moderate Basque nationalist party (the PNV) and the Scottish National Party, for instance, campaign for 'Independence in Europe'. This translates as a seat at the Council of Ministers, not the existence of a sovereign nation-state in the traditional sense. This is what moderate European micro-nationalism means in the post-national era.

Subsidiarity has updated the concept of decentralisation, as discussed below. No longer must arguments be made for the devolution of power from the nation-state. Instead the nation-state itself must defend its legitimacy against claims from communities demanding greater control over decision making. For this reason, modern European nationalist parties and regional movements rely less on nationalist rhetoric and more upon arguments of democracy and utility. The enduring legacy of subsidiarity within the EU may be the removal of the nation-state as the paradigm within which all other constitutional mechanisms must be framed. It gives the possibility of a more rational basis upon which the territorial governance of Europe can be constructed.

It is into this new constitutional environment that the regional governments emerge. The development of post-war government has seen the creation of a plethora of sub-national units of government, both democratic and non-democratic, in the name of decentralisation. However, this change has all been achieved under the assumption that sovereignty still lies at the national level alone, with other units gaining their legitimacy from and being limited by the national tier. Regional interests are invariably seen as beneath national ones, while international relations have remained exclusively under national control. This made any study of the region as a new type of authority difficult. For this reason, the regions have often been seen as another type of local authority, merely operating within the national paradigm and regarded as inferior to it. This analysis is wrong. The region is a *sui generis* form of non-sovereign authority, filling a gap in the territorial organisation of government which the nation-state cannot fill. The principle of subsidiarity gives such institutions a form of legitimacy independent of, and untarnished by, the nationalist myth.

2.2.2 Deconcentration and decentralisation

The administration of government cannot be achieved from a single central institution. To this extent the Member States of the European Union have accepted the logic of the subsidiarity concept. They have been less keen to apply the democratic elements that the concept implicitly demands. From the earliest recorded examples, officials have been designated to oversee the administration of government in the provinces of the nation-state. Such deconcentration of government does not imply democratic accountability. 'Deconcentration' is not a term regularly used in discussions of territorial governance in the United Kingdom. The term, taken from French, describes the administration of territorial units by centrally appointed government institutions. Despite its ignorance of the terminology, the UK was and continues to be one of the greatest proponents of this method of governance.

Unlike decentralised institutions, deconcentrated institutions are accountable to central government, not to the territory that they serve. Although some democratic element may be present (in an advisory or subsidiary capacity) deconcentration is a method of more efficiently administering national government policy, not delivering democratic accountability. Deconcentrated authorities are the territorial representation of the central state.

Territorial deconcentration comes in many guises but it remains a feature of government in most European Member States. The classic European example, and one that has been readily exported, is the French *préfet*. These national civil servants continue to administer the field services of the French state on a *départemental* basis. Until 1986 they also exercised *a priori* control over French local government (see Chapter 6).

Regional deconcentration (explored more fully in Chapter 3) is a more recent phenomenon, but one that is now common across the Member States of the EU. In the administration of the UK, examples of regional deconcentration have a longer history, however. The Secretary of State for Scotland, a centrally appointed official entrusted with significant powers to administer the governance of Scotland, dates back to the 19th century, but in post-devolution Britain, the tradition of deconcentrated regional authorities is most obvious in the regions of England. English regional government continues to be administered in this manner, with a number of government departments having regional field agencies and administrative agencies (Tomaney, 2000). In 1994, a degree of rationalisation saw a number of field agencies brought together in a series of regional Government Offices. These continue to administer national policy on a regional basis, under the authority of a regional director appointed centrally. Alongside this rationalisation of deconcentrated regional government, England has also experienced a proliferation of regional quangos (quasi autonomous non-governmental organisations). Most significant of these are the Regional Development Agencies, created in 1999.

In those EU countries which lack a regional tier of decentralisation (Greece, Ireland and the Portuguese mainland), deconcentrated regional administration remains the norm. In many other cases regional deconcentration preceded regional decentralisation (see Chapter 3), while those states which have engaged in regional decentralisation often continue to operate deconcentrated authorities in tandem with the democratic institutions. In the United Kingdom, the territorial departments for Scotland, Wales and Northern Ireland continue to operate, although their responsibilities (particularly in the former case) have been significantly reduced. Only in the federations of Austria, Germany and Belgium does the central government lack a specific presence in the region. Even in these cases, field agencies for specific national responsibilities still exist. The continued existence of these authorities in systems of regional decentralisation is often a source of friction between the regional government and the Member State.

2.2.3 Regionalism and decentralisation

The acceptance of a need for deconcentrated government does not bring with it an acceptance of its democratisation. Langrod went as far as suggesting that local government does not mean local democracy while a system without democracy is not necessarily undemocratic (Smith, 1985). This statement is fundamentally flawed. If governance is divided territorially and parts of this system are not democratically accountable, this section of the system is undemocratic. Regional deconcentration by definition creates a democratic deficit.

The literature of democratic decentralisation argues for this principle as a good in itself. It brings with it a 'democratic climate' and thus a more 'true' version of democracy through greater participation in governmental decision making. By such involvement, Mill (1861) and de Tocqueville (1835) saw its potential for educating the populace in politics, thus creating the democratic intellect required for democratic governance. Others such as Ylvisaker and Dahl see this greater participation leading to greater unity and equality within the system, with smaller groups having a voice denied them at the higher level (Smith, 1985). Utilising these general arguments for more local forms of territorial government as justifications for regional decentralisation is not without controversy, however. The consistently low turnouts at local (and in some cases regional) elections in many countries undermine the claimed educative benefits of decentralisation, particularly as Mill placed such emphasis on the act of voting as the measure of such an educative process. Although local and, by extension, regional government can play a role in developing a democratic culture, it is not clear that such a culture is a prerequisite, nor that decentralisation itself necessarily leads to it.

Less controversial are two perceived advantages of decentralisation that are particularly apposite to the regional tier. Smith describes these as accountability and responsiveness (Smith, 1985). Democratic governance at the lowest level possible increases the responsiveness of government (Mill, 1861, p 376). By placing government within a regional or local context, issues pertaining to a specific geographical area can be discussed more fully, and responses tailored to specific needs. In a national context, local or regional issues are swamped amidst consideration of more general issues. The existence of a regional or locally elected tier potentially allows the electorate in a smaller territorial unit to express its policy choices more clearly. Policy preferences differ from individual to individual and also from area to area. Thus, decentralising the decision making powers of government to a lower level will reflect more accurately the policy priorities demanded by the area's population.

When national elections are held, the dominant issues in such campaigns will be those common to the entire national territory. Alternatively, issues which are the concern of the more populous regions may be raised to national importance. In either case the issues of concern in specific localities, particularly in peripheral or less populous territories, will be less prominent. This leads to a government that is responsive only to certain issues and specific territorial concerns. Although national issues are important, specific regional concerns and those of the periphery must also be addressed if the government is to represent the whole electorate. Without this condition, national politics will dictate the policies pursued at regional level. In the worst case, some regions of a democratic nation-state may vote for a set of policies opposed by more populous areas. In a unitary state this will result in the policy priorities of the more populous areas being represented in the national government, and thus applied nationwide, while the opinions of less populous regions can be disregarded. The permanent exclusion of such populations from the national policy arena leads to frustration in the excluded region and may translate into movements for territorial defence. Such movements will often demand that greater decision making authority be held in the region or locality.

This scenario was clearly demonstrated in the United Kingdom during the 1980s and 1990s. During this period the electorates of significant areas of UK territory expressed preferences for policies which were clearly at odds with those followed by the national government. Areas with relatively clear regional boundaries, particularly Scotland, the north east of England and Wales, voted consistently for parties of the left but their policy choices were buried by the overwhelming support for the policies of the Thatcher government found in the Midlands and the south east of England. Mitchell has argued that this situation led directly to the growth of support for devolution, not as a means of defending the Scottish nation, but rather in defence of the welfare state (Mitchell, 1996). A similar situation was experienced in Belgium, where the more prosperous and populous region of Flanders returned representatives from liberal parties while Wallonia returned members predominantly from the left. As in Scotland, the result was a movement of regional defence in Wallonia and eventually demands for economic regional autonomy for the south of the country.

The increased responsiveness created by a democratic regional tier brings with it an increased level of democratic accountability. Regional or local tiers of government can be held more accountable for regional or local policy decisions. That discretionary decisions will be taken at the regional level is beyond dispute, as the existence of regionally deconcentrated agencies makes clear. Even without these bodies, discretionary decisions affecting the individuals of one region will be taken by national governments. Without the existence of a regional level of decentralisation within the Member State, such administrative decisions and general issues of managerial competence will not be tested at the ballot box. The regional decisions of national ministers or their officials will only be challenged if the national electorate regards the regional policy error as relevant. Even mismanagement and significant errors of judgment will only be held accountable at the ballot box if they make national headlines. The more centralised a system of government, the less accountable to the electorate it will be.

2.2.3.1 Regionalism and democracy

Although the arguments advanced above apply equally to democratic local and regional levels of government, one of the most enduring arguments is unique to the regional tier. Built upon the arguments explored above and advanced by those such as Jefferson and de Tocqueville (de Tocqueville,

1835), this can be termed the classic federal theory of decentralisation. According to this thesis, a devolved system of government not only encourages accountability but actually acts as a defence against authoritarianism. Jefferson described the defence of States' rights (meaning the regional tier) under the US Constitution as 'the surest bulwarks against anti-republican tendencies' (Smith, 1985, p 26). This idea of decentralisation protecting liberal democracy is referred to as the 'countervailing power' argument by Wolman (1990, p 35). Put simply, it is not healthy for democracy if power is held exclusively in the hands of one level of institution.

The most common federalist method of controlling the central state relies on the fact that the autonomy of the regional units in certain specific spheres can limit the authority of the centre. Where the central state lacks authority, particularly over enforcement institutions such as the police or the judiciary, attempts at authoritarian forms of government are far more difficult to achieve than in a state where central control over these areas is absolute. This theory of a 'countervailing power' is most evident in the constitution of the United States, but in Europe the principle was most obvious in the constitution of the Federal Republic of Germany. Heavily influenced by the United States model and the lessons learnt from the Nazi takeover in 1933, the post-1945 West German state left the majority of powers concerning the police, the judicial system and education in the hands of the regional *Länder* authorities (Schweitzer *et al*, 1984).

The perceived democratic benefits of regional or federal government have not gone unchallenged, however. In particular, significant criticism has been levelled at Mill's assumption that ideas of individual liberty can be logically applied to a group or community. Although the liberty of a community (in our example, the region) may guarantee the community's freedom against encroachment from the centre, these critics have argued that this will not necessarily assure the liberty of the individual within this community. As a result it is wrong to portray regional decentralisation as a democratic virtue.

Riker used the example of the United States to show how individual liberty could be restricted within a community or region against the policy of the central state. His example of the southern states of the US showed how constituent states could oppress minorities within their borders largely against the wishes of the federation. In this example, far from defending democratic principles, the system of regional government allowed a tyranny of the majority within the region. The argument is certainly persuasive (Riker, 1964).

Fesler also cast doubt on the assertion that decentralisation will bring about increases in accountability and responsiveness of government. Rather than leading to increased levels of democratic legitimacy, smaller units of government are more vulnerable to domination by local élites. If this is the case, regional governments are responsive primarily to the demands of regional élites. The increase in accountability discussed above may therefore only apply to powerful interests within the region and not the electorate as a whole (Fesler, 1965).

The evidence for the arguments of Fesler and Riker is difficult to ignore, but is it fair to describe these problems as a consequence of decentralisation and, by extension, regionalisation *per se*? There can be no doubt that the federal system of the US allowed the existence of laws abhorrent to the majority of US citizens to develop in specific regions. Nevertheless, to say that this was a consequence of the federal system itself is a significant further step. If all governments, from local to federal, were covered by effective restrictions regarding human and civil rights, the racist laws of the south might have faced effective challenge earlier than they did. With reference to the concept of subsidiarity discussed above, such rights should be universally applied across a territory encompassing an area far beyond that of the nation-state. That protection of universal civil and human rights varies between nation-states, in the name of sovereignty, is as wrong as any differences that occur within them.

There is a significant difference, however, between the abuses of a national government and those of the institutions of a regional tier. While a region will be subject to a degree of national control or influence, and vice versa, the hard-bordered sovereign nation-state will know no significant political challengers to its policy (Mill, 1861). A centralised system can deny democracy throughout a territory, just as a regional unit can within a decentralised system. In the latter case, there is a significant difference, however. If one tier of government abuses its power, others exist to challenge it. In addition, a collapse of democracy at one level does not necessarily mean the end of democracy in the territory as a whole. Reservoirs of democratic legitimacy with constitutional authority will remain at other levels to challenge the threat.

Criticisms that a regionalised government will be susceptible to local élites are also valid, but as with the arguments examined above, the same charge can apply to the national level. The domination of government by minority interests is a problem that exists in democratic systems of government from local to national. That such dominance can exist at any governmental level suggests that the issue is wider than Fesler portrays it. It concerns more fundamental questions about democratic government, rather than the territorial organisation of the state.

The major democratic criticisms levelled against regional devolution are valid, but only to the extent that they apply to government in general. All systems of democratic government must guard against the domination of power structures by élites as well as the abuse of human rights by a majority. This can occur in the smallest town council or the highest multinational structures. To avoid it we need democratic systems designed to avoid minority domination and based upon rational norms of human rights. This is well beyond the scope of this book, and is not an issue of territorial government.

2.2.4 Self-determination, identity and regionalism

A 'sense of place' is a rather unscientific concept, and somewhat hard to quantify. It is nevertheless one that has had a profound effect on the development of regional government. Indeed, it could be argued that this abstract notion has been the single most important influence on the development of a regional tier. With the self-determination of peoples recognised as a fundamental right in the UN Charter (1948, Arts 1, 55 and 56) and the International Covenant on Civil and Political Rights (1966, Arts 1(1) and 2(2)), to both of which the UK is a signatory, identity has assumed an international legal persona. Although originally interpreted as applying only to colonial territories, a wider view of applying the principle generally has emerged since the 1960s. Recently, Rosas has argued convincingly that there now exists a right of internal self-determination (Rosas, 1993). In this situation, the emergence of a political will in favour of regional government has far reaching consequences for international law.

Since the 1960s it has become increasingly obvious that the territorial identities of many populations have not been completely fulfilled by the nation-state paradigm. That decade was marked by an apparent upsurge in European sub-nation-state identities in conflict with the nation-state itself. The development of this phenomenon has been described as 'micro-nationalism'. This saw territories within existing states developing nationalist movements to challenge the legitimacy of the national tier and demand the recognition of their territory as a nation-state in its own right (as examined in Chapter 1). In tandem with this, regionalist movements also emerged. Although accepting the legitimacy of the national identity of the parent state, these movements demanded that the distinctive nature of their regions be recognised in the institutions of the state. In addition to the more publicised examples such as Catalonia and Scotland, regional identities took on a political aspect in much more unexpected areas such as France.

This territorial aspect has continued to be a feature of European politics, with regionalist parties securing varying degrees of electoral success in Belgium, France, the UK, Spain and Italy. Regional government offers a way of addressing these issues whilst retaining the unity of the national state. Although originally perceived as a challenge to the nation-state, regionalism may actually have become its saviour.

2.3 A RATIONALE FOR REGIONS

The region, as explored above, is a concept of government that sits uneasily within the nation-state paradigm. It is this failure to fit with conventional models of government that makes it so difficult a concept to define. It is at once both an intermediate level of government, reliant on the national level, and a level of legitimate government in its own right. It does not lay claim to the sovereignty of the nation-state, but does possess a degree of independent policy making power or limited sovereignty. It is thus distinct from both the national and local levels, but reliant upon each of them. In this it bears some similarities to the European level. It too is a sui generis model, beyond the national paradigm, relying not on the mythical concept of the nation for its legitimacy but on rational concepts of utility.

As in the example of the European Union, the concept of subsidiarity has proved useful in legitimising the regional tier. Although much less romantic than national myths of derring-do, subsidiarity offers a far more rational basis for the legitimation of territorial government. Many regions, like the EU, may lack a national myth, but their utility as a unit of government suited for the delivery and development of specific policies is difficult to refute. The acceptance of regional deconcentration by European Member States further strengthens such arguments. Once the utility of the regional tier is accepted, it proves difficult to deny it democratic accountability. Nevertheless, although the pressures for democratisation of the regional tier are common throughout the 15 Member States, the development of the regions in 13 of them was undertaken for particular reasons related to the specific history of the nation-state and its regions. The result was a Europe-wide regional revolution but not necessarily a European one.

The concept of the region, unlike that of the nation-state, does not come with a 'one size fits all' model. The arguments presented above, although driving the regional revolution across Europe, have impacted very differently across Member States. Regional models reflect the individual circumstances of each Member State and its regions. Based on rationality and utility, the models adopted reflect the problems the regions are expected to solve (for example, micro-nationalist pressures) or the perceived advantages the regions could bring (such as democratising regional administration). These specific drivers have left their mark on the models of regional government that make up Europe's 'third level'.

CHAPTER 3

THE REGIONAL REVOLUTION

The years since 1945 have witnessed the rapid evolution of regional government in Western Europe. There is no one reason why such a revolution occurred, but it is clear that the development of regional structures reflected a crisis faced by the traditional unitary nation-state in the post-war world. Nation-states appeared unable to deliver effective government or to satisfy the interests of their populations. These issues cannot be addressed purely on a national basis and, for the reasons explored in Chapter 2, a democratic regional tier offered an alternative. The challenges to the sovereign nation-state therefore led to the growth of the non-sovereign region. The use of this level in resolving some of the problems that have faced the nation-states is the theme of this chapter. An appreciation of these drivers of the regional revolution is vital for an understanding of the various regional systems that exist in the EU today.

The first stirring of the regional revolution occurred in the immediate aftermath of the Second World War. The collapse of democratic regimes in the 1930s, and the ensuing years of carnage, had a profound effect on democratic ideas in Western Europe. The ease with which democratic regimes were overthrown was seen by many as a system failure (Czechoslovakia was the only Eastern European democracy by 1939). One aspect of this system failure was perceived to be the over-centralisation of power. By placing too much power in the hands of too few, the system was vulnerable to overthrow at the centre. No institution outside the central government was capable of protecting the constitutional order. The constitutional response was to follow the sage advice of Jefferson and create a 'countervailing power' through the division of sovereignty along federal or regional lines.

The regional revolution cooled somewhat after the initial impetus of post-war constitutional reform, but by the 1970s the issue of regional identity and its political representation was again becoming a significant issue. The allegation that the nation-state has failed to address the interests of communities within its borders has been a consistent feature of many nation-states in the post-war period. Regional cultural defence became increasingly transformed into a broad political agenda that brought the regional issue into the national political agenda. In almost every Member State of the EU, regional movements challenged the legitimacy of national authorities to exercise sovereignty over significant areas of their territory. These groups, and the rise of regionalism they represented, played a significant role in the development of regional government. The impact of such movements was more subtle than their limited political support might suggest. Regional autonomy presented a political outlet for such non-national identities without necessitating secession from the nation-state.

The final driver in the development of regionalism was the need to administer and develop particular areas of policy on a regional basis. The concept of functional regionalism recognised the need for a tier of deconcentrated administration between local government and the central state. Accepted and implemented in most European states, it led to the development of various types of regional management unit. In most cases these units of regional administration lacked direct accountability to their electorates.

By developing these units of regional management, central governments tacitly accepted the failure of the central state to administer the entire territory as a single entity, and recognised the need for a regional tier. The failure to make these new bodies regionally accountable created strains on the system which, in most cases, proved unable to sustain. In cases where regional movements already existed, the creation of these deconcentrated and non-elected units of regional governance gave further impetus to the regional cause.

Combined, the three drivers described above were responsible for the development of the regional tier throughout the EU. The nature of this development was such that by 2000 some form of democratic regional government existed in 13 of the 15 EU Member States. These regional governments, to greater and lesser degrees, still reflect the pressures that originally brought them into existence. Even in those larger Member States which lack a regional democratic tier (particularly Greece), regional administration is the norm. The same is true of states such as Portugal and the United Kingdom where the regional project covers only part of the Member State territory. The regional revolution has therefore had an impact far beyond the states traditionally associated with regional forms of government.

3.1 REGIONAL GOVERNMENT AND THE DEFENCE OF DEMOCRACY

In Germany, Italy, Spain and Portugal, the regional issue came to the fore during the attempts to create a sustainable democratic system in the aftermath of right-wing dictatorships. During the 1930s, the short lived democratic structures in each of these states collapsed, to be replaced by authoritarian rule. In each case a combination of fascist and nationalist movements was able to topple the legitimate democratic institutions. Only in Spain did the attempt encounter significant resistance. Even here, the forces of the democratic government were defeated by the authoritarian forces ranged against them. With this exception, the fascist takeovers were achieved by semi-constitutional means. Though intimidation was part of the Nazi arsenal, it is an unavoidable fact that the party that gained the most votes in the German elections of 1933 was Hitler's NSDAP (the National Socialist German Workers' Party).

The fact that several pre-1930 democracies had been overthrown by democratic methods, or at least with the support of large sections of the populace, was not lost on the constitutional framers of the new democratic regimes (Cassese and Torchia, 1993; Montserrat, 1993; Paterson and Southern, 1991, pp 144–46). One of the prime objectives of the post-fascist constitutions was to make an authoritarian takeover impossible. With this in mind, a federal or regional structure was seen as desirable. As explored above, the federal argument for decentralisation saw the existence of legislative bodies, with control over certain state institutions, as a counterbalance against the power of the central state. In addition, the argument advanced by those such as Andrew Fletcher (Daiches, 1979) that a decentralised state was less able to engage in war than a centralised nation-state struck a chord. This provided a further reason for considering a federal or pseudo-federal system. The fact that Fletcher's ideas were advanced in the early 18th century shows the enduring resonance of such ideas. The Europe of 1945, like that of 1703, was tired of war.

With these arguments in mind, regional devolution became an integral part of the constitutions of the new democratic states. The constitutions of Germany and Italy (1949 and 1948 respectively) predate those of Spain and Portugal (1978 and 1976) by almost 30 years, but the emphasis placed on the regional devolution of power is strikingly similar.

Although the framers of the new constitutions may have accepted the benefits of a division of the state along territorial lines, the constitutional provisions that reflected this did not always come to fruition. Implementation of these provisions, once some degree of normality had returned, proved problematic. Although the German Federation was established from the outset, Italian regionalisation was not implemented until 1970 while in Portugal only the two offshore regions of the Açores and Madeira had been established by 2001. In most cases, further incentives were needed to force the hand of the recently constituted national governments.

The part played by regional movements in opposing the authoritarian regime was significant in both Italy and Spain. In these states, regional institutions and movements opposed the authoritarian takeover and the regime it implemented. Such moral and practical arguments for a degree of regional devolution helped to back up the intellectual case for regional government. In Italy, anti-fascist partisans had operated in most of the Mediterranean islands and parts of the periphery (particularly the Valle d'Aosta) throughout the war. The Italianisation policies of the fascist government had led to opposition in the non-Italian speaking parts of the state from the outset. As the war came to a close, however, regionally based resistance achieved a number of successes, and in Sardinia the fascist regime was overthrown prior to Allied occupation. The lack of central control over Italy in the post-1945 chaos meant that in many cases the regional resistance movements presented the new Italian government with something approaching a *fait accompli*. They had therefore no choice but to grant special concessions to these areas or risk secession (Spott and Wieser, 1986, p 222). In response to this, four special regions were created (Valle d'Aosta, Sardinia, Sicily and Trentino-Alto Adige), all negotiating their own constitutions or statutes. A fifth, Friuli-Venezia Giulia, was added in 1964. In those regions where no such pressures existed, the constitutional provisions remained a dead letter.

It was in Franco's Spain that the regionalist movements played the greatest role in the struggle against the authoritarian regime. During the Spanish civil war both Euskadi (the Basque country) and Catalonia were granted autonomy under provisions contained in the 1933 republican constitution. Both governments, and large sections of their populations, fought a bitter and ultimately doomed struggle against the nationalist forces (Gonzalez, 1987). The opposition of these regions to the nationalist regime came with a heavy human price. With the final fall of Barcelona, and thus the end of the republics of both Catalonia and Spain, many Catalans and Basques fled across the border to France. The Catalan *Generalitat* remained a government in exile for the entire period of Franco's dictatorship.

During the fascist regime itself, all vestiges of Catalan and Basque culture and institutional independence were removed, and both languages were banned in public. Not surprisingly, the Basque and Catalan regions became a focus for resistance to the regime. This was mainly peaceful in Catalonia, but the Basque response was violent (Clark, 1980). The success of the Basque terrorist group ETA in damaging the fascist regime should not be underestimated. The attacks on Franco's authority seriously undermined the government's attempts to present Spain as successful and settled under the dictatorship. Furthermore, the assassination of Franco's Prime Minister and second in command, Admiral Carrero Blanco, in 1973 effectively spelt the end of the dictatorship (Clark, 1980; Minority Rights Group, 1985). With his replacement dead, Franco was now left without an heir. The grooming of the future king, Juan Carlos, proved to be the regime's final mistake.

The role of regional governments and movements in overthrowing authoritarian regimes gave great weight to claims for regional autonomy after democracy had been restored. By challenging the previous authoritarian regimes, the regional movements had acquired a moral claim for autonomy and in some cases presented the government with such severe practical problems that their demands could not be ignored. The success of these opposition movements against the authoritarian regimes had been notable. If the new democracy failed to deliver change, the regional movements were liable to damage the legitimacy of the fledgling state. If these nation-states were to continue as a single unit, regional concessions would have to be granted.

In France and Belgium, the years 1940–45 (and, in the case of Belgium, 1914–18) also had an impact on the regionalist debate, but in these states the post-war consensus saw regionalism as an ally of authoritarianism rather than democracy. Some regionalist movements allied themselves with the Nazi takeover, and it was the national level that was seen as resisting the fascist occupiers.

In return for their support, the Nazi regime granted a facade of autonomy to both Brittany and Flanders. In Brittany this led to the creation of a Breton 'army' and assembly. Both had little support or independence (Fortier, 1980, pp 145–46). Some Flemish parties also followed this path, notably the Nazi *De Vlag* and the nationalist *Vlams National Verbond*, by collaborating with the Nazis as a means of increasing their powers against the Walloons (Cullen, 1990, p 350). The Walloon organisation *Rex* followed a similar strategy. This association between some regionalist groups and the occupying Nazi forces had a detrimental effect on moves towards regional decentralisation in the post-war period. Rather than the centralised nature of the state being seen as a contributing factor in the rise of fascism, it was the regional bodies themselves that were seen as supporting the Nazi occupation.

This was, of course, a gross oversimplification. Nevertheless, in the eyes of the political élite and sections of the populace, collaboration could be neatly associated with the regionalist movement. Such an association was in the interests of the leaders of post-war France and Belgium, as it avoided embarrassing questions about the role of many national officials and individuals during occupation.

The post-war perception that regionalism was a reactionary concept severely weakened calls for regional decentralisation in these countries. There was little support in France for creating a structure that many considered a threat to democracy. The fact that the Vichy regime had dabbled in regional deconcentration did not help matters. Nevertheless, even in those states where arguments for regional government received a serious setback, economic and cultural issues soon brought regionalism to the fore once again.

3.2 THE 'RISE' OF REGIONAL IDENTITY

There can be little doubt that the rise of regionalist or micro-nationalist movements throughout Western Europe has been one of the most significant developments in the European political scene in the past 30 years. These organisations have played a significant role in the development of regional government. Although persuasive arguments existed for the establishment of regional government, as outlined in Chapter 2, it was the perceived threat of regionalist movements to the existing political orders that persuaded centralised nation-state regimes to move down the regional road (Smith, 1985, p 48). In extreme cases, regional political parties became so powerful that regional devolution was inevitable; the question was only how it should be achieved and the form it should take. In other cases the regional movements have been less successful and their impact more subtle.

The literature on Western European regionalist movements is immense (see, for example, Lawrence, 1973; Rokkan and Irwin, 1982; Foster *et al*, 1980). However, although academic interest in the subject is relatively recent, regional identities within the nation-states of Europe are not a recent phenomenon. Despite the best efforts of many centralised regimes to homogenise the territory under their control, Europe is littered with regional and national identities that do not correspond to nation-state borders. In France, there is a patchwork of regional affinities corresponding to the pre-1789 provinces, as well as those which cross into neighbouring nation-states. Similarly, in Germany, Greece, Italy, the United Kingdom, Spain, Belgium, Portugal and the Netherlands, there exist regional and national identities of varying strengths within the present nation-states.

In some cases, these identities are based on language, such as the various dialects of Occitan in southern France and Euskerra in the Basque area of modern Spain. The Dublin-based European Bureau of Lesser Languages recognises 40 languages in the European Union (in addition to the 11 official ones); in total, 50 million people out of Europe's population of 344 million speak at least one of them. In other cases, such as Bavaria and Scotland, affinity is to a previously independent state and the distinct institutions and culture that remain. Sometimes, as in Catalonia and Brittany, regional or micro-national identity is due to a combination of the above factors (Petrella, 1980). These regional identities are neither more nor less organic than those of the nations explored in Chapter 1. The populations of many regions have strong identities, whatever their genesis, that exist either in parallel with national affinities or to the exclusion of them.

If micro-national or regional identities are not new, then neither is support for regional movements nor resistance to nation-state regimes. After the unification of Italy (1860–70) regional revolt in areas of the new nation-state was widespread. The Piedmontese control and centralisation imposed on the fledgling state caused some of its citizens to turn to violent rebellion (Gildea, 1987, p 197). Similarly violent methods had been used in Spain (Gildea, 1987, p 229), France (Rudé, 1964, pp 139 and 144) and Scotland, the last uprising being in 1820 (Ellis, 1989). The most successful of these violent uprisings was of course in Ireland, where insurrection led to the secession of part of the United Kingdom. Even in this case, most of the population supported the option of what would now be called 'regionalism' rather than outright secession. It was only the UK Government's insensitive handling of the 1916 rebellion that drove the mass of the Irish population into the nationalist camp.

By the mid-20th century, European regional unrest of the type explored above seemed largely consigned to history. Regional identities, though continuing to exist, were rarely politicised in the democracies of Western Europe. Organisations of regional defence were primarily concerned with specific cultural issues and, exceptionally, the protection of regional economic interests. Their engagement with wider political debates on governance was rare. In Occitania, for example, organisations campaigned for the defence of the Occitan language, but these groups had little or no interest in political affairs. The groups that did put a political complexion on regional issues were generally seen as parochial or eccentric and enjoyed little support. Those political parties or movements campaigning on a platform of regional government or autonomy were very much peripheral to the political debate. The nation-state was safe in its paradigm as the only unit of political territorial organisation.

Since the 1960s, the debate surrounding regional questions has undergone dramatic change. It is this metamorphosis of opinion that is seen as the 're-awakening of regionalism'. This phrase is misleading, however, as it suggests that this phenomenon was something new. In fact, as has been shown above, regional identities had never gone away. What occurred was a change in the nature of the regional organisations. Rather than an increase in regional affinity, there seems to have been a widespread politicisation of the territorial question. The focus was no longer on a single issue such as language or culture but instead on the achievement of some degree of regional control over regional affairs.

Increasingly, Western European regional movements turned to the democratic process to achieve their goals. This does not mean that the success of regional parties is necessarily a good indication of support for regional government. Indeed many regional parties have been spectacular failures, most notably those standing in French elections, with the exception of Corsica (Beer, 1980; Boisvert, 1988). In the regional elections of 1982, the Corsican regional parties achieved around 12% of the votes cast. This placed the moderate UPC (*Union du Peuple Corse*) as the joint second largest party (with seven seats) in the assembly. Even this can hardly be regarded as hugely significant.

In France at least, the weakness of regional political movements does not seem to reflect popular opinion on the regionalist issue. According to opinion polls, 55% of the French population supports an increase in the powers of regional government, despite the minimal support for regional parties (*Le Monde*, 13 October 1991). Nevertheless, the notable success of some regional political parties, particularly in Belgium, the United Kingdom and Italy, has given many nation-states little choice but to compromise.

3.2.1 The politicisation of regionalism

The politicisation of the regional question has had one of two effects. Depending on the strength of the regional movement in question, centralised states have found it necessary either to create entirely new structures of regional government or to democratise existing regional structures.

Spain has seen some of the strongest regionalist and micro-nationalist parties in recent years. Catalonia and Euskadi are the most quoted examples, for good reasons. Following the end of the Franco dictatorship, the moderate Catalan and Basque nationalist parties (the CiU and PNV respectively) were, and continue to be, the largest in the regions concerned. In addition, other nationalist movements also operate within these regions, some with significant success (HB, the political wing of ETA, consistently polls around 10% in Basque regional elections). In post-regional Spain, further regionalist parties have emerged, with varying degrees of success. In the Canaries, the regionalist party now dominates the regional assembly. The strength of these movements is a reflection of the strength of regionalist feeling, particularly in the outlying regions of the Spanish state, and means that regional demands cannot be ignored by the central state. Such central arrogance could drive these movements towards more extreme demands and even separatism. The strength of the regionalist parties is a further reason for the independence granted to the regional tier in the Spanish system.

Outside Spain, the impact of regional parties has been less dramatic, but their very existence has still made regionalist demands for autonomy difficult to ignore. In Belgium, moderate nationalist parties grew at such a rate that there was little choice but to create some sort of regionally devolved structure as they demanded. Failure to do so would possibly have encouraged more extreme nationalist parties (such as the right wing *Vlamsblok* in Flanders) and thus endangered the continued existence of the nation-state itself. In other states, however, the process has been more subtle.

The Scottish National Party (SNP) has never exceeded 30% of electoral support in Scotland at a general election. Nevertheless, their limited successes have had a profound effect on the politics, and ultimately the constitution, of the UK. Fear of the nationalist revival in the 1970s (when the SNP briefly held 11 out of Scotland's 70 seats) forced all the UK parties to pledge support for devolution at various points during the late 1960s and 1970s. In the case of the Liberal party, this was merely a confirmation of a long standing policy of creating a federal UK. Labour too had a long history of supporting the principle of home rule for Scotland, but an equally long history of conveniently forgetting the policy commitment when in power. The success of the SNP forced Labour to rediscover the policy they had previously championed. The Conservatives, by contrast, had never supported constitutional change to accommodate Scottish or Welsh difference, and acceptance of the devolutionary principle represented a major policy change. In the 1968 'Declaration of Perth', Edward Heath took the plunge in an attempt to arrest the decline of his party in Scotland, and committed the Conservatives to the devolution project, albeit in a very limited form (Marr, 1992). Without the shift of stance initiated by the leadership of the UK parties (often to the incredulity of their activists in Scotland who had been fighting so bitterly against the SNP), a continued drift of support to the nationalists was regarded as inevitable. Although support for regional government existed in all the UK parties prior to the *volte-face* of the 1970s, it was clearly the threat posed by the SNP (and to a lesser extent the Welsh nationalist party, *Plaid Cymru*) that drove the mainstream UK parties to embrace such reform. In the event, of course, devolution had to wait as the nationalist threat diminished in the aftermath of the failed referendums of 1978. Although the SNP has never come close to achieving its stated aim of creating an independent Scotland, the impact of the national parties in both Scotland and Wales is clearly far greater than their limited electoral success would suggest.

In France, regionalist movements have had little or no direct electoral impact, yet they too succeeded in getting the reformed French left to accept at least some of their demands. In Scotland, the UK parties adopted a regionalist stance to draw votes from the nationalists, but the French PS (*Parti Socialiste*) pursued a different tactic. As part of the project to unify the left and return to power after a decade of opposition, the PS wooed several regionalist movements into the fold. To do so, they pledged to introduce democratic decentralisation, and thus increased their base of electoral support (Keating and Hainsworth, 1986, pp 43–50). This was a policy which, it should be noted, already had significant support within the traditional ranks of the PS itself. The success of the PS in the 1982 elections led to an immediate implementation of their regionalisation programme, although the policies implemented were not as radical as the regionalist movements might have wished (Schmidt, 1990, p 110).

In the UK, the election of the Labour government in the spring of 1996, with its accompanying raft of constitutional reforms, was no guarantee in itself that the devolution project would be completed. Labour had been elected several times before on a platform of home rule, but in 1996 there were two major differences. First, the vast majority of the Labour Party in Scotland was now firmly behind the proposals put forward by the constitutional convention, in which they had a significant stake. Secondly, the unspoken threat of the nationalists lurked in the shadows. If Labour did not deliver, the SNP's assertion that reform within the UK was impossible would be confirmed. Such an outcome carried the threat of a split in the Labour Party and a surge in support for the SNP. Equally, without the heightened profile of the Scottish and Welsh issues, one doubts whether the English regional question would have been seriously considered.

Throughout Europe, the politicisation of regional issues has changed the parameters of debate. The nation-state is no longer the only legitimate outlet for political identity. As the constituent regions of Europe have achieved higher prominence, the 'rise' of regionalism has placed the territorial legitimacy of the nation-state on the political agenda. Ironically, however, the reforms that have been introduced to assuage micro-nationalist and regionalist demands are portrayed not as a threat to the nation-state but as its saviour.

3.3 FUNCTIONAL REGIONALISM

Unitary democracies in post-war Europe have experienced further regional stresses unconnected with issues of regional identity. In particular, the post-war growth of welfare provision by the central state and the emergence of economic planning gave an unexpected boost to arguments for regional decentralisation. The change in the role of government led to a reassessment of the role of both central and local authorities. The traditional levels of government were perceived to be incapable of delivering these new aspects of government policy. For this reason, central governments were forced to introduce regional tiers to cope with new public responsibilities. Such levels of authority, by their very creation, were a recognition by nation-state governments of the need for a regional tier of governance. Although in Scandinavia, the new institutions were directly accountable to their electorate from the outset, in the majority of cases the development of functional regions was not accompanied by any direct democratic accountability to the regional population. The existence of these authorities, unaccountable to the population they served, soon raised issues of democratic accountability and legitimacy.

3.3.1 Economic regionalism

The growth of economic planning in the post-war period had a significant impact on the development of European regional government. The majority of Western European governments, following the French indicative model of planning, created the need for some type of regional structure (Sharpe, 1993, p 12). This form of economic planning utilises territorial planning organised on a regional basis. This required regional organisations to draw up and administer the plans. Where no regional tier of government existed, regional institutions had to be created.

The French model, developed in the 1950s, required the creation of regional economic areas across French territory. Without these, a realistic plan could not be developed, as the needs of one region differed markedly from those of another. In a parallel development a number of *forces vives* movements, particularly in Brittany, sprang up. These voluntary institutions created a regional co-operative framework for interest groups including political, business and employee organisations. Demanding greater regional autonomy in the field of economic development, these bodies were a challenge to the unitary state, particularly as they attracted traditional supporters of the conservative right.

The French government's response was to tame these bodies by incorporating them into their new regional structure. This was achieved through the establishment of the CODER (*Commission de Développement Économique Régional*) regional development committees in 1964. These boards, replacing the SDRs (*Société de Développement Régional*) established in 1955, consisted of 25% elected representatives, 25% government appointees and 50% professional nominees. Their tasks were minimal, and consisted mainly of advising the regional Prefect on regional portions of the national plan (Keating and Hainsworth, 1986). Despite the fact that the government-appointed Prefect took all the important decisions, there was, by 1964, a definite regional structure emerging in France. The regional Prefect, established in 1964, was the executive of an administrative region, one of 22 CARs (*Circonscription d'Action Régionale*) advised by the region's CODER. Son of CODER lives on in the form of the Economic and Social Committees, which form part of the current regional structures.

In the UK, Italy, Germany, Belgium and the Netherlands, a regional level of administration was established as a vital element in the economic planning system, although the extent of democratic involvement varied widely. Even in Spain, a degree of indicative planning was introduced by the fascist regime (Richardson, 1975). In Germany, Belgium and the Netherlands, existing tiers of government (the *Länder* and the provinces) were used as the regional elements in the national plan, but in the UK and Italy this was not possible. Although in theory, the Italian state was designed as one incorporating a number of devolved regions, in fact only the five 'special status' regions had been established. In the UK, of course, no such regional devolution was even planned.

The regional component of the Italian national economic plan was supplied by Economic Planning Committees during the 1960s (Zariski, 1987, p 128). In the UK, this was achieved with the creation of eight English planning regions and one each for Scotland, Wales and Northern Ireland. The institutions in these regions closely mirrored those developed in France, with a nominated (and advisory) representative council and an executive board of civil servants. These were to advise and report on the regional portion of the eventual national plan (Keating and Rhodes, 1979, p 5). The common feature of the regional structures in France, Italy and the UK was the advisory nature of the democratic element. The centre was unwilling to delegate such power to a democratic sub-national institution.

In the examples of Germany, Belgium and the Netherlands, the existence of a tier capable of contributing regional input to the national economic plan meant that these authorities themselves became the regional planning authorities. In the German case, the economic planning role of the *Länder* was constitutionally secured in the Basic Law, and therefore the *Bund* had little choice but to develop such policies in co-operation with the regional tier. The growth of national planning had little lasting impact on the structure of these states, but did enhance the role of the regional level. In unitary states the effect was twofold. The central government recognised the need for a regional authority, and created the regional institutions necessary for it to function. This in turn gave further impetus to regional movements and enhanced regional identity. More importantly, it invited the question as to why regional authorities, if they were necessary, were not democratically accountable. Ironically, these effects far outlived the fashion for indicative planning which faded as nation-states lost confidence in their ability to manage their economies amidst the crises of the 1970s.

3.3.2 Welfare and service regionalism

Although the use of economic management in post-1945 Europe enhanced regional identity and created tensions which ultimately proved difficult to sustain, the impact was not uniform across Western Europe. In states such as the Netherlands and Belgium, where the provinces were capable of supplying the regional element of the national plan, the tensions were less evident, while in smaller states such as Denmark, the regional planning episode had virtually no impact whatsoever. In these countries, and indeed in many of those unitary states mentioned above, the regional question was raised by the growth of the welfare state and increased pressure on governments to provide diverse services at optimum levels of efficiency and accountability.

In Scandinavian countries, the growth of the welfare state, although supported by the mass of the population, caused a degree of concern on democratic grounds. The centrist nature of welfare provision meant little democratic accountability below the level of the nation-state. Both Denmark and Sweden reorganised the regional level as a direct result of this concern (Hansen, 1993, p 312). Prior to the reforms of 1970, the Danish regional level had been controlled by the state and headed by a Prefect. The existence of such a regional administrative tier again gave ammunition to those wishing for democratic regional devolution. In the event this tier was democratised and granted responsibility for several welfare and health services.

The situation in Belgium, the Netherlands and the UK was less clear cut. Although welfare and service regionalism occurred in these countries, it was only in Belgium that regional governments emerged, and in this case it was due more to ethnic divisions and regional identities than to the factors discussed above.

Regional administration in England remains common in a number of policy areas, including policing, where several local authority jurisdictions are under the auspices of one police authority. In fact, regional offices and field agencies of government have been a consistent feature of modern government throughout the UK, as Keating and Rhodes showed in their study of the West Midlands in the 1970s (Keating and Rhodes, 1979). In their example the Ministry of Agriculture, sections of the Department of Trade and the then Department of Industry, as well as the Department of the Environment, all operated regional offices. By the year 2000, regional deconcentration in England was even more pronounced and complex (Tomaney, 2000).

In England this has not, until recently, led to a demand for the democratisation of the regional tier of government. One reason for this could be the non-coterminous nature of their territorial boundaries. Although the regional planning boundaries have often been used in discussions surrounding English regionalism they are by no means universally accepted (Sharpe, 1993a). The regional units, at least until recently, have also been relatively anonymous and as such are generally ignored by the population. A combination of these factors may have led to the neutralisation of the English regional debate.

The decision by the Conservative government to rationalise a number of regional field offices and administrative agencies into a series of Regional Government Offices has changed this. By creating a single regional entity, the government inadvertently made the task of the regional lobby easier. The coming of devolution to Scotland and Wales, coupled with the creation of the Regional Development Agencies with significant spending power, has led to a far more visible democratic deficit at the regional level. Whether this will be translated into significant pressure for regional reform in England remains to be seen. A number of regional campaigns have been established in several English regions, most notably in Yorkshire and the North East. These have achieved some measure of support, and a Government White Paper on the English regional question is due to be published in early 2002 (*Hansard*, col 127, 23 October 2001).

In Scotland and Wales the existence of fixed and mostly non-contentious borders gave a greater regional identity to the established deconcentrated authorities. The Scottish Office and, to a lesser extent, the Welsh Office exercised authority over a diverse range of visible policies. Whereas in England these powers were distributed throughout Whitehall, or even to their regional offices, in Scotland and Wales they were, to a large extent, transferred to Edinburgh or Cardiff; perhaps more importantly, the population perceived this to be the case even when it was not (Leicester, 1996). The regional persona of these deconcentrated government bodies was therefore much higher. This in turn served to highlight the lack of direct democratic control over them.

3.3.3 Functional regionalism and accountability

The existence of regional institutions to govern economic planning, welfare and services gave significant impetus to calls for democratic regional government. By setting up these sub-national bodies, the central authorities accepted the efficiency arguments of decentralisation. By creating them at a regional level they conceded the need for the existence of this tier. In a democracy it then follows that such regional bodies should be directly responsible to the regional population they serve.

The creation of these regional institutions in an effort to deconcentrate power led to a visible democratic deficit at the regional level. If regional institutions are necessary, as the central governments of France, Italy, the UK and Denmark (among others) accepted, it is reasonable to suggest they should be democratically accountable to those who will be affected by their decisions. In the cases of Italy, France and Denmark this argument proved irresistible. Only in the UK did the central government refuse to make such regional institutions democratic. Even this opposition was ended in relation to Scotland, Wales and Northern Ireland in the wake of the devolution reforms. It may soon prove equally difficult for the UK Government to resist such claims for democratic accountability in the regions of England.

3.4 CONCLUSION: THE CONSEQUENCES OF THE REGIONAL REVOLUTION

The development of regional government in Europe has not been a simple process. Several factors have combined to pressurise central authorities into regionalising their nation-states. Underlying all these developments, however, has been the failure of the centralised nation-state to represent adequately the interests of a proportion of its population. With a devolved system of government, more of these interests can be satisfactorily addressed.

The interests of democracy have not been fulfilled by the centralised nation-state. Authoritarian regimes were created throughout the European nation-states of the 1930s and it needed the cataclysm of the Second World War to restore democratic systems. In a regionalised system, such a process is perceived as less likely, with power being devolved to several tiers rather than concentrated at one all-powerful level.

In a similar vein, the democratic aspirations of self-determination have not been addressed by the nation-state, and the identities of many people have only been partially represented if at all. The politicisation of these issues in the 1960s has led to the increasing calls for self-determination or *autogestion* (self-management) now evident throughout the Member States of the European Union. These interests are usually expressed not through demands for nation-state status, but rather for regional autonomy within the wider state and the European Union.

Finally, centralised European nation-states have found it increasing difficulty to deliver the increased economic and welfare responsibilities now demanded by their populations. The need for a regional tier (and indeed other forms of governance) has now been accepted by all European central governments. If such levels are created but not accountable to the region they govern, this leaves them open to claims of being undemocratic, adding further fuel to the regionalists' argument.

The current patchwork of regional governments has been created through a combination of the factors described above. Under the principle of subsidiarity, it has been accepted that certain functions and tasks are best performed by a government elected on a regional basis. This is certainly not to say that the region should be the only, or indeed the most important, level of government. This would merely recreate the problems of the 'hard-bordered' nation-state explored in Chapter 1. The region has a part to play both in delivering particular services and policies and in representing the interests of the regional population. Since 1945, the evidence for this argument has become overwhelming, causing several nation-states to devolve varying degrees of authority to democratic regional authorities throughout the EU. This may have been as much a response to the threat posed by such tensions on the nation-state as any active support for the principle of regional government, but the effect has been the same. Regional governments now form a new and distinct 'third level' of government across the territory of the European Union. The structures, operation and consequences for European governance of this third level are the subject of the remainder of this volume.

Part 2

The Practice of Regional Governance

CHAPTER 4

EUROPE'S FEDERATIONS

Three Member States of the European Union classify themselves as 'federations' in their constitutional documents (Switzerland, Europe's oldest federation, remains obstinately outside the EU). Although there continues to be some debate as to what this term actually means (as discussed in Chapter 2), for our purposes their self-definition is enough to merit their being discussed as a distinct group of regional systems.

The youngest and perhaps the most unusual is Belgium. Created to manage the community conflicts that have beset the Belgian state almost since its inception, it has several features which distinguish it from other federal systems. The Austrian and German federations, by contrast, were both created in the aftermath of military defeat under significant influence from beyond their borders. With the exception of the Austrian Tyrol (and possibly Bavaria) their regions do not represent distinct ethnic or cultural identities within the state.

The very different origins of these systems have resulted in a significant number of differences between them. Nevertheless, there are several distinctive features of these systems which set them apart from the other regionalised systems discussed in this volume. Most importantly, in each of the federal systems the regional tier has a constitutional status as part of the national level of government. This constitutional 'equality' plays out very differently in the three European federations discussed below.

4.1 THE BELGIAN FEDERATION

4.1.1 Regionalism in Belgium

On 17 February 1994, King Albert II signed the new Belgian Constitution. In doing so he formally created Europe's youngest and arguably most unusual federation. Although the story of Belgium's transformation from traditional unitary state to innovative federation began in the 1970s, the roots of the story go back to the foundation of Belgium itself. To understand the present constitutional settlement one must first understand the complex history of the Belgian state.

Although some may challenge the premise that nations are a mythical concept (as discussed in Chapter 1), even the most ardent nationalist would have difficulty in claiming that the Belgian state was anything other than an artificial construct. The word Belgium comes from the Latin name for this far flung district of the Roman Empire, *Gallia Belgica* (Belgic Gaul). Occupied by Julius Caesar in the 1st century BCE, it marked the edge of Roman expansion in this area of northern Europe, a fact that has shaped the political development of this area of Europe to the present day. The term itself was not used in modern times until it was plucked from obscurity in the 18th century to describe the provinces of the 'Spanish Netherlands' that make up the modern Belgian state.

The Romans left a lasting inheritance. Belgium lies across a linguistic fault line that has divided Europe for over a millennium. To the west lie the Romance languages (directly influenced by Latin), to the east those of the Germanic family. The Belgium of today continues to reflect this linguistic division. To the south of a line that bisects the country lies the predominantly French speaking area, collectively referred to as the Walloon provinces or, more recently, Wallonie (*Wallonia*). The Walloons actually speak one of three Wallonian dialects (Walloon, Picard or Gaumais) which differ markedly from standard French. To the north of this line lies the predominantly Dutch speaking territory of Flanders. The Flemish speak a series of dialects which are very close to standard Dutch (the written language is identical). Brussels is now a predominantly French speaking island (though not necessarily Walloon) surrounded by Dutch speaking territory. A third much smaller territory in the south east of the country is home to a predominantly German speaking population. Until the Belgian Constitution of 1831, these areas had never been ruled as a single entity. The German speaking areas were not added until 1919.

All these provinces (particularly those of modern day Flanders) had participated in the Dutch revolt, and for a brief period (1757–58) formed part of the United Provinces after the pacification of Ghent. Despite this, the relationship between the predominantly Roman Catholic Flemish and Walloon provinces and their Calvinist-dominated northern compatriots was never cordial. The relationship was made possible only by the confederal nature of the short lived constitution. In response to the Union of Utrecht, the Walloon provinces seceded and sought reincorporation into the Spanish crown (1579). This was soon followed by Spanish reconquest of Flanders (1580). In both cases, religious differences drove a wedge between the 'Belgian' provinces and their co-conspirators.

The provinces of the Spanish Netherlands were to remain separated from their Dutch cousins under the rule of the Hapsburg crown (first Spanish and then Austrian) for the next two centuries. In 1795, the armies of the French Revolution effected a marriage of sorts after they seized control of both Wallonia and Flanders before occupying the United Provinces of the Netherlands in 1798. This unification of the Low Countries was to continue in the aftermath of the Napoleonic era with the creation of the United

Netherlands, a monarchy under the rule of the Calvinist house of Orange. The consequences of such a constitution seem somewhat inevitable in hindsight. In September 1828, the mainly Catholic élites of the southern provinces briefly put aside their linguistic differences and allied with the predominantly French speaking liberals to press for concessions from the Dutch regime. The regime responded by promising a recall of the parliament (the States General) while simultaneously sending troops to Brussels. This approach backfired, and when the Dutch troops arrived, they found the population of Brussels barring their entry and preparing for a defence of the city. Other cities sent men and aid to the rebels and something akin to a national rising seemed imminent. William III called for aid from the great powers which had established his kingdom in 1815. Their surprising response was to trumpet the cause of independence and a neutral 'Belgium'. The British in particular feared that opposing the rebels might cause them to look to France for aid, and saw the benefits of a nominally neutral but pro-British country on the borders of their French rivals.

In 1830, the Kingdom of the Belgians was duly proclaimed. The events of the 'September Days' had seen Europe's youngest nation-state stumble to independence almost by accident. Nevertheless, despite the Walloon-Flemish alliance that had made the September rebellion possible, the new state was a far from united political entity. To quote the rather melodramatic words of Jules Destrée, the Walloon socialist leader, '*Laissez-moi vous dire la vérité, la grande et horrifiante vérité: il n'y a pas de Belges*' (Let me tell you the truth, the great and horrifying truth: there are no Belgians).

Despite the clear cultural split that existed within the country, the Belgian state of 1830 was strictly unitary. Based around Brussels and its French speaking élite, the only recognised language was French. This failure to recognise the linguistic divide and the fact that the majority of the population was Flemish (as it still is) was a recipe for conflict. The linguistic situation was further complicated by the addition of the German speaking districts of Eupen and Malmédy to Belgium under the Versailles Treaty of 1919.

Resentment within the Flemish majority grew steadily from the mid-19th century, and the Belgian state was gradually forced to address the Flemish issue. With the establishment of universal suffrage in the aftermath of the First World War, the Flemish majority soon began to exercise its numerical superiority through the ballot box. Although the collaboration of Flemish nationalists with the occupying German forces meant political concessions would not be delivered, this period did see the end of discrimination against the Flemish language and the permanent establishment of a language border in 1963 (Delmartino, 1993, p 44). Of symbolic importance was the official publication, in the same year, of the Belgian Civil Code in Dutch.

The emergence in the 1970s of economic as well as linguistic divisions within Belgium added a further variable to the situation. The Walloon provinces had been one of the first regions to industrialise and, in common with most other European industrial regions, they experienced a collapse of their industries in the late 20th century. By contrast, the less developed Flanders, with an economy based on light industry and commerce, weathered the economic storm rather well, emerging as the richer partner in the Belgian state. As the Walloon electorate turned increasingly to parties of the left, the national government increasingly followed neo-liberal policies aimed at reducing both the involvement of the state in the Belgian economy and its crippling national debt. The result was resentment amongst the Walloon electorate and calls for economic autonomy for the south (Thomas, 1990).

The reforms that eventually led to the creation of the Belgian federation began in 1970. Through what eventually became a three stage process, culminating in the new constitution of 1994, the Belgian unitary state slowly became a federation. The impression given may be one of organised reform but organised chaos may be a more accurate description. The entire process was developed on an ad hoc basis, with no clear vision in 1970 as to the final settlement. The priority at a time of linguistic tension and unrest was the survival of the state and prevention of a crisis developing into intercommunal violence. Whatever criticisms can be laid at the door of those who designed the Belgian state, they at least achieved these primary goals.

The initial pressure for reform came from the Flemish. Although defended by a number of constitutional provisions, they still feared for the future of Flemish culture and the Dutch language, given the global importance of French in comparison with Dutch. This was reflected in increased support for Flemish regionalist political parties. The Flemish regionalist party *Volksunie* gained nearly 10% of the vote in 1968, while the French regionalists (the *Rassamblement Wallon* and the *Front Wallon*) collectively gained nearly 6%. Further evidence of the influence of language in Belgian politics was to be found in the national parties themselves, which began to divide internally along linguistic lines (Fitzmaurice, 1996, p 48).

In 1970, primarily as a result of Flemish demands, the Belgian state was divided into three cultural regions to represent the three linguistic populations (Flemish, French and German). In each of these a cultural council comprising the regional members of the national parliament (the Chamber of Representatives) was given limited responsibilities in the fields of education and culture. The Brussels-Capital region was to remain bilingual. The boundaries of these linguistic regions were enshrined in a Special Majority Act which cannot be altered without the agreement of both Flemish and French representatives in the Belgian Parliament (Art 59 of the 1970 constitution, now consolidated in Art 4, Belgian Constitution). In tandem with this development, three Regional Councils (Brussels-Capital, Flanders and Wallonia) were established, again comprising the national members of parliament operating a dual mandate (the Belgian Region is capitalised to distinguish these specific institutions from the generic regional tier). Unlike the cultural regions, the powers of these bodies were not enshrined in the constitution, which denied them legislative power. These Regional developments in particular were as a result of Walloon desires for greater regional autonomy in economic matters (Thomas, 1990).

These reforms, although overshadowed by more recent constitutional amendments, marked a fundamental shift in the Belgian Constitution. In his opening address to parliament on 18 February 1970, Prime Minister Eyskens elegantly summed up the change. 'The unitary state', in his words, had been 'overtaken by events' (Alen and Ergec, 1998, p 11).

The constitutional reforms of 1980 saw the creation of three 'Cultural Communities' (henceforth referred to as 'the Communities') based upon the already extant cultural councils. These Communities were responsible for the educational and cultural policies previously devolved to the cultural councils, with a number of new responsibilities relating to health and social policy. These were the personalisables, powers that directly relate to the individual. The most important of these was health. In tandem with the elevation of the Communities to something akin to a truly devolved government, the regions were given a far greater role, close to that accorded to the Communities. Under pressure from the Walloons, the three economic Regions were also given legislative powers and constitutional status alongside the Communities. This structure largely survives to the present day.

Further reforms were instituted as a result of the Cockerill-Sambre crisis of the early 1980s (Covell, 1987, p 70). The Walloon steel giant Cockerill-Sambre was in severe financial difficulty by the early 1980s, and an independent consultant estimated the cost of rescue at over BEF11 bn (approximately £1.1 bn), a bill that the Flemish members of the national parliament were unwilling to foot. The compromise gave a fixed sum to regional representatives in the national government to spend on the national industries in their territory. Any extra funding for such fields was to be found from regionally computable sources of national revenue. Ironically, neither Regional executive wished this power to be devolved due to the expensive nature of economic support and the realisation in Flanders that their shipbuilding and mining sectors were also in financial difficulties (Covell, 1986, pp 274–75). This proved to be an unsatisfactory and temporary solution, and most of these powers were formally transferred to the Regions in 1988.

The final two stages of the Belgian reform process took place in 1988 and 1993. The 1988 series of reforms saw further expansion of Regional and Community powers including the crucially important devolution of greater financial resources and the introduction of interregional solidarity payments. This reform also saw the establishment of the Brussels-Capital Region which, although agreed under the reforms of 1980, was not established for a further eight years. The 1988 agreements also set in motion the negotiations that were to lead to the final set of constitutional changes five years later.

The final reform proved the most difficult to agree on. The 1993 St Michel Accords, signed between the governing coalition parties and their allies, led to the formal federalisation of Belgium and the rewriting of the constitution. The latter was necessary due to the large number of changes that had taken place in the previous twenty years, creating a highly convoluted constitutional document. The practice of adding new amendments to alter existing amendments made the document particularly confusing. For example, the provisions now found in Art 3 (originally 107d) concerning the establishment of the Regions has never been amended due to Walloon fears that any alteration could be used as an excuse to dismantle the tripartite system of Belgian federalism. Nevertheless, the Regions of today bear little resemblance to those created in 1970, having accumulated a large degree of constitutional power. In particular they now have the authority to undertake primary legislation (something barred without explicit constitutional authority). This was achieved by the creation of enabling provisions elsewhere in the constitution (Art 39, Belgian Constitution) which allowed extra powers to be granted to the Regions through special majority laws (now under Art 4, Belgian Constitution). The continued use of these special provisions makes study of the Belgian Constitution extremely confusing.

The 1993 accords and the constitutional amendments that followed them were intended to represent the final destination of the constitutional reform process, with further changes being necessary only to complete the processes agreed at St Michel. The rumblings of discontent within the more regionalist elements (particularly in Flanders) made this prediction increasingly unlikely, and on June 29 2001 a further package of regional reforms was approved. This, the St Polycarpe agreement, grants even greater responsibilities to the regional tier in the fields of agriculture, foreign trade and local government, as well as increased powers of taxation and extra federal grant funding for Communities. Nevertheless, the federal system established in 1994 appears likely to remain the framework for any further reform, at least for the foreseeable future.

4.1.2 The national framework

Article 1 of the 1994 Belgian Constitution states that 'Belgium is a Federal State, composed of Communities and Regions' (Art 1, Belgian Constitution). By this statement, the Belgian unitary state of 1830 was finally pronounced dead, although, like the Soviet leaders of the 1970s, its practical demise had occurred decades previously. In its place was a new state built along federal lines.

Figure 4.1: Structure of territorial government in Belgium

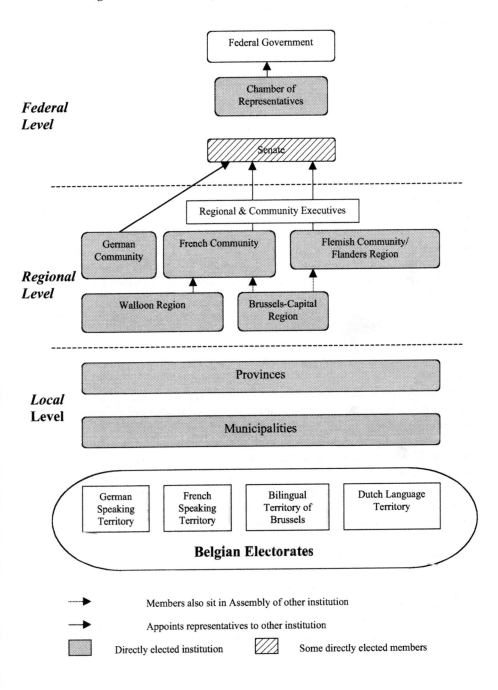

As will already have become clear from the above discussion of the reform process, the territorial organisation of the Belgian federal state is highly complex. Although Belgium has a population of only 10 million, there are five types of democratically elected government (municipalities, provinces, regions, Communities and the federal government), as shown in Figure 4.1. It is incorrect to describe these as tiers of government for two reasons. First, the federal and regional governments are constitutionally equal; secondly, the Belgian regional level comprises two functionally distinct forms of government, Communities and Regions. These constitutionally separate institutions function in distinct policy spheres. Most importantly, their territorial boundaries are not coterminous. This latter property makes the Belgian federation unique.

The organisation of local government remains a federal responsibility and as such is uniform throughout the Belgian state. The most basic unit of governance is the municipality, of which there are 589, a significant reduction of the 3,000 that existed prior to reform in 1970. Above this local level lie 10 (originally nine) provinces which until 1970 formed the 'regional' level of the Belgian state. As a result of the federal reforms, the bilingual province of Brabant has been divided into Flemish and French parts. Within the Brussels-Capital Region (formerly part of this province), the Regional government has taken on formerly provincial powers. The continued relevance of this level has been seriously questioned as a consequence of the constitutional reforms (Delmartino, 1993).

The regional institutions are explicitly guaranteed by the Belgian Constitution. The three Communities are entrenched by Art 2, and the Regions by Art 3. In addition, the four language territories (French, Dutch, German and bilingual) are guaranteed under Art 4. The boundaries of these territories may be altered only by a special majority of the Belgian Parliament. This requires a majority of each language group's representatives in each house to support the motion. In addition the overall majority in each house must be two-thirds of the votes cast, and a majority of each language group's representatives must be present. The language groups were established by an ordinary *loi* of 3 July 1971 (*Moniteur Belge*, 6 July 1971). This 'dual key' mechanism is utilised elsewhere in the structure of the Belgian Constitution, and has been emulated in the procedures of the Northern Ireland Assembly (see Chapter 7).

The federal executive is limited to 15 ministers, with equal representation from the two main language groups, not including the Prime Minister (Fitzmaurice, 1996, p 91). The federal executive is responsible to the newly streamlined lower house, or Chamber of Representatives (150 members reduced from 212). This directly elected chamber previously shared its legislative role with the Senate (or upper house) but the position of the latter chamber has changed markedly in the aftermath of the federal reforms.

One particularly unusual feature of the Belgian legislative process is the *sonnette d'alarme* (alarm bell) procedure. Introduced in 1970, the procedure allows three-quarters of either the French or the Flemish representatives in the Chamber of Representatives to delay a bill for up to 30 days (Art 38, Belgian Constitution). Although not strictly part of the federal structure, it is further evidence of the bipolar regionalism so prevalent in the Belgian political system (Swan, 1988, p 376).

Regional statutes are referred to as *loi*, Community statutes as *décret* and Brussels Regional Statutes as *ordinances*. The various regional bodies have full legislative and administrative autonomy within their fields of competence. Belgium has no equivalent of the German concept *Bundesrecht bricht Landesrecht* (federal law overrides regional law, discussed more fully below) and as a result Regional *loi* and Community *décret* have equal constitutional status to federal *loi* (Alen and Ergec, 1998, p 21). This principle of legislative equality between the federal and regional tiers has been heavily criticised by some commentators (Cullen, 1990, p 356), but for Regions and Communities it has proved crucial in negotiations with the federation. Although the equality of laws has led to significant difficulties within the Belgian system, the success or failure of such an extreme level of decentralisation surely depends upon whether one regards the needs of the federation as paramount. The supremacy of federal law can lead to creeping centralisation, as in the case of Germany and concurrent competencies (see section 4.2.4).

The minor exception to this rule applies to specific Brussels Regional *ordinances* (primarily related to planning) which are open to veto by the federal government and to judicial review in the administrative courts. This is due to the city's importance as the capital of Belgium and the *de facto* capital of the European Union (Special Majority Law, 12 January 1989).

The equality of laws between the federation and its component parts means that disputes between the various levels of regional government and the federation must be handled primarily through negotiation and consensus. Disputes between Regional and Community legislatures are dealt with in the Senate, while disputes involving the federal authorities are referred to a conciliation committee. This committee consists of the Prime Minister, the Regional and Community presidents and a selection of national and regional ministers. Decisions are taken unanimously and not by majority. By placing such emphasis on unanimity, however, the system reduces the autonomy of individual regional and community authorities by relying on political horse-trading to achieve a solution (Fitzmaurice, 1984, p 429).

If negotiations fail, the matter may be referred to the Court of Arbitration. This court, which is Belgium's constitutional tribunal in all but name, is somewhat unusual. Only half its members are jurists, the other half being retired politicians. The name of the court (and its composition) reflects Belgian sensitivity over explicitly accepting judicial supremacy over the legislature (Cullen, 1990, p 355). As with everything else in Belgium, the composition of the court is divided along linguistic lines, with half the members coming from each major language community. The small German community does not figure in these quotas, a fact which emphasises the bipolar nature of the Belgian federal system. The court has held that contradictions in the Belgian federation are impossible, given the principle of equality explored above (Alen and Ergec, 1998, p 21). Instead, it will adjudicate only as to whether a decree or law is beyond the competencies of the relevant institution, as laid out in the constitutional and special majority laws (in effect using the *ultra vires* principle as understood in the United Kingdom). As such it is the final arbitrator in disputes over constitutional competencies.

Due to the delicate political nature of this task, the court is not obliged to give reasons for its judgments. In 1988, the court's authority was expanded to include review of legislation for compatibility with three rights elucidated in the Belgian Bill of Rights (Title II, Belgian Constitution). The somewhat eclectic collection of equality, education and academic freedom (Arts 10, 11 and 24, Belgian Constitution) once again reflects the particular tensions within the Belgian state.

4.1.3 The Belgian Regional level

The three Belgian Regions, Flanders (*Vlaanderland*), Wallonia (*Wallonie*) and Brussels-Capital, are territorially defined entities (see Figure 4.2) with responsibility primarily in the fields of economic and social affairs. The two large regions were first established in 1980, while controversy surrounding the exact nature of Brussels-Capital delayed its establishment until 1988.

Figure 4.2: Belgian Regions and Communities

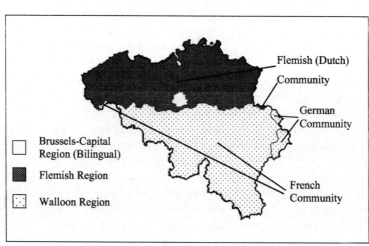

Operating in parallel with Regions are the three 'Cultural Communities' (French, Dutch and German). These are, in theory, non-territorially defined entities empowered to make decrees concerning cultural or 'personalised' matters. The French phrase is *les matières personalisables*, which does not easily translate into English. It refers to matters concerning the individual, which are defined as including Health, Education and Culture while excluding economic matters.

In practice, the French Community comprises the population of Wallonia (not including the nine German speaking municipalities) and the French speaking population of Brussels. The Dutch Community comprises the population of Flanders and the Dutch speaking population of Brussels. Due to the sensitivity of the issue, census data on Dutch and French speakers living in Brussels is unavailable, but estimates put the split at around 85:15 in favour of the French. The German Community makes up the trio and comprises the nine German speaking provinces in the east of the country. Dutch, French or German speaking individuals who reside in areas other than those outlined above are citizens of the Community they reside in, although some 'special rights' are accorded to non-native speakers in specific municipalities along the linguistic border. In practice, therefore, the Communities have become territorial regions, although these regions are somewhat soft around the edges. Only within the borders of the Brussels-Capital Region have Community responsibilities retained their non-territorial basis.

The Belgian regional institutions do not possess individual regional statutes or constitutions. Instead, the Belgian Constitution and its accompanying special majority laws provide the constitutional basis for all the various federal and regional institutions. This is another distinctive feature of the Belgian system, as in formal federations it is common for the institutions of the regional tier to be established under regional constitutions, established within the framework of the national document. As will be seen below, non-federal regional structures are also commonly established under individual regional statutes, with the consent of the national tier. To some extent, recent reforms have brought the Belgian regional tier closer to this practice, and a limited degree of organisational autonomy now applies to the Flemish and Walloon Regions and respective Communities under Arts 118(2) and 123(2) of the Belgian Constitution (amended in 1995). Further flexibility has been introduced as a consequence of the St Polycarpe agreement (see section 4.1.1). Such decisions must be approved by the relevant legislative branch by a two-thirds majority. This limited constitutional autonomy does not apply to the German Community or the Brussels Region.

The members of the larger regional councils originally held a dual mandate representing their electorates both in the Belgian Chamber of Representatives and in the Regional and Community legislatures. Only the

Brussels-Capital Regional Council and the German Community Council were directly elected from their inception. Since 1993, all the regional legislatures (now called Parliaments) have been directly elected. Each Regional and Community Parliament is unicameral and comprises between 25 and 124 members (see Table 4.1), each with an executive accountable to it. The executives need not be elected from its council, and in the most recent elections the Regional presidents have come from the national parliament through party deals struck at the federal level. Only the German Community does not follow this practice.

The Belgian Constitution has provisions for the various Regional and Community institutions to merge or delegate power to each other. In Flanders this has already happened, with a single parliament and executive taking on the responsibilities of both the Flanders Region and the Dutch Community. Formally, the institutions of the Flanders Region undertake the duties of the Dutch Community although, in an example of the soft-bordered nature of the Belgian system, Brussels members are barred from matters of a purely Regional nature. It is unlikely that the French Community and the Walloon Region will follow a similar path. The differences between the French speakers of Brussels and their Walloon co-linguists are far greater than between the Dutch speaking populations. This lack of unity amongst the French speaking populations at least partially explains the limited transfer of powers from the French Community to the Walloon and Brussels-Capital Regions (Polet 1999, p 23).

Table 4.1: Composition of Belgian Regional Parliaments

Community/Region	Size of Parliament	Executive (maximum)
Flemish (R and C)	124	11
Wallonia (R)	75	7
Brussels-Capital (R)	75	5
French (C)	94	4
German (C)	25	3

In practice, only one regional election is held in both Flanders and Wallonia (except in the territory of the German Community). The Flemish Parliament and the Walloon Community Council comprise the elected members of the regional parliaments and representatives from the Brussels Parliament (six on the Flemish Council and 19 on the French). The German Community Parliament and the Brussels-Capital Regional Parliament remain directly elected by their respective populations.

The German Community is responsible for Community matters within the nine German speaking municipalities in the east of the country. This territory is entirely within the region of Wallonia, and the Region may transfer powers to the German Community if both governments agree to such a proposal. As yet, there is little evidence of this happening. Nevertheless, with a population of only 80,000 represented by a parliament of 25 and an executive of three, the German speaking population of Belgium must be one of the most protected minorities on the planet.

There are a few differences in the organisation of the Brussels-Capital Region that merit special mention. The Communities have jurisdiction over the relevant language speakers in the Brussels-Capital Region. In practice, however, the authority of the Communities in the Brussels area is delegated to Community Committees. These consist of the representatives of the relevant language groups in the Brussels-Capital Regional Parliament.

This structure applies only to institutions, primarily schools. 'Personalised' matters are administered by the Brussels United Assembly, although in practice this is the Brussels Council by another name. The executive of this body is referred to as the Brussels United College but it too is merely the Brussels Regional government in a different guise, the only difference being that the chairman may not vote. Decisions taken in both Brussels executive bodies are reached by consensus, so the chairman's lack of a vote is relatively unimportant. The major difference in the United Assembly is that any ordinances approved must achieve a majority in both language groups, although only 11 of the 75 members are Flemish (Van Ginderachter, 1993, p 7).

The over-representation of the Flemish within Brussels (50% of the Regional executive), and their disproportionate power in the Brussels Assembly, is the result of a political bargain between the representatives of the two language groups. The Flemish parties accepted a 50:50 split of the national executive in exchange for a similar split in Brussels. The Flemish represent 60% of the national population but less than 20% in Brussels. This imbalance made a negotiated bargain possible.

Special treatment has been granted to the predominantly francophone municipalities in the Brussels suburbs of the Flemish Region, as a well as a number of municipalities along the borders between Communities (including the entire German Community). These were established under a constitutional law passed using the special majority method outlined in Art 4 (see section 4.1.1). Individuals in these municipalities are able to vote for French speaking senators, and enjoy special language privileges in relation to schooling and official documents (Leonard, 1992, p 25). This latter point has continued to be a source of political controversy. The Flemish Government claims that these privileges are only temporary while the French Community (and the populations of these municipalities) regard them as protected in perpetuity (Polet, 1999, p 41).

4.1.4 Regional participation in the federal institutions

Table 4.2: Composition of the Belgian Senate

Method of appointment	Senators
Directly elected by Flanders Regional electorate	25
Directly elected from Walloon Regional electorate	15
Elected by and from Dutch Community Council (dual mandate)	10
Elected by and from French Community Council (dual mandate)	10
Elected by and from German Community Council (dual mandate)	1
Co-opted by Dutch speaking directly elected members	6
Co-opted by French speaking directly elected members	4

One Flemish and six French speaking senators must be from the Brussels region.

In common with other European federations, the regional tier in Belgium has a formal role in national decision making. The second chamber of the Belgian federal parliament (the Senate) is an assembly of Communities and Regions, in practice if not in name, as shown in Table 4.2 (Alen and Ergec, 1998, p 29). As part of the reforms of 1994, it was reduced from 184 members to a mere 75. The reforms also significantly altered (and reduced) its role in the legislative process. Its primary purpose is now to represent Regional and Community interests at the federal level and to act as a limited chamber of reflection, although it may still initiate legislation (Leonard, 1992, p 24). Its most significant power is the ability to delay legislation by 60 days at the request of a mere 15 members. During this time amendments may be proposed, but the power of approval remains with the lower house. Senate approval is only required in four specific circumstances (Art 77, Belgian Constitution):

(a) changes to the constitution;

(b) linguistic laws;

(c) legislation which purports to grant powers to international or supranational organisations;

(d) the organisation of the judiciary.

The Senate is also endowed with exclusive authority to intercede in disputes between the regional legislatures. Although it gives the Belgian Communities a voice in the national framework, the Belgian Senate does not have the pivotal role in regional or federal relations which is accorded to the German *Bundesrat* (see section 4.2.5). The Senate's inability to veto national legislation is in tune with Belgian attempts to segregate federal and regional powers. The lack of a legal hierarchy means that the Belgian Regions and Communities (unlike the German *Länder*) have less need for collective power in the Senate to protect their interests.

4.1.5 Regional responsibilities

The competencies assigned to the Belgian Regions and Communities are contained within the relevant Articles of the new constitution (Arts 127–30, Belgian Constitution) and a series of constitutional laws passed under Art 134 using the procedure laid down in Art 4. These competencies are, in the main, exclusive. The intention is a vertical division of powers but, in practice, the retention of significant powers at the national level, combined with the equality of regional and federal laws, has resulted in a system which requires a high level of co-operation between the various governments. Some commentators have gone as far as questioning whether the Belgian system is actually federal, while others doubt whether such co-operation will continue as the system develops (Deelen, 1994; Erk and Gagnon, 2000).

It is envisaged that all unassigned powers will eventually be devolved to the regional governments in a 'subsidiarity' clause, but as yet the competencies of the Regions and Communities remain positively defined. As most competencies already seem to be allocated to either the regional or the federal tier, the effect of such a clause is likely to be minimal.

Although Belgium is the most regionalised state in Europe, the federal level retains a number of key competencies. Principal amongst these are defence, the police, the justice system, social security and public health. In addition, those areas of international and European affairs not granted to the regions are still held centrally. The federation also retains a responsibility to safeguard the economic and monetary unity of Belgium. This latter responsibility encompasses a number of additional powers, including monetary policy, prices and incomes policy, and control over a number of key sectors such as banking, the professions and company law.

Most supply side economic issues are now the responsibility of the Regions. Such authority, though extensive, excludes a number of key reserve powers deemed necessary to ensure the continued operation of a single market (see Table 4.3, p 73). In many ways the Regions are only in a position to alleviate the effects of national policies. It would certainly be difficult for a region to pursue a macroeconomic strategy entirely at odds with the federal level. Increasingly, this capacity is also limited by European Union restrictions on the use of state aid.

The Court of Arbitration has also recognised the federal government's role in protecting the Belgian internal market. The Regions are therefore barred from any economic policy that would harm the internal market of Belgium. Further federal competencies in areas such as company and labour law are also retained at the national level, in the name of the internal market (Delmartino, 1993, pp 58–59).

Regional authority is nevertheless exercised over a significant range of economic competencies within the Belgian federation. The fact that federal competencies have also been lost to the European Union (by some estimates, up to 80% of economic regulation emanates from this source) has led some academics to suggest that the federal government has been all but removed from the economic arena (Van Ginderachter, 1993). This conclusion seems premature. More emphasis needs be placed on the co-operative nature of the new Belgian federal model. For example, to describe a competence such as energy as 'exclusive' when the authority of the Regions is tempered by federal responsibility in such fundamental areas of policy as the national grid and pricing seems erroneous (Covell, 1986, p 279). In wider areas of strategic energy policy too, the region cannot make large macroeconomic policy decisions without federal approval. For instance, the Region may wish to move towards coal rather than nuclear power to save an ailing coal industry or for environmental reasons. However, under the present structure, such an option would be difficult to implement due to federal control over both national energy policy and the nuclear industry. In energy policy, as in much else in the Belgian federation, there is in practice a requirement for co-operation between the Regions and the federal government. During such negotiations, which are explored in more detail in Chapter 11, the federal level holds significant leverage through its 'residual' regulatory functions.

Table 4.3: Belgian federal reserved competencies and powers

Regional exclusive competencies	Federal reserved powers
Planning and land use	Review over decisions relating to Brussels
Environment	Minimum environmental standards
	Water distribution and treatment standards
	Species conservation
Energy	The national grid
	Nuclear power and fuels
	Energy pricing
Employment	Limited reserve powers
Housing	
Economic and industrial policy	
Transport and public works	Brussels airport
	Infrastructure policy
Local government	Supervision of Brabant provinces
Regional export promotion	National export promotion
Scientific research	National scientific research

Community exclusive competencies	Federal reserved competencies
Education	School leaving age
	Minimum educational qualification standards
	Staff pensions
Cultural policy	Right to broadcast national government statements on radio and television
	National cultural bodies
Health	National healthcare framework legislation
	Framework legislation on:
	(a) CPAS (social assurance scheme)
	(b) Less able people
	(c) Prisoner rehabilitation
	(d) Youth policy

The limits of Belgian Regional autonomy in the economic sphere, at least prior to 1988, are well documented by Covell. In 1985, the socialist government of the Walloon Region abandoned its policy of state intervention and investment, which it had pursued contrary to the policies of the conservative-liberal government in Brussels. A lack of financial resources and the fragmentation of policy control in vital areas were key to the region's difficulties (Covell, 1986, pp 272–74). Today, the Region's economic powers are more extensive but it is still a moot point whether a single Region could pursue an economic strategy substantially different from the federal one. Despite the principle of exclusivity found in the Belgian division of functions, the continued placing of economic powers at different levels, including the EU, makes co-operation the key to any successful economic strategy.

The Communities exercise authority in the areas of culture, social policy, health and education. The federation remains the dominant partner in social policy and retains a significant role in health policy, while the Communities are the dominant policy makers in education and cultural policy. This division of powers reflects the principle that 'personalised' matters should be handled by the Communities (Art 128(1), Belgian Constitution). Health is included in the list of 'personalised' matters in the Special Institutional Reform Law of 1980, but Community competence excludes authority over health insurance and organisation of hospitals (Art 5.1(I)1, Special Institutional Reform Law, 8 August 1980). This law also specifically excludes principles agreed in other constitutional legislation (in other words, legislation passed under Art 4 of the constitution). These principles lay down the fundamental framework governing the performance of health policy.

'Cultural matters' are a key competence of the respective Communities under the Special Institutional Law 1980 introduced under Arts 127(1)1 and 130(1)1 of the constitution. These include libraries, museums, the arts, youth policy, professional retraining, heritage, broadcasting, the media, sports and tourism (Special Institutional Reform Law, 8 August 1980, Art 4, Belgian Constitution). Responsibility for language in their regions is also enjoyed by the Flemish and French Communities in relation to public administration and employee relations. The latter *décrets* do not have the force of *loi* in those municipalities which fall within one Community territory but are adjacent to a different Community.

The areas in which the Communities exert greatest authority are without doubt education and the media. Education falls almost exclusively under the competence of each respective Community (see Table 4.3), with a few basic principles being guaranteed by the national level (Arts 127(2) and 130(3), Belgian Constitution). This leaves curriculum, staffing and general education policy firmly under Community control. There is no longer a Belgian Ministry of Education. Equally, the Belgian broadcasting authorities are divided along linguistic lines. As a result, all broadcasting matters are handled at Community level (Special Institutional Reform Law, 8 August 1980). Since 1989, responsibility for written media and regulation of advertising has also passed into Community hands (Fitzmaurice, 1996, p 150).

4.1.6 Does the new Belgium have a future?

In the aftermath of the new constitution, Brussels experienced its biggest public demonstration for many years. Much larger than the Flemish separatist marches of 1990 and 1991, it was mounted in support of the continuation of Belgium and against outright separatism (Leonard, 1993, p 18). On this evidence at least, reports of Belgium's demise appear to be greatly exaggerated.

The devolution process has not always proved popular or indeed rational. The devolution of agriculture to the Regions led to the original 10 farms (apparently there is now only one) within the Brussels region having a ministry all of their own. (*The Economist*, 31 October 1992, p 52). More importantly it meant that agricultural investment funds, as well as the Agricultural Export Promotion Service, are now regionalised. The regionalisation of foreign trade has also meant a division of the export promotion budget. These reforms were strongly opposed by the business community (Deelen, 1994, p 12). In the world of international trade, the division of such resources is perceived to weaken Belgium's presence abroad.

Despite these caveats the Belgian system appears to work, while the Regions and Communities continue to exercise a remarkable level of autonomy for a sub-national level of government. An example of this has seen the Dutch government negotiating with Flanders, not Belgium, over the proposed high speed rail link to Amsterdam (Delmartino, 1993, p 10). However, just as there are few areas where the regions have no involvement whatsoever, there are also few where they operate exclusively, notwithstanding the constitution's assertion to the contrary. Even in areas such as health, which are formally exclusively regional functions, there is significant federal involvement (in this case concerning hospitals). With the exception of language and education, the watchword of the Belgian federation is co-operation. This encourages a consociational approach to the issues of the day, although some have argued that this has begun to weaken (Fitzmaurice, 1996, p 224). It also brings with it significant difficulties concerning accountability and democracy. As Scharpf has noted in relation to Germany, such co-operative arrangements can produce a policy dynamic in themselves, unconnected with the issues concerned (Scharpf, 1988). In addition, the role of the regional parliaments is diminished as such arrangements flourish. Co-operative arrangements almost exclusively involve the executive branch of government.

The dual nature of Belgian federalism adds a particularly Belgian slant to this argument. Although Belgium is formally a federal state with four constituent territories (Brussels, Flanders, Wallonia and the German Community), each with varying powers, in practice Wallonia and Flanders dominate the federal system and the political scene. This occurs to the extent that the smaller regions can be ignored in the scrupulously even-handed division of federal posts. For example, both the federal government and the Court of Arbitration are divided 50:50 along linguistic lines. No explicit provision is made for the German Community. This leads to a *ménage à deux*, to quote Robert Polet, whereby something granted to one Region or Community must be seen also to be granted to the other, whether it is necessary or not (Polet, 1999). One (surely apocryphal) tale concerns a canal in Flanders that leads nowhere. It is said this was built after demands from the Flemish Government for a new canal after the Walloons received federal assistance to build one. One seriously doubts that the canal actually exists (although in Belgium, one always hesitates to doubt such tales entirely) but the story illustrates the popular perception of how this polarised federation operates.

The Belgians nevertheless remain united by a number of factors. Perhaps the most practical of these is the 'Brussels question'. The importance of Brussels within Belgium is obvious, accounting as it does for around 10% of the national population. For the Flemish, Brussels is Flemish soil and, perhaps more importantly, the hub of the regional economy. Yet it is clearly no longer a Flemish city and there is no chance of its becoming one. To complicate matters further, although the *Bruxellois* may have some affinity with their French speaking brethren in Wallonia, this is more an alliance of necessity to protect their language rights against the more extreme notions of some Flemish politicians than any tie of true affection. As neither the Flemish nor the Walloons will allow the other region to acquire the city, responsibility must be shared.

In cultural terms, too, a number of important institutions remain Belgian in character. The popularity of the Belgian monarchy (especially the recently deceased king) is a particularly powerful uniting force. The role of sporting identity also should not be underestimated. In football in particular, Walloons and Flemish are all Belgians. When the Flemish Minister of Sport proposed a Flemish 'national' team, the ensuing outcry nearly cost him his job (Van Ginderachter, 1993).

Possibly the strongest uniting factor comes from beyond the borders of the Belgian state itself. An independent Wallonia or Flanders would be a very small player in the European game, and political domination by her neighbours would be a likely consequence of a Belgian split. Few Walloons, Flemish or German speakers desire unification with their respective linguistic counterparts across the border, with the consequence of becoming a minority in a larger state with less autonomy than they currently enjoy. For the time being, therefore, Belgium remains, to quote the words of Theo Lefèvre (a former Belgian Prime Minister), 'a happy country comprising three oppressed minorities' (Swan, 1988, p 365).

4.2 THE FEDERAL REPUBLIC OF GERMANY

4.2.1 Federalism in Germany

There could hardly be a greater contrast between the genesis of the Belgian federation and its German federal neighbour. The complexity of the Belgian system stems from the political realities that surrounded and indeed drove its creation. It is a product of a highly complex political situation, and as such reflects the compromises necessary to ensure that all sides of the political debate agreed to the new constitutional settlement. The German federation and the *Grundgesetz* (Basic Law) upon which it is built arose from the political wasteland that existed in Germany after the Second World War. Although conscious of the Allied powers looking over their shoulders, the framers of the Basic Law were faced with a rare opportunity. They had the chance to create a system of government from a constitutional *tabula rasa*. To a greater extent than any other European constitution, the German system represents an attempt to create a 'scientific' system of government without the constraints of political bargaining. This goes some way towards explaining the influence that the German system has had on regional and federal government elsewhere in Europe and on the institutions of the EU itself. It also explains why successful aspects of the German system have proved so difficult to reproduce elsewhere.

Although the Federal Republic of Germany only dates from 1949, federation and confederation are not new concepts in German constitutional history. From its very inception, modern Germany has eschewed the unitary model in favour of federal, confederal or regional arrangements. Even prior to its final 'unification' in 1871, many German speaking states had been intermittently united to varying degrees through economic and political unions. The Holy Roman Empire, the Napoleonic Confederation of the Rhine and the German Confederation are but three examples. The year 1871 was a watershed, nevertheless. The 'unification' of Germany, after the Franco-Prussian war, represented the culmination of efforts by the Prussian Chancellor Otto von Bismarck to exert Prussian domination over the whole of central Europe. In Bismarck's opinion there was 'nothing more German than the development of Prussia's particular interests' (Gildea, 1987, p 197). This was achieved at the expense of the other German speaking empire, Austria. After suffering economic exclusion from the German customs union at the hands of Prussia and then military defeat in the contrived war of 1866, Austria was sidelined. The 'unification' of Germany was not a natural unification of the German speaking people but the expansion of the Prussian continental empire (Gildea, 1987). Not only did it fail to incorporate all the German speaking peoples, it also clung tenaciously to territories occupied by non-German speakers (Poles and Danes, for example). This was empire building, not 'liberation' (see Craig, 1981, pp 1–37).

The establishment of Prussia's German empire in 1871 came at a constitutional cost. A degree of sovereignty was pooled in a *Bundesrat*, which represented the governments of the German states, and a significant degree of autonomy was retained by the 25 previously independent states (in some cases even including peacetime defence). Nevertheless, Prussia dominated the *Bundesrat*; the King of Prussia became Kaiser, and Prussia possessed the military might to impose its will upon the other member states. As Kaiser Wilhelm II commented, 'I have eighteen army corps and I can handle south Germans' (J Steinberg, taken from Gildea, 1987, p 207). Nevertheless, although Prussia was clearly the power behind the imperial Germany, even it was unable to dominate the states it acquired entirely.

The tradition of regional or federal constitutionalism has continued to the present day with the brief and catastrophic exception of the periods 1914–18 and 1933–48. These periods of centralism must be regarded as an exception in German political history. Nevertheless, although the German federal tradition runs deep, the current Federal Republic has little in common with its antecedents.

The Federal Republic's Bonn constitution of 1949 made a number of clean breaks with prewar German constitutional tradition. Most noticeably, the German states (or *Länder*) which now make up the federation have little similarity to those that existed prior to 1933. There are two reasons for this. First, the Allied powers (and some Germans) perceived the existence of a single Prussian state, dwarfing its partners, as a destabilising factor, particularly in the previous Weimar Republic. A significant amount of blame for the collapse of the republic was placed upon its constitution, and the imbalance caused by the dominance of Prussia was perceived as part of this. Secondly, the historical territories of the German federation were extremely heterogeneous, comprising a patchwork of states with enormous variations in both size and population. It was deemed preferable to create new states with more 'rational' boundaries.

The influence of the Allied powers on this process should not be ignored. Although it would be wrong to portray the German Basic Law as a settlement imposed upon the German delegates, the opinions of the victorious powers were influential. The United States in particular perceived great democratic advantages in a federal system with a strong regional tier, while the lack of a credible opposition meant that the Prussian state could be divided without protest. In practice, the Russian occupation of much of what had previously been eastern Prussia meant that a *de facto* division of the territory was already in place. The result was a territorial structure that bore little resemblance to the historical territories of Germany. With the exception of Hamburg, Bremen and Bavaria, the postwar *Länder*, if they reflect anything, reflect Allied zones of control in the aftermath of the war. This has not stopped these *Länder* using the symbolism of the prewar entities and their antecedents in creating regional identities that have, over time, become extremely strong. Only one pre-unification German state is rarely mentioned; the name Prussia has all but disappeared from the Federal Republic which it ultimately created.

4.2.2 The federal state

Germany is probably the most studied of all the regional or federal systems within the European Union. There is good reason for this. Apart from being the oldest modern federation in Western Europe (until 1993, Germany was the only federation within the European Community), it is perceived as a success. This made the Federal Republic the most obvious model for other European countries that began to move towards regionalised structures in the 1980s and 1990s.

Although substantially amended, the constitution ratified by the postwar *Länder* and signed at Bonn on 23 March 1949 remains the constitutional document of the Federal Republic. Only the Bavarian constitutional assembly refused to ratify it, arguing that it was overly centralist in tone. The German constitution's unusual title, *Grundgesetz* (or Basic Law) betrays its original purpose as a temporary constitution to be used until the reunification of Germany. When reunification did arrive, over 40 years later, redrafting the constitution was never seriously considered. The *Länder* of the former German Democratic Republic wanted to join the rich and successful Federal Republic, not change it. In constitutional terms at least, a new Germany was not created.

Article 20(1) of the Basic Law confirms federalism as one of the three fundamental principles that underpin the modern German state. It states unequivocally that 'The Federal Republic of Germany shall be a democratic and social federal state'. As a consequence of this, substantial portions of the Basic Law relate to the federal structure, the role of the *Länder* and the relationship between them and the federation (or *Bund*). The Basic Law also places federalism among the 'eternity' clauses at the heart of the constitution. These are laid down in Art 79(3) of the Basic Law (which may never be amended):

> Amendments of this Basic Law affecting the division of the Federation into *Länder*, the participation on principle of the *Länder* in legislation, or the basic

principles laid down in Arts 1 to 20, shall be inadmissible. [Art 79(3), Basic Law.]

Federalism is thus placed alongside human rights (which are contained in Arts 1–20 of the Basic Law) and social democracy as a principle fundamental to the German state. Nevertheless, although Art 79(3) guarantees the *Länder* and their involvement in the federal legislative process for 'eternity', or at least for as long as the Federal Republic continues to exist, it does not guarantee the existence of any particular *Länder*. In contrast to the situation in Belgium and Austria, it is the federal principle, not the regions themselves, which lie at the heart of the German system. This was shown very clearly by the original wording of Art 29 of the Basic Law, which placed a duty on the federal government to review the number and size of the states with a view to reorganising them when required:

> The federal territory must be reorganised to ensure that the *Länder* by their size and capacity are able to fulfil the functions incumbent upon them. Due regard shall be given to regional, historical and cultural ties, economic expediency, regional policy, and the requirements of town and country planning. [Art 29, Basic Law.]

In the event, despite the Allies' presumption that the arbitrary nature of the *Länder* boundaries would make them flexible, only one substantive amendment to the regional map has been made (the creation of Baden-Württemberg, against the wishes of the majority of the population of Baden, in 1952). The obligation on the Federal government to reorganise the sub-national units of the German state was removed in 1976, when 'must be reorganised' in Art 29 was replaced by 'may be reorganised' (Schweitzer, 1984, pp 162–63). With this subtle change, the boundaries of the 1976 *Länder* were made all but permanent. Over the 50 years since the Basic Law's inception, the present organisation has become increasingly entrenched and, although the possibility of reducing the 16 *Länder* is intermittently raised in the press, the issue is all but dead. The most recent evidence of this was provided by the attempt to merge the *Länder* of Berlin and Brandenburg in the aftermath of unification, as provided for in Art 118a of the Basic Law. The proposal was rejected by the people of Brandenburg in a referendum in 1996.

Figure 4.3: Structure of territorial government in the Federal Republic of Germany

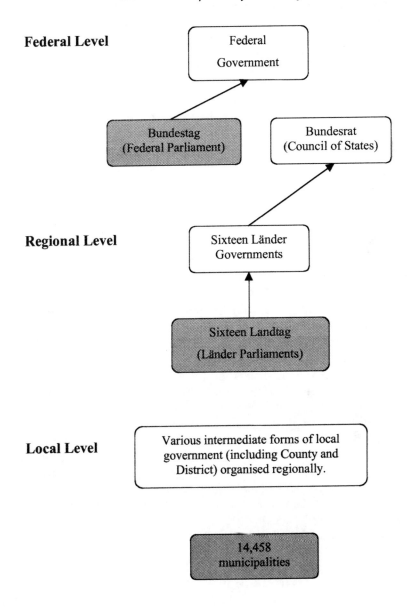

Federal Level

Federal Government

Bundestag (Federal Parliament)

Bundesrat (Council of States)

Regional Level

Sixteen Länder Governments

Sixteen Landtag (Länder Parliaments)

Local Level

Various intermediate forms of local government (including County and District) organised regionally.

14,458 municipalities

Directly elected level

Appoints other institution

At the apex of the German system lies the federal level or *Bund* (see Figure 4.3). The federal legislative branch comprises two deliberative chambers, the *Bundestag* (the lower house) and the *Bundesrat* (the upper house). The 645 members of the *Bundestag* are elected by universal suffrage through a combination of first past the post and the d'Hondt list system of proportional representation (50% by each method). This is the primary legislative chamber of the federation. It is this chamber which elects and holds the federal executive to account. The second chamber or *Bundesrat* is sometimes referred to in English as the 'council of states' or 'federal council'. This chamber comprises members of the *Länder* governments and as such is unique in Europe. Overseeing the Federal Republic and its constitution is the Federal Constitutional Court (*Bundesverfassungsgericht* or *BVerfG*). The judges are elected by two electoral colleges comprising the *Bundesrat* and a committee of *Bundestag* members, and are appointed for non-renewable terms of 12 years.

Although the federal principle and *Länder* involvement in federal legislation are recognised as part of the federal structure (Art 20 and Art 79(3), Basic Law), Art 31 of the Basic Law makes it clear that '*Bundesrecht bricht Landesrecht*' (federal law overrides regional law). In contrast to Belgium and in common with the non-federal systems, a clear hierarchy of laws exists in the German federal system. Where legislation is lawfully enacted by both the regional and the federal level in the same area, the federal legislation will apply. This led some more conservative authors (notably of the Anglo-American school) to discount Germany as a federation (Wheare, 1953).

Early German academic discussion focused on the relationship between the *Länder* and the *Bund*. Some argued that the *Länder*, as an arm of the national state, were constitutional equals of the *Bund*. How could this be squared with the concept of *Bundesrecht bricht Landesrecht*? The answer was the concept of *Dreigliedrig*, whereby the German state consisted not of two tiers of government (*Länder* and *Bund*) but of three. Under this theory, espoused by Kelsen and Nawiasky among others, the German federation or *Bundesstaat* (the *Länder* and *Bund* combined), not the *Bund*, was the highest authority. The fact that most *Bundesstaat* powers were granted to the *Bund* was merely coincidental (Blair, 1981, p 159). After briefly flirting with this concept in the South West State case of 1951 (1 *BVerfGE* 14) and arguably the Concordat case of 1958 (26 *BVerfGE* 246) (Kommers, 1997, pp 71–78), the constitutional court abandoned the principle. Instead it explicitly recognised the traditional two tier concept of *Zweigliedrig* in the Territorial Reorganisation case of 1961 (13 *BVerfGE* 54) (Davis and Burnham, 1989). This equated the *Bund* with the *Bundesstaat* and recognised the *Länder* as inferior constituent units.

4.2.3 The *Länder* as the regional tier

Each *Land* has a constitution that establishes the structure of government within the region. Although it must be compatible with the *Grundgesetz* (Art 28(1), Basic Law) the constitution of each *Land* is the sole responsibility of the regional institutions. Each *Land*, with the exception of Schleswig-Holstein, has a constitutional court at the apex of its constitutional structure. These courts, not the *BVerfG*, adjudicate on *Länder* constitution matters. Only in Schleswig-Holstein are *Länder* constitutional disputes handled by the *BVerfG*. Although a significant degree of organisational autonomy is granted to the regional authorities, in general *Länder* institutions followed the federal model (Paterson and Southern, 1991, p 147).

In strict constitutional terms, it can be claimed that Germany does not possess a regional tier of government at all. This is the stance taken by the *Länder* themselves. *Länder* politicians are national figures who represent regionally defined areas. To this extent the theory of *Dreigliedrig* still has some political relevance. Notwithstanding the status of their leaders in German political life, the *Länder* are regional institutions. Unlike the Belgian system, the German system has an implicit hierarchical structure. The constitutional court's rejection of *Dreigliedrig* theories meant that the *Länder* have an inferior level of authority within the German federation.

One of the most obvious features of the German federation is the lack of uniformity in governmental structures. As each *Länder* has its own constitution, it may develop local government structures dependent upon individual circumstances and policy. The only exception to this rule is the case of the municipalities, which cover the entire country and enjoy very limited protection under the Basic Law (Art 28(2), Basic Law).

The 16 *Länder* (see Figure 4.4) can be divided into two groups: *Stadtstaaten* (city-states) and *Flächenstaaten* (area states). There are only three city-states (Hamburg, Bremen and Berlin), with the 13 other *Länder* belonging to the latter category. Since 1998, the regional legislatures or *Landtage* (termed *Abgeordnetenhaus* in Berlin and *Bürgerschaft* in Hamburg and Bremen) have been directly elected unicameral institutions. Until 1998, the Bavarian Senate was the only *Länder* second chamber, comprising indirectly elected representatives from various economic and social institutions, but this was abolished in the reforms of that year. Each *Landtag* elects a Minister President and executive from among its members.

Figure 4.4: The German Länder

A: Schleswig-Holstein

B: Mecklenburg-West
   Pomerania

C: Lower Saxony

D: Saxony-Anhalt

E: Brandenburg

F: Saxony

G: Thuringia

H: Hesse

I: North Rhine-
   Westphalia

J: Rhineland-Pfalz

K: Saarland

L: Baden-Württemberg

M: Bavaria

N: Hamburg

O: Bremen

P: Berlin

Flächenstaaten executives comprise a cabinet of between nine and 15 ministers, headed by the Minister President. Executive power in *Staatstaaten* is vested in a similar body, termed the Senate, which is headed by a mayor (*Bürgermeister*) in Berlin and Hamburg, and a Senate President in Bremen. Some ministries are common to all *Länder*. For example, ministers of interior, finance, economy, transport, labour, social security and education are to be found in each state. The interior minister is the most important ministerial post. This minister is responsible for all police and judicial matters, and, more importantly, any authority not specifically granted to another ministry. The ministries within each *Land* may also vary according to custom or to the specific needs of the *Land*. Bremen, for example, has a minister for ports and harbours.

Local government structure varies significantly from region to region, but the basic unit of local governance is the municipality. In the city-states of Hamburg and Berlin, the only sub-regional unit is the *Bezirk* (district). In Bremen, the unusual territorial coverage of the *Land* (which is divided into two isolated territories) has made the creation of two 'autonomous municipalities' (Bremen and Bremerhaven) expedient. In the *Flächenstaaten,* many different intermediate levels exist between the municipal and *Land* levels.

4.2.4 Regional responsibilities

The powers of the *Länder* are not specifically defined anywhere in the Basic Law. Instead, Art 30 grants the regional tier a general competence, sometimes referred to as a 'subsidiarity clause'. This states:

> The *Länder* shall have the right to legislate in so far as this Basic Law does not confer legislative power on the *Bund.*

This clause gives a clear and constitutionally guaranteed general competence to the regional tier. This method of defining all regional functions negatively was unique in Europe until the advent of devolution in the United Kingdom. Regional legislative competence in the Federal Republic, as in the case of the Scottish Parliament, is entirely based on the principle of 'general competence', rather than the principle existing in addition to specified responsibilities. Unlike the UK example, however, this clause explicitly places a degree of sovereignty at the regional level.

The Basic Law lists the functions that accrue exclusively to the *Bund* in Art 73. This list is surprisingly short and includes foreign affairs, defence, citizenship, freedom of movement, postal service, telecommunications, air transport, the federal railways and property rights. Further authority is granted to the *Bund* in relation to the co-operation of police forces. The limited nature of the functions specified as federal in this Article, together with the general competence clause in Art 30, gives the impression that the *Länder* enjoy something approaching complete autonomy on domestic issues. This perception is misleading, as the federal powers listed in Art 73 are not the only areas in which the *Bund* is permitted to operate.

Article 74 of the Basic Law lists an extensive range of responsibilities known as the 'concurrent powers'. These include wide areas such as public welfare, economic affairs, agriculture and fishing. These powers, according to the Basic Law, are to be exercised concurrently by both the *Bund* and the *Länder.* In practice most of the 'concurrent powers' listed in Art 74 have become governed purely by federal legislation. To discover why, we must return to the *Bundesrecht bricht Landesrecht* (federal law overrides regional law) principle found in Art 31 of the Basic Law.

The strict delineation of federal and regional legislative power means that the provisions of Art 31 apply only when *Land* legislation strays into areas of federal territory. In those areas in which the federal government has no jurisdiction (primarily culture, policing and education), the principle does not apply, but where the *Bund* and *Länder* share responsibility the effect is to allow the *Bund* to dictate legislation in these areas. This is what happens in relation to the concurrent powers listed in Art 74. In practice, Art 31 has meant that the *Bund* has taken on responsibility for these competencies.

The role of the *Länder* in the exercise of concurrent powers is defined in Art 72(1):

> Where concurrent legislation is concerned the *Länder* have the right to legislate as long as and to the extent that the *Bund* does not exercise its legislative powers.

In theory, the *Bund* can only exercise its powers in these areas when a number of criteria are fulfilled. The Basic Law defines these in Art 72(2). Until 1994, the federation could only intervene in areas of concurrent responsibility when:

1 a matter cannot be effectively regulated by the legislation of individual *Länder*; or

2 the regulation of a matter by a *Land* law might prejudice the interests of the other *Länder* or of the people as a whole; or

3 the maintenance of legal or economic unity, especially the maintenance of uniformity of living conditions beyond the territory of any one *Land*, necessitates such regulation. (Art 72(2), Basic Law.)

In practice, however, these criteria have become constitutionally meaningless. The reason for this can be found in the constitutional court's attitude to intervening in support of them. After some brief flirtation with examinations of *Bund* grounds for intervention in particular concurrent fields, the constitutional court retreated to a position whereby it all but refused to adjudicate on the interpretation by the *Bund* of Art 72(2) (Hesse Salary case, *BVerfGE* 34, 9; see Blair, 1981, pp 78–85). Instead, it regarded the issue of when concurrent powers may be exercised by the *Bund* as a political rather than a judicial matter and thus Art 72(2) became something of a dead letter. The *Bund* has therefore been free to assume such powers through the normal federal legislative process. In practice, a combination of Art 31 and the attitude of the court to Art 72(2) has left the *Bund* free to assume the extensive list of powers found in Art 74 as well as those explicitly assigned to it under Art 73.

As a result of *Länder* pressure, the principle found in Art 72 underwent a degree of amendment in 1994, as did a number of Articles related to it. Under the revised Article, the *Bund* may only use its concurrent powers:

> ... if and to the extent that the creation of equal living conditions throughout the country or the maintenance of legal or economic unity makes federal legislation necessary in the national interest.

As a result of this amendment, necessity is required for interventions by the *Bund* in concurrent fields. A further amendment to Art 72 introduced the possibility for the *Länder* to claw back some of the concurrent powers already lost to the *Bund*. This states:

> It may be determined by federal law that in cases where federal legislation is no longer required pursuant to paragraph (2) of this Article it may be replaced by *Land* legislation. [Art 72(3), Basic Law.]

These attempts by the *Länder* to introduce the principle of subsidiarity into the exercise of concurrent powers would be meaningless were it not for the explicit attempt to force the constitutional court to adjudicate in these issues. Article 93(1) now places decisions regarding the necessity of *Bund* actions explicitly within the remit of the constitutional court. The purpose of this is to force the court out of its current position of claiming that such arguments are political and thus unsuitable for their deliberation. Whether the court will oblige on such a politically sensitive issue remains to be seen, although some authors were not optimistic (Leonardy, 1994, p 14).

Although *Länder* legislative functions are now largely limited to those implicitly guaranteed by the constitution (principally education, police and broadly defined cultural matters), the regions play a significant role in German life far beyond these limited fields. The *Bund* is constitutionally prohibited from establishing all but a few field agencies as defined in Art 87 of the Basic Law. These are primarily limited to the foreign service, federal finance administration, the post office, defence, the *Bundesbahn* (federal railways), air transport and, under Art 88, federal waterways (within limits). With these exceptions, the *Bund* must rely on individual *Länder* to implement federal legislation. Under Art 83, the *Land* ministries are, by default, the administrators of almost all domestic policy. Within the limits imposed by federal legislation, much of which requires *Länder* approval, such administration is largely exercised without federal interference.

It was intended that most *Länder* executive autonomy would be exercised under Art 84 of the Basic Law. This defines the limits that the *Bund* may place upon the *Länder* when they are implementing federal legislation in their own right. Such limits may only be placed through legislation and not by executive decree, unless approved by the *Bundesrat*. Article 85 deals with the *Länder* acting as the agent of the *Bund*. This occurs when the *Bund* is financing more than half of the costs of the legislation. Increasingly this Article, rather than Art 84, has been utilised, raising the question of whether the *Länder* are losing their executive autonomy in return for federal cash. On the other hand, the limits imposed upon the *Bund* under Art 85 remain significant. Although administrative decrees may be used to direct the *Länder*, these may only be addressed to the *Länder* governments and not directly to the administrative agencies, again leaving significant scope for executive autonomy (Art 85(3), Basic Law). The restrictions imposed on

Bund supervision are such that the regions continue to enjoy substantial independence even when they are administering policy as the agents of the federal government.

In 1969 a new type of responsibility was introduced into the Basic Law. This was the concept of 'joint tasks', of which economic development was the first. Under a new Article of the Basic Law (Art 91(a)), a joint task committee was established to oversee the development of a federal outline plan for economic development, within which each *Land* could exercise its discretion. Neither the federal government nor a majority of the regions can be outvoted on the joint task committee, and in general a wide consensus is achieved (Klemmer, 1989, p 405). The extension of the joint tasks (this category now includes the previous regional responsibilities such as the development of higher education and agricultural development) has led to accusations that the *Bund* has acquired increased influence. As its votes are administered as a block, it need only convince a few *Länder* to back its stance to be successful. On the other hand the focus on consensus in the joint tasks and elsewhere has led to a 'joint decision trap' whereby decisions are taken which attract the support of a number of executives, rather than being taken for the good of the federation (Scharpf, 1988).

Table 4.4: Federal and Länder *responsibilities*

Exclusive *Länder*	Joint tasks	Federal framework powers	Federal direct legislation administration
Education	Economic development	Higher education	Armed forces
Police	Agriculture	The press	Nuclear energy
Local government	Development of higher education	Hunting and nature conservation	Air transport
Media		Regional planning and water management	Federal railways
Culture			Postal services and tele-communications
			Federal bank
			Federal waterways

Broadly speaking, therefore, we can divide the responsibilities of the *Länder* into distinct groups (see Table 4.4): policies for which the regions are exclusively responsible, joint tasks, where the regions operate within nationally agreed frameworks (which they participate in creating), concurrent tasks (which in practice amount to very little) and areas of regional executive autonomy. It is important to realise, however, that such an analysis misses a key factor in German federalism. Although significant scope for regional autonomy remains within the German system, this only explains part of the regional tier's importance within the Federal Republic. The power of the German regional level comes primarily through collective action. However, the decisions taken through such processes will be national and will apply to all regions. Regional policy autonomy is thus restricted and transferred to a national body. While it is true that the national body contains regional representatives, this cannot disguise the fact that it is not an organ of regional autonomy. It is this co-operative structure that is the hallmark of the German system of federalism. The key institution within this structure, and indeed in German federalism itself, is the *Bundesrat*.

The co-operative nature of German federalism means that the scope for purely regional legislation is very small, and most regional autonomy is executive in nature. The involvement of the regional tier within federal policy making is extensive, and few decisions can be taken at the federal level without the consent of at least a majority of the *Länder*. This leads to national decisions being taken with the involvement of regional executives, and reduces the role of regional legislatures in the exercise of regional autonomy. Despite this, the German *Landtage* have all the hallmarks of a legislative chamber, and are not particularly well suited to controlling a powerful regional executive.

4.2.5 Regional involvement in the federal policy process

The *Länder* are unique amongst European regions in having a formal and extensive role in the federal legislative process. This is achieved through the institution of the *Bundesrat*. The *Bundesrat* is unique amongst upper houses in the European Union in having no directly elected representatives. It is entirely the creature of the regional executives and as such has become a pivotal institution in the operation of German federalism. It is composed entirely of members of the *Länder* governments, whose respective voting strengths are loosely based on population lines. As the main purpose of the *Bundesrat* is the representation of *Länder* interests at the federal level, larger states are under-represented while the small states enjoy influence proportionately greater than their size (each *Land* government having a minimum of three representatives), as shown in Table 4.5 below.

The members of the *Bundesrat* are members of *Länder* governments. In theory, these are specifically appointed individuals within each *Länder* government, but in practice the use of alternates means that the subjects being discussed at each *Bundesrat* session will dictate which ministers will attend. The ministers themselves (not their officials) are the only ones capable of voting and each *Land* must do so as a single block according to the instructions of the *Länder* government.

The framers of the Basic Law clearly envisaged an important but strictly limited role for the *Bundesrat*. Most bills must be referred to the *Bundesrat* but, although amendments can be proposed and bills delayed, in most areas *Bundesrat* approval is not required. The objections of the *Bundesrat* may be overturned in the *Bundestag* by a simple majority. Only in a short list of specific areas, and when the responsibilities of the *Länder* are affected, does the upper house have a power of veto (by a two-thirds majority). The framers of the constitution clearly saw this power as necessary to protect *Länder* interests while not being too burdensome a requirement on the *Bund*.

In practice, the role of the *Bundesrat* has expanded far beyond that originally intended for it. This has occurred primarily as a result of the federation's attempts to regulate *Länder* executive actions rather than merely create frameworks for *Länder* policy delivery. To do this requires the consent of the *Bundesrat*. This has created the situation where over half of all laws passed between 1949 and 1980 required *Bundesrat* consent (Blair, 1981, p 93). In recent years the percentage has been slightly higher, averaging between 52% and 60% per annum (*Bundesrat*, 1992).

The impact of this on German federalism is difficult to overemphasise. The ever greater requirement of *Bundesrat* consent has put a powerful weapon in the hands of the regional tier. The requirement of *Länder* consent through the *Bundesrat* has allowed the *Länder*, when acting collectively, to demand concessions in return for their support on major issues. The result has been ever greater involvement of the regional tier in federal decision making, but at the expense of individual *Länder* autonomy. The German regional tier clearly remains powerful, but perhaps only when it acts collectively.

Table 4.5: Länder *representation in the Bundesrat*

Land	Seats in *Bundesrat*	Population (millions)
N Rhine-Westphalia	6	16.7
Bavaria	6	10.9
Baden-Württemberg	6	9.3
Lower Saxony	6	7.2
Hesse	4	5.5
Rhineland-Pfalz	4	3.6
Berlin*	4	3.3
Saxony*	4	5.0
Schleswig-Holstein	4	2.6
Mecklenburg-West Pomerania*	4	2.1
Thuringia*	4	2.5
Saxon-Anhalt*	4	3.0
Brandenburg*	4	2.7
Saarland	3	1.1
Hamburg	3	1.5
Bremen	3	0.7

* post-1990 Länder

4.2.6 Where now for the Federal Republic?

The constitutional guarantees given to the federal system in the Basic Law, coupled with widespread public support, makes wholesale reform of the Federal Republic virtually unthinkable. Even the boundaries of the regions themselves, although lacking any formal constitutional protection, are all but secure. Nevertheless, the system is far from perfect, and faces a number of significant challenges as it enters the 21st century. The most significant of these are the challenges posed by co-operative federalism, the issue of regional finance, and the relationship between the *Länder* and the European Union.

German regions are involved in a wide range of policies, but the extent of regional independence is less clear. The extensive use of joint tasks and the high number of decisions taken between *Länder* executives reduces the scope for variation between regions. In addition, use of these methods has led to the adoption of non-optimal policies based on bargaining rather than problem solving. The result of the bargaining process can be that regional representatives protect their own perceived interests (often financial) when the problem requires a more rational solution.

The increased use of co-operative methods of decision making within the German system is raising significant problems within the federal system itself. In particular, greater reliance upon intergovernmental forums for decision making in the Federal Republic leads to ever greater power being passed to the executive level at both the federal and the regional tier. Decisions taken collectively are often presented to the deliberative chambers as a *fait accompli*, leaving the parliament concerned with only the option of rubber-stamping the decision or discarding it altogether. The nuclear option is, of course, rarely used and the *Landtage* in particular tend to accept the negotiated settlements provided by the *Länder* government (especially as the government, by definition, will hold a majority in the *Landtag*). The directly elected chambers at both federal and regional levels become emasculated by these decision making processes. The inability of the elected chambers to hold the executives effectively to account is further hampered by the culture of secrecy which continues to surround the German government. There is as yet no right to information at federal level, while the freedom of information legislation enacted by Berlin, Brandenburg and Schleswig-Holstein remains minimal. However, it is noticeable that this subject, long neglected in Germany, is beginning to be taken seriously, with the current SPD-Green coalition committed to the introduction of such legislation at the federal level. As yet, these proposals have not progressed past consultation with the *Länder*.

The second challenge to the federal system receives far more public attention in Germany than the democratic problems highlighted above. The financing of the regional tier continues to be an area of significant conflict between individual regions. The issues revolve, primarily, around discussion of how to finance financially weak *Länder* through the equalisation process (see Chapter 9). Still regarded as a fundamental principle of the German system, equalisation nevertheless continues to cause significant friction within the regional tier. The poorer states (particularly those from the east) clamour for a bigger slice of the German economic pie, while the rich states demand more financial responsibility and less equalisation. This issue has rumbled on for as long as the Federal Republic itself has existed, with repeated references to the constitutional court. There is no sign that it will be conclusively solved in the near future.

Finally, and perhaps most crucially, there are challenges that come from beyond the borders of the federation. In particular, how can the institutions of the German regional tier fit within the Member State-dominated structures of the EU? At present the regional level is very much the poor relation in the European decision making structure, a situation which the powerful German *Länder* find unacceptable. With the help of their regional allies in Belgium and Spain, the German *Länder* have managed to bully their way into the European decision making process (see Chapter 8), through the Committee of the Regions and the representation of regions at the Council of Ministers. More progress has also been made on the domestic front, with the *Länder* now having a formal role in decision making at the national level in relation to the EU (Art 23, Basic Law). Nevertheless, such mechanisms remain limited, and suffer from the problems of intergovernmental decision making discussed above.

These problems are discussed more fully in later chapters, but one common thread is worth noting here. Although much of the literature on German federalism portrays its problems as a German phenomenon, in practice they are repeated across the EU. This occurs not only amongst the other European federal states, but also amongst those formally classed as regional. Possibly because Germany is the oldest regionalised state in the EU, it encountered the problems outlined above earlier, and as a result they are more evident in the Federal Republic than elsewhere. Whatever the reason, the issue of democratic accountability, finance and the European Union are themes that will be returned to again and again in this volume. The *Länder* are no longer alone.

4.3 AUSTRIA

4.3.1 The development of Austrian federalism

The modern history of Austrian federalism is a history of Austria itself. The Austrian provinces have a history that can be dated back to the Ostmark (eastern march) of the Frankish Empire in the 8th century. These provinces prospered for several centuries as the heartland of Europe's most enduring empire. This was brought to an end by the defeat of the central powers in 1918 and the final collapse of what had become the Austro-Hungarian Empire. After the collapse of 1918 and the settlement of 1919, all that remained of the defunct empire was a rump of seven German speaking 'Austrian' provinces. These remnants of the Austro-Hungarian leviathan became the Austrian republic. With the creation of two new provinces within this territory (including Vienna), these nine *Länder* remain the regional level of the Austrian federation today.

The first republican constitution of 1920, although establishing federalism as a principle of the Austrian state, created a very centralised structure, federal in name only. In common with so much in Austrian history since, this was a result of compromise between the two major parties (represented today by the Christian Democrats and the Social Democrats). As such, it followed the principle of federalism advocated by the Christian

Democrats while bowing to the centrist demands of the Social Democrats. The resultant federation without federalism was significantly reformed in 1925 to give greater autonomy to the regions and to create something approaching a true federation. It nevertheless remained weak, with the central government retaining its role as the superior partner with exclusive responsibility for almost all legislation. The principle role of the *Länder* was the administration of such legislation, often under executive order from the federal ministries.

Although the principles of the 1920 constitution (and its amendments of 1925) have survived to this day, the Austrian republic proved less resilient. Faced with the loss of its empire, the rump Austrian state sank into poverty and starvation. Food aid was delivered by western agencies during the period 1919–20, and a huge loan was extended to the Austrian government by the League of Nations in 1922 to stave off imminent economic collapse. The situation was made no easier by the inherent friction between socialist Vienna and the largely conservative provinces. By 1933, less than 13 years after it had been proclaimed, Austrian democracy was finally snuffed out by the Christian Democrat Chancellor, Engelbert Dollfuss. Facing electoral defeat within a year of taking office, he allied with the Austrian fascists, abolished the federal parliament and ruled by decree. Opposition was banned, and the Social Democrats forcibly crushed in 1934 along with the federal states. The assassination of Dollfuss in July 1935 was followed by *Anschluss* with Hitler's Germany in 1938, and with it war and defeat at the hands of the Allies.

In the years following the Second World War, the status of Austria remained in a state of flux. The onset of the cold war led to the country's occupation by the Allied powers for a decade after the Nazi defeat, and only after the Treaty of Vienna did the USSR agree to reunite the country and grant it independence under a number of conditions (principally neutrality). Eastern Austria was the only region from which the USSR withdrew after 1945.

In the years immediately following the Nazi defeat, Austria was perceived as more sinned against than sinning and for this reason, amongst others, did not suffer the same constitutional fate as Germany. The 1920 Austrian republic was not considered to have failed in the way that the Weimar Republic had, which is rather surprising given the Dollfuss takeover of 1933. For this reason the post-1945 document was based upon a re-enactment of the prewar structure. The perception in the 1950s of Austria as victim (however inaccurate) allowed the prewar federal system to re-emerge phoenix-like from the ashes, without being associated with the horrors of the period 1934–45. An example of the speed with which Austria was rehabilitated into the international community can be seen in the events of 1957. In this year, the Austrian Government championed the cause of the German speaking Tyrolese living in Italy against the efforts at 'Italianisation' being perpetrated by the Italian government. It is almost inconceivable that Germany would have been able to intervene in a similar dispute so soon after the end of hostilities. Although both had been subject to the Nazi regime, the contrast with Germany could not have been greater.

4.3.2 The Austrian federal system

The Austrian republic is a federal state comprising the nine *Länder* (or provinces) established in 1920. The federal legislature is bicameral and comprises the *Nationalrat* and the *Bundesrat*. The *Nationalrat* is elected by proportional representation on a nationwide basis. This chamber appoints both the federal Chancellor and the executive as a whole. The *Bundesrat*, comprising the representatives of the *Länder*, is the inferior house in the bicameral system.

The *Länder* comprise the regional tier of the Austrian system. Beneath them lie two levels of local government or administration. With the exception of Vienna, each *Land* is divided into a series of Gemeinden (municipalities). These directly elected local authorities possess a significant degree of constitutional protection under Chapter IV(C) of the Austrian Constitution (Arts 115–20). This grants them responsibility for 'all matters which exclusively or mainly concern the local community personified by a municipality and which can be dealt with by the community within its local boundaries' (Art 118(2), Austrian Constitution). In addition to this general competence, further responsibilities can be delegated to them by both the *Länder* and the federation. Between the local and regional tiers lies a tier of *Bezirke* or administrative districts. These units of administrative deconcentration are, depending upon the administrative duties they perform, responsible to both federal and *Länder* ministries. However, the appointment of the director of the district is in the gift of the regional premier, and the overall responsibility for the districts lies within the responsibilities of the *Länder*.

A unitary system of local government and administration operates within the cities. The status of a city in Austria is defined by charter. Today these can be awarded to towns with a population of over 20,000 at the instigation of the *Länder* and with the approval of the *Bund*. In these cases, the city government also assumes the administrative responsibilities of the district.

The exception to the above structure is the city-state of Vienna. As both city and *Land* it undertakes the responsibilities of all sub-national levels of government within a single set of institutions. Due to the fact that its status as a city predates its recognition as a *Land* by several centuries (Vienna did not become a province until 1920), the city authorities formally undertake the role of the region, not vice versa.

The prominence of the federal principle within the Austrian Constitution contrasts sharply with the reality of Austrian federalism. This has led some commentators to describe it as one of the world's most centralised federations (Elazar, 1991, p 31). Formally this is clearly the case, but, as with much else in Austria, appearances can be deceptive. In particular, provincial identities remain strong, and regional leaders have a significant profile in Austrian politics. To some extent the pervasive nature of party politics in Austria means that regional influence is exerted through these channels rather than through the visible mechanisms of the federal state. This, of course, does not necessarily aid federalism as such, and creates a series of problems, not least of which is a lack of accountability. To some extent the success of the far right FPO in recent Austrian elections can be explained as a protest against this system and the 'Red-Black' coalition that has dominated Austrian politics since the war. In the light of this it is perhaps more correct to describe the Austrian regions as 'politically well endowed but constitutionally weak' (Morass, 1997, p 76).

At first glance, the Austrian Constitution appears to back up its fine words of federal principle with practical federalist features. In particular, the German federation's principle of *Bundesrecht bricht Landesrecht* (federal law overrides regional law) is a notable absentee from the Austrian system. This places the Austrian *Länder* in a position not dissimilar to the Belgian regions and Communities, and distinct from the *Länder* of Germany. In practice, the effects of this equality of legislation are minimal. Article 10 of the Austrian Constitution provides a detailed enumeration of the powers granted exclusively to the federation. The series of Articles that follow grant further legislative powers to the federation, with executive autonomy lying with the *Länder* in some cases (Art 11), and the implementation of laws within federal frameworks in others (Art 12). As in Germany, a subsidiarity clause (Art 15(1)) grants all powers not explicitly granted to the federation to the *Länder*. Collectively these clauses grant little in the way of legislative power to the *Länder*. In practice, therefore, Austria, like Germany, is primarily an executive federation. There are significant differences, however. The area left for *Länder* legislative freedom is far less in Austria than in Germany, while the extent of joint responsibility and thus co-operation between the *Länder* and *Bund* is greater. There are in fact few areas in which either level can direct policy without reference to the other.

Unlike the German *Länder*, the executive authority of the Austrian *Länder* can be significantly limited by the actions of the federal government. Through the concept of *Mittelbare Bundesverwaltung* (indirect administration) a large number of federal administrative tasks are handled by the *Länder*, which are directly responsible to the relevant federal ministries for their delivery. The scope for autonomy in the administration of federal tasks is therefore less than that in Germany.

All this paints a picture of administrative decentralisation rather than true federalism and devolution of policy choices to the regional tier. As mentioned above, however, this picture can be misleading. The political power of the *Länder* institutions, and particularly of the *Landeshauptmann*, is such that provincial issues play a significant role in the Austrian political system.

4.3.3 The Austrian regional tier

As already stated, the regional tier in Austria comprises the nine largely historical provinces established by the Constitution of 1920. These are guaranteed by name in Art 2(2) of the Constitution (Burgenland, Carinthia, Lower Austria, Upper Austria, Salzburg, Styria, Tyrol, Voralberg and Vienna). In fact, the Austrian state itself is defined as the collective territory of these *Länder* rather than the *Länder* being divisions of Austria (Art 3(1), Austrian Constitution).

The constitution of each *Land* defines its institutions and organisation, and includes such matters as the voting methods for provincial elections. In Voralberg, for example, voting in regional elections is compulsory. In contrast to Germany, Austria has no *Land* constitutional courts to adjudicate on provincial constitutional questions. Some commentators do not even class the *Land* constitutions as such since constitutional authority lies at the federal level. Nevertheless, as they organise the administration of the *Länder*, these documents are the *de facto* constitutional documents of the provinces. As in Germany, the regional tier is part of the national level of government and thus has theoretical equality with the *Bund*. The *Länder* also possess independent legal status in private law, which allows the operation of the region outside the sphere of specific competencies assigned to it. This can be important in the practical utilisation of their general competence contained in Art 15(1) of the constitution.

Each Austrian *Land* has a unicameral legislature (numbering between 36 and 56 members) from which is elected the *Landeshauptmann* or provincial governor. The *Landeshauptmann* chairs the regional executive or *Landesregierung* which comprises a number of councillors (ministers). The *Landeshauptmann* performs a dual role that is unlike any other European regional premier. On the one hand, the governor is head of the *Länder* executive and as such is accountable to the *Landtag* for the direction of *Länder* policy. He or she is also head of the federal administration within the *Land* and as such is responsible to the federal government for the implementation of its policies.

It is this dual role, particularly in relation to the implementation of federal policy, that gives the *Landeshauptmann* a pivotal role in the Austrian federal structure. The *Landeshauptmann*, not the *Landesregierung*, is responsible for the administration of federal tasks, although individual ministers (*Landesräte*) can be delegated specific administrative tasks by the federation. Even in these cases governors remain personally responsible for the indirect administration system as a whole. In this task they are aided by the Director of the *Amt der Landesregierung* (regional government office) rather than one of their political deputies. This civil servant heads the regional Civil Service but, in the case of indirect administration, is designated as the assistant to the *Landeshauptmann*.

The legislative competencies granted to the Austrian *Länder* are significantly fewer than those granted in the other federations, and accrue to the *Länder* primarily as a result of the general competence they enjoy under Art 15(1), although a few powers are granted to the *Länder* explicitly. As in Germany, those areas not specifically granted to the *Bund* are exclusively regional. In Austria these amount to a short list; exclusive regional responsibilities are limited to regional planning, building regulations, nature conservation, culture, sports, ambulance and fire services, local government organisation and civil defence. In addition to these, policies on social welfare, hospitals and nursing homes are developed by the regional authorities within the frameworks established at the national level (which can be extensive). These exceptions apart, the competencies of the Austrian *Länder* are largely executive in nature. Although many of the responsibilities that the regions possess come from the fact that the *Bund* has no field agencies in most areas of policy, the regional governor must act (in contrast to the German system) upon detailed instructions received from the federation.

The result of this system is that the mass of provincial power lies with the provincial executive and the person of the provincial governor. The *Landtage* are sidelined, having only a limited role even in holding the provincial executive to account. This has led to calls for the direct election of the *Landeshauptmann* (Leitner and Neuhold, 1999, p 296) and for change to a presidential system in the provinces. As yet these calls have not been heeded. Such a change would require the amendment of the federal constitution and as a result is unlikely to occur in the near future. It is interesting to note that similar calls have been seriously addressed in the Italian regional system (see Chapter 5).

4.3.4 The future of the Austrian federation

The domination of the major parties in the Austrian federation has meant that the federal system has never operated in the manner expected. The Austrian *Länder*, in any case, lack the constitutional levers granted to their powerful neighbours in Germany. Their presence in the Austrian *Bundesrat* is only through the appointment of representatives by the *Landtag*, and this institution does not have the powers granted to its German namesake. It has therefore been possible for the federal state to bypass the regional tier, although regional views have significant influence within the political system.

The weakness of the Austrian regional tier has begun to change with Austria's accession to the EU. Ironically, while membership of the EU has caused significant problems for the German *Länder*, their Austrian counterparts have apparently benefited from the experience. Rather than providing a threat to *Länder* competencies, it has given the regional tier the opportunity to press for greater influence in decision making at the national and European levels. Whether the constitutionally weak Austrian *Länder* will continue to develop as Austria settles into the EU's structure remains to be seen.

The success of the Austrian regions in gaining access to EU decision making reflects the ability of the Austrian regions to operate in the international sphere generally, which has been significantly greater than their domestic competencies might suggest. Early recognition of the need to allow such activities came through a constitutional amendment of 1988 (Art 16(1)–(3), Austrian Constitution), which allows the *Länder* to undertake treaty negotiations unless the *Bund* states an objection within eight weeks of being notified. Although this allows a national veto, it does mean that the Austrian regions are specifically authorised to undertake international relations unless specifically barred from doing so. With the entry of Austria into the EU, other significant constitutional amendments have been approved in this area. Most notably, a new constitutional clause gives the Austrian *Länder* a role not unlike that applying to their German cousins (see Chapter 8). In particular, the *Bund* will adhere to a common regional opinion in European matters that affect their competencies (Dertnig and Handstanger, 1992). In the Austrian case, the EU appears to be reinvigorating a long established but moribund regional tier.

4.4 ARE THE FEDERATIONS DIFFERENT?

Perhaps the most noticeable fact arising from the discussion of Europe's three federations presented above is the significant degree of difference between them. Although a number of factors distinguish these regional systems from those discussed in later chapters, these factors are few. It is true that all three possess a formal role for the regions in the national decision making process, a theoretical equality with the national level, and constitutional protection from abolition and interference by the central state, but apart from these the similarities between the federations are not great.

The involvement of the regional tier at the national level varies significantly and is based upon entirely different principles. In Belgium, the equality of legislation between the federation and the regional authorities makes intergovernmental co-operation a necessary part of the Belgian federal structure. However, such co-operation happens in the semi-formal and informal meetings that take place between the ministers and officials of the various levels. The Senate's role in representing the regional viewpoint is minimal. We can contrast this with the role of the German *Bundesrat*. This is the key to regional power in the German federation. Since *Länder* legislative autonomy is limited under the principle of *Bundesrecht bricht Landesrecht* the regional tier requires access to the federal legislative process. This is provided collectively in the *Bundesrat*. The regions of Belgium, by contrast, do not require such access, holding as they do exclusive legislative authority in their fields of competence.

In fact, the constitutional differences between Europe's federations are as great as any similarities. Although formally they stand distinct from the constitutionally protected regional governments of the non-federal states, in practice the individual federations have as much in common with their non-federal cousins as they do with each other. Although the federations do enjoy some advantages, notably their independence of finance (see Chapter 9), these do not necessarily relate to their federal status. Even the formal constitutional guarantees which are present in federal regions have their parallels in non-federal regions, although the latter may be attained through political rather than constitutional means. This is particularly true in the constitutionally guaranteed regions, and it is to these that we now turn.

CHAPTER 5

THE CONSTITUTIONAL REGIONS
OF THE EUROPEAN UNION

Outside the three federations of Belgium, Germany and Austria discussed in the previous chapter, a further four Member States of the European Union have a tier of regional government that is enshrined in the constitutional documents of the state. These four (Italy, Spain, Portugal and Finland) do not class themselves as federations; the regions are seen as a territorial division of the state, not an integral part of a federal or national level. In two of these examples, Italy and Spain, the regional tier covers the entire territory of the Member State, although both systems exhibit high degrees of asymmetry. Two further Member States, Portugal and Finland, have guaranteed regional autonomy to island archipelagos within their territory (the Açores, Madeira and Åland). Given their asymmetry, none of these systems could be classed as federal in the formal sense.

In these examples the regional tiers, although lacking formal equality with the central state, still exhibit significant levels of legislative autonomy (at least formally). Spain in particular, although lacking many of the formal properties of federalism listed in Chapter 2, is arguably a federation in practice. As will become clear, there are more similarities between these non-federal regions and their formally federal cousins than there are significant differences. Nevertheless, the lack of regional influence at the national level of decision making has been a significant weakness for the constitutional regions. In Spain, this constitutional weakness was diminished by the importance of regional parties in the national parliament. To an even greater extent than in the federal examples of the previous chapter, the formal constitutional status of these regions must be taken in the context of the political and economic factors within which they exist.

5.1 ITALY

5.1.1 Regionalism in Italy

Despite the relative youth of the Italian nation-state and the wide cultural differences that exist within its borders even today, regional or federal forms of governance have not been a feature of Italian government. Prior to 'unification' in 1860–70, modern Italy was divided into eight independent states, with the former territory of the Venetian Republic under Austrian control. Despite its political and cultural diversity, Italy took the path to a unitary state. Plans for a confederal or regional state were discussed several times during the wars of 'unification' but the death of Count Cavour, their last influential advocate, saw the end of efforts to develop a federal or regional Italy (King, 1987, p 328).

The concept of a centralised Italy has been a powerful one amongst successive generations of Italian politicians. This reached its zenith under Mussolini, and it was partly as a backlash to the fascist years that the new constitution of 1948 for the first time proposed that Italy should be a regional state. In some regions, the framers were given little choice in the matter. Many peripheral regions had opposed the fascists throughout Mussolini's regime and had suffered at the hands of the 'Italianisation' policies instigated by his government. The regional resistance movements were themselves the *de facto* government in the postwar chaos, and the threat that such regions might join co-linguists in adjacent countries or move towards independence was very real. The response of the new republic was the creation of four (later five) autonomous regions within the state itself. The regions which benefited from these special arrangements (Sardinia, Sicily, Trentino-Alto Adige, Valle d'Aosta and in 1963 Friuli-Venezia Giulia) each has an individual statute passed as an 'organic' law. These organic laws have a status on a par with the constitution itself. The 1948 Constitution explicitly recognised these regions and their special status under Art 116.

The genesis of regional government in the rest of the Italian Republic was less straightforward. The three main parties that drew up the constitution of 1948 (the precursors of the communist PCI, the socialist PSI and the Christian democratic DC) had very different views on regional reform. The DC pressed hard for a strong form of regionalism, bordering on the federal model being discussed in Germany. In contrast, the PSI and PCI, expecting to dominate national politics, were less keen to see power devolved to a regional tier. The left's view prevailed and the compromise reached saw regional powers limited to what were regarded as 'secondary' powers such as vocational training, planning and regional transport. There was to be no significant regional role in the development of economic and social policy as envisaged by the DC (Leonardi and Nanetti, 1981, p 97).

The resultant constitution envisaged a mild form of regional devolution, providing for a significant, though limited, regional tier of legislative authority. Appearances can be deceptive, however, and, as explored in more detail below, the constitutional provisions do not by any means tell the whole story of Italian regionalism.

Title V of the Italian Constitution, which contains the regional (and local) government provisions, lacks clarity. There is no mention, for example, of how the regions are to be elected. Was this to be by direct election (as most assumed) or by indirect appointment? It was intended that such gaps in the constitutional provisions would be filled by a number of *disposizioni transitorie* or 'transitory provisions' drawn up in tandem with the constitution and, most crucially, by ordinary legislative acts of the Italian Parliament (or administrative decrees of the Italian Government). Only when the latter were enacted would the constitutional provisions and their accompanying documents come into effect. The fact that one of the *disposizioni transitorie* envisaged elections to the regions within a year of the constitution being enacted was evidence that progress towards regionalisation was expected to be swift (Leonardi and Nanetti, 1981, p 97).

The elections of 1948 delivered a surprise result, and the Christian democrats were returned as the largest party with both the PSI and the PCI excluded from national politics. The DC, on assuming the reins of power, immediately cooled its ardour for regional government. The required national legislation was repeatedly delayed, and the regions, with the exception of the special regions, failed to materialise. To all intents and purposes, the regional constitutional provisions became meaningless. Even in the case of the special regions, the results of regionalisation were disappointing. Although it had been assumed that the special statutes guaranteed a significant degree of legislative freedom to the new regions, and in the case of Valle d'Aosta even a special tax regime, decisions of the constitutional court deemed that such provisions needed further confirmation by national legislation. Such legislation was not forthcoming. The level of autonomy of the special regions was therefore far lower than their supporters had envisaged.

In 1953, one of the two 1948 bills introduced as the basis for a regional tier was rewritten. This now envisaged that, should the regional tier ever be created, it would be merely an administrative adjunct of the national state, such were the limitations placed upon it. This legislation, piloted through the Italian Parliament by Mario Scelba (the Minister of the Interior), seemed to signal the final nail in the coffin of Italian regionalism. However, such predictions of its demise proved premature. In 1960, the political landscape of Italy began to change, and the issue of regionalism re-emerged in Italian politics.

1960 saw the start of what became known as *l'apertura a sinistra*, or the opening to the left. This saw the rehabilitation of first the socialists and later the communists into Italian national politics. Over a decade of opposition had persuaded the left of the benefits of decentralisation and it had performed a volte-face over the regional question. As it became clear that the exclusion from power at the national level had become entrenched, the left (particularly the PCI) began to see the creation of a regional tier as a means of achieving significant political power. This became an ever more tempting prospect for the left in general (and the PCI in particular) as communist support grew across the 'red belt' which divided the country (Zariski, 1987, p 105).

The left presented the implementation of regional government as a priority, considering it a way both to reinvigorate a stagnating political structure and to allow socialist politicians the chance to govern at regional level. The Fanfani Government of 1960–62 began the process by substantially altering the provisions of the Scelba Law; however, the reforms again foundered as opposition drove the pro-regional Fanfani from government. Finally, in 1968, and only after the longest filibuster in its history, the Italian Parliament passed a bill to allow the holding of regional elections (Leonardi and Nanetti, 1981, p 102). 20 years after agreeing the regional constitutional provisions, the same parties had finally agreed to implement them.

Further bills followed, dealing with regional finances (Law 281/1970) and the transfer of regional personnel (Law 775/1970), and in January 1971, after regional elections the previous year, the 15 'ordinary' Italian regions were born. At this point the fragile coalition that had piloted the reforms collapsed, as first the communists and then the socialists refused to endorse DC proposals to transfer only strictly limited powers to the regions. These draft decrees gave the regions only an eclectic mix of partial powers taken from the list found in Art 117. Policy making was to remain centralised, with the regions, in the words of some Italian commentators, to be little more than 'giant municipalities' (Giannini, 1963, quoted in Cassese and Torchia, 1993, p 99).

On 4 July 1972, the Andreotti Government asked for an extension to the deadline, which it had itself included in Law 775/1970, to transfer personnel to the regions. The PSI and the PCI used this opportunity to attack the minimalist approach of the DC government to regionalisation. The result was the defeat of the government's request for an extension in the Senate. Instead, the Senate amended the legislation to grant further responsibilities and personnel to the region, under the influence of the newly elected regional presidents.

Defeat at the polls in favour of the left in 1975, along with the increasingly pro-regionalist stance of the chamber of deputies and the Senate, led to pressure from the Italian Parliament, not the government, to review the transfer of power to the regions. The result was Law 382/1975, which paved the way for all the powers outlined in the constitution to be granted to the regions by decree. In addition, the regions were to possess full legislative power in their areas of responsibility within the limits of European Community and national legislation. Most importantly, the government decrees to transfer power were to be reviewed both by the regions collectively and by the Italian Parliament (through the Interparliamentary Committee on the Regions).

The endgame of this tortuous process saw a draft set of decrees rejected by both parliament and the regional authorities. The log jam was removed by an agreement that all sides would accept any amendments made by the interparliamentary committee. In fact the government reneged on this agreement and some powers were withheld (particularly in the area of agriculture and in relation to the funding of welfare organisations).

Nevertheless, DPR (Presidential Decree) 616/1977 saw the final piece of the regional jigsaw fall into place. This remains the main source of regional authority. The scope of the decree was such that in 1981, three years after its enactment (on 1 January 1978), Leonardi and Nanetti confidently stated that the 'massive transfer of powers had made the regions one of the key centres of political authority in the country' (Leonardi and Nanetti, 1981, p 108). Whether they would stand by this statement in the light of two decades of experience is extremely questionable.

In fact, the years following the regional reforms proved disappointing and led to a degree of disillusionment amongst the regionalist lobby. Although the regions existed, their practical powers proved very limited. Depending on the method of assessment, between 80% and 90% of their budget was allocated directly to projects by the national government (Engel and Van Ginderachter, 1993). The framework laws within which the regions could exercise their legislative authority also proved highly restrictive. They were so tight that it has been argued that the central ministries had actually increased their hold on certain areas of policy (particularly health) in the aftermath of the reforms (Sanantonio, 1987). The hostility of the constitutional court to regional autonomy created a further hindrance to regionalism. The overall picture led Hine to conclude that Italian regionalism was little more than the regional administration of centrally imposed policies (Hine, 1993).

Perhaps most importantly, the regional issue had ceased to be of major concern at the national level. The entire regional process had been a consequence of national politics, and the development of the Italian regions had largely been at the mercy of national trends. Without a sponsor at national level, the regions soon slipped off the political agenda. To add to this, the centralised nature of Italian politics meant that many regions were tightly controlled by the relevant national party hierarchies.

Despite these difficulties, regional success stories did emerge. Emilia-Romagna, in particular, became something of a celebrated example of those northern regional governments which had made a difference (Leonardi and Nanetti, 1990). With these exceptions, regional policies varied little from region to region, and regional elections were little more than national opinion polls. By the late 1980s, further regional reform was not on anyone's agenda.

The regional front built up by the northern regions in the 1970s continued through the medium of the Regional Presidents' Conference, and this institution began to present reform proposals in the late 1980s. These included the granting of greater legislative power to the regions, financial autonomy, involvement in the European Union decision making process, and the participation of regions in national politics through a regionally organised senate. These proposals were introduced into the national parliament by the regions (using a power granted to them under Art 138(2)), but it was not until the 1990s that the political situation would give the regions an opportunity to implement at least some of their demands.

The changing political climate in the late 1980s and the 1990s saw the creation of new regionalist parties in Italy. Autonomist parties already had a significant presence in a number of the special regions (the Union Valdotaine had been the natural party of government in Valle d'Aosta, for example), but now regionalist parties outside the 'special regions' began to make a significant impact upon the electoral scene. The success of the Northern League in winning 17% of the northern vote in the 1992 general election, with a programme built around 'federalism', thrust the regional issue back to the top of the national agenda. Nevertheless, the League's programme is based upon northern resentment of southern subsidisation. As such its limited appeal lies in the north alone, and even here support for their particular scheme of federal 'super states' is limited. It is noticeable that some of the League's bitterest rivals are the autonomist movements of the special regions.

The emergence of the League, and the ongoing political crisis that destroyed much of the post-1948 political establishment (many regional politicians were also implicated in these scandals) was nevertheless used by the regional governments. Most notably the successful constitutional reform referendum of 1993 included three proposals to give greater powers to the regions. Most importantly, agriculture and tourism were transferred almost *en bloc* to the regions, as was the administration of environmental protection. In separate developments, the regions have been permitted to undertake direct links with European institutions without the prior permission of the government while regional financial provisions have also been reformed. A significant difference in these reforms is that they came not as a result of national political bargaining, but from pressure applied by the regions themselves.

Despite the advances made in the 1980s and 1990s, the Italian regions remain relatively weak in European terms. The regions themselves, and those who favour regionalism in Italy, certainly wish to take the regional reforms further. The question is whether the limited reforms that were achieved in 1993 and 1994 at a time of central weakness will be able to be repeated when national parties regain their strength, as they surely must. It is perhaps not a good omen for the regions that when the new Presidential Conference of 1995 published its proposals for *Le Regioni Italiane Verso il Duemila* (the Italian regions in the year 2000), their demands were broadly those they had campaigned for in the 1980s. *Plus ça change ...*

5.1.2 The national framework

Italy is a regionalised state as confirmed by the opening Article of Title V of the constitution: 'The Republic is divided into regions, provinces and municipalities' (Art 114, Italian Constitution). This bold statement of intent is not dissimilar to those one finds in the opening Articles of federal constitutions such as the German Basic Law and the Belgian Constitution. The image of a semi-federal state is further strengthened by the strong words that are found in Art 115. This confirms that 'the regions are constituted as autonomous territorial bodies with their own powers and functions according to the principles established by the constitution'. Given that the constitution goes on to enumerate these principles one would be forgiven for concluding that the Italian regional structure is at least comparable to the federations examined in Chapter 4. If ever one needed an object lesson in the misleading nature of constitutional interpretation taken out of context, Italy can provide it.

The constitutional provisions of Title V remain the fundamental basis upon which all the regions rely for their constitutional legitimacy. Article 116 confirms the status of the special regions, while Arts 117–119 of the constitution establish an 'ordinary' regional regime with extensive autonomy. Nevertheless, the framework provided in Arts 114–133 has enough ambiguities to require further legislative enactment. This not only delayed the establishment of the regional governments but also placed their final structure in the hands of the centre. The enabling legislation, which was enacted principally in the 1970s, created a system well short of the regional ideals found in the constitution.

The regions are part of a single system of territorial government that encompasses the entire Italian state (see Figure 5.1). Italy is divided into 8,100 municipalities, 103 provinces and 20 *regioni* or regions (see Figure 5.2). One of these regions is uniprovincial (Valle d'Aosta) and two provinces are 'autonomous' (Trento and Bolzano). Since 1971, these two autonomous provinces have exercised most of the powers previously held by the region of Trentino-Alto Adige which they comprise (Council of Europe, 1993, p 7). Within the 20 regions, there are two specific varieties. Each of the five 'special' regions possesses an individual constitutional statute with a status equal to that of the Italian Constitution (Art 116). In theory, these regions enjoy greater autonomy than their 'ordinary' counterparts. The 15 'ordinary' regions are established by 'ordinary' statute under the constitutional provisions of Title V of the Italian Constitution.

Deconcentrated national offices exist at both the provincial and regional levels. The provincial Prefect administers the field services of the national government at the provincial level, while the regional commissioner's role is the supervision of all local authorities, including the regions (Zariski, 1987, p 112). The national level of government comprises two elected chambers, an executive council of ministers (headed by the Prime Minster) and a directly elected president as Head of State. The chamber of deputies is the primary legislative body and is elected by proportional representation on a national basis. The Senate is the upper house (although it has similar powers to the chamber of deputies) and is directly elected on a regional basis, with each region represented by a minimum of seven senators (the exception to this is Valle d'Aosta, which has only one). Although it is elected on a regional basis, it does not represent the regional executives or legislatures. In this regard the Italian system mirrors the United States Senate rather than the German *Bundesrat*. In common with the US example it divides along national party lines and is, in practice, a national rather than a regional institution.

All constitutional adjudication in Italy is undertaken by the Italian Constitutional Court, including matters relating to the regional state. Regional governments have recourse to this judicial remedy if they feel that the national authorities have impinged upon their constitutional rights but until recently the court consistently took a pro-centre stance. This discouraged regions from using this facility (the so called 'flight from the court') and led to a growth in national power over the regions (Zariski, 1987, p 114). However, recent decisions suggest a change in the attitude of the court, and regional authorities seem to be returning to the court to uphold their rights against the national government.

Figure 5.1: Territorial government in the Italian Republic

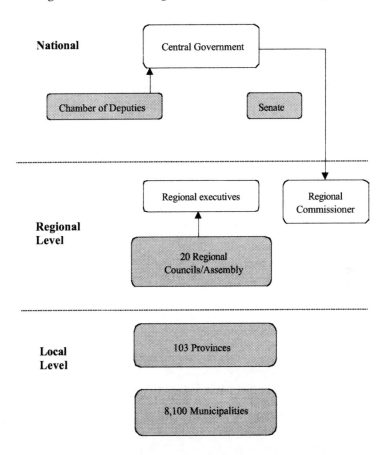

A priori supervision of the regional tier is exercised by the national government. This is undertaken by the state commissioner for the region. Regional legislation does not become law until this centrally appointed official signs the relevant bill. This must be done within 30 days unless the government wishes to object, in which case the bill is referred either to the constitutional court (which may annul it) or, if the bill in question presents a conflict of interest with the state or other regions, to the national parliament (Council of Europe, 1993, p 31). The latter process has never been used. In practice, the jurisdiction of the court has expanded to include such conflicts of interest (Zariski, 1987, p 114). Financial and administrative supervision of the regional tier exists through the regional accounting courts and *tribunale amministrativo regionale* (TAR) respectively (Hine, 1993, p 262).

Figure 5.2: The Italian regioni

'Special' regions:
A: Valle d'Aosta
B: Trentino-Alto Adige
C: Friuli-Venezia Giulia
D: Sardinia
E: Sicily

'Ordinary' regions:
1: Piedmont
2: Lombardy
3: Veneto
4: Liguria
5: Emilia-Romagna
6: Tuscany
7: Umbria
8: Marches
9: Lazio
10: Abruzzi
11: Molise
12: Campania
13: Basilicata
14: Apulia
15: Calabria

The *regioni* do, however, possess certain unusual powers to influence the national authorities. For example, individual regional councils can initiate legislation in the national parliament, which can bring regional issues to national attention. Perhaps most unusually, the presidents of the special regions may attend the meetings of the Council of Ministers to state their region's case. The Sicilian president may even vote and has the rank of minister in the national government (King, 1987). In practice, however, these powers are of little importance. They are rarely used and the national government does not encourage their application (Zariski, 1987, p 103).

Examination of the framework laws associated with the constitutional provisions of Title V (and their interpretation by the court) makes it clear that the Italian system is a limited system of constitutional regionalism. It is far removed from the federal systems of Belgium and Germany, and even from the Spanish regional structure which it influenced. The regions are clearly a subordinate level of government, while the constitutional situation is further undermined by the continued dominance of the national parties and bureaucracy.

The 'special' regions are in a slightly different situation. These regions are founded upon much more detailed and individualised 'organic' statutes. The statutes give a number of specific functions to the special regions, including police and linguistic powers to the French speaking province of Valle d'Aosta. However, as with the regional provisions in the constitution proper, the statutes of the special regions can be equally misleading. Due to an early and controversial decision of the constitutional court, special region powers required national legislation to enact them. Since their enactment, much of the necessary legislation has not been forthcoming, leaving special regions in a very similar situation to those governed by 'ordinary' law (Zariski, 1987, p 103). The major difference has been the greater financial autonomy enjoyed by the special regions.

5.1.3 Regional structures

Each region has a deliberative assembly of between 30 and 80 members elected by proportional representation. Until 1995 (Law 43/1995), these were elected from provincial constituencies, limiting the development of regional political structures. However, as part of the wider reform of voting procedures in Italy, and at the request of the regional presidents, the regional assemblies are now elected on a region-wide basis. The size of the assembly varies according to the size of the region concerned. This body is referred to as the regional council (except in Sicily where it is termed the regional assembly).

Within the limits of the constitution the 'ordinary' regions are largely free to organise their own structures. Under Art 212, each region must have a council, and a president elected from it, although most regional electorates now elect the regional president directly (Loughlin, 2001, p 226). The president heads a regional *giunta* that has primary responsibility for the administrative functions devolved by the national government. Aside from this, each region is free under Art 123 to devise a regional statute or 'constitution' that reflects the singularities of the region. In practice, there are few differences between ordinary regional statutes.

Although drawn up by the regional assemblies (requiring an absolute majority for their approval), the regional statutes require the approval of the Italian Parliament to become law. The regions are thus granted a measure of influence as regards the organisation of their structures but, unlike the situation found in most federal systems, the final say on the matter still lies with the national authorities. Structural innovation is therefore at the mercy of a national veto. When the 'ordinary' regions were first established in 1971, many hoped that their statutes would reflect a move towards greater participatory democracy in Italy and reduction in the power of the existing political élite. There were some limited innovations. For example, standing committees at the regional level are required to hold public hearings on regional acts. The relationship between the regional executive and regional council also has some slight differences from the national model. Of particular note are the inability of the *giunta regionale* (the regional executive) to dissolve the regional council and the council's power to approve or remove individual members of the executive body (at national level, the parliament is presented with a shortlist of candidates prepared by the Prime Minister). With these small exceptions, regional politics did not herald the new political dawn that the reformers had envisaged. The regions largely developed structures that mirrored national practice (Zariski, 1987, p 108).

The *giunta regionale* was, until the reforms of 1996, drawn from the council. It consists of the regional president, the deputy president, and a number of assessori, not limited by national law. In Lombardy, for example, the 1990 *giunta* consisted of 15 of these regional 'ministers' (Hine, 1993, p 261). It is general practice for the regional government to organise itself into departments headed by *assessori*. The giunta departments are generally reflected in standing committees set up by the council to monitor the activities of the executive. Unlike at the national level, however, the regional executives were intended to be a truly collegiate body, with the individual assessori responsible only for implementing *giunta* decisions. Since 1999 for ordinary regions (Constitutional Law 1/99), and since 2001 for most special regions (Constitutional Law 2/2001), the regional president is directly elected in the region, with 20% of council seats also being allocated to the president's list. Valle d'Aosta and the autonomous province of Bolzano have retained the previous system of elections.

5.1.4 Regional responsibilities

Article 117 of the Italian Constitution lays down the broad legislative limits of the regional governments. These include local police forces, health, urban planning, tourism and agriculture as well as any other legislative functions delegated by constitutional law. Article 118 complements Art 117 by granting the accompanying administrative powers to the regional level. This is accompanied by a caveat that local administrative matters may be allocated directly to the provinces and municipalities, and in most cases it is these bodies to which the region will delegate most administrative functions. Article 119 is potentially the most important to the regions, guaranteeing as it does 'financial autonomy', although this is only 'within the forms and limits laid down by the laws of the Republic which co-ordinate this autonomy'. Regional taxes are also guaranteed by this Article, as are quotas of state taxes according to the 'needs of the regions'.

In practice, the central government's minimalist interpretation of Arts 117–119, coupled with a pro-centrist approach by the constitutional court, has rendered these Articles almost meaningless. The wording of Art 117 requires national legislation to establish the 'limits of the fundamental laws of the state' in all of the areas of legislative competencies given to the regions. Article 117 therefore lists the maximum legislative competencies that may be granted to the regions by ordinary national legislation. The actual limits of regional competence are defined by national framework laws.

The most important of these framework laws is DPR (Presidential Decree) 616, which was passed in 1977 after achieving the approval of the Italian Parliament. More recent legislation (including Law 59/1997 and DPR 112/1998) has expanded the regional responsibilities provided for under the 1977 decree. Individual acts of the national parliament may also give scope for regional legislation. The limits are generally narrow, however, and always decided by the central state. Despite constitutional appearances, therefore, Italian regions have no general competence, being instead limited by national framework legislation.

Article 118 has proved equally ineffective, as the central state has consistently given significant authority directly to the local authorities in an effort to bypass the regional tier. This phenomenon can be explained by the ease with which the central bureaucracy can control local government, and by the influence of the local government associations (in comparison with the regions) at the national level. The financial autonomy guaranteed by Art 119 has also proved to be illusory, with tax sharing (guaranteed by Art 119(2)) conspicuous only by its absence from the Italian system. The taxes assigned to the Italian regions are extremely limited.

The legislative and administrative actions of the regional governments are further limited by Art 120 (free movement and single market provision) and, more crucially, by Arts 125 and 127. These Articles outline the operation of the administrative and legislative *tutelles* which are operated by a regional commissioner (Art 124). The tutelles allow regional actions to be reviewed by the national government, in the person of a regional official. Administrative acts may be reviewed by the official on procedural and substantive grounds. In the latter case, however, such review may only cause the regional legislature to re-examine the act; in the former, such decisions will be referred to the administrative courts. In legislative cases, however, the regional commissioner (on the orders of the national government) may submit acts to the constitutional court in cases of alleged illegality, or to the Italian Parliament in cases of a conflict with national or other regional interests (Art 125). In practice, however, the position of the constitutional court has made the latter method surplus to requirements, and it has never been utilised.

5.1.5 Where now for the Italian regions?

In the wake of the institutional crisis that engulfed Italy in the 1990s, a Bicameral Constitutional Committee (with representatives from the Senate and the chamber of deputies) was established to bring forward proposals for the reform of the state. One aspect of this was the future of the regional system and the question of whether Italy should become a federation. In the event it reported to parliament in 1998 with a list of proposals which would strengthen the existing regional structure while eschewing any moves towards a truly federal structure or alteration of the existing regional boundaries. Opinion polls suggest that the population itself supports such reforms, with around two-thirds of the population supporting a regionalist or federal structure based upon the existing boundaries (Loughlin, 2001, p 220). The support of the population is crucial, as the reforms as a whole will require approval by referendum.

The reforms, if instituted, will give greater leeway to the regions by restricting the legislative authority of the state to a list of exclusive powers, while defining the state's role in developing framework legislation more tightly. The committee's reforms also proposed the direct election of the regional president. This represents the first direct election of such a post in the EU. As such it may point the way for the increasingly executive-focused role of the regional tier. The final major proposal is to allow regions with 'ordinary' status to move to 'special' status through negotiation with the central government. Ironically, this would allow greater divergence of regional structures and authority within the Italian state at a time when the Spanish state (from which this idea came) is attempting to remove such variations.

The reform package was accepted in its entirety by the parliament of 1998, and incorporated in constitutional laws 1/1999 and 2/2001. Despite doubts expressed about whether the Italian population had the appetite for further reform, voters turned out in sufficient numbers to approve a further regional reform on 7 October 2001 (by a two to one majority). This will grant further legislative powers to ordinary regions. The recent successes of the *Polo della Libertà* alliance led by Silvio Berlusconi may further complicate the future of Italian regions. Berlusconi's partners, the unpredictable Northern League, are continuing to agitate for further regional devolution although not along the lines of current boundaries. The roller coaster ride of Italian regionalism seems set to continue.

5.2 PORTUGAL

5.2.1 Portuguese regionalism

As the oldest state in Western Europe (its frontiers dating back to 1267), Portugal claims to be the most homogeneous. There is some evidence to substantiate this claim. In particular, it is the only state in the European Union to lack any minority languages (European Bureau of Lesser Languages Report, 1994). Nevertheless, this state of 10 million people has significant differences within its borders, not least of which are the isolated archipelagos of the Açores and Madeira. Even on the 'homogeneous' mainland, the issue of regional government has, until recently, been a live one.

In 1974, the Portuguese army overthrew the fascist regime that had run the country for 40 years. This paved the way for a reintroduction of democracy under a new constitution promulgated in 1976. The new regime was immediately faced with the question of how the island groups of the Açores and Madeira should be governed. The population of both these islands had exhibited a desire for autonomy over several centuries, and in the case of the Açores, a guerrilla movement had conducted a campaign of violence to achieve its declared goal of independence. To some extent, this activity was fuelled in the conservative Açores by fears of a far left government on the mainland. The organisation briefly re-emerged in 1986 when the Portuguese President initially refused to ratify the new Açores flag and anthem, but has largely lain dormant since the island's autonomy was granted (Elazar, 1991, p 201).

To assuage the desires of these regions, both island groups were granted the status of autonomous regions, with legislative assemblies and regional executives. On the mainland, plans to introduce limited regional government did not proceed smoothly. In the aftermath of the authoritarian and centralist Salazar regime, the Portuguese Constitution contained many concessions towards decentralisation and direct democracy at the local level. These proposals included provisions for the creation of 'administrative regions' (s VIII, Portuguese Constitution). The legislation necessary to translate the constitutional provisions into concrete institutions did not emerge, however. As in Italy, the original enthusiasm for decentralised government in the aftermath of dictatorship soon dissipated as the main political parties took the reins of national power.

At the time of writing, the mainland regions do not exist, and it is far from certain that they will ever be established. With an extremely homogeneous culture and minimal regional affinities, it is hard to see where the impetus for such change will come from. Although there is opposition to the current structure of deconcentrated administration, it has failed to ignite widespread interest amongst the Portuguese populace.

In the absence of any meaningful regional pressures the central government seemed content to continue with a system of deconcentrated administration, but in 1991, a regional framework law was enacted (as required by Art 225, Portuguese Constitution). Under this legislation, the basic structures of the regions were mapped out. They were to have significant administrative powers in a number of fields including economic development, planning, environment, infrastructure and education. The regional assemblies (of either 46 or 61 members) would have comprised both directly elected members and members indirectly elected by the municipal councils (two-thirds and one-third respectively). This legislation was the first necessary step to the establishment of the administrative regions. The next step required by Art 226, the establishment of individual regions, was not forthcoming. Article 226 of the 1976 Constitution would also have required a majority of municipal councils in each region to support the region's creation. No procedures were introduced to meet this requirement.

The 1997 constitutional reforms moved the goalposts of regional reform. The new Art 226 required a majority of the national electorate to approve the regional reform through a referendum. Only those individual regions that approved the reform in that referendum would have regional government introduced. The referendum itself was brought forward in 1998. It proved to be a disaster for the regionalist cause.

The regional referendum of 8 November 1998 was merely the first stage in what would have been a long procedure to establish individual regions. Applications for regional status could only come from a local government initiative. This in itself would be unlikely in several regions given the opposition of many local governments to regional reform. The proposed structure could have led to an asymmetrical system of regionalism on the Portuguese mainland, but the obstacles placed in the way of regional reform emphasised the hostility of significant parts of the Portuguese political élite to the regional aspect of the 1976 constitution.

The referendum itself failed to gain the required 50% turnout to make its results binding (Mira, 1999), but those who did bother to vote delivered a possibly fatal blow to regional reform in Portugal. By 63.5% to 36.5%, the electorate rejected administrative regions for mainland Portugal (Corte-Real, 1999). Only in Alentejo did voters approve the establishment of a regional government for their region.

The results revealed some interesting anomalies, which go some way towards explaining the results. The autonomous regions of the Açores and Madeira both voted heavily against the proposals. This was curious for a number of reasons. First, the reforms did not apply to the island archipelagos as they already enjoyed a degree of self-government as 'autonomous regions' of the Portuguese Republic. Second, the provision of autonomy to these islands has proved popular. So why should they vote against such reforms in the rest of Portugal?

The answer to this question helps to explain the referendum result itself. It appears that the electorate voted largely along party lines. Only in the communist-dominated territories of Alentejo and Setúbal were votes in favour of the reforms recorded (Setúbal is not classed as a region, instead being amalgamated with Lisbon which voted against the reforms).

Elsewhere, including the island regions, votes went against the reforms. During the campaign itself, pro-regionalist politicians (particularly from the ruling socialist party) were conspicuous by their absence. The lack of commitment shown by the two major parties thus condemned the referendum to failure (Mira, 1999). One even suspects that the referendum was called merely to allow the regional reform process to be stopped. It is noticeable, for example, that the creation of the much stronger autonomous regions of Madeira and the Açores was not deemed to require a referendum. In this case, the parties had done a deal and implemented it. The failure of the referendum, by contrast, has allowed the governing socialist PSP to declare that discussion of regional reform will not be on the political agenda for many years to come (Corte-Real, 1999, p 326).

5.2.2 The national framework

The territory of Portugal is divided into 275 municipalities and 4,005 parishes. Above these democratically elected local governments, the Portuguese Constitution continues to envisage the creation of a tier of 'administrative regions' on the mainland, but in practice only the autonomous regions of Madeira and the Açores have been established as yet.

The constitution describes an asymmetrical system comprising the autonomous regions of the Açores and Madeira (see section 5.2.3 below) and the 'ordinary' mainland regions, with the possibility of some variance between ordinary regions. This structure mirrors the regional system developed in Spain and Italy but, as yet, remains merely an aspiration within the Portuguese Constitution. For the reasons discussed above, the administrative regions have not been constituted. The parallel with Italy's experiences in the period 1948 to 1970 is difficult to avoid. The constitutional protection of the municipalities against the non-existent regional institutions is further emphasis of the tensions created by the issue of regional government in Portugal (Art 257, Portuguese Constitution).

At present, the regional level is occupied by five Regional Co-ordinating Commissions (CCRs) operating as deconcentrated administrations within the boundaries of the would-be regions. 18 districts make up a further level of administrative deconcentration, while a further 52 'technical support structures' exist between districts and the municipalities.

The net result is a confused system of undemocratic sub-national administration on the Portuguese mainland. Had the regions been established the situation would have become more streamlined, as the region would have replaced the CCR and the district as the level of regional co-ordination and planning. Given the referendum result, however, there is little chance that the Portuguese Constitution's regional provisions will be enacted in the foreseeable future.

5.2.3 The autonomous regions

For the present, the autonomous regions of the Açores and Madeira are the only examples of democratic regional government in Portugal. The status, powers and structures of the two Portuguese autonomous regions are set out in s VII of the Constitution. The deliberative body of each region is a unicameral regional legislative assembly elected by the population of each region by proportional representation (Art 235, Portuguese Constitution). The regional president is elected from this body and leads a regional executive, which he or she appoints. Local government in the islands is identical to that on the mainland, with a two tier system of municipalities (Madeira having 11, the Açores 19) and parishes (numbering 52 and 134 respectively).

The central government is represented in each autonomous region by the Minister of the Republic. This post is filled by a presidential appointee proposed by the national government. Once appointed, the minister has powers not dissimilar to those of the modern French regional Prefect or the Italian regional commissioner. There is also a degree of similarity with the roles of the UK Secretaries of State for Wales, Scotland and Northern Ireland (Art 232, Portuguese Constitution).

Although the Minister of the Republic's role has been described as the 'executive authority' in the region, this is slightly misleading (Elazar, 1991, p 200). This executive authority is limited, in practice, to those areas where the central government continues to exercise direct administrative authority in the autonomous regions. In areas within the competence of the regional governments, it is the regional executive that is the executive organ in practice. In this respect the Minister of the Republic is similar to the French regional Prefect, as both are the head of centrally organised field services in their territorial area. Further similarities are evident in the control that these ministers exert over the regional authorities. Like the Prefect (see section 6.1.2), the Portuguese minister may exert ex post facto supervision over the region. If the minister suspects a regional decree to be unconstitutional, it can be referred to the constitutional court. However, in Portugal, the powers of control are significantly stronger than in the French example.

Under Art 235, the Minister of the Republic may refuse to sign a decree of the regional legislature, even if it is adjudged within the constitution, if he or she does so within 15 days of having received either the decree or the decision of the court. In this case the minister's veto may still be overruled, but only if an overall majority of the regional legislature backs the decision after it has been reconsidered. In this case, the minister must sign the decree within eight days of the assembly's verdict. Until the signature is obtained, the legislation is not considered law. Although only a delaying measure, this suspensory veto power is something that even the French Prefects no longer possess.

In practice, the delaying power is much greater than this description suggests. The attitude of the constitutional court is such that referral of a regional legislative enactment to the court generally means its immediate demise. Although the Portuguese Constitution grants such autonomy to the regions, the court's interpretation of the concept of the 'unitary' state, given primacy in Art 6(1) of the constitution, is such that it will not allow any but the most inconsequential regional legislation to stand.

The similarity with Scottish or Welsh Secretaries in the UK system of government comes from the minister's dual role as member of the cabinet (see Chapter 7). Whenever regional issues or issues concerning the interests of the region are discussed, the Minister of the Republic has a seat in the Council of Ministers, and in this role also exercises full ministerial powers (Art 232, Portuguese Constitution).

Although the autonomous regions are guaranteed by the constitution, there are distinct limits to this autonomy. The statutes of autonomy were originally approved (and can be subsequently amended) by the Assembly of the Republic, the Parliament of Portugal. Although amendments are proposed by the regional legislature (as were the original statutes), the final decision lies with the assembly (Art 228, Portuguese Constitution). This therefore weights the hand of the central state heavily in any discussions over structural independence. Furthermore, under Art 236, the Portuguese President may dissolve the regional authorities completely and place their functions under the control of the state representative in the region. There is no mention in this Article as to how long such a dissolution would be allowed to continue, or indeed any elaboration on the reasons the president must give, merely that the regional authorities had acted 'contrary to the constitution'. Although such a draconian power would seem to hang over the island authorities, one suspects that political realities make this particular sword of Damocles rather rusty.

Due to their geographical isolation, the autonomy granted to these regions is relatively extensive. With the caveat that significant legislative freedom will not be accepted in the Portuguese system, all aspects of domestic affairs are handled regionally. Health, education, tourism and transport, for example, are all handled by the regional governments. The lack of legislative power has left the legislative branch of the regional institutions at a disadvantage, with most of the activities of the region being handled by the executives. In the Açores, the election in 1999 of a minority socialist administration has increased the degree of control that the legislative assembly has been able to exert.

5.3 SPAIN

5.3.1 Regionalism and the Spanish state

As one of Europe's most diverse nation-states, Spain would appear to be a prime candidate for a regional or federal structure. Within its territory of over 500,000 km^2, there are a number of distinct regional cultures and widely spoken regional languages (notably Basque, Catalan and Galician). Significant numbers of Spanish citizens (particularly in the Basque country and Catalonia) do not regard themselves as Spanish, while in many other areas such as the Canaries, the Balearic Islands, Andalusia and Valencia, regional identities remain strong. This is reflected politically in significant support for regionalist parties in all these territories. If this were not enough, the economic diversity of the Spanish peninsula also invites decentralisation, with the peripheral northern regions in particular being far more economically developed than the south and the centre. Such differences are not exclusive to any particular area of the Spanish peninsula, but are repeated across the territory; Spain is more of a sub-continent than a country.

Before the 18th century, this cultural reality was repeated on a political level. Until the uniting of the crowns of Aragon and Castile in 1569, the territory of modern Spain had never been governed as a single political entity. Even in the centuries that followed, outwards impressions of unity were somewhat misleading. Although under the crown of a single monarch, Spain remained a patchwork of kingdoms and principalities. Spain was, in effect, a federation of kingdoms. Under the Castilian monarchy, the individual states continued to exercise significant autonomy. Nevertheless, the period from 1569 to 1701 witnessed growing friction between an increasingly absolutist Spanish monarchy and some of their kingdoms where more limited ideas of government prevailed. This tension exploded in the aftermath of the transfer of the Spanish crown to the Bourbon dynasty in the shape of Philip V. Under the Treaty of Partition, the great powers had agreed that Archduke Charles of Austria would succeed Charles II of Spain (the last Spanish Hapsburg), but on his deathbed, Charles reputedly ignored the Treaty and handed the crown to Philip, grandson of Louis XIV of France.

The subsequent war of the Spanish succession saw a grand alliance, brokered by William of Orange, comprising England, the Netherlands and Austria, pitted against Castilian Spain and France. The Catalans, alongside their allies in Mallorca, Aragon and Valencia, declared for Charles, distrusting the absolutist tendencies of the Bourbon dynasty. Despite the famous victories of Eugène and Marlborough, Philip remained on the throne. The Treaty of Utrecht confirmed that, as Louis had said all along, this was a war about trade, not succession. Britain and the Dutch gained a significant number of territories abroad while Austria gained territory in Europe. Philip's rebellious territories were promptly abandoned by their erstwhile allies. In the aftermath, only the Basques and Navarre retained any degree of special treatment. 1713 saw the end of the other Spanish states, as Castile now ruled supreme on the peninsula.

The political diversity evident in Spain until 1713 partially explains the cultural diversity that remains such a feature of the Spanish state today. It also explains the strong tradition of regional and federal thought that runs through Spanish politics. Nevertheless, although ideas of regional and federal government have a long history in Spain, practical application of such concepts was rare and short lived.

The constitutional history of Spain from 1713 to 1976 has been dominated by unitary and authoritarian forms of government. In the minds of many, the two are not entirely unconnected. In 1876 and again in 1931, the democratic republican constitutions included elements of federal or regional government. In both cases, the democratic republics were short lived, and authoritarianism returned.

The modern Spanish state was established after the collapse of the Franco dictatorship in 1976, and its structure reflects the lessons learnt from this period of Spanish history and the failed republic that preceded it. The current structure of *autonomías* or 'autonomous communities', established under the Constitution of 1978, owes much to the constitution of 1931. Article 1 of the 1931 Constitution stated *inter alia* that the 'the Republic is an integral state, recognising the autonomy of municipalities and regions'. This was not a federal republic but one which envisaged self-governing territories within it.

In practice, of course, the civil war meant that little of this principle was put into effect. Catalonia, Euskadi (the Basque country) and Galicia had successful referendums, but only in the former example was there time to establish anything approaching regional autonomy. In the case of Euskadi, by the time the Basques were granted their autonomy the nationalist forces were already advancing into the Basque country. Basque support for the republican regime won them little more than a few weeks of regional government and an abiding hatred of the fascist state. Galicia, a conservative stronghold, fell to Franco's forces almost immediately, giving no time for the region's autonomy to be implemented. Valencia, Aragon and Andalusia also drew up autonomy statutes, but did not progress to the referendum stage before war broke out (Merino-Blanco, 1996, p 19).

Regional government was a key demand of the more regionalist areas of Spain in the aftermath of the Franco regime. However, the establishment of the first regional governments in 1979 (Euskadi and Catalonia) had the unexpected effect of encouraging other areas not noted for their strong regional affinities to press for regional autonomy. This 'domino effect' lasted until 1983, when the final areas of the Spanish mainland became autonomous communities. The last few were under direct pressure from the central government to become regions despite an ambivalent electorate. The centre perceived that such regions would be a centripetal counterbalance to the centrifugal forces being exerted by the peripheral and non-Castilian regions, particularly Catalonia and Euskadi, but also Valencia and Andalusia (Cuchillo, 1993). The Spanish north African enclaves did not achieve their particular brand of autonomy, authorised under a transitional disposition, until 1995. The creation of this regional tier has led some authors to describe Spain as a federation in all but name (Börzel, 2000; Elazar, 1991, p 227; Colomer, 1999; Heywood, 1995, p 162).

5.3.2 The Spanish regional state

Spain is a regionalised state as confirmed by the Spanish Constitution:

> The constitution is based on the indissoluble unity of the Spanish nation ... and guarantees the right to autonomy of the nationalities and regions of which it is composed and the common links that bind them together. (Art 2, Spanish Constitution.)

This Article explicitly guarantees the autonomy of the constituent regions of the Spanish state. It also, somewhat unusually, recognises both the Spanish nation and the 'micro-nationalities' that exist within it. Although this has no practical effect, it is a clear recognition of the diverse nature of the Spanish state. It was, nevertheless, not sufficient in the eyes of the moderate Basque parties who demanded that the traditional rights of self-government enjoyed by the Basque provinces (the *fueros*) be explicitly recognised in the constitution (Newton and Donaghy, 1997, p 117). The resultant boycott of the referendum on the constitution in the Basque country meant it was the only region of Spain to reject it.

Today the territory of Spain is divided into 17 regions or *autonomías* (see Figure 5.3). The importance of the regional level to the modern Spanish state is emphasised by its structure being described as the United State of the Autonomies, as in judgment 32/1981 of the Spanish Constitutional Court (Aurrecoechea, 1989, p 74). It is not a uniform structure, however, and the Spanish model of regional government outlined under s VIII of the constitution is very different from those found elsewhere in the European Union. The section does not lay down a detailed structure for the regional tier, instead listing the broad principles of regional government and methods by which it can be created. In this it clearly owes some debt to the Italian constitutional system. There are clear differences, however.

Figure 5.3: The Spanish autonomías

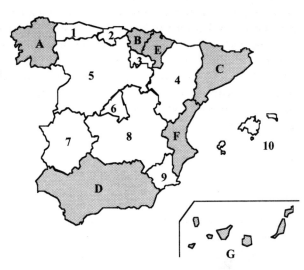

High Autonomy Regions:
A: Galicia
B: Euskadi (Basque country)
C: Catalonia
D: Andalusia
Medium Autonomy Regions:
E: Navarre
F: Valencia
G: Canaries
Low Autonomy Regions:
1: Asturias
2: Cantabria
3: Rioja
4: Aragon
5: Castilla y León
6: Madrid
7: Extremadura
8: Castilla-La Mancha
9: Murcia
10: Balearic islands

Unlike the Italian system, which foundered so seriously on the need for the central state to create the regional structures outlined in the constitution, the Spanish Constitution defines the methods by which prospective regions themselves may move towards regional government. This 'organic' system of regionalism defines the methods by which territories may establish *autonomías*. The key to this structure is the *Estatuto de Autonomía* or statute of autonomy, which is granted to each autonomous community. The three methods by which the statute could be established were:

(a) The second transitional provision (Title XII, Spanish Constitution);

(b) Art 143;

(c) Art 151.

The second transitional provision applied only to:

> ... the territories which in the past have, by plebiscite, approved draft Statutes of Autonomy, and which, at the time of the promulgation of the constitution, have provisional regimes of autonomy. These territories may proceed immediately in the manner provided in Art 151(2), when agreement thereon is reached by an absolute majority of their pre-autonomous higher collegiate organs, and the Government is duly informed. The draft statutes shall be drawn up in accordance with the provisions of Art 152(2) when so requested by the pre-autonomous collegiate organ. (Title XII(2), Spanish Constitution.)

In practice this applied to the regions of Catalonia, Euskadi and Galicia, which had approved statutes of autonomy under the Spanish Republic of 1931–36. The provisional regional governments of these regions (which in the case of Catalonia had sat in exile during the entire period of the Franco dictatorship) were authorised to move towards a high level of autonomy as outlined in Art 151(2) of the constitution. The statute drawn up by these provisional bodies was then forwarded to the *Cortes* (the Spanish Parliament) and submitted to a regional referendum for approval.

The second procedure (Art 143) was designed to be the most common method of establishing an *autonomía*. This offered a *vía normal* (normal route) to regional government which came with the proviso that full autonomy would not be achieved for five years after the *autonomía* had been established (Art 148(2)). According to this Article, provinces with 'common historical, cultural and economic characteristics' could move to self-governing status after an initiative was taken by two-thirds of the interested municipal councils (which must represent a majority of the provincial population for each province within the proposed region). Following the drawing up of the statute, by a body comprising local politicians and members of the *Cortes* for the territory, it was passed to the *Cortes* for enactment as an 'organic' law.

The final procedure, Art 151, was included in the constitution at the behest of representatives of regions (particularly Andalusia) which wanted the chance to move to the higher level of autonomy offered to Catalonia, Euskadi and Galicia without the five year waiting period set out in Art 148(2). This was seen as the exceptional route for autonomy, and under it the successful region could follow a *vía rápida* or 'fast track' to high autonomy. To achieve this, the prospective *autonomía* needed to pass a series of difficult obstacles. These included requirements for the regional initiative to gain the support of three-quarters of the municipalities in each province (representing a majority of the population in each province), the support of each provincial council, and the support of an absolute majority of voters in each province through a referendum. Once the initiative had been successful, the members of the *Cortes* for the region concerned would convene as a constitutional assembly to draw up the regional statute. After negotiation with the *Cortes*, a further referendum was then necessary to approve the statute, which again must be successful in each province (though not by absolute majority). After such a successful referendum, the draft law would be passed to parliament for ratification as an organic law.

It is far from clear that the framers of the 1978 constitution expected the entire Spanish territory to be regionalised. In particular, the extensive procedures required for high autonomy made the *vía rápida* unlikely. Nevertheless, somewhat to the government's surprise, Andalusia almost immediately instigated procedures (which were ultimately successful) under Art 151 which were followed by initiatives in Valencia and the Canaries. The national parties' response to this rush for autonomy was an attempt to stop the creation of any more high autonomy regions, and to impose tighter controls on all regions already created, through the autonomy pact of 1982 (Cuchillo, 1993). Andalusia was the only region granted autonomy under Art 151 after a special law was passed allowing the low turnout in Segovia to be ignored. A constitutional court decision (STC 70/83) in effect forced the government to accept partial Art 151 status for the other applicants.

Although the organisation of local government is defined to some extent by the constitution, there are significant variations in local structures across the peninsula. The basic level of sub-national authority is the municipality, of which there are 8,032. These vary in population from four citizens (Cerveruela) to three million (Madrid). Although these cover the entire territory of the Spanish state, a further 3,000 sub-municipal units have been created at the instigation of either the population concerned or the local municipality. Creation of these units requires the consent of the relevant *autonomía*. The *mancomunidades* (municipal associations) are a further feature of local administration that can be found throughout Spain. These deal with specific municipal policy areas collectively and, as with sub-municipal units, are subject to regional legislation.

Above the municipal level lie 50 provinces, which date back to the Napoleonic reorganisation of the state. The provincial councils are indirectly elected from the municipalities within their territories. In uniprovincial regions (the Balearic islands, Asturias, Cantabria, Madrid, Murcia, Navarre and Rioja), the institutions of the *autonomía* and the provinces are combined. Only in the Canaries have the provinces been abolished and replaced by island councils. With this exception, the provincial authority continues to operate separately from, though sometimes uneasily with, the regional tier.

Deconcentrated agencies of the Spanish state exist at each of the three principal levels of sub-national territorial authority (municipalities, provinces and autonomías). In the case of the regional level, a government delegate is appointed to head the state administrative services and co-ordinate activities with the regional authorities (Council of Europe, 1993).

At the apex of the Spanish constitutional system stands the monarch as Head of State. In this role he or she must remain politically neutral and protect the institutions of the state. This latter duty proved to be no mere formality during the events of 1981. During the failed coup, the king played a pivotal role in denouncing the actions of the rebels while ordering that the army stay in its barracks. The crown (even formally) is not the executive of the Spanish state. This role lies specifically with the president and his ministers, whom he appoints. Collectively they comprise the *consejo de ministros* (council of ministers). The president alone is responsible to the *Cortes*.

The bicameral *Cortes Generales* is the legislative branch of the Spanish state. The *Congreso de los Diputados* (chamber of deputies) is the principal legislative chamber. The upper *Senado* (Senate) has not proved a successful institution in the Spanish state. Created primarily as a home for Francoist politicians fearful of losing office after the end of the dictatorship, it was nevertheless styled as a chamber of regional representation. It has never fulfilled this role, with only 51 of the current 259 seats being appointed by the *autonomía* parliaments, the other 208 being directly elected from provincial constituencies. The elections are held in parallel with elections to the chamber of deputies; in practice this means that majority in the *Senado* tends to reflect the majority in the *Congreso* (Russell, 2000, p 82). This has proved unsatisfactory to all concerned, and reform of the *Senado* continues to be on the agenda.

5.3.3 The *autonomías* as regional government

In formal constitutional terms, the 17 *autonomías* of the Spanish state, which comprise the regional tier, can be divided into two distinct groups. The first group consists of the high autonomy regions sometimes described as Art 151 regions. These four *autonomías* achieved autonomy either through the second transitional provision (Catalonia, Euskadi and Galicia) or the Art 151 *vía rápida* to regional government (Andalusia). The remaining 13, sometimes described as low autonomy regions, achieved autonomy through the slower constitutional procedure found in Art 143. In practice, the constitutional distinctions have been blurred by further transfers of power to a number of individual Art 143 regions. The Canaries and Valencia were granted powers particularly in the fields of health and education, while Navarre enjoys a special financial status similar to that of Euskadi (see section 9.2.1) and significant powers beyond those held by other Art 143 regions. These three *autonomías* now represent a third, intermediate level of autonomy between the high level (Art 151) and the low level (Art 143) regions.

Each *autonomía* is defined by an individual statute of autonomy, which is, in essence, the regional constitution. These are *leyes organicas* (organic laws), which require the consent of both houses of the Spanish Parliament (including an absolute majority in the chamber of deputies) to be amended. The vote of the *Senado* is not required if the president of the *autonomías* has given consent (Art 155, Spanish Constitution). This procedure also gives the national government the ability to force an autonomous community to take an action to fulfil a constitutional obligation. Further caveats to regional independence exist in the cases of crisis or rebellion. Each statute of autonomy includes a clause whereby the national authority can assume control in such situations (Clark, 1985, p 7).

Each *autonomía* has a directly elected legislative assembly and an executive elected from it. The elections to these bodies follow the same method (the d'Hondt) but the dates vary across Spain. The 'big four' high autonomy regions (Andalusia, Catalonia, Euskadi and Galicia) held their first elections independent of any organisation from the centre. Because of the fixed nature of the electoral calendar, these four continue to hold their elections separately. Other elections can take place on these election days, as has happened in relation to the Andalusian elections and elections to the European Parliament. The other 13 *autonomías* hold their elections collectively, often in conjunction with other institutions.

The organisation of the deliberative body and the regional executive branch of the *autonomías* are defined in the relevant statute of autonomy. The members of the regional executive are invariably drawn from the legislative branch, and the executive is always headed by the regional president. The specific organisation of these executives varies significantly between regions. The Art 151 high autonomy regions have larger executives, as one would expect, comprising 14 members, although Euskadi only has 11. The low autonomy regions are limited to a total of 10, although the specific portfolios are not nationally prescribed.

5.3.4 Regional responsibilities

As the Spanish system of regional government is not uniform, regional responsibilities vary considerably across Spain. The reasons for some variations are rooted in the history of the regions themselves, and it is helpful to bear this in mind when studying their functional autonomy. The Catalan civil code, for example, which covers a limited list of subjects (mostly in areas of family law) is under the authority of the Catalan legislature. Interestingly, the Spanish code still applies in Catalonia but is set aside when contradicted by the regional law. Equally, the Catalan civil code is not territorially restricted, as a Catalan citizen may be covered by it in any other region, or indeed nation-state (Villiers, 1999). More generally the Catalan statute places much greater emphasis on cultural and language issues that that of Andalusia, for example, where support for regionalism was based on economic arguments rather than any sense of cultural identity.

Each *autonomía* has an individual relationship with the central state. This results in a complex division of functional responsibilities, with legislative responsibilities lying regionally in some territories and remaining under central control in others. This bears some resemblance to the Italian structure and the asymmetrical autonomy granted to the 'special' regions, although the distinctions are greater. Unlike in Italy, however, every region is defined by a distinct constitutional statute, including those with lesser autonomy. In practice, though, there are considerable similarities between the statutes of some regions.

All the regions enjoy legislative as well as administrative responsibilities, but there is no 'general competence' of the type seen in Germany. Some regions have compensated for this limitation by resorting to their status in private law ('dominium' power as described by Daintith) to develop policy in areas that fall strictly outside their constitutional remit (Daintith, 1989). Regional functions are positively defined and in theory such regional responsibilities are exclusive. In practice, such clear vertical functional divisions have proved problematic.

Despite the potential for difference across Spain, the majority of low autonomy Art 143 regions exhibit a sufficient degree of similarity to be discussed collectively. The powers devolved to these regions are primarily in the sphere of economic development. The most significant of these responsibilities are regional public works, regional transport (railways and roads completely with the region), agriculture (within the limits of the national economic plan), forestry, water (including canals), spatial planning and environmental protection (Art 148, Spanish Constitution). A few cultural matters are also handled by all regions, such as promoting regional culture generally and teaching in the language of the autonomous community (Art 148(1), Spanish Constitution). This competence is especially relevant to lower autonomy regions which have a distinct culture and language (such as the Balearic islands) but where education remains a national responsibility. Other cultural areas open to all regional governments are sport, regional museums, libraries, art galleries and promotion of tourism.

The functional responsibilities granted to all Spanish regions, though significant, are not extensive, and some authors have likened them to local government competencies in a traditional unitary state (Donaghy and Newton, 1997, p 136). This view seems slightly exaggerated. Few local governments have legislative authority over such a range of fields, or the constitutional protection afforded to the Spanish regions in the exercise of this authority. Nevertheless, co-operation remains the key factor in Spanish regionalism. Powers over economic development and agriculture in particular must be exercised within nationally set objectives. This effectively turns these 'exclusive' regional powers into powers exercised under national framework laws.

The minimum level of functions afforded to the Spanish regions under the constitution has been significantly added to in the case of many high or medium autonomy regions. The greatest example of this is in the field of health. Six of the 17 *autonomías* have responsibility for the provision of health services. These are the high autonomy regions (Andalusia, Catalonia, Euskadi and Galicia) and the medium autonomy regions of Valencia and Navarre (Solé-Vilanova, 1990, p 212). The remainder may offer extra services above the basic standard of healthcare provided by the national government (Council of Europe, 1993, p 37). An example of the scale of autonomy enjoyed by those regions with authority over their health service is given in the Catalan statute:

> It is the responsibility of the *Generalitat* of Catalonia to develop and implement the basic legislation of the State on internal health matters ...

> The *Generalitat* of Catalonia may organise and administer for these purposes and within its territory, all the services connected with the matters previously expressed and shall supervise institutions, organisations and foundations as regards health and social security matters. The state shall reserve for itself the inspection facilities that will enable it to fulfil the duties and powers contained in this Article. [Art 17, Catalan Statute of Autonomy.]

This power is not an exclusive power but the central government's role is limited to basic legislation on standards of care. The policy used to achieve it is at the discretion of individual *autonomías*.

The persecution of non-Castilian cultures and languages by the Francoist dictatorship, and the use of education to 'Castilianise' Spain, led to demands in non-Castilian regions for the decentralisation of education in the new democratic state. To some extent this was conceded in the constitutional settlement, but as yet only the seven high and medium autonomy *autonomías* (Andalusia, the Canaries, Catalonia, Galicia, Valencia, Euskadi and Navarre) have responsibility for education within their regions. The Spanish government retains a responsibility to ensure compatibility between qualifications and free universal education (Art 149(1)30, Spanish Constitution). This should leave the seven communities which have acquired this competence with exclusive responsibility for the provision of all levels of education including curriculum. In practice, the central state remains influential in its role of ensuring compatibility of educational certificates (something achieved through regional co-operation in Germany). Notwithstanding the continued role of the central state in Spanish education, there is no longer a single Spanish education system. Having said this, it should not be forgotten that the national government remains education provider in the majority of Spanish regions (though not over the majority of population). This is not a state of affairs that the national government wishes to perpetuate.

In Euskadi and Catalonia, autonomous police forces have been established under their respective statutes (Art 17, Basque Statute of Autonomy; Art 13, Catalan Statute of Autonomy). The creation of the Basque police force was a major concession in the attempt to defuse the violent situation left behind by the fascist dictatorship. The distrust felt by Basques towards the *Guardia Civil* was intense and justified. To avert further bloodshed a separate Basque police was established. Originally very restricted in its remit and with limited manpower, it has since developed substantially. It now operates as a fully fledged police force within Euskadi and has had some significant successes against the terrorist and extortion activities of ETA. This success has proved a poisoned chalice for the Basque police. The violence has continued (with increasingly little political context) although ETA now kills Basque policemen as well as Spanish ones. The Catalan police force is much smaller and limited in its scope than its Basque counterpart, being used primarily for the policing of issues related to the *autonomía* (Art 18, Catalan Statute of Autonomy). A similar situation is found in the new force established in Galicia. Although the *autonomía* police forces are responsible to the regional governments for financial and administrative matters, final responsibility for these forces lies with the Ministry of the Interior in Madrid.

There is less variation between the higher autonomy regions and their compatriots in other spheres of policy, although significant differences do exist in particular policy fields. Euskadi, for example, has exclusive authority over savings banks and credit institutions, internal trade, industry, transport, ports and airports (Art 10, Basque Statute of Autonomy). Although in theory exclusive, the Euskadi constitutional statute is typical in limiting most of these functions by a number of caveats. For example, banking controls must be within the established national guidelines, and internal trade regulations must not infringe pricing policy, free movement of goods or competition rules. Other functions such as transport policy are subject to specific reserved powers retained by the centre and laid down in the constitution, for example:

> ... the merchant navy and the registering of ships, lighting of coasts and signals at sea; general purpose ports; general purpose airports; control of the air space, air traffic and transport; meteorological services and registration of aircraft. [Art 149(1)(xx), Spanish Constitution.]

This example exposes a phenomenon that reappears regularly in Spanish constitutional law. The regional statutes often appear to contradict the national constitution (in this case, the ports and airports are listed as exclusive powers under the Basque Statute while Art 149(1)(xx) states that they remain a national competence). This is particularly true in relation to the Basque and Catalan statutes. The limitations placed upon the 'exclusive' powers of the Basque and Catalan governments in these areas of contradictory competence give the national government the power to enact framework laws.

The functions undertaken by the Spanish *autonomías* are broad, and the impression given is of a relatively autonomous regional tier, although one which operates within very different parameters depending on the region in question. The variety of regional functions is the most striking feature of the Spanish system, with health and education regionalised in large sections of the country but operating under direct national control in the rest.

Nevertheless, the extent of regional autonomy can be misleading, with the term 'exclusive' often being applied to areas of regional authority where the national tier retains a significant co-ordinating role. In addition, regional policies must operate under the constraints of both European and national monetary and fiscal policies over which the regions have little influence. The poorer regions, in particular, are open to national influence through the use of grants-in-aid. As ever, a significant degree of co-operation is required to make this complex system work in practice.

5.3.5 A federal Spain?

The future of the Spanish regional system is a constant subject of debate in Spain. This was particularly true during much of the 1980s when the moderate nationalists in Euskadi and Catalonia (the governing parties in both regions) held the kingmaking power in the *Cortes*. Although this power was successfully employed by the Basques and Catalans to gain significant concessions from the Spanish Government, it also had the effect of creating resentment in Spain towards the 'special treatment' granted to the northern provinces. This interregional resentment is a particular feature of the Spanish system and one that makes the development of a truly federal system difficult to envisage in the near future.

Spanish regions do not tend to co-operate in their dealings with the centre, and until recently they even lacked the institutions to do so (see Chapter 12). Instead they have concentrated on bilateral dealings with the centre. This has the advantage of creating clearer lines of democratic responsibility for decision making, but it can seriously weaken the regional hand. There is no real concept of regional solidarity in Spain, as there is in Germany or Italy (the Spanish regional leaders do not regularly meet), and instead a culture of competition exists. The clearest example of this can be seen in relation to the challenge of Europe.

The Spanish regions have long campaigned for representation within the Spanish delegation at the Council of Ministers, and the government has recently been willing to concede this. However, the Catalans and Basques demand individual representation at the council, not merely a collective regional representative. Whatever powers are granted to the mass of Spanish regions, the Basques and Catalans are likely to demand more. Unless and until a true accommodation can be struck between the micro-nationalist aspirations of the northern regions and the regionalist demands of the others, the Spanish system will continue to be driven by this competitive rather than co-operative dynamic.

5.4 FINLAND: THE ÅLAND ISLANDS

5.4.1 Åland: an international region

Although part of the territory of Finland, the Åland islands are home to a Swedish speaking population and were, until 1809, part of the Swedish state. Despite the rural isolation of the islands, the population has not enjoyed a quiet life. Occupying a strategic position in the Baltic Sea, the islands have a history of military conflict, particularly between the Swedish and Russian Empires. During this period, the islands changed hands several times and were the subject of several local rebellions against Russian occupation. In 1809, the Swedish Empire finally accepted defeat in the east and formally ceded the islands (along with the Grand Duchy of Finland itself) to the Russian state under the Treaty of Fredrikshamn. The Russians immediately set about fortifying the islands, but during the Crimean war proved unable to defend them against attack from a combined French and British force. Under the ensuing peace treaty, the islands were returned to Russia, but declared a demilitarised zone, a status they retain to this day.

In the wake of the Russian revolution, the islanders declared their independence from Russia under the principle of self-determination, and expressed a desire to return to Swedish rule. Neither the newly independent Finnish state nor Soviet Russia accepted this declaration, and fighting broke out between Russian and Finnish units which had been illegally stationed on the islands. After the intervention of Sweden and Germany, the demilitarised status of the islands was re-established and a de facto parliament was established to govern the islands. This institution refused to accept Finnish offers of limited autonomy, and declared its intention to seek reunification with Sweden. Finland responded by arresting the leaders of the Åland assembly and prosecuting them for treason.

The referral of the dispute to the League of Nations in 1921 took place against this volatile backdrop, and it became a celebrated example of peaceful international dispute resolution. In the event, of course, it proved to be one of few successes for the League. Nevertheless, it is for this reason that the name of the Åland islands is known far beyond their isolated shores.

The settlement of the Åland dispute resulted in the creation of a demilitarised, neutral and autonomous region with guarantees for the culture and language of the population under the sovereignty of the Finnish State (Decision of the Council of the League of Nations on the Åland Islands, 697, September 1921). The neutrality of the islands was confirmed by the 1921 Convention On The Non-Fortification And Neutralization of The Åland Islands, signed by all the major powers and the neighbouring states. The essential principles of the Autonomy Statute were enshrined in a treaty between Sweden and Finland and guaranteed by the League (The Åland Agreement in the Council of The League Of Nations, 701, September 1921). This settlement, and the Autonomy Acts that are guaranteed by it, remain the basis of Åland autonomy to this day. Åland therefore has the unique distinction of being the only European region to have its status guaranteed not only by a domestic constitution but also by international law.

5.4.2 The regional institutions

The Act of Autonomy of Åland is an 'organic' law of the type found in Italy and Spain. It enjoys a status equal to that of the Finnish Constitution itself and, most importantly, cannot be altered without the agreement of the Åland Parliament (the *Lagting*). The current Act, which is the third, dates from 1993. This gives significantly more legislative autonomy to the regional institutions than its 1951 and 1920 predecessors.

The Parliament itself, which first sat in 1922, comprises 30 members elected by proportional representation. Finnish political parties do not operate in Åland, and a distinct Åland party democracy has developed. The *Lantråd*, or First Minister, is appointed by a majority of members after consultation with all parties in the assembly. Minority governments are not permitted. The executive, which comprises no more than seven members (and may have as few as five), is appointed by the *Lantråd* and heads the Åland administration.

The Finnish Government is represented on the islands by a provincial governor. The governor is appointed by the Finnish President in agreement with the speaker of the *Lagting*, as stipulated in the Swedish-Finnish agreement of 1921. If such agreement is not forthcoming, the *Lagting* will provide a list of five candidates from which the president may chose the governor. Uniquely, therefore, the government representative in the region is appointed with the agreement of the region itself.

The role of the governor is primarily to act as a conduit between the region and its parent state rather than its keeper. He or she undertakes the formal duties of the Head of State in Åland (for example, the opening and closing of parliament), but the most significant role is as head of the Åland delegation. This body comprises two members elected by the *Lagting* and two by the Finnish Government, with the governor as its chairman. This institution can be referred to by the Finnish Government in relation to Åland matters, but it is primarily used to handle the financial relationship between the regional institutions and the central state. This includes the regional block grant (the principles of which are laid down in the Autonomy Act), tax reimbursements, and emergency payments required by the region in the event of economic or natural disaster. It may also advise the president to annul an Act of the Åland Lagting if it falls outside its legislative autonomy. The president is not obliged to heed such advice.

Within the region, 12 municipalities make up the local government tier. A regional council comprising representatives of the local authorities, of the type that makes up the regional tier on the mainland, also exists in the islands (see section 6.2.3). However, as the functions of these councils are largely in the hands of the regional institutions in Åland, the regional council is responsible only for the few field functions which remain the responsibility of the national state. A similar situation applies to the Åland Health Service district although, as this is a devolved matter, it is the regional rather than the national government to which the council is responsible.

5.4.3 The responsibilities of the autonomous region

The core responsibilities recognised in the original agreement of 1921 remain at the heart of Åland autonomy today. However, the Autonomy Acts of 1951 and now 1993 have significantly increased the responsibilities of the regional authorities. Given the genesis of the Åland region it is not surprising to find education, cultural matters, the preservation of heritage and the police being exclusively regional matters. Beyond this, however, health, local government, regional development, transport, postal services and broadcasting (the latter two only since 1993) are now all largely exclusive legislative powers within the regional territory (s 17, Åland Autonomy Act). In fields such as telecommunications, decisions of the national government which affect Åland must have the approval of the regional government (s 27(40), Åland Autonomy Act).

The Finnish central state only retains exclusive responsibility in the fields of international affairs, defence and currency issues, but retains supervisory powers in a number of other areas including public health and agriculture. The autonomy of the region is nevertheless substantial. The supervisory powers of the central state are minimal in relation to Åland legislation. This legislation can only be overruled if found to be contrary to the Act of Autonomy, or damaging to the security of Finland, by the Supreme Court of Finland or the Åland delegation. In such a case, the president may exercise his or her veto.

The financial status of the island is also extremely secure, enshrined as it within the Autonomy Act itself. At present this guarantees Åland 0.45% of the Finnish budget per year (s 47, Åland Autonomy Act). There is also provision for the retention of national taxes raised on the islands if the income from any one of them exceeds 0.5% of the total Finnish yield in that tax. Increases to the Åland block can be agreed through the Åland delegation, but the 0.45% figure cannot be reduced.

The short Autonomy Act of Åland (which runs to only 79 sections) outlines a regional regime with extensive autonomy. Guaranteed by international treaty and domestic constitution, the regime itself stands as one of the most protected in the EU. The regional institutions are financially secure and cannot be overruled by the central state except in extreme circumstances. The only formal role that the regional institutions lack is involvement in the national legislative process. The Åland Government does have the right to be consulted (s 28, Åland Autonomy Act), and in practice the bundle of constitutional powers that the island institutions enjoy means that even in the most international of matters their opinions cannot be ignored.

5.4.4 Åland: the European region

The unique constitutional position of Åland (its autonomy being recognised in both international and domestic law) has had a significant impact on its recent development, particularly as Finland entered the European Union in 1995. Treaties entered into by the Finnish state do not apply to the Åland islands to the extent that they deal with regional competencies, unless the assembly assents to the application of the implementation statute. In addition, treaties which contradict the Åland Statute of Autonomy can only apply if the procedure for amendment of the statute is utilised. This left Åland in an extremely strong position when Finland applied for membership of the EU.

In fact, Åland was given the option not to join the EU, under provisions enshrined in the Accession Treaty (Art 25, now Art 227(5), EC Treaty). It did join at the same time as Finland, but retained a number of specific derogations from the EC Treaty. Most importantly, the islands (and ferry traffic through their territory) lies outside the zone of tax harmonisation for indirect and excise duties. Additional derogations include restrictions on the ability of non-Åland residents to purchase property on the islands. Aside from these permanent exemptions from EU provisions, the island authorities have ensured a significant voice at the negotiating table (Chapter 9a, Åland Autonomy Act).

In areas within the legislative authority of Åland, it is the Government of Åland that prepares the position of the national government in relation to a policy's application in the archipelago. The Åland Government is also entitled to participate in the preparation of the Finnish position in the Council of Ministers, although the final say on this lies with the national government. Nevertheless, in keeping with their recent history, the island institutions have a significance far beyond that which their small population would normally allow.

5.5 THE CONSTITUTIONAL REGIONS: FEDERATIONS IN THE MAKING?

The development of constitutional regional structures in Europe represents an attempt to reconcile increasing calls for regional autonomy with a desire to retain the borders of the nation-state. Because of this, all these examples exhibit significant asymmetry between those regions which demand greater self-determination and those which ally themselves with the central state. This can be contrasted with the symmetrical nature of the German and Austrian federations and, to a lesser extent, that of Belgium. Nevertheless, as these structures have developed, many of these regions have exhibited similarities with their federal cousins and, in some cases, have enjoyed significantly greater policy independence.

The links between the autonomy of regional units and their constitutional status is therefore more complex than may appear at first. A pattern has emerged through the brief analysis of the constitutional regions given above. Those regions that have a constitutional or political lever are able to exhibit the most independence of action and make their voices heard at the national and European levels. Those that lack such political or constitutional leverage can find their formal status undermined. The nature of these levers can vary as the above examples show. In Spain, it was the strength of regional political parties, particularly in the 1990s, that ensured a significant degree of autonomy was devolved. In Åland, the international status of the region is a powerful negotiating tool for the regional authorities in their dealings with Finland.

In contrast to these examples, the weakness of the regional political parties in Italy and the pro-centrist approach of the constitutional court have allowed the central state to limit the power of regional institutions through financial and other means. A similar situation has been seen in Portugal, although the change of government allowed the autonomous regions to push for greater financial security.

The constitutional status of individual regions is therefore only part of the story. Formal aspects of regional autonomy can be undermined or strengthened, depending on non-constitutional factors. The question then arises as to whether the formal constitutional status of the region makes a difference. Can regions which lack constitutional protection entirely operate as autonomous regional governments? To examine this, we shall now turn to those regional governments of the European Union that lack a formal constitutional status. Do these 'local government' regions operate in a manner that would justify their inclusion as examples of regional government?

CHAPTER 6

REGIONS AS LOCAL GOVERNMENT

The final constitutional category of regional governments is made up of those which lack any constitutional status whatsoever. Instead, they form part of the structure of local government in the Member State. As a consequence they lack constitutional protection and legislative power, deriving their authority entirely from executive powers devolved by the central state. Some might question whether these are true political regions as defined in Chapter 2. In some cases, this criticism is valid, but in most cases the role they perform is one of policy maker and co-ordinator. This role is beyond that of the traditional local level of government. Although not enjoying the more formal legislative autonomy of their constitutional cousins, these administrative regions nevertheless offer a level of regional accountability and have the potential to develop distinct policies tailored to their populations.

6.1 FRANCE

6.1.1 French regionalism

The French system of regional government, introduced in the wake of the election victory of the PS (Socialist Party) in 1981, was the most dramatic change in French sub-national government since the beginning of the Third Republic. The reforms introduced by Gaston Defferre revolutionised the whole system of French local governance rather than just the regional tier, but the most controversial parts of the decentralisation reforms concerned the creation of democratic *régions*. The importance of the regional project to the socialist legislative programme was due, at least in part, to the grand alliance the socialists had constructed in their long march to power. Alongside those who favoured the Girondist tradition from within its traditional ranks, the PS also attracted regionalists and those who favoured autogestion (literally, 'running oneself') through their promise to reform the territorial governance of France.

There were also practical reasons for the socialists' change of heart. During their political isolation the left had made significant gains at the local level, and socialist councillors who had experienced the impotence of local government wanted it reformed. As is often the case with such promises to decentralise, the ardour of the central party cooled somewhat once the goal of national power had been achieved. This was particularly true once their opponents began to win at the local (and eventually regional) level. Possibly as a result of this, the grander schemes of the regionalist movements were ignored, leaving the regions as local government bodies with no legislative power.

The situation was further complicated by the Corsican question. The culturally distinct Mediterranean island has had an uneasy relationship with the French state since its purchase from Genoa in 1768. By the early 1980s, a small but violent independence movement was active on the island, and democratic movements in favour of home rule were acquiring increased support. For this reason, the socialist manifesto of 1981 gave priority to the creation of a Corsican 'assembly' in advance of the larger regional plan for mainland France. The manifesto included the overseas *départements* of Martinique, Réunion, Guadeloupe and Guyane. Although officially part of the EU, these territories are not included in this study because of their territorial isolation from the continent.

The creation of democratic regional government in Corsica was also perceived as something of a test case for wider regional reforms, but the idea was misconceived. Corsican culture and identity places it apart from mainland France despite the mantra that France is an 'indivisible republic'. In addition, the unrest that had occurred sporadically since the 1970s obviously set the Corsican experience apart from that of the mainland. Less well known (at least outside France), but equally important to any solution to the Corsican question, was the political control exercised by the Corsican 'clan' system. Two clans have controlled Corsica through patronage and electoral fraud for decades, and although they compete vehemently against each other they have co-operated frequently to ensure that they continue their hegemony (Boisvert, 1988, pp 208–09). Changes to the Corsican system of government were an attack on clan dominance, and as such the clans opposed them. Ironically, therefore, many of the strongest opponents of the reform were Corsican 'notables' with positions of influence within the ranks of the national parties.

Many myths surround the pre-1982 French system of territorial government. The most common is that of the 'one and indivisible republic' first proclaimed by the Jacobins in the 1790s. This centralisation of France had long been the goal of rulers in Paris and the Jacobins were merely more successful than the preceding monarchy. Although at first glance this centralising tendency continued almost unbroken up to the 1980s, closer inspection exposes the inaccuracy of this view.

Within France a large proportion of local power was exercised in an informal manner, and wielded by the 'notables'. A notable was described by Grémion as:

> ... a man who disposes of a certain power to act on the apparatus of the state at certain privileged levels and who, by a reverse effect, sees his power reinforced

by the privileges which these contacts confer, in so far as they are sanctioned by results. [Keating, 1983, p 237.]

These politicians hold a collection of local and national elected posts under the *cumul des mandats* system. Under this arrangement an individual can acquire several elected posts at once. The influence of these 'local' politicians was presented as evidence that local power in government was strong.

However, Theonig casts doubt on the idea that any strictly local power existed within the system. The power lay with the notables, not the locality (Keating and Hainsworth, 1986, p 12). These individuals controlled the periphery through a complex series of networks. This 'honeycomb' system removed power from the local electorate and led, in the 19th century words of Lamennais, to 'apoplexy at the centre and paralysis at the periphery' (Hayward, 1983, p 24). Altogether, this created a *société bloquée* with inefficient local government and administration.

Another key player in the pre-1982 system was the Prefect, a centrally appointed civil servant who exercised a joint role as both executive of the local council and representative of the central state in the locality. In this role the Prefect had the power to veto any decisions of the local *conseil général*. Debate continues over how this power actually affected the independence of the *départemental* level. Some described the relationship between the elected representatives and the Prefect as one of mutual dependence rather than one of control by the latter over the former.

Keating gives the apocryphal example of a mayor who, when required to take an unpopular decision, took the popular one instead. Privately, however, the Mayor asked his Prefect to veto the decision. When the Prefect duly obliged, the Mayor then publicly criticised him for obstructing local democracy, thus saving his own political skin while still taking the unpopular decision (Keating, 1983, p 239).

Although this particular tale may be an urban myth, it does illustrate the symbiotic relationship that existed between the government's representative and the locally elected delegates. Clauzel (himself a Prefect) argued that in practice the tutelle was rarely used. The Prefect and the departmental president acted in the pursuit of common interests for the good of the territory for which they were responsible. The system itself recognised the possibility of such a relationship. In an effort to avoid it, Prefects and sub-Prefects were transferred every two years to avoid their 'going native' (Keating and Hainsworth, 1986, p 9). Laignel on the other hand suggests that such an interpretation is fundamentally wrong. The *tutelle* gave the Prefect an almost total veto over the *départemental* and regional decisions and in this way he or she was the dominant partner in such relationships (Rousseau, 1987, p 185).

The economic changes of the 1960s laid the foundations for the subsequent reforms. Regional interests began to organise themselves into lobbying groups (*forces vives*) comprising businessmen, trade unionists and politicians, amongst others. In response, the government created a tier of centrally appointed CODERs (*Commission de Développement Économique Régional*), primarily as a method of controlling these *forces vives*. These bodies were deconcentrated tiers of administration, and the *conseils régionaux* which followed them in 1972 were merely advisory (Rousseau, 1987, pp 172–73).

The lack of regional democratic control exercised over these bodies led to demands for their democratisation. By creating the CODERs, government had created a form of regional government but could come up with no plausible reason why it should remain detached from the regional electorate. The resentment was further increased when these regional bodies encouraged economic developments at odds with local wishes, such as the commercialisation of the Mediterranean coast (Keating and Hainsworth, 1986). National decisions such the attempt to close the Corsican rail network and the proposed dumping of waste off the Corsican coast further alienated the periphery. Boisvert has gone as far as suggesting that these blunders by the state were inevitable given its centralised nature (Boisvert, 1988).

The left capitalised on this 'unexpected rebellion' of the French periphery (Beer, 1980) by placing local and regional reform at the heart of their programme of government. French constitutional history is littered with the wreckage of previous attempts at regional reform, but Defferre believed that speed of implementation would be the key to the success of his reforms. By rushing a series of enabling *lois* through the French Parliament, he was able to defeat the likely opponents of the reform before they could regroup in the aftermath of their electoral defeat.

Defferre's policy required a degree of compromise to ensure that the reforms were passed swiftly through the Senate. The French Senate (colloquially referred to as the house of notables) is indirectly elected by the *communes* (the smallest units of local government). It has an inbuilt conservative majority because of this, and is the power base of the very notables who risked losing influence through the decentralisation reforms. To buy off these opponents, proposals for the reform of the *cumul de mandats* were watered down.

Defferre's method had a second problem which became obvious in the years following the reform. By leaving the technical aspects of the reform to later executive decrees, he left the ultimate shape of the regions in the hands of the government. As the opposition began to gain ground in the periphery, the support of President Mitterand and his government for the regions became somewhat muted. The right then began to demand the speedy implementation of the promised reforms (which they had previously opposed). The government finally acceded to this demand in 1985. The results could not have been worse for the socialists. The party that introduced regional government to France received little thanks, with only two of the 21 mainland regions returning socialist majorities. These events nevertheless convinced the right of the benefits of regionalism. This was of crucial importance, as the right, on returning to power, left the local and regional reforms largely intact (Keating, 1986).

Despite the limited nature of the regional reforms, the regional tier has proved relatively popular in France. Opinion polls consistently show that the reforms have strong support among the electorate, which favours more decentralisation to the regional tier (*Le Monde*, 13/14 October 1991). The success of the regions in the field of education has certainly helped this process, as has their apparent thrift. With the exception of their unpopular decision to invest in new assembly buildings, their use of their limited resources appears to be successful. Although they remain a background player in the French system, their profile is far higher than suggested by the 2% of national spending that they control.

6.1.2 Regions in the French state

The French system of sub-national government in metropolitan France comprises three tiers of democratically elected authority. France is divided into 36,551 *communes* of varying sizes and populations. These boundaries reflect historical divisions that are no longer relevant, and lead to the situation that Marseille (population one million) is a *commune* as is Vernassal (population 300). Above this level are the 96 Napoleonic *départements* and, since 1982, 22 *régions* including Corsica (see Figure 6.1). A further system of regional and local government exists for French overseas territories, the *Départements Outre Mer* (DOMs) and *Territoires Outre Mer* (TOMs). Each level has a deliberative council and an executive drawn from it.

The French *régions* are a branch of local government, and as such have no specific standing under the French Constitution. Instead, they are founded on a number of *lois* (primarily Acts of 2 March 1982, 7 January 1983, 22 July 1983 and 24 February 1984). In addition to lacking constitutional standing (and by definition legislative power), this classification places the regions on an equal footing with all other branches of local government. Due to the lack of a hierarchy in the French sub-national government structure, all authorities are treated as equal under the law. Although the *région* is territorially larger than the *département*, it has no inherent authority over it, which in turn has none over the commune. All are classed as *collectivités territoriales*, giving them formal equality as local authorities under the national umbrella. Until 1986, the regions did not even enjoy such equality with the other democratic tiers, being classed merely as *établissements publics*, and as such were inferior to the *départemental* and *communal* tiers. The practical effect was to deny them the general competence afforded to these two levels and instead limit their functions to specific duties (Keating, 1983, p 237).

Two levels of deconcentrated administration (the prefectures) operate in parallel with the region and department. The regional Prefect (who is also the Prefect for the department in which the regional capital is situated) is the representative of the state, and as such administers all deconcentrated regional functions. Although this represented an increased role for the regional Prefect, the national ministries were slow to hand over the required powers. By 1985, 300 deconcentration reforms had been put forward, with 75% being approved. Of these, only 12% had been implemented (Schmidt, 1990, p 323). The Act of 6 February 1992 on the Territorial Administration of the Republic attempted to improve the situation regarding prefectural authority. In areas such as education (which has its own hierarchical structure) the Prefect exerts no authority.

The role of the Prefect has changed dramatically at both the regional and departmental levels since the reforms of 1982. Prior to the programme of reforms, the Prefect, at all levels, was the executive of the relevant local authority and exercised *a priori* control over decisions taken by the conseil général (the democratically elected council of the *département*). Under national legislative provisions, Prefects now have *ex post facto* authority to refer any acts to the local *tribunal administratif* (administrative court) if they regard them as *ultra vires*. However, the region may also bring an action for unwarranted interference against the Prefect if it feels it is being improperly controlled, or impeded, in its duties (Mazey, 1993, p 66).

The Prefect also oversees the regional budget. If the Prefect feels that the regional council has not fulfilled its budgetary obligation, he or she may refer the matter to the *chambre régionale des comptes* (regional audit court). Such references may only be made in specific circumstances, for example when the deficit of the region is over 5% of operating income or when the region has failed to include items of expenditure that are obligatory. In the latter case, the final decision lies with the *conseil d'état*. The status of a particular head of expenditure is an administrative rather than an accounting matter.

In effect, the French regions operate under a distinct administrative and economic sub-constitution within the French Republic. Although the Prefects remain the representatives of the state in the regions, their formal role is more ombudsman or constitutional watchdog than active participant in regional decision making. Nevertheless, it appears to be common practice for regional presidents to consult with the Prefect to assess a decision's administrative or financial legality prior to its approval by the regional council (Mazey, 1993, p 71). This brings Prefects back into the regional decision making process, though the extent of their practical influence is difficult to assess. This is not universal practice however, and in some cases Prefects have been shut out of regional discussions altogether (Schmidt, 1990, p 321).

The restrictions within which the regions operate are statutory, and the national authorities have no legal right to interfere in the region's policy choices outside these legislative rules. The legal framework within which the French regions must work is substantially tighter than that of most constitutional regions, and the restrictions placed upon the regions may be altered unilaterally by the national level at any time. Whether political realities always allow such control to be exercised is another matter.

French regions do possess limited rights in relation to their abolition or alteration under the current legal framework. In particular they have the right to be consulted before any changes are made to their titles or territorial limits, and regions may also request to be amalgamated after their councils have voted in favour of such a move. This provision only covers the amalgamation of regions and not their reorganisation. The latter is something that many traditional regions such as Brittany would find desirable. The current region of Bretagne does not include the Breton *département* of Loire-Atlantique, whose territory was part of the ancient Breton state.

Some regions have tackled the artificial nature of certain boundaries themselves. In the Languedoc-Roussillon region, for example, the regional authorities created separate offices and institutions in the two areas. The geography of Languedoc and that of Roussillon have created two separate economies, which led the region to indulge in 'administrative deconcentration' within its own borders (*The Economist*, 13 April 1985).

6.1.3 The regional tier

The French *régions* are the only regional governments in the EU to operate a bicameral system of decision making. The *conseil régional* (regional council) is the primary chamber and is directly elected from *départemental* constituency lists. The *départemental* nature of the electoral constituencies has not aided the development of a regional political culture. In Corsica the *conseil* is referred to as the 'Corsican Assembly', but despite its title its role is, at present, not much greater than that of mainland region examples. The council (or assembly) is the only qualified decision making body in the *région*. It is the only legally competent body to decide regional policy, but in practice extensive use is made of sub-committees to scrutinise decisions prior to discussion in the full council. The *conseil* also elects the regional president as its chairman. This individual alone exercises the limited executive powers of the region.

The second chamber of the French *région* is the Economic and Social Committee. This body is a remnant of the deconcentrated regions that had existed prior to 1982. It comprises indirectly elected regional stakeholders drawn from the business community (35%), trade unions (35%), welfare, cultural and consumer associations (25%). A further 5% of each region's Economic and Social Committee consists of regional 'experts' appointed by the Prime Minister's office. The committee must be consulted on all policies proposed by the regional council, and issues advisory opinions upon them. The committee may also call extraordinary meetings to discuss wider issues affecting the region, and present such opinions as they see fit to the *conseil régional* itself. In practice the committee, in common with its senior partner, makes extensive use of sub-committees in its work.

Formally, there is no cabinet system of government at the regional level. Instead all executive authority rests with the person of the president. In practice, the regional councils appoint several vice-presidents who behave as the executive of the region, notwithstanding legislative assertions to the contrary (Mazey, 1993, p 68). A 'standing committee' (representing the various party strengths in the council) carries out a number of executive functions in relation to the council. This includes setting the agenda for discussion, as well as the dates of full council meetings.

The Corsican region, established under separate legislation, exhibits a number of characteristics that set it apart from the mainland regions (*Loi* 13 May 1991 superseded the provisions applying to Corsica in *Loi* 2 March 1982). Nevertheless, this does not yet place it in the category of a 'special' region such as those found in Italy or Portugal. The Corsican statute has no constitutional status and can be amended in the same way as any other *loi*, while the Corsican Assembly, despite its grand title, is a local government council, having no legislative authority. Institutionally there are a number of idiosyncrasies, such as the existence of advisory councils including a *conseil de la culture, de l'éducation et du cadre de vie en Corse* (council of culture, education and quality of life) and a committee on Corsican broadcasting which advises the assembly. Unlike the mainland Economic and Social Committees, appointments to both these bodies are made by the French President. The government has claimed that this remains necessary to avoid domination by clan interests (Boisvert, 1988, pp 358–60).

Figure 6.1: The French régions

French Regions

A: Bretagne
B: Basse-Normandie
C: Haute-Normandie
D: Picardie
E: Nord-Pas-de-Calais
F: Pays de la Loire
G: Centre
H: Ile de France
I: Bourgogne
J: Champagne-Ardenne
K: Lorraine
L: Alsace
M: Franche-Comte
N: Poitou-Charentes
O: Limousin
P: Auvergne
Q: Rhône-Alpes
R: Aquitaine
S: Midi-Pyrénées
T: Languedoc-Roussillon
U: Provence-Alpes-Côte d'Azur
V: Corsica

6.1.4 The role of the French *régions*

Defferre wished to divide functional authority into self-contained blocks, each of which would then be given to the relevant level along with the necessary finance (Le Galès, 1994). In practice, this idea was almost impossible to implement.

Although the socialist government's programme for regional government was influenced by pressure from micro-nationalist and regionalist movements, the primary reason for the creation of the regions was to democratise the regional planning process. As one would expect, economic development continues to dominate functional powers at the regional tier. After the reforms of 1982, the function of drawing up regional economic plans was passed from the CODERs to the newly democratised regions. Indeed, it could be argued that all other regional powers were intended to be ancillary to this primary function. The extent to which the region was linked to the economic planning process was emphasised by Rocard (the minister for planning) in 1981:

> In effect, planning and regionalisation are inextricably linked, like two sides of a coin. Without planning, regionalisation would degenerate into petty interests;

conversely, without regionalisation, planning would tend to become a uniform and centralising straitjacket. [Kofman, 1985, p 17.]

Regional involvement in the planning process operates at a number of levels. The regions are free to construct regional economic plans within the confines of this national plan. The region also acts as the main conduit for the implementation of the regional plan. The only legal restrictions on the region's independence in establishing its own economic plan are that it must not contradict the national plan or another regional one. Consultation with the Prefect is compulsory for the region when creating the regional plan. This is no mere formality however, as it is the Prefect who represents the region in the national planning process (Baume and Bonnet, 1994, p 7). In practice this legally imposed solidarity is of far less impact than national influence by financial means. Regions may suffer financial loss if they do not follow the objectives set out at national level (Keating, 1983, p 248). The national government will only financially support projects that match its own objectives.

The establishment of the regional plan is the framework for the region's wider economic role. Within the confines of the plan, the region may use its powers of financial intervention to encourage economic development. This can consist of financial aid to 'healthy' enterprises as well as all forms of indirect aid such as loans, tax concessions, sale of land to enterprises and loan guarantees (Schmidt, 1990, p 124). The only formal restrictions placed upon these activities are that they must not limit freedom of trade and industry or the legal equality of citizens. The national government may also impose maximum limits on direct investment in specific companies as well as limiting the total expenditure by a region on this type of activity. All assistance to companies given by the regions must be within the context of regional and national plans and EU restrictions on state aid (Keating, 1983), while all direct investment must be within nationally set frameworks (Keating, 1986).

Most economic intervention occurs through the *contrat du plan* for each region. This is a contract negotiated between the national government and the region, and includes input from other local authorities and private enterprises. The document commits the region and the central state to financing certain projects over a five year period (the first set ran from 1984–88 inclusive) when another contract is agreed upon. This amounts to a five year commitment to grants-in-aid, thus giving financial incentives to those regions which finance projects that the central government also supports.

Although economic planning is no longer fashionable in most western economies, it has continued to play a significant role in French economic policy. The practical change has been one of emphasis. More stress is now placed by the national government on public-private partnerships in preference to direct public intervention (Mazey, 1993). Le Galès noted an increase in funding to the centrally controlled regional development agencies (DATAR and DIV) as evidence of increased national intervention in economic development (Le Galès, 1994). Whether this is to the detriment of the regional element is unclear.

The use that regional governments have made of their economic powers has varied significantly. Some of a more liberal complexion have been content to act in a co-ordinating role while others have invested heavily in major infrastructure projects (for example, Nord-Pas-de-Calais) or indigenous industries (Midi-Pyrénées and Bretagne) (Mazey, 1993). Overall, intervention has been less heavy-handed than previous excursions by the state into economic development. Emphasis has been placed on co-ordination of regional projects rather than direct regional involvement. The result has often been the establishment of mixed-capital companies, under regional supervision, with the aim of developing the projects deemed necessary for regional development.

Transport is a further area of significant regional policy. With the introduction of LOTI (*Loi d'Orientation des Transports Intérieurs*), control over regional rail services passed to the regions, although the national trunk routes remain the exclusive preserve of the French national rail company SNCF. The regional authorities and SNCF now negotiate agreements on the running of services on local routes, with the regions integrating the rail services into a public transport network (in practice SNCF run most bus services anyway). Government involvement in subsidisation and infrastructure improvement is now administered regionally (*Le Monde*, 22 and 23 March 1992).

In all these areas of policy, the key to regional involvement remains co-ordination. As Michel Rocard stated at the very birth of the regions in 1982, '*dans la domaine économique, la région exerce en principe une fonction de pilote*' (in economic policy, the region acts principally as a guide). Little can be achieved without the involvement of other partners and tiers of local government.

One further authority which falls within the regional sphere is the administration of secondary education (the lycées). This authority is entirely administrative, with curriculum and education policy remaining tightly controlled by the national government. Regional involvement in the *lycées* is widely credited with averting a crisis in secondary education provision. After a period of neglect, the secondary school system was unable to cope with the large increase in pupil numbers which occurred in the early 1980s. The regions, after being granted authority over what many saw as a poisoned chalice, embarked upon an extensive building and refurbishment programme which has broadly been regarded as a success. The lack of regional resources available to finance it led to the use of innovative public-private partnerships such as the METP (*Marchés d'Entreprise de Travaux Publics*) schemes (Douence, 1994, p 22). The regions have also invested heavily in professional training, which accounted for 42% of total regional spending in 1992 (Engel and Van Ginderachter, 1993, p 75). Although high in regional terms, 80% of the cost of this has primarily been met by national funding through specific grants (Douence, 1994).

A key factor in the development of the regional responsibilities examined above has been their general competence to act for the good of their territory in any field not specifically allocated to another level. This is a power enjoyed by all *collectives territoriales*. The strict division of tasks between national, regional, *départemental* and *communal* government should ensure the practical operation of such a principle is limited.

In fact the regions in particular have involved themselves in areas which are, strictly speaking, beyond the remit of regional government. This has allowed the *régions* to establish a foothold in French cultural life. In addition to using their statutory power to support regional museums and libraries, many regions have established drama studios, orchestras and *fonds régionaux d'art contemporain* in spite of their questionable competence for such projects (Council of Europe, 1998). Universities too benefited from regional expenditure before higher education became an area of some regional responsibility. The common thread with all these projects has been their regional focus (Douence, 1994, p 20). The regions are therefore acting as a reservoir for, and defender of, France's diverse regional interests. This tendency cannot help but encourage the growth of regional identity, intentionally or not, further enhancing the status of the *régions* in French society. The national government has found it politically difficult to restrict these actions, and revisions to the 1982 reforms have generally accepted and formalised these encroachments.

6.1.5 The end of the 'one and indivisible republic'?

Although the regions have made their presence felt in the fields of economic development and transport, the jury is still out on their overall impact. In particular, debate continues as to whether the use of *contrats du plan* ensures that national finance is spent on regional priorities, or whether their use means that the region's policy choices are driven by the need for national finance (Le Galès and John, 1998; Rogers, 1998). On the mainland at least, the one and indivisible republic remains intact, although it now has a distinctly regional flavour.

The clearest threat to the Jacobin state comes from Corsica. This region has greater authority in the field of education and culture than those in metropolitan France. Control over these responsibilities was a major issue amongst the population of the region, and the national government was obliged to make concessions in its attempt to appease the micro-nationalist movements on the island. Primary amongst these were Corsican language education (controlled by the region), a Corsican university, and powers in the field of broadcasting (Boisvert, 1988, p 366). These were substantially expanded under a new statute introduced in 1991 which raised the Corsican region's formal status above that of a metropolitan *région* to a *sui generis* institution within the French state (Engel and Van Ginderachter, 1993). Further devolution to Corsica was proposed in 2000 and approved by the Corsican Assembly in December of that year. The reforms remain limited, however; the assembly will only have secondary powers of legislation within its specified competencies, and only when justified by the island's circumstances. It will also be allowed to establish formal international links with its neighbours. Despite the limited nature of the reform proposals, the emotive pull of the indivisible republic had already led to one high profile resignation over the issue by the end of the year. The *loi* designed to implement these proposals is currently progressing slowly through the French Parliament. Although the chamber of deputies approved the new Corsican statute in the spring of 2001, the conservative Senate is currently mauling the proposals.

Although the proposals themselves have attracted support in Corsica, recent opinion polls by *Paris Match* found that only 17% of Corsicans favour outright independence (although 43% of French people questioned expressed support for the idea). Corsicans may disapprove of the indivisible republic, but they remain tied to France. Perhaps the Corsican experience will, in time, persuade metropolitan France that it need not remain doggedly wedded to its mythical unity.

6.2 SCANDINAVIAN FORMS OF REGIONAL GOVERNMENT

The issue of regional government in Scandinavia raises some interesting questions. In particular, the small population of all the Scandinavian countries prompts one to question whether there is a need for regional government at all. In addition, are the systems of middle government (between the local and national) really regional in the sense of the institutions discussed above? These conceptual issues are too complex for this volume, but the Scandinavian experience of regional government can add to our discussion for a number of reasons.

First, it must be remembered that although the population of Scandinavia is small (Sweden has the largest population, with eight million inhabitants), the areas of both Finland and Sweden are vast. Sweden, for example, is larger than Germany. Secondly, traditions of local governance and democracy in Scandinavia are very strong. In fact, their adoption of representative forms of government predates those of the United Kingdom by several centuries. This traditional of local autonomy has led to the creation of units of government, particularly in Denmark, which, although small in population and limited in area, exercise an exceptional degree of autonomy and financial independence. If nothing else, the Danish example proves that significant devolution of both financial and functional autonomy to small units of governance is possible and does not weaken the state.

In the sections that follow, the various forms of local government region developed in Scandinavia are examined, but another example of Scandinavian soft-bordered governance deserves a brief mention. Norway, Sweden and Finland (as well as Russia) are the only countries in Western Europe to be home to a nomadic people, the *Sami* (or Lapps). The *Sami* of northern Scandinavia, in common with most nomadic peoples, have been forced to adapt to the alien nation-states which were imposed around them. This led to a loss of their land and exploitation of their natural resources.

In response to *Sami* demands for recognition, three *Sami* 'parliaments' were created. These parliaments were established under the laws of the three nation-states and operate differently. The oldest, the Finnish, was established in 1973, but it remains only an advisory council. The Swedish *Sameting*, established in 1993, represents the Sami people in an advisory capacity and also acts as an administrative arm of the Swedish state in relation to a number of *Sami* projects. The two roles do not easily coincide. The Norwegian *Sami Thing*, established in 1989, is the closest to a regional government of the type examined above. It currently has responsibility for *Sami* language education, and a number of other budgets are allocated to it by the state. The Norwegian statute is intentionally open-ended to allow further devolution of authority in the future.

Although these entities do not yet correspond to the regional model examined in Chapter 2, they do exhibit a number of interesting features. Most interestingly, they are elected according to a language rather than a territorial franchise. In addition, they often speak with one voice for the *Sami* people as a whole. In this respect they represent an intriguing use of soft borders on the periphery of Europe, and may soon become a further element in the 'third level' of the European Union.

6.2.1 Regionalism in Denmark

Denmark, with a population of just over five million, has the third smallest population of any Member State of the European Union. It is less populous than many regions in the EU (Bavaria and Catalonia for example) and has a long history of political, cultural and linguistic homogeneity. The European mainland of the Danish state is therefore not a prime candidate for political regionalism. The Danish overseas possessions of the Faeroe islands and Greenland are a different matter, but these are both geographically and politically outside the territory of the European Union. Nevertheless, Denmark has created a further tier of authority between the national and local authority levels which merits the attention of this study. These *amter* (described as 'counties' in the official translations) are small by the standards of most of the other authorities examined. The largest has a population of 606,689 and the smallest a mere 45,554. Nevertheless, they possess a level of responsibility that would make many larger authorities envious. For this reason they are of greater interest than their size might suggest.

The history of Danish local self-governance, based on the *kommuner*, goes back to the 13th century. Although the *amter* have existed since 1662, it was not until 1841 that these authorities acquired a measure of democracy through an elected council (Andersen, 1993, p 5). In 1970, a major reform of the Danish system of local government granted increased powers to the *amter* and created something like the structure we see today. In conjunction with this, the numbers of local government units were reduced. These reforms were introduced not for cultural or economic reasons but rather to counter fears of over-centralisation as a result of the expansion of the Danish welfare state.

As the Danish concept of the welfare state expanded so did the central government's role in managing it. By the 1960s, it was becoming increasingly obvious that many rural local authorities were unable to cope with the new burdens being placed upon them. This led to a number of related problems. First, the central government began establishing agencies to undertake those duties which local authorities could not manage. The result was a centralisation of power in the hands of deconcentrated agencies. Secondly, the quality of service provision in those fields that remained in the hands of the lower levels varied significantly, particularly between urban and rural areas (a postcode lottery, to use a UK analogy). The logical response of those *kommuner* that couldn't effectively manage the services was to enter into a large number of inter-*kommuner* executive agreements. These further reduced local accountability over the responsibilities that remained nominally under local control.

The response to these criticisms was the introduction of a newly empowered 'county' or regional tier (the *amt*) and a simultaneous reduction in the number of *kommuner* to allow them to undertake their duties without relying on either the national or regional tiers for support (Bogason, 1987, pp 47–48).

6.2.1.1 The national framework

The Danish system of territorial government comprises 275 *kommuner* (municipalities or communes) which are divided into 14 *amter* (counties or regions). In addition, the cities of Frederiksberg and Copenhagen have unitary authorities exercising the powers of both levels. Special home rule arrangements exist between Denmark and the devolved territories of Greenland and the Faeroe islands.

A tier of deconcentrated national authority operates in parallel with the *amter* level of sub-national government. Prior to the 1970 reforms, this Prefect (or *Statsamtmand*) was the chief executive of the deconcentrated regional tier, but the role has changed dramatically in the past 30 years. The main function of this office today is to supervise the activities of the *kommuner*, a role fulfilled in conjunction with the *amter*. Somewhat unusually, this official also acts as the judicial tribunal of first instance in cases concerning family law (Council of Europe, 1993; Andersen, 1993).

Neither the regional nor the local level of government enjoys specific constitutional protection, although the existence of local self-governing authorities is guaranteed under Art 82 of the Danish Constitution. The *amter* are defined by Acts of the national government, while supervision of the regional tier is limited to questions of *ultra vires*. The role of watchdog is not held by the Prefect over the *amter* but lies solely with the national Ministry of the Interior in Copenhagen. Decisions about the legality of regional actions are taken by the ordinary courts, whose decisions are binding in these matters (Fitzmaurice, 1981, p 76).

The lack of constitutional protection can leave the *amter* vulnerable to control by national government, and the national authorities have in the past imposed restrictions on regional finance policies. As the regional tier acquired greater legitimacy, and developed networks within the national government, it has become politically harder for the national government to impose restrictions. It is convention in Denmark today that any such restrictions that the national government wishes to impose will be preceded by a voluntary agreement between the local and regional authorities (Council of Europe, 1993). This has been particularly evident in the case of limits on *amter* income tax rates. The use of these agreements confirms the regional authorities' involvement in the national policy process on matters concerned with their autonomy.

6.2.1.2 *The* amter *as the regional tier*

The deliberative body of each *amt* is a directly elected assembly of between seven and 31 members. The national legislation requires the council to consist of an odd number of members, but within these limits the council is free to organise its procedures internally. The chairman of the council is the *amt* mayor, elected from within its ranks. He or she represents the *amt* in its dealings outside its boundaries and is regarded as its head. As such the chairman is responsible for executive duties concerning the administration of the *amt* authority (Bogason, 1987, p 53; for post-1989 changes, Andersen, 1993).

The executive body of the *amt* is appointed from within the council. It consists of a financial committee and one or more standing committees responsible for specific policy areas. The role of the former encompasses more than just financial matters; it administers the county's staff and acts as the regional planning authority as well as preparing the budget. Its chairman is the mayor of the *amt*.

The other committees implement policies as directed, as well as preparing policies for approval in the deliberative chamber. All parties are represented in the committees in proportion to their power in the full chamber. The full council can, in theory, make decisions on any matter concerning the county under its general competence, but in practice few decisions are undertaken in the assembly. Instead, powers are delegated to the relevant committee, which acts on the council's behalf. A few restrictions are placed upon the *amt* in its decision making. Some decisions must be taken in the full council chamber (taxation, approval of the budget, committee structures and membership, agreements with other authorities) while the finance committee's duties are set out in statute. Any member of a committee may demand that a decision be taken in the full chamber (Council of Europe, 1993, p 7).

The Danish regional tier is a branch of local government and as such has no legislative authority. Its executive responsibilities are wide, although it often fulfils the role of co-ordinating other bodies rather than acting itself. As already mentioned, the reforms of 1970, which saw the creation of the modern *amter*, were primarily a response to the over-centralisation of welfare services in the Danish state. For this reason *amter* competencies remain focused on the fields of welfare and healthcare. Even the boundaries of the *amter* reflect health service management considerations more than any other factor (Hansen, 1992, p 312). Nevertheless, in their 30 years, the authority of the *amter* has expanded substantially from this welfare orientated beginning.

The specific responsibilities assigned to the *amter* are complemented by a general competence to act in any policy area unless specified otherwise in law. This right is not constitutionally guaranteed, and its boundaries are set by ordinary laws at the national level, but it may not be limited by an executive decree (Andersen, 1993, p 10). The strong Danish tradition of consensus and local self-government means that such restrictions are generally negotiated rather than imposed. The stated policy of the national government in recent years has also been to legislate minimally in areas of local and regional government responsibility. The belief that locally operated services are more efficient and more democratic underpins the political scene in Denmark, regardless of party. For this reason, minimum frameworks have been set by the national authorities in many areas, with the *amter* (and *kommuner*) left free to develop policy within them.

As the decentralisation of health and social services was the primary rationale behind their establishment, it is no surprise that the Danish *amter* enjoy a high degree of responsibility in these fields. The extent to which health remains the key function of the *amter* is clear from their expenditure in this area. In 1992, this amounted to 49% of their total budget (Andersen, 1993, p 19). The Danish health service is administered entirely by the *amter* and *kommuner* levels, with the regional level playing the dominant policy role. Within national frameworks which establish minimum standards of care and service provision, the *amter* organise the health service within their territory. This has led to a situation in which some counties pay non-profit making companies to provide hospital services (5 hospitals in 1993) while others provide patient care directly. In 1992, the *amter* developed a system whereby patients could use a hospital of their choice anywhere in Denmark. These policies are regionally initiated and negotiated (with occasional national encouragement).

Although the *amter* began life in an effort to decentralise the Danish welfare state, they have increasingly played a role in the economic lives of their regions. Since the local government reforms of 1970, legislative amendments have given the *amter* competence to act in economic areas previously addressed nationally. The most significant transfers occurred in 1972 (maintenance and construction of roads), 1978 (public road transport), 1990 (agriculture) and 1992 (economic development). Tourism, hunting, fishing, forestry and conservation have also been added to the list of *amter* competencies (Andersen, 1993). Since 1982 the regions have also had responsibility for the development of regional plans, although the *kommuner* plans continue to be the detailed spatial planning documents in the Danish system (Council of Europe, 1993). Since 1992, the *amter* have also been responsible for the creation of regional economic plans. The national government made this possible by granting the *amter* authority to set up development agencies, co-finance EU projects and establish companies providing business services (Andersen, 1993).

Although the *amter* are now the dominant authority in public road transport and maintenance, co-operation between regions has been a major factor. Most *amter* have moved away from road building and have instead concentrated on pedestrian and cycle usage. The latter has led to the completion of a 3,000 km network of cycleways throughout the country (Andersen, 1993). This suggests that a meaningful group of powers has been transferred to the *amter*, allowing a major shift in policy to be undertaken.

6.2.1.3 The amter *as regional government*

The Danish *amter* are general purpose regional authorities and, despite their small size and lack of legislative function, have a degree of functional autonomy at least comparable with the *régions* in France. The comprehensive nature of powers granted in each policy area leads to a noticeable lack of functional fragmentation. For example, healthcare is entirely within the regional sphere of competence as is, to a large degree, road transport. This allows policy shifts without reference to the national tier.

The *amter* are nevertheless local government regions and, in common with the regional tier in France, are not regarded as superior to the *kommuner*. Many of the tasks they undertake are within a strict national framework and rely on co-operation between levels to be successful. The tradition of local autonomy in Denmark ensures that such co-operative mechanisms are successful, and that the national government rarely exercises its authority to curtail the general competence of the *amter*. The trend in Denmark continues to be one of decentralisation (at least officially) rather than centrally controlled services.

6.2.2 Sweden

Despite being the third largest Member State in the EU, Sweden has a system of regional government that is rather less developed than that found in Denmark. The situation is currently in a state of flux and it is this reform process, due to be completed in 2002, which is of particular interest to this study.

Sweden is a traditional unitary state, and legislative power is held exclusively at the national level. Nevertheless, local government and regional administration has a long history in Sweden. The regional level, the län (or county), dates from 1634, and the current territorial organisation of 24 counties has changed little since this date. The constitutional recognition of local and regional levels of government is included in Chapter 1 (ss 1 and 7) of the 1974 *Regeringsformen* (Instrument of Government), one of the four fundamental texts of the Swedish Constitution.

Although the *län* has a long history as a unit of territorial administration, its role as a unit of democratic government began only in 1862. Even then, the *Landsting* (or regional council) was relatively anonymous until the national health service reforms of the 1970s. As in Denmark, the growth of the welfare state brought with it increased government involvement in the lives of citizens. The 21 *Landstinget* (three municipal councils, Malmo, Goteborg and Gotland, undertake the responsibilities of the regional tier in their cities) offered a ready-made unit of democratic regional government to provide the services of the expanded state. The health service origins of the *Landsting* are still evident. Around 80% of *Landsting* expenditure is on health. Their other responsibilities include aspects of education (primarily colleges), tourism, public transport and culture. All the latter responsibilities are undertaken in close co-operation with the 286 municipalities (*kommuner*). Most of the region's activities (around 70%) are funded through direct taxation. The *Landstinget* are free to set the rates of regional income tax without nationally imposed limits (Hansen, 1992, p 317). In line with Scandinavian traditions of government, it is not uncommon for the regional councils and the national government to agree collectively on tax limits. A further 18% of income comes from grants allocated by central government. The nature of these grants changed substantially in 1993 when the predominantly specific grants were replaced by block funds.

The regional level of administration (the *Länsstyrelsen*) operates in tandem with the *Landstinget*. Headed by a provincial governor (the *Landshøvding*), the *Länsstyrelsen* or regional board is responsible for administering a large range of government policy, including regional planning, roads, education, fisheries, agriculture and public health amongst others. The 14 member boards themselves comprise regional councillors elected on a four-yearly basis (on the same cycle as those of the regional councils themselves), but the governor is appointed by the central government for a six year term. The governor, whilst remaining a servant of the central state and therefore responsible to the national government, has increasingly been regarded as a regional advocate in the central administration (Langset, 1999, p 350).

A further regional tier exists in the form of single function boards. Although much reduced in recent times (their powers being transferred to the regional administrative board), these regional quangos continue to deliver national policies for their respective departments. With the proliferation of these boards, as well as various general purpose authorities which exist between the municipalities (including inter-municipal organisations) and the national level, the commission on government reform has described Swedish intermediate government as a 'regional muddle' (State Commission Report, 1995). In response to this 'muddle' a series of reforms is proposed for 2002. The method by which this reform process is being undertaken deserves some attention.

As the result of legislation introduced in 1996 (1996/97:36 Regional Government Organisation Bill), a series of trials was organised in Skåne, Kalmar, Gotland and Västra Götaland to examine a number of options for regional government. In Skåne, the existing *Landsting* has been granted increased powers through the abolition of the regional board. In Kalmar, the new powers have been granted to a new, indirectly elected body (comprising members of both the municipal councils and the *Landsting*). Gotland has seen the new powers allocated to the existing municipality. Västra Götaland is an entirely new region, taking on the responsibilities of four existing counties and a number of other responsibilities currently handled by the regional boards.

The government's stated intention is to create a democratic level better suited to the responsibilities currently being decentralised by the central state. The reform is not without its critics, however. Some see it as a threat to traditionally strong municipal autonomy in Sweden (Langset, 1999, p 364). Previous reforms to the *län* and municipal levels, which were portrayed by the central government as decentralising, have been criticised for the degree to which financial controls replaced formal legal ones (Elander and Montin, 1990). In the light of this we must wait until the final reform, due to be implemented later in 2002, emerges. Only then will a true assessment of this Swedish example of the regional revolution be possible.

6.2.3 Finland

Finland, as is often the case, is something of an exception to the Scandinavian norm. Although it has experienced similar pressures on its system of government to those found in Sweden and Denmark, its response has been very different. Finland is also the only Scandinavian country to incorporate some form of constitutional region within its borders. The special case of the Swedish speaking Åland islands was dealt with in Chapter 5.

Finland has been divided into *lääni* (provinces) and municipalities since it gained its formal independence from Russia in 1919. This division of government is guaranteed by the constitution, but the current structure of six *lääni* was only introduced 1997 (a reduction from 12). Only the municipalities are directly elected. Each province is headed by a governor, whose appointment lies in the hands of the president. These are political appointments for a maximum of eight years, with few officials being appointed to such posts. The governor is responsible to the Ministry of the Interior for the administration of the province, and to specific national departments for the delivery of their policies.

A series of regional quangos is also responsible for a number of specific functions across Finnish territory. Economic development is largely administered through 15 employment and business development centres, while 13 environment centres deliver a number of national policies including environmental protection, land use and water management.

A tier of regional government was introduced in 1993, but not at the level of the province. As part of an ongoing reform package, which includes the rationalisation of regional administrative offices, 19 regions now cover the Finnish mainland, while a further 22 health service regions have been established. In both cases, the regions form part of the municipal level of government and are, as such, very different from any other regional level found in Scandinavia or the EU. Regional councils are indirectly elected from the municipal authorities, which also provide the bulk of their finance (a limited amount is provided by the state). In most cases, municipalities elect their representatives to the regional assembly for a four year term (in line with the electoral calendar of the municipalities). In two cases, the participating municipalities have agreed that the membership of the assembly will vary according to the issues under discussion. These seats are generally allocated on the basis of population, but some regional assemblies are established on the basis of the economic contribution of the various municipalities (Mäki-Lohiluoma, 1999, p 339).

The statutory tasks of these regions are relatively limited, and their only independent role is to construct regional development plans. In practice, however, their responsibilities as a regional level of municipal co-operation mean that they also engage in aspects of a number of areas including tourism, cultural affairs, education and energy supply. Health service management is also a task undertaken at the regional tier, though not through the regional councils. Twenty-two health service districts cover the country, and are responsible for the management of the hospital services within their area. A further five hospitals are managed outside this system (through the universities) and act as the focus for serious and specialist treatments in their areas. Each health district is run by councils whose members are elected from the municipalities within the health district's area of responsibility. These representatives also have four year terms. As with the regional councils themselves, these health service districts receive a significant degree of their funding through the municipalities (around one-third), with a further 30% provided directly by the state. The remainder is provided from health insurance schemes and by the individuals concerned.

The regional tier in Finland, although developed under the same pressures as those seen in Sweden and Denmark, has responded by creating a formal tier of inter-municipal organisation to deliver regional services, although the regional services of the state also continue to play a significant role. The result is a regional system that is fragmented and confused. This presents significant problems in terms of accountability and transparency. The regional system remains under scrutiny in Finland, and may face further reform in the near future.

6.3 THE NETHERLANDS

6.3.1 Regionalism in the Netherlands

If for no other reason than completeness, the final system to be examined is that of the Netherlands. Despite the small size and population of the Netherlands, this territory has a long history of regional and even federal government. Unlike other European states with a similarly distinguished regional pedigree, little of the nation's federal past has survived. Until 1798 the Dutch state was styled the 'United Provinces of the Netherlands'. This title reflected the state's genesis as a confederation of seven semi-independent provincial governments, united more through a desire to throw off Hapsburg rule than through any love of their neighbours. The state remained highly decentralised until its demise under the advancing armies of the French Revolution in 1798. For many 18th century advocates of decentralised government, this was the model to be emulated, although its questionable success was a poor advertisement for would-be federalists.

The French victory led to the formation of the Batavian Republic, a centralised unitary state based upon the French republican model. Although a monarchy was restored in 1814, the centralised model introduced by the French was retained. This proved a significant factor in the September Days of 1828, which saw the Belgian provinces leave the new kingdom (see section 4.1.1). The system lasted only until 1848, when the revolutionary upheaval of that turbulent year resulted in a new constitution that remains the basis of the modern Dutch state. The constitution of Johan Rudolf Thorbecke abandoned the previous federal structure completely, replacing it with that of the 'decentralised unitary state' (Toonen, 1993, p 122). This remains the basic philosophy of the Dutch system of government.

6.3.2 National structure

Dutch sub-national government comprises two levels of authority, with 647 *gemeenten* (municipalities) organised within 12 *provincies* (provinces). Between these levels, areas of municipal co-operation have been established, along with a few metropolitan unitary authorities. These are often referred to as 'regions' by Dutch writers, but their size and responsibilities do not correspond to the wider European concept of regional government. At present, the closest parallel to a European concept of regional government exists at the provincial level.

In addition to the Dutch decentralised tiers of sub-national government, there exists a series of 120 non-democratic deconcentrated agencies (Toonen, 1993). These operate on many levels both above and below the provincial tier, and cover such policy areas as labour, planning, education, housing and social insurance. 140 'water boards' also operate in certain parts of the Dutch mainland. These boards can also have responsibility for transport and communications. In these cases it is common for more than one board to cover overlapping territories, each board being assigned a certain portion of functional authority (Kortmann and Bovend'Eert, 1993, pp 34–37). The water boards, which are elected from a limited franchise, exercise authority within the limits established by the province (Dutch Ministry of Foreign Affairs, 1980, p 33).

Although Dutch people identify closely with the province, the political activities of this unit of government are largely irrelevant. It is generally seen as too large to cope with local issues and too small to address regional problems. Thus, units of deconcentrated administration take on the responsibility for the regional organisation of many policies. This reduces the democratic credentials of the regional tier and increasingly makes the provincial tier irrelevant. In response to this, there have been attempts to create a system of four 'euro-regions' to reflect current economic and cultural realities in the Netherlands (North, South, West and East Netherlands). However, attempts to introduce these units have so far failed. In 1987, the Dutch Government produced proposals to reorganise the sub-national system by creating a regional level and increasing the number of provinces. They were never implemented, and debate continues in the Netherlands as to how the system can be best structured. Until such changes are instituted, the province will remain the 'regional' level.

6.3.3 The regional tier

The modern Dutch province bears little resemblance to its illustrious ancestor, although Dutch citizens still retain a significant degree of loyalty to their province. Chapter 7 of the Dutch Constitution gives a very limited constitutional status to both the provinces and municipalities (Art 123, Dutch Constitution). Article 124 grants the administrative organs of local governments the power 'to administer their own internal affairs', but in practice this provision means very little. In practice, the powers and responsibilities of the local and regional levels are defined by ordinary Act of Parliament.

Article 132 does offer some small comfort in that a provincial decision may only be quashed if it conflicts with national law or is against the national interest. In these cases the power is wielded by the national government exercising the 'royal decree'. The proviso that a decision must be against the public interest gives a large degree of discretion to the national government in its dealings with the provinces. In addition, Art 132(3) gives the option that provincial decisions may require *a priori* approval by another body if this process is approved by the national parliament.

The Dutch Constitution, though dealing with the provincial tier and guaranteeing its existence, does not protect its autonomy from encroachment by the state. Instead the structure and responsibilities of the provinces are mostly covered by the *provinciewet*. This statute is the collective 'constitutional document' of the provincial tier and is approved by the Dutch Parliament. The position of the Dutch province, despite its constitutional status, bears some resemblance to the French *région*. Unlike the *région*, however, the Dutch province remains subject to *a priori* supervision by the state authorities, while its decisions may also be annulled for reasons other than their illegality.

The province consists of a directly elected assembly and an executive branch which is only semi-accountable to the regional electorate. The assembly (or *provinciale staten*) is elected by proportional representation from the provincial electorate. The executive branch (*gedeputeerde staten*) consists of the Queen's Commissioner, appointed by the central government, and a 'cabinet' of between three and nine assembly members. It had been previous custom for the executive body to represent the parties' electoral strength in the assembly itself. Recent practice has moved away from this consociational approach to a more political cabinet model, with the majority coalition partners filling all the executive positions and leaving the opposition parties outside the executive altogether. Recent law concerning sub-national government in the Netherlands forces provincial executives at least to consult the minority parties, in an effort to reverse this trend (Kortmann and Bovend'Eert, 1993, p 27).

6.3.4 Are the provinces regions?

As a result of their constitutional status, the provinces enjoy an executive general competence but one exercised under the possibility of national executive control. Provinces may create bylaws in any area not assigned to parliament, but the *tutelle* makes this power reliant on central government discretion. In addition, bylaws may only by used in the interests of the province and may not become involved in areas 'relating to the private interests of their residents'. The autonomy they exercise is always open to central control. Any measure of the provinces can be annulled by the central government on the grounds that it conflicts with other laws or the general interest (Harloff, 1987, p 101). It is up to the courts to decide whether such an infringement has occurred (Kortmann and Bovend'Eert, 1993, p 30).

The functions handled by the provincial authorities are limited to the supervision of water authorities, river transport, and some responsibilities in relation to spatial planning and road maintenance (Council of Europe, 1988). Provinces also have authority to organise regional gas and electricity supplies, although the delivery of these services is generally a municipal responsibility (Toonen, 1993). Limited responsibility for care of the mentally ill and environmental protection also lie with the provinces (Engel and Van Ginderachter, 1993, p 90).

Even in fields such as spatial planning, the provinces only provide a general plan which must conform to the national one. It is the municipalities that create the actual zonal plans defining areas for specific uses. This mirrors the situation in most of the fields mentioned above. Few are exercised without municipal or national involvement.

The power and role of the Dutch provinces is therefore minimal. The fields in which they exercise authority are rarely exclusive and generally unrelated, leaving little room for coherent policy. They are in consequence largely irrelevant to the Dutch political system. The role of the Dutch provinces has increasingly been to implement national policy. To this end, most provincial spending is undertaken on behalf of other agencies and funded directly by them. They are therefore examples of the meso governments recognised by Sharpe (Sharpe, 1993) but are not true 'regions' in the sense defined in Chapter 2.

6.4 ARE LOCAL GOVERNMENT REGIONS REALLY REGIONS?

There can be no doubt that the regional governments explored in this chapter comprise a group apart from those examined in Chapters 4 and 5. Lacking a formal constitutional status, they do not possess the ability to enact legislation (although the Dutch provinces can enact bylaws); their power is rooted entirely in the administrative autonomy accorded to them by the central state. Is it therefore correct to consider them alongside the powerful legislative regions examined previously?

The lack of an ability to create legislation is perhaps not the restriction it might at first appear. In practice, regional legislation plays only a limited role in the development of regional policy by regional governments. In most cases, the areas of exclusive regional legislative authority are minimal, with most decisions relying on executive action and co-operation between levels of government (for example, see section 4.2.4 above on regional responsibilities in Germany). In many cases, regional legislative power relies upon national framework legislation, as in Italy and Wales (see section 10.5.1 below). As these examples show, the real limit for local government regions lies in the positive definition of their administrative functions by national legislation. These frameworks can be strictly defined, and in extreme cases such as the Dutch provinces render any discussion of regional autonomy practically meaningless. This is not always the case, and the local government regions may be granted significant autonomy in their spheres of competence. In the case of France and Denmark, this is underpinned by an administrative 'general competence' (see Chapter 10) and a high degree of financial autonomy (see Chapter 9).

Overall, although local government regions are significantly different from their more illustrious legislative cousins, they are still part of the wider process whereby decision making moves away from the central level, making regional diversity within the Member States possible. Although the possibility for regional variation in legislation within the state does not exist, the local government regions, in their role as policy maker and co-ordinator, clearly offer the potential for the development of distinctive regional policy, and in this respect are clearly part of the regional revolution.

CHAPTER 7

DEVOLUTION IN CONTEXT: REGIONAL GOVERNMENT IN THE UK

Although the devolution of power to democratic institutions within the United Kingdom forms the context for this book, it is not the main purpose of this volume to explore these systems in detail. Despite the youthful nature of these institutions, some good attempts at early analysis are provided by Burrows (2000) and Hazell (2000) amongst others. This short chapter cannot hope to emulate these texts. Instead it provides a brief outline of the various systems that operate in the United Kingdom from a comparative perspective. As such it acts both as a conclusion to this part of the volume and as a starting point for the comparative chapters that follow.

The history of regional government in these islands is one of curious contrasts. Although the United Kingdom was for decades amongst the most centralised states in Europe, its territory has a long history of regionalism. The mainland of this archipelago is divided into three 'nations' which remain culturally distinct. Scotland and (to a lesser extent) Wales have national histories that include long periods of political independence. Even after their union with England, significant policies within the former states continued to be administered separately. This allowed the institutions of the peripheral 'nations' of the British state to develop distinct identities. In the case of Scotland this even extends to the systems of education and law. If this were not enough, the island states (Jersey, Guernsey and the Isle of Man) and the province of Northern Ireland have all experienced political devolution. In the case of the islands their relationship with the British Crown has always been through such arrangements. In Northern Ireland, home rule lasted from 1922 to 1972.

For a centralised unitary state, the United Kingdom has exhibited a remarkable degree of cultural and administrative, if not political, decentralisation. Elazar went as far as recognising aspects of the United Kingdom Constitution as federal (Elazar, 1991). As in the example of Belgium (see section 4.1), to understand the complex constitutional arrangements of the United Kingdom, including the current devolved state, one must understand the history that created the state itself.

England, Scotland and Wales were independent states in the medieval period. Wales was incorporated into what is now the English Crown in the 13th century after an expensive invasion and campaign of pacification. Although rebellions occurred after this period, most notably in 1400–14 (during which Owain Glyn Dwr reigned as a sovereign prince), Wales was dominated by its larger Norman neighbour. Scotland, in contrast, did not succumb to the aggressive foreign policy of Edward I as applied in Wales.

Financially weakened by the costs of pacifying the Welsh and constant wars on the continent, Edward was unable to hold the Scottish state by force of arms. The Treaty of Edinburgh of 1328 finally recognised its independence. Edward's policy had turned a friendly neighbour into a bitter enemy, an animosity that has never entirely dissipated.

For the next three centuries, the Scottish and English states co-existed, not always peacefully, but the Scottish state was eventually bound to its larger English neighbour through two separate unions. The first, in 1603, united the Crowns of the two states, but it was not until 1707 that the Parliaments of Scotland and England were joined to create the Parliament of Great Britain. The machinations that led to this union are too complex to enter into here, but suffice it to say that this was no 'freely negotiated bargain'. The funds used to pay for the 'management' of the Scottish ministry led to political scandal in Westminster in the years that followed, while private correspondence from the period shows that, had diplomacy failed, Scotland would have been brought into the English fold by force of arms (Hopkins, 1992). Although constitutionally it was a union of equals, there can be no doubt that, as Henry VIII had predicted, the greater had drawn the lesser.

The union state was completed by the Act of Union of 1801, which abolished the semi-autonomous Irish Parliament (there was, and continues to be, some debate on its actual status) and incorporated Irish members into the British Parliament. By this Act, the United Kingdom of Great Britain and Ireland was formed, but this is not the United Kingdom of today. In 1922, after two years of armed conflict, the government in London ceded 20 of the 26 Irish counties to the newly created Irish Free State. From this point, the United Kingdom of Great Britain and Ireland was reduced to that of Great Britain and Northern Ireland. It is this incarnation of the British state which survives to this day.

With the exception of Northern Ireland, the United Kingdom has always operated as a unitary state. This political unity has not translated into cultural unity, and cultural and institutional diversity left a series of fault lines within the unitary structure. Over time, this led to the development of the Secretary of State system whereby Scotland, Wales and Northern Ireland were administered separately (although not in the same way) under Secretaries of State appointed by the United Kingdom Government. In England, no such post existed, but the development of regional planning and the perceived need for a tier of regional administration has led to the development of non-elected regional bodies since the 1960s.

In the 1970s, a number of factors, most notably the growth of nationalist parties in Wales and Scotland, brought home rule (or as it was now called, devolution) to the forefront of the political agenda. Although officially Labour Party policy since 1912, it was not until the minority Labour Government of the late 1970s required the support of nationalists that it acted. In the light of the Kilbrandon Commission, devolution proposals were brought forward and entered the statute books in 1978 (Scotland Act 1978; Wales Act 1978). To be implemented, the Acts required approval by referendums, which took place in 1979. In Wales, the limited executive devolution proposals were roundly rejected. In Scotland, although the proposals achieved a narrow majority, this was not enough. An amendment introduced by George Cunningham (the Scots-born MP for Islington), and supported by Labour MPs from the north of England, required that 40% of those registered to vote must support the proposals. On an ageing electoral roll, this threshold was not achieved. The result was a disaster for the pro-devolution lobby. The nationalists withdrew their support from the minority Labour government, which collapsed. The Conservatives, led by Margaret Thatcher, were returned to power and devolution appeared dead. Their promise to deliver 'something better' than the devolution proposals of 1978 proved to mean a continuation of the status quo.

Less than 20 years later, devolution was back on the agenda. In referendums held in the wake of the Labour Party's landslide victory of 1997, first Scotland and then Wales (by the slimmest of majorities) approved new devolution schemes. These were very different from those rejected in 1978. In a further change, the constitutional reform programme of the Labour Government now included regional government for England itself, should demand exist. It is this reform of the United Kingdom that is the focus of the rest of this chapter and which informs the context of this book.

7.1 THE DEVOLUTION PROCESS

In what has become something of a cliché, Ron Davies MP, the former Secretary of State for Wales, was credited with the comment that devolution was 'a process, not an event'. In this, the UK's experiences of devolution reflect those found in continental Europe. The systems of regional and federal government established on the continent have not proved static. In each case, the establishment of the regional system proved to be only the starting point for that system's development. The paths which these regional systems took were not predicted by those who framed the systems, nor by their contemporary commentators. It would be extremely unusual if Davies' comment had not been borne out in the United Kingdom, and in the limited time in which the devolution process has been under way, his analysis has proved correct. What should perhaps surprise us, given the examples explored above, is that anyone should have thought otherwise.

The devolution reforms were instituted through a series of Acts of the Westminster Parliament (Scotland Act 1998; Government of Wales Act 1998; Northern Ireland Act 1998). These devolution Acts were drafted and driven through the legislative process within two years of Labour's taking office.

The individual nature of the devolution statutes has led to some comparisons with the Spanish example of asymmetrical regionalism. The similarities are explored more fully below, but there are significant differences in their genesis that are worth exploring first.

The devolution statutes are in effect the constitutions of the regional governments. This places the Scottish, Welsh and Northern Irish regional institutions on what appears to be a par with the tradition of regional constitutions found in Austria, Germany, Spain and Italy. This can be distinguished from the Belgian model, which defines the various regions and 'Cultural Communities' under the Belgian Constitution and its accompanying organic laws. In practice, the situation in the United Kingdom is closer to this latter model than at first appears.

Although the three devolution Acts create distinct regional systems with varied responsibilities and powers, the involvement of devolved bodies in the creation of these Acts was minimal. In the Spanish example, the national constitution and its transitional dispositions created a structure by which a regional 'convention', in negotiation with the central institutions, drew up the regional statute. This was not the case in the UK. The Acts of the Westminster Parliament which created the devolved system are entirely the creatures of the UK legislative process.

Nevertheless, an informal process of regional negotiation took place in the form of the Scottish Constitutional Convention and the Northern Ireland peace process. The Convention brought together the Labour Party and the Scottish Liberal Democrats as well as representatives from smaller parties, interest groups and local government. The final report of the convention, 'Scotland's Parliament: Scotland's Right', formed the basis of the devolution legislation. However, the document was vague in parts due to the need to keep the two main political parties involved in agreement (Constitutional Convention, 1992 and 1996). The devolution legislation, when enacted, was therefore the UK Government's interpretation of the principles outlined in the convention's reports.

In Northern Ireland, the genesis of devolution reflects a peculiar dichotomy. Neither nationalists nor unionists were particularly committed to a devolution project. Although the Ulster Unionist Party favoured devolution as party policy, its reasons for doing so could be traced back to 1922. Devolution was seen as a method of defending the six counties' place in the United Kingdom, not fulfilling a demand for greater regional autonomy. Nationalists and republicans by contrast would like to see the six counties amalgamated with the Republic. For Northern Ireland, devolution was a method of reconciling these two contradictory positions, and only formed part of the complex settlement that is found in the Good Friday agreement. The devolved institutions created in Northern Ireland reflect the demands of the various parties to these negotiations (particularly the Ulster Unionist Party, Sinn Fein and the Social Democratic and Labour Party).

Despite the informal regional consultation (which was almost totally lacking in Wales), the genesis of the devolution Acts bears little similarity to the Spanish or even the Italian examples. The legislation that underpins devolution in the UK is centrally established and centrally controlled with little formal input from regional representatives. Despite impressions to the contrary, the UK's system of devolution reflects the Belgian model more than the asymmetrical systems.

This has a further impact on the organisation of the devolved institutions themselves. It will be recalled that the German *Land* constitutions can be amended by each *Land* under procedures set out in the constitutions themselves. The larger framework of the federal state remains defined by the Basic Law, but within these limits regional institutions are free to organise their structures. This is not the case in the UK. The devolved institutions are defined by devolution Acts themselves. This includes the size of the parliament (or assembly), methods of election, and proceedings of the parliament. No process exists for the devolved assemblies to undertake modification of the Act. In addition, the UK government appears very reluctant to engage in any amendments, fearing it will lead to further calls for change to what it regards as a completed process.

The speed with which the devolution legislation was brought forward and enacted is almost unheard-of in the UK. There was good reason for this. The Scots, and to a lesser extent the Welsh, were holding the Labour Government to promises made before the election to introduce the legislation within one year. Many of the Labour Party's own supporters were smarting from its decision to put the devolution proposals before a referendum without consulting its Scottish party (this after the Labour Party had originally explicitly ruled out such a course). Memories of 1979 lingered, as did repeated unfulfilled promises of devolution or home rule. A further reason was the desire to get the legislation through before the opposition could regroup, and to ensure that the referendums took place in the afterglow of the Labour Party's resounding victory (although the referendums took place on the basis of the White Papers, not the legislation itself).

The result was a situation not unlike that found in Spain, particularly in relation to Catalonia and Euskadi (the Basque country). As in these examples, the speed with which the legislation was rushed through has left anomalies and gaps that may prove problematic. As in the Spanish examples, this is particularly true in relation to the powers granted to the various devolved authorities, which are not always coherent. The attempt by the UK Government to portray the devolution settlement as a completed process may be difficult to sustain as the system develops.

7.2 THE INSTITUTIONS OF THE DEVOLVED STATE

As described above, the devolution process in the UK has played out very differently across its various constituent parts. This has led some to describe the resulting structure as asymmetrical and to compare the UK's structure with the Spanish system of autonomías. Although there are lessons to be learnt from the Spanish example, it is dangerous to draw the comparisons too closely. The UK practises an extreme form of asymmetrical devolution, if it can be truly described as such, where the largest state has no regional tier. There is no overarching legislation, constitutional or otherwise, as seen in Spain. This has led Burrows to coin the phrase 'haphazard' (rather than asymmetrical) devolution to describe the UK's unique regional structure. This she sees as emerging from a pragmatic rather than a principled approach to regional government (Burrows, 2000, p 27). This creates a flexible structure, which could be an advantage as the devolution process progresses. It also creates a structure that is open-ended. As the UK lacks a traditional court to define the limits of this process, the comparison with Spain appears very weak indeed.

7.2.1 The devolution Acts

The devolved state rests upon three Acts of the Westminster Parliament (Scotland Act 1998; Government of Wales Act 1998; Northern Ireland Act 1998). Strictly speaking, therefore, the devolved regions of the UK cannot be described as constitutional regions, having no special status within the UK Constitution. In practice, the institutions outlined in the devolution Acts are easily distinguished from the local government regions explored in Chapter 6. In particular, all the devolved assemblies and parliaments have some form of legislative authority.

The Acts themselves outline the structures of the devolved parliaments (or assemblies) and their executives. The statutes are relatively detailed in outlining the structures of these institutions, including the numbers of representatives who will sit in the deliberative chambers. As mentioned above, the individual nature of these statutes draws some comparison with the individual *Land* constitutions of Germany and the regional statutes used in both Italy and Spain. The fact that they remain ordinary Acts of the Westminster Parliament raises a number of constitutional issues.

The principle of parliamentary sovereignty continues to dominate constitutional thought in the United Kingdom. Under such a principle, no parliament can bind its successor. Each of the devolution Acts can therefore be altered unilaterally by the actions of the UK Parliament. Can we really view the devolved institutions and the Acts that they rest upon as anything more than powerful local government?

The impact of the doctrine of parliamentary sovereignty should be viewed in context, however. The devolution process was approved by referendum, and the political legitimacy of the institutions (particularly in Scotland) is high. Significant amendments or repeal of the devolution Acts in Scotland or Wales would almost certainly invigorate the nationalists and threaten the union which British parties claim to defend. In the case of Northern Ireland, the devolved settlement is part of the wider Good Friday agreement and any attack on the assembly would risk a return to sectarian violence.

The constitutional nature of European regions can be overemphasised, too. Even the Italian special regions can have their regional statutes unilaterally altered by constitutional amendment carried in both chambers of the national parliament. In Spain too, the organic status of *autonomía* statutes, which means that the Acts must be passed in both chambers of the *Cortes*, is of limited practical value. The Spanish electoral system ensures that the Spanish government almost always controls the second chamber, making the 'organic' nature of the *autonomía* statutes rather academic. Should the governing party decide to alter a regional statute, it could do so, particularly if it allied with the national opposition as is common practice in Spain over autonomy matters. What protects the Spanish regions is not their constitutional status *per se* but their political legitimacy.

In the UK, the legitimacy of the devolved institutions, in the form of their referendums, the strength of the regional institutions themselves, and the ever-present threat of the nationalist parties, makes their abolition extremely unlikely. In practice, therefore, sovereignty has been transferred. Westminster would only be able to take it back in the event of 'pathological circumstances' such as those which developed during the 1960s in Northern Ireland (Bogdanor, 1998, p 12).

7.2.2 The devolved legislatures

The devolution Acts established assemblies in Northern Ireland and Wales, and a parliament in Scotland. These terms are somewhat misleading, however, as the structures and powers of the two assemblies have little in common. The Scottish Parliament and the Northern Ireland Assembly are empowered to enact primary legislation, while the Welsh Assembly has authority over secondary legislation and executive actions delegated by Westminster. To some extent, these differences are reflected in the structures themselves, with the Welsh Assembly operating as both 'legislature' and executive of the devolved institution. The Scottish Parliament and its Northern Ireland counterpart operate a more traditional cabinet model.

The directly elected Scottish Parliament, with its attendant institutions, is the closest of the devolved bodies to the traditional Westminster model.

Currently, 129 Members of the Scottish Parliament (MSPs) sit in the Scottish Parliament, but this number is not defined in the Scotland Act itself. Instead, the number of seats is linked to the number of Scottish MPs elected to the Westminster Parliament. Each Westminster constituency returns one MSP, except for Orkney and Shetland, which return one MSP each (although they share an MP). A further 56 MSPs are elected on a regional list basis. The regional allocation incorporates a degree of proportionality.

The Welsh Assembly, although much smaller than its Scottish counterpart, utilises a similar method of election. 40 of the 60 Assembly Members (AMs) are elected on a 'first past the post' basis from Westminster constituencies. A further 20 come from regional lists elected on the basis of European constituencies. The 109 member Northern Ireland Assembly is elected by single transferable vote (STV) from 18 constituencies, as defined in the Northern Ireland Act. The use of STV was already established in Northern Ireland both for local government and European elections. The size of the Northern Ireland Assembly is large, given the population of 1.5 million that it governs.

The linkage in Scotland between the regional parliament's size and its representation in the national parliament is unique. It also brings with it a potentially difficult problem. The devolution of power to Scotland and Northern Ireland in particular has led to Scottish and Northern Irish MPs having less of a role at Westminster. This also raises the 'West Lothian Question', made famous by Tam Dalyell MP. Members from the devolved regions are able to vote on subjects which are devolved and thus, as discussed in the Westminster Parliament, concern only England. In addition, Scotland, Wales and Northern Ireland remain significantly over-represented within the House of Commons. It is therefore expected that the House of Commons representations of the devolved regions will be reduced. The result of this will impact directly upon the size of the Scottish Parliament, which will automatically be reduced.

The Scottish Parliament, in particular, might find it hard to fulfil its role effectively with a reduction in membership. It is likely to end up with the same number of members as in Northern Ireland, for a population three times as large. To change this will require the Westminster Parliament to amend the Scotland Act. This is something that the Scotland Office and the UK Government appear unwilling to do. The UK Government wishes to present the devolution settlements as completed processes approved by the respective regional electorates. This is disingenuous, as it was the principles contained in the White Papers that were tested by referendum, not the statutes themselves. In addition, the Government's proposal to replace the three territorial Secretaries of State with a single minister would also require amendments to the devolution Acts.

The use of proportional representation in the devolved chambers has had a profound effect on government in these regions and on politics in general.

The Westminster tradition of 'first past the post' leads to the consistent election of governments, often with significant parliamentary majorities, who achieve less than 50% of electoral support. Coalition governments are therefore unusual and rarely survive for long. The ill-fated 'Lib-Lab pact' of the late 1970s, although not a formal coalition, is the only recent example of this. By contrast, the Scottish four party system ensures that achieving a single party majority in Scotland will prove very difficult. Even in the Welsh Assembly, where the proportional element is smaller, the rise in *Plaid Cymru* support denied the Labour Party a majority. In Northern Ireland, the structure of the executive, which is discussed below, must reflect party strengths in the assembly itself. By definition, therefore, the Northern Ireland executive is multi-party.

As a result of the introduction of proportional representation, coalition politics have become the norm in the devolved institutions. This is something that the Westminster system has not yet come to terms with. The coalition nature of devolved politics does not fit well with the Westminster model, with its emphasis on executive secrecy and unity in cabinet. This becomes difficult to sustain when the executives of the devolved institutions are not of the same party.

7.2.3 The devolved executives

The Scottish executive is the closest to the traditional cabinet model. The cabinet is appointed by the First Minister and is responsible to him or her. This position is elected by and from the parliament itself. Individual ministers are responsible only to the First Minister and cannot be removed individually by the parliament. The Scottish executive (the executive itself has used the term 'cabinet', and controversially floated the phrase 'government' in 2001) thus reflects a typical legislative regional government model of the types found in the federal and constitutional regions explored in previous chapters.

The Northern Ireland executive reflects the consociational nature of the Good Friday agreement. The Northern Ireland First Minister and Deputy are appointed collectively through the special majority system outlined above. These posts are tied together by s 16 of the Northern Ireland Act. The resignation of one of them, whether forced or voluntary, will require the resignation of the other, and the posts will need to be reappointed. In practice, the need for a special majority will mean that the First Minister will generally be from a unionist party and the Deputy from a nationalist or republican party. The ministers themselves are not chosen by the First Minister and Deputy. Instead, the Northern Ireland Act designates that the ministers are appointed according to the d'Hondt method of proportional representation. This method, which favours larger parties, operates a number of rounds of voting. In the first round the number of votes for each party (in this case, the number of assembly seats) is counted and the highest receives the first post. In the second round the party which won the first executive post has its representation halved. The party with the highest number of seats by this formula now gains an executive post. The rounds continue, with each party having its divisor increased by one for each of the executive posts it receives. When the 10 posts were filled (a number agreed between the First Minister and Deputy), three UUP, three SDLP, two DUP, and two Sinn Fein made up the first executive.

The actual posts are chosen by the parties in the order that the seats were awarded, thus preventing the largest party from 'cherry picking' the best cabinet seats. Somewhat to the surprise of observers, the first Northern Ireland executive had Sinn Fein ministers at the head of the Northern Irish Ministries of Education and Health, with the largest budgets in the province. It was perhaps the intention of the unionists to provide the republicans with a poisoned chalice, but this is only conjecture. The nature of the Northern Ireland executive means that collective responsibility is absent. It follows a model of government used at the federal level in Switzerland, but has no parallel in regional governments elsewhere.

The final executive model used in the UK has closer parallels to European local government regions. As explained in more detail below, the Welsh Assembly is charged with executive powers, and lacks the primary legislative powers granted to the Scottish Parliament and the Northern Ireland Assembly. Such legislative authority as it has is limited to secondary legislation in areas delegated to it by Westminster. All the powers devolved to the Welsh regional institutions are allocated to the assembly. Thus executive power is vested in the assembly, not in the executive committee which is elected from it. This committee merely exercises those functions delegated to it by the assembly. In effect the assembly exercises, in a deliberative chamber, powers which had previously been exercised by a number of government ministers.

The assembly executive is not a true executive in the Westminster mould or that of other regional governments. Although the Welsh example has more significant powers, its practice of placing executive power in the hands of the deliberative chamber is closest to the model followed by the French *régions*. The effect of this structure on the workings of the assembly is significant.

The assembly elects a First Secretary, who in turn appoints a number of assembly secretaries with responsibilities for all the functions of the Welsh Assembly (s 56(3), Government of Wales Act 1998). Together these make up the cabinet of the Welsh Assembly. Powers can be delegated by the assembly to these individuals, but they remain the servants of the assembly. There are assembly committees for each of the subject areas which include the relevant assembly secretary. These committees discuss and decide policy rather than just hold the assembly secretary to account.

The powers of the assembly cabinet, because they are delegated to it by the assembly, can be revoked at any time. This can occur *en masse* or can be directed at a single secretary. In a minority administration, in particular, this makes the relationship between the executive and the legislative branch far closer than is traditional. The clearest example of this system in action came during the first year of the assembly's operation. Alun Michael, the First Secretary, attempted to run the assembly (in which his Labour Party formed a fractious minority) along Westminster lines. The results were a shock for the national Labour Party in London. After an incident in which Michael was accused of failing to fight Wales' corner in negotiations over European structural funding, he lost a vote of no confidence by the assembly. Although this had no formal effect, the next step would have been for the assembly to revoke the powers delegated to the First Secretary. In the event, he stepped down and Rhodri Morgan was appointed by the assembly. The assembly in effect chose its own leader, not one put forward by the largest party.

The Welsh model provides the potential for greater control of executive affairs than in the traditional regional government model. Given that executive functions are crucial to the region, the Welsh example appears to have much in its favour. The German regional legislatures (*Landtage*) in particular have found themselves emasculated by the steady growth of intergovernmental relations and executive power. The Welsh model, drawing as it is does upon UK local government methods of executive accountability, may offer a way forward.

The Welsh model is not all wine and roses, however. In practice the standing orders of the Welsh Assembly give the executive committee significant leverage over the deliberative body. The committee structure in particular, which ties the executive and the assembly together, has not functioned as the 'powerhouse of the assembly' as Alun Michael expected (Assembly Record, 7 December 1999). Osmond has put the failure of committees to hold the executive to account down to their infrequency of meetings and the lack of experience of most Assembly Members. The fact that Ron Davies (the former Secretary of State for Wales), during his short chairmanship of the Economic Development Committee, managed to prise a number of damaging admissions from the relevant civil servants concerning the use of European funding in Wales, emphasises this point (Osmond, 2000).

In fact, this exposed a wider problem with the Welsh model. The executive committee is the gatekeeper for most government information. It is not required to release information or advice from officers to the wider assembly and has the only direct line to the officials of the Welsh Civil Service. The executive committee has been able to use its monopoly of information to undermine the assembly and its committees. Papers to be considered by committees often arrive just prior to committee meetings (Osmond, 2000). The clearest example of the rift developing between the assembly and its executive committee is the appointment of an independent legal advisor to the Presiding Officer of the assembly, distinct from the office of Counsel General.

The continued use of Westminster-style information regimes, therefore, has led to a Westminster-style model developing in Wales, even though the institutions were set up to avoid this. Some have severely criticised this development, maintaining that the assembly is not designed for such a role. This is true, of course, but it is worth remembering that, however imperfect the current situation may be, the decisions taken in the name of the assembly still receive far more scrutiny now than they ever did under the previous regime of deconcentrated administration.

7.2.4 Institutions of intergovernmental relations

The remnants of the deconcentrated system of administration are still visible in the posts of Secretary of State for Scotland, Wales and Northern Ireland, which remain UK cabinet posts. Although stripped of much of their pre-devolution power, they remain responsible for relations between the devolved institutions, in addition to exercising a limited number of *tutelles* and representing the interests of the relevant regions of the UK at cabinet level. Their long term future remains in doubt, however, and the relationship between these individuals and the devolved institutions has not been terribly cordial (particularly in the examples of Scotland and Northern Ireland).

The Northern Ireland example is unique, as the Secretary of State retains significant powers of control, as well as having a responsibility to continue the peace process which underpins devolution. In Scotland, the two post-devolution incumbents appear to have viewed their purpose as watchdog of the Parliament, which led to some 'turf wars' between the devolved institutions and the UK ministers. At the time of writing, the senior partner in the governing coalition in both Scotland and Wales is of the same political colour as the governing party in the United Kingdom. The consequences for relations between the Secretaries of State and the devolved institutions when the Scottish executive and the United Kingdom government are no longer of the same party can only be guessed at, but they are unlikely to improve.

Intergovernmental relations in the devolved system, although monitored by the Secretaries of State, are based primarily upon a system of bilateral links between the devolved executives and the various Whitehall departments. The devolution Acts are surprisingly silent on the issue, leading to an informal system of concordats which have no formal legal status. They may have created a 'legitimate expectation' to be followed, but this hypothesis has yet to be tested. This has some similarity with the pattern of intergovernmental relations found in Spain, but the constitutional weakness of the UK's devolved institutions make the informality more of an issue. In Spain, the national government has little choice but to enter into relationships with the autonomías; however, the UK Government may view this only as an option.

At the apex of this intergovernmental system is the Joint Ministerial Committee. This institution, established under the Memorandum of Understanding, comprises ministers from the various devolved governments and the UK Government. It offers a forum for inter-executive discussion and has been used extensively by the UK Government to advance its policies. The agenda of these meetings is established by the central government. The extent to which the meetings will operate successfully when the parties involved are not of a like mind is difficult to assess. At the time of writing, devolved institutions appear to feel that their opinions are valued, particularly in technical matters (Hazell, 2000). Nevertheless, the informal nature of this system may make it vulnerable to the strains that will arise as the political balance changes within the various assemblies and parliaments.

The inter-executive nature of relationships between the devolved institutions and the centre is also reflected in the only formal intergovernmental institution that has been established. The British-Irish Council (or 'Council of the Isles') was established as part of the Good Friday agreement, and incorporates representatives from the governments of all the states and nations that make up the British Isles (including the Republic of Ireland). Although emerging as a unionist proposal to balance the republic-assembly links of the agreement, the establishment of such a body makes a lot of sense. Indeed, it comes as a surprise to many foreign observers that such an institution has never been established in the past. These institutions and their operation are explored more fully in Chapter 11.

7.2.5 Dispute resolution

Intergovernmental relations are inextricably linked to dispute resolution mechanisms (see Chapters 11 and 12). In the UK example, it is expected that most disputes will be resolved through the intergovernmental relationships briefly mentioned above. If these fail, or if an individual wishes to challenge the actions of the devolved institutions or their executives, the Judicial Committee of the Privy Council has been nominated as the final court of appeal.

The Judicial Committee undertakes the role of a constitutional court in what the devolution Acts euphemistically describe as 'devolution issues'. This institution has some history of resolving devolution disputes. The

Government of Ireland Act (1922) empowered this body to adjudge upon Acts of the Northern Irish Parliament, although only one was actually heard. It is nevertheless a curious beast with several features that distinguish it from equivalent bodies in the European Union.

The most notable feature of the Judicial Committee, and one which may not be grasped by the electorate, is that it can only adjudicate on the actions of the Scottish, Welsh and Northern Irish institutions, not on the actions of the centre. It is therefore the constitutional court of the devolved institutions, but not of the UK. As such it undertakes a role not dissimilar to that of the *Länder* constitutional courts, but significantly different from the constitutional court of Germany, or its counterparts in Spain or Italy. It is in effect a watchdog whose function is to ensure that the regional institutions stay within their legislative limits, not to police the national government's transgressions. Politically, this may prove a difficult role to sustain.

In practice, the institution (as it sits for devolution issues) will comprise the Judicial Committee of House of Lords under a different name. The reason for avoiding explicit reference to the House of Lords is political. The House of Lords, as part of the UK Parliament, is not a suitable forum for the discussion of devolution matters. This, in tandem with the Judicial Committee's historic role in the Northern Ireland devolution settlement, and in relation to former colonies and Commonwealth countries, made it the easiest choice. Whether it is the best choice is another matter. The judiciary of the UK remains in the gift of the Lord Chancellor, a political appointee and minister in the UK Government. Such cross-fertilisation between the political and the judicial spheres is unique in Europe. It will become increasingly difficult to sustain in the UK, particularly as UK judges take on a more overtly political role in their policing of the Human Rights Act 1998 and the devolution settlements. It is noticeable, for example, that the Lord Chancellor has refrained from sitting as judge since the Human Rights Act came into force. The appointment of individuals to what is in effect a constitutional tribunal solely by the national government would prove highly controversial in the regional states discussed above. When intergovernmental disputes in the UK reach the Judicial Committee it may prove equally problematic.

7.3 DEVOLVED RESPONSIBILITIES

The various devolved institutions do not have the same responsibilities. To this extent the similarity with asymmetrical systems is clear. In practice, the devolved institutions can be divided into high autonomy and low autonomy, along the lines of the Spanish example. The Scottish and Northern Ireland devolution Acts grant high autonomy to their institutions. These regions are granted primary legislative power through a general competence found in both Acts. The powers of the Scottish Parliament are defined through s 28(1), which states that, 'subject to section 29, the parliament may make laws, to be known as Acts of the Scottish Parliament.' In effect this is a 'subsidiarity' clause of the type found in Germany. The restrictions to this can be found in s 29. These include some aspects unique to the UK example.

Section 29 refers to Sched 5 to the Scotland Act, where the mass of exclusions are to be found. This is Scotland's version of Arts 73 and 74 (applying to *Länder*) of the German Basic Law. These matters are reserved to the Westminster Parliament, and any legislation of the Scottish Parliament which transgresses these functions is *ultra vires* (s 29(2)(b), Scotland Act 1998). In contrast to the German example, the Scotland Act recognises only reserved and non-reserved powers. Concurrent powers are not part of the Scottish system. Schedule 5 is an impressive list, covering a significant range of subjects far longer than its German counterparts (or indeed Art 179 in Spain). The list of general exceptions includes most areas of the constitution, foreign and European affairs, the Civil Service and defence. In addition to these general exceptions, a long list of specifically reserved matters is included. These include fiscal, economic and monetary policy (Sched 5 A1, Scotland Act 1998), most aspects of energy policy (Sched 5 D), railways (Sched 5 E2), social security (Sched 5 F1) and broadcasting (Sched 5 K1). In effect the Scottish Parliament has been given power over those areas previously handled by the Scottish Office. The most important of these are health, education, local government, police and the law. The last of these in particular is subject to specific and eclectic restrictions (such as laws relating to handguns, misuse of drugs laws and business law). As in Germany, the general competence in practice is far more limited than may at first appear. Significant powers remain at the national level, and co-operation in many areas will be the norm.

In addition to Sched 5, s 29 lists a number of other limits on the power of the Scottish Parliament. Most important of these are actions of the devolved institutions which contradict European Community law and Convention rights. Scottish legislation, unlike that of the Westminster Parliament, will be *ultra vires* if it is contrary to those aspects of the European Convention on Human Rights incorporated in the UK law by the Human Rights Act 1998. In effect this means that the European Convention is the Scottish Parliament's Bill of Rights, but not that of the UK Parliament.

The Northern Ireland Act is more complex in its devolution of legislative power than its Scottish counterpart. Although operating a negative definition of powers, of the same type employed in Scotland and Germany, the Northern Ireland Act recognises three distinct varieties of policy. To confuse matters, the terminology applied in Northern Ireland is different from that used in Scotland.

The equivalents of Scottish reserved powers are described under the Northern Ireland Act as 'excepted' powers. These powers cannot be transferred to the Northern Ireland Assembly or its executive without amendment of the Northern Ireland Act itself. These are not dissimilar to the powers reserved to Westminster in the Scotland Act, although there are a number of omissions. Most of these are to be found in a further list of powers described as 'reserved' by the Northern Ireland Act. These include police, public order, firearms, financial services, criminal justice and others. At present, Northern Ireland Assembly legislation in these areas requires the consent of the Secretary of State to become law. Powers that are not within these lists are described as 'transferred'.

Reserved powers can be transferred if cross-party support within the Northern Ireland Assembly is evident. This particular innovation has parallels with the 'dual key' procedure found in the Belgian Parliament (see section 4.1.2). By this method, particular actions of the Northern Ireland Assembly must gain both a 60% majority of Assembly Members and 40% of designated unionist and nationalist members. This method is utilised for elections of the First Minister, Deputy First Minister and Presiding Officers, for transfer of powers from the reserved list to the transferred list, and for approval of the assembly's budget. If 30 Assembly Members sign a petition relating to a specific measure, this too must be submitted to the special majority procedure. This latter measure has similarities with the Belgian 'alarm bell' procedure (see section 4.1.2).

At present, the only low autonomy region in the UK system is Wales. The Welsh Assembly has no primary legislative power and, as already described, is a very different animal from the Assembly of Northern Ireland and the Parliament of Scotland. Unlike the high autonomy regions, its powers are positively defined and are executive or secondary in nature. The Welsh Assembly has no general competence even in its executive role. For the most part it performs the functions which were formerly exercised by the Secretary of State for Wales. These functions are now exercised by the assembly as a whole, although often, as explained above, through the executive committee.

The Government of Wales Act does not list the powers of Welsh Assembly. Instead, these powers are defined in secondary legislation (primarily Orders in Council), which for the most part transfer the responsibilities of the Secretary of State to the assembly. Further powers can be transferred by legislation passed at Westminster. This places the Welsh Assembly in a position not dissimilar to the Italian 'ordinary' region. The Government of Wales Act is therefore closer to an Italian regional statute than that of a Spanish *autonomía*, as the powers are not defined in the primary legislation itself. In Italy, the principal legislation that performs this function of transferring powers is DPR 616/1977. In Wales, The National

Assembly for Wales (Transfer of Functions) Order 1999 (SI 1999/672) is the key piece of legislation.

In both cases regional powers are established by executive order of the national government, and operate within primary legislative frameworks established at the centre. The Welsh Assembly, as in the case of its Italian counterparts, must rely upon initiatives from the national level to develop its competencies. In effect, the Welsh legislature remains in London. As in Italy, the relationship between the assembly and the national government will be close and complex. To some extent this is reflected in the ability of the assembly to request the Secretary of State to introduce Welsh legislation at Westminster, but this power is persuasive only.

7.4 DEVOLUTION IN CONTEXT

The UK's system of haphazard devolution does not fit neatly into the constitutional ideal types discussed in previous chapters. The majority of the UK remains governed directly from London; there is no constitutional pretence that the regional tier is the equal of the national level in the UK, and there is no formal involvement of the devolved institutions in national decision making. It is, therefore, not a federal system of the classic type explored in Chapter 4. Nevertheless, there are significant similarities between the European federal systems and devolution. The legislative competence granted to Scotland, in particular, is far in excess of that granted by Germany and comparable to that found in Belgium. The general legislative competence granted to Scotland and Northern Ireland is also paralleled only in the Federal Republic of Germany.

Even more similarities can be found between the constitutional regions and the devolved institutions. In particular, the use of regional 'statutes' to define the powers and institutions of devolution is common amongst the regions of Spain, Italy and Portugal. Nevertheless, significant differences remain. In particular, the defining constitutional feature of these regions is the constitutional protection of the regional tier. This is entirely lacking in the UK example.

All the current institutions of devolution have legislative powers in excess of those given to the local government regions, but again some significant similarities are evident. The institutions of the National Assembly for Wales have much in common with local government regions, although their powers mirror the weaker constitutional regions of the European Union. The English regions, should they be established, would be clear examples of local government regions in the UK.

The UK system is therefore something of a *sui generis* structure with a number of similarities with particular aspects of European systems. It also remains unfinished. Despite central government attempts to present the devolved system as a 'done deal', it is clearly a process. Over time, the UK's system of devolution will develop. In the case of Wales, the pressure for change is already growing, leading one author to describe the assembly as a 'constitutional convention by other means' (Osmond, 2000). If this can of worms is opened, there may be greater pressure on the central government to alter the devolution settlement in Scotland too. The prospective devolution of power to English regions is a development that may cause centripetal forces to develop further.

The exact path that the devolution process will take remains in the realms of hypothesis. Nevertheless, we can be aided in our quest by examining the paths taken by other regional systems of government. Operating under a common European Union umbrella, how have more mature regions developed? In the remaining chapters of this book we attempt to aid this discussion by focusing on a number of key aspects of devolution in the states of continental Europe. Although these do not give us definitive answers as to where devolution in the UK will lead us, they go some way towards helping us to know what to expect. In particular they allow us to understand the place of the United Kingdom's devolution settlement in the context of the evolving European regional level.

Part 3

Comparing Regional Governance

CHAPTER 8

BEYOND THE BORDERS:
REGIONAL GOVERNMENTS AND
INTERNATIONAL RELATIONS

International affairs may seem an unusual subject to discuss in the context of regional government. Yet the satisfactory resolution of international responsibilities is a key area of conflict in most regionalised states. The classic federal distribution of powers places international affairs within the domain of the nation-state level, with regional or devolved governments having responsibility for domestic affairs. This traditional concept of 'layer cake' federalism is fundamentally flawed. Although the national tier may be given the authority to engage in international relations, and to enter into agreements on behalf of the state as a whole, does this include the ability to impose such agreements on the regional level within their fields of domestic competence?

If the answer is yes, the autonomy of the regional tier is seriously threatened and the constitutional division of authority undermined. Such a scenario gives the central state the opportunity to sidestep constitutional restrictions on its autonomy in the name of international relations. In extreme situations, the central state might be eager to enter into international agreements which place restrictions on regional autonomy if the agreement coincides with national policy preferences. This option would be particularly attractive when central imposition of such policies would be unconstitutional.

If the answer to the question is no, regions are in effect handed a veto over such agreements within their fields of responsibility. This would leave the central government unable to guarantee the enforcement of those international agreements it has entered into. In such situations the central state is left in a difficult legal position, as the failure to implement a treaty due to constitutional difficulties is not a recognised justification under international law (Art 49, Vienna Convention on the Law of Treaties).

The international issue only proves to be a constitutional dilemma in those states where the regional tier has constitutionally protected legislative autonomy. In the EU, this includes Austria, Germany, Spain, Italy, Belgium and Portugal. In Scotland and Northern Ireland, the issue is constitutionally simple but politically complex. International and European Union affairs remain the responsibility of the UK Government (Sched 5(I)7 Scotland Act 1998; Sched 2(3) Northern Ireland Act 1998). In addition, the continued acceptance of Westminster sovereignty (s 28(7), Scotland Act 1998; s 6, Northern Ireland Act 1998) adds further weight to the constitutional argument in favour of the UK Government's control over the international and European arenas. Nevertheless, despite the constitutional position, there must be a serious question mark over whether UK Government interference in devolved matters in the name of international affairs would be politically acceptable.

The resolution of this dichotomy has been fundamental to the practical development of almost all the constitutionally defined regions. Although each European system has handled the conundrum differently, a common factor has been the involvement of the judiciary. Such resolutions remain highly political. Although the legal question may be whether or not the central level's constitutional authority to make treaties includes the power to implement their provisions, the political question centres on the fundamental role of the region in the structure of the state.

The importance of the international issue has intensified within most Western European states in the light of the continuing development of the European level of governance. Most Member State governments continue to regard European Union matters as 'international' under national constitutional provisions which generally allow for minimal regional involvement. Recently, Belgium and Germany have moved to separate European and international matters and, in both cases, the pressure for such a change has come from the regional tier. Retaining European matters within the 'international' bracket (and largely outside regional influence) is in the interests of the central state.

If the international competence of the national level is held to include the ability to impose such obligations on the regional tier, and EU matters are classed as international, then regions will find their competencies limited by European legislation (negotiated by the Member State) over which they themselves have no influence. The sphere of political autonomy granted to the region by the national constitution can be reduced almost at will by the decisions of the Council of Ministers or the Commission. As the supremacy of European law is all but accepted in all Member States, the supremacy of such law over the constitutional divisions within the state is clear (see *Costa v ENEL* [1964] ECR 585 and subsequent cases). Only the German Constitutional Court continues to question this doctrine, most notably in relation to the protection of human rights, but more recently in relation to the role of *Länder* in European decisions. Although the Bavarian Government failed in its attempt to force the federal government to vote against a directive in the council (2 *BVerfGE* 1/89; see Herdegen, 1995), the court confirmed that European law could be reviewed to ensure that it did not infringe the Basic Law (Foster, 1996, pp 69–70).

Member State delegations may use regionally held powers as convenient bargaining counters within the Council of Ministers, given that their domestic influence over them is minimal. With national constitutional restrictions offering no practical defence against European legislation, regional involvement in the European decision making process has become a priority for the regional tier.

Again, there is another side to this argument. Should European competence not include implementation, the Member State could be left in an extremely weak position. Failure to fulfil an international treaty obligation can be troublesome and cause complications in the field of international relations in the long term, but the obligations of a European Union Member State increase these problems considerably. The European Court of Justice has made it abundantly clear that the Member State will be responsible for failure to implement EU law by a regional government (*Commission v Italy* [1970] ECR 961, *Commission v Italy* [1983] ECR 1057, and more recently *Commission v Spain* [1998] ECR I-3301; see also Aurrecoechea, 1989, p 90 and Hopkins, 1996). If a Member State cannot guarantee compliance it will be open to constant challenge by the Commission and rebuke by the ECJ. This occurred frequently in Belgium, particularly in relation to the actions of the government of Wallonia, until the most recent Belgian constitutional reforms (see, for example, *Commission v Belgium* [1998] ECR I-4291 and [1998] ECR I-5063). The Francovich decision (*Francovich v Italy* [1991] ECR I-5357) and its subsequent jurisprudence also brings with it the possibility of financial loss to the Member State as a result of the actions of its regions.

8.1 RESOLVING THE 'INTERNATIONAL QUESTION'

As the oldest federation in the EU, it is hardly surprising that Germany was the first Member State to encounter the international affairs problem. The issue was central to the crucial Concordat case of 1957 (8 *BVerfGE* 309). The case revolved around the government of Lower Saxony's pursuance of a policy of non-denominational education and, in consequence, the end of separate schooling for Roman Catholic pupils. For this purpose, it introduced an Act to bring the region's Roman Catholic schools within the mainstream non-denominational system. Although education is an exclusive responsibility of the *Länder*, the federal government challenged the constitutional validity of this action on the grounds that it was contrary to the Concordat of 1933. The Concordat was an international treaty, agreed between the German Government of the time and the Holy See, guaranteeing the right of Roman Catholic children to separate education. Significantly, it clearly encroached upon one of the few exclusive areas of postwar *Länder* sovereignty. The case raised a number of issues, many of them political. The *Bund* was attempting to use this international Concordat to further its own policy agenda. The federal government's use of a Nazi-sponsored treaty to control the actions of the democratic *Länder* was a separate but rather unsavoury aside to the dispute. The German Constitutional Court, in rejecting the argument of the *Bund*, made it clear that this case went far beyond the facts as presented and asserted that the federal authorities did not have the power to impose a treaty obligation upon the *Länder* in areas where the latter possessed legislative autonomy.

The German court rejected the view that treaty making competence and implementation are one and the same, and in doing so followed the 'Canadian model', as propounded by the Judicial Committee of the Privy Council in the Labour Conventions case of 1937 (*Attorney General for Canada v Attorney General for Ontario* [1937] AC 326). The facts of this case revolved around an attempt by the Canadian Dominion Government (the federal level) to implement a 'new deal' programme in Canada. Lacking domestic legislative authority in the area of industrial relations, the federal government attempted to implement a number of International Labour Conventions (of which Canada was a signatory) directly through federal legislation, claiming that such legislation was required to fulfil Canada's international obligations. The government of Ontario, alongside other opposition provinces, challenged the actions of the Dominion Government.

In its decision, the Privy Council drew a clear distinction between the formation and the performance of treaty obligations. Formation was an executive act, but any changes to domestic law demanded by such an act would require legislative action. There was no reason why the same principles should not apply in both unitary and federal (or regional) states. Atkins summed up the court's view as follows:

> In a unitary State whose Legislature possesses unlimited powers the problem is simple. Parliament will either fulfil or not treaty obligations imposed upon the State by its executive. The nature of the obligations does not affect the complete authority of the Legislature to make them law if it so chooses. But in a State where the Legislature does not possess absolute authority, in a federal State where legislative authority is limited by a constitutional document, or is divided up between different Legislatures in accordance with the classes of subject-matter submitted for legislation, the problem is complex. The obligations imposed by treaty may have to be performed, if at all, by several Legislatures; and the executive have the task of obtaining the legislative assent not of the one Parliament to whom they may be responsible, but possibly of several Parliaments to whom they stand in no direct relation. The question is not how is the obligation formed, that is the function of the executive; but how is the obligation to be performed, and that depends upon the competent Legislature or Legislatures. [*Attorney General for Canada v Attorney General for Ontario* (1937) at 348.]

The German court's decision to resolve the issue along these lines still left a major constitutional problem in the Federal Republic, just as the Privy Council's decision had in Canada. How can the central government conduct international relations if it cannot guarantee the implementation of any agreement reached? The German Constitutional Court addressed this issue by reference to the principle of federal comity (or *Bundestreue*), which the court recognised as an obligation on the part of the *Länder* to take its duty to the federation as a whole 'particularly seriously' in this case. This was far short of an obligation to implement, and could hardly be regarded as a satisfactory conclusion in itself. The case left the *Bund* unable to impose treaty provisions on the *Länder* within their areas of autonomy, while the *Länder* themselves could not enter into international agreements in these areas without *Bund* approval (see section 8.2).

The participants in the Spanish autonomy negotiations of the late 1970s and early 1980s seem to have learnt at least partially from earlier German experiences. Thirteen of the 17 *autonomías* ('autonomous communities') address the issue in their autonomy statutes, and thus the role of the constitutional court has been reduced. Nevertheless, variations between regional statutes, and the omission of treaty implementation provisions in some cases, has caused constitutional confusion. In the statutes of the Basque country Euskadi (Art 27(3), Statute of Autonomy), Catalonia (Art 27(3)), Andalusia (Art 23(2)), Aragon (Art 40(2)), Castilla-La Mancha (Art 34), the Canary Islands (Art 37(2)) and Madrid (Art 33(2)), the position is relatively clear. Their statutes stipulate regional implementation of all international treaties concluded by the central government but concerning areas included in their sphere of autonomy. The central state cannot use international treaties to increase its *de facto* legislative powers, but equally the regions are subject to international obligations made on their behalf. The situation of the Spanish autonomías is not as strong as that of the German *Länder*. The Spanish regions have no authority to refuse to implement international obligations in their fields of autonomy, as the Concordat case granted to the *Länder*, but the implementation of such obligations is a regional responsibility and not a national one.

Five other Spanish regions deal with treaty implementation in their statutes, namely Asturias (Art 12, Statute of Autonomy), Extremadura (Art 9(1)), the Balearic islands (Art 12(1)), Castilla y León (Art 28(7)) and Navarre (Art 58(2)). These five grant their regions administrative competence in the implementation of international obligations, but the legislation required for such implementation lies at the national level (Aurrecoechea, 1989). As a consequence of these variations, the central government argued that any international implementation functions not assigned to the regions were retained by default by the centre under Art 149(1)3 of the Spanish Constitution, which allocates competence for international relations to the national tier. Article 93 of the Spanish Constitution, which grants the national authorities the ability to 'guarantee compliance' with legislation from an international organisation, was used as further evidence of the constitutional intent of the drafters. Article 93 was drawn up specifically with the European Union in mind.

The Basque statute of autonomy added a further twist to the already complex constitutional situation by barring international treaties or agreements from altering the region's powers and competencies without the statute itself being altered (Art 20(3)). This was an attempt to stop central encroachment of regional powers by stealth through the use of the international competence found in Art 149(1)3 Spanish Constitution. Article 20(3) does not apply to agreements made under the provisions of Art 93 of the Spanish Constitution.

In a landmark judgment of 1982, the Spanish Constitutional Court followed the decisions of both the Judicial Committee of the Privy Council and the German Constitutional Court to the extent of recognising a distinction between treaty making power and implementation authority. To some extent it also attempted to address the loose ends left by this approach. The court asserted that clauses in autonomy statutes giving implementation powers to the regions were 'a logical consequence of the territorial organisation of the state' rather then exceptions to the rule of central implementation (Judgment 44/1982). The argument was strengthened by Spain's monist approach to international law whereby a treaty, once ratified, becomes part of the domestic law and therefore liable to internal rules of implementation. The effect of Art 93 is therefore to allow the central state to implement international (and specifically European) obligations only if a region has failed to do so. This view is widely held in Spanish academic circles (see Aurrecoechea, 1989, p 97, note 61).

Both the German and Spanish courts defended the autonomy of the region against encroachment by the state. Similarly, both failed to answer fully the problems this approach entails. In the Spanish case, although no specific mention was made of the 'guarantee clause' in Art 93, the existence of this Article has enabled a weight of academic opinion to interpret the court's decision as having the effect mentioned above, thus at least partially squaring the circle. In Germany, no such clause existed, and instead the principle of *Bundestreue* was urged upon the parties to resolve the stalemate.

The political response to the German court's decision was the Lindau Agreement between the *Länder* and the *Bund* (Blair, 1981, p 171). Signed in 1957 as a direct result of the Concordat decision, this agreement makes federal acceptance of obligations in fields of *Länder* exclusive competence conditional on their approval. In addition, the *Länder* are to be kept informed of international negotiations affecting their interests to allow their views to be expressed. A permanent *Länder* commission was established for this reason (Blair, 1981, p 171). A Spanish agreement reached in December 1985 between the regions and the central state broadly reflects its German counterpart (Aurrecoechea, 1989, p 99, note 64). Unlike their German partners, however, the Spanish have only settled the issue with regard to the European Union, the most pressing manifestation of the problem. Even here, the regions' role is merely to implement European obligations and to be informed of European negotiations; they do not possess the veto power of the German regional tier.

The opposite approach to the Canadian model can be seen in Italy. In its decision of 24 July 1972, the Italian Constitutional Court accepted the legality of a decree giving jurisdiction for implementation of European legislation to the central government despite the inroads that this would make on the regional autonomy guaranteed by the constitution. The newly established Italian regions were convinced that the extensive EC involvement in agriculture (one of their main competencies) would be used by the state to reduce their already limited independence. The court's decision claimed that, since the Italian government took responsibility for international affairs, it followed that it required the ability to guarantee compliance (Court decision 142, 24 July 1972). The judgment concluded that no powers could be conferred on the regions to implement international obligations unless the national level had a system to ensure compliance should the regions fail to act. Although this case set the tone for the constitutional court's centrist leanings, the judgment did give the possibility of compromise. This was implemented in 1977 when, during the transfer of the bulk of regional powers under DPR 616, Art 6 transferred the implementation of EC obligations, within their competencies, to the regions concerned (Condorelli, 1986, p 147). The court's decision was adhered to by instituting an internal supervisory mechanism to ensure regions complied with EU legislation. The system applied to European Union obligations is now accepted in Italy as applying also to international obligations in general.

The system as now enforced gives regions the right to implement international treaties in the areas where they hold competence. In the case of EU regulations, the regions implement these directly and set up any administrative structures as required. Where directives are concerned, the regions operate within framework laws established by the national parliament. These framework laws contain detailed default clauses that apply if the region fails to pass its own legislation. If the region develops its own legislation, the national legislation is set aside. If the region does not do so, the default clauses established by the national legislation come into force. Unlike the Spanish example, it is not left to the regions to establish the legislation themselves. If, however, regional action is necessary (for example, the establishment of an agency) and not forthcoming, or if the regional legislation is found to contradict EU law or an international treaty, the Italian government can, after a time limit and consultation, enforce compliance on the region.

Belgium reflects a far more radical solution to the international question. In Belgium, treaties are negotiated by the individual Regions and Communities, thus removing the implementation problem completely. When treaties involving the competencies of Regions and Communities are negotiated by the federal state, they must be approved by the relevant regional legislatures. This sidesteps the difficulties of the Canadian solution.

By devolving international relations along with other competencies, the Belgians have constructed a simple but effective solution. The problems that it brings with it are examined in the next section.

Although the approach taken by the different EU Member States has varied, the bias has been towards the Canadian model developed by the Privy Council. Even in Italy, where this course was not followed, subsequent events have emasculated the decision somewhat. In both Spain and Germany, the courts' support of a narrow interpretation of 'international relations' led to a blocked process that forced politicians to negotiate a viable working relationship. The result has been that the Spanish autonomías and the German *Länder* have the authority to implement international obligations and, at least in the case of the *Länder*, have some involvement in their negotiation.

Despite all the political compromises, the issue remains an area of conflict between most regional and national tiers. Only Belgium has actually grasped the nettle and devolved international relations along with domestic competencies. Political considerations make this approach unlikely in other states. In the longer term, however, it may be the only satisfactory solution.

8.2 INTERNATIONAL AGREEMENTS

The question of what actually constitutes international persona is a complex one and far beyond the scope of this volume. Nevertheless, the most practical manifestation of such a status is the ability to undertake formal treaty agreements. Amongst the Member States of the European Union, only the federal regions possess such a capacity. In Germany, this authority is enshrined in Art 32(3) of the Basic Law but its operation is somewhat restricted. With the exception of Concordats (Treaties with the Holy See), all *Länder* treaties must have the approval of the federal government (Art 32(3), Basic Law). This limited authority has been exercised by several *Länder*, notably Bavaria and Baden-Württemberg, particularly in the field of environmental protection (Harris, 1983, p 566, note 12). Although the federation has supported such actions, such agreements remain at the discretion of the *Bund*.

A similar situation is observed in Austria, although Art 16 of the Austrian Constitution restricts regional treaties to states and regions which border the Austrian Republic itself. The federal government of Austria has an eight week period prior to the signing of the treaty when it can exercise a veto. This time limit is only of limited importance, as the federal government can also unilaterally demand that such regional treaties be revoked (Art 16(3), Austrian Constitution).

In Belgium, the situation is markedly different. Both Regions and Communities have the constitutional authority to conduct international relations in any area under their competence, although such agreements may not be entered into contrary to the international policy of the Belgian state (Art 167(3), Belgian Constitution). This provision would apply if the federation had imposed sanctions on the state in question. The degree of international persona granted to the Belgian regions is a logical extension of the Belgian equality of laws principle. The Belgian federal level lacks authority to legislate in the areas of Regional or Community competence, and so has no power to impose international obligations on the Regional and Community governments. Direct regional and Community involvement is therefore required to ensure that Belgium has an international persona in the areas in which they hold exclusive competence. Many of Belgium's national partners have had difficulty in coping with this state of affairs, and a number are clearly uncomfortable with it. To some extent this reflects unease at encouraging a regional presence on the international stage that may be demanded by troublesome provinces in other states. For this reason, the Belgian federation has experienced some difficulties in projecting its domestic structure into the international arena (Senelle, 1999).

Although the Austrian, German and Belgian regions are the only ones to enjoy formal treaty making competence in the European Union, a number of others do have a formally recognised place in the treaty making process. A few Spanish *autonomías*, for example, have a recognised but limited role in affairs beyond the borders of the Spanish state. As in the Federal Republic of Germany, formal international relations are entirely the responsibility of the central state (Art 97, Spanish Constitution). In contrast to the German example, however, no exceptions to this rule apply. The formal influence of Spanish regions is limited to a right to lobby the central government on specific issues as listed in the individual statute of autonomy. Catalonia in cultural issues (Art 27(4), Catalonian Statute of Autonomy), Andalusia in assistance to emigrants (Art 23(3), Andalusian Statute of Autonomy), and Aragon in border issues (Art 40(1), Aragon Statute of Autonomy) all enjoy this limited right. Some regions also have a formal right to be informed of treaties which affect matters of specific relevance to them (these include Euskadi, Catalonia, the Canary Islands, Andalusia, Madrid, Murcia, Asturias and Navarre).

The only other European regions to enjoy any formal involvement in international affairs are Madeira and the Açores. The situation in the Portuguese autonomous regions is more settled but no less confusing than that in Spain. The Portuguese Constitution grants the island governments the right to 'participate in the negotiation of and enjoy the benefits derived from international treaties and agreements which may concern them' (Art 227(1)r, Portuguese Constitution). This grants the islands a limited right to involvement in treaty negotiations that concern them. For example, the government of the Açores was involved in agreements between Portugal and the United States over the use of their islands by the US military. However, in such cases, the final say still lies with the national government.

There is therefore a clear split between the federal states and the constitutionally defined regions in this field. Even the most devolved authorities have only procedural rights when it comes to the field of treaty relations. Formal substantive rights to enter into international agreements, and veto those agreements that adversely affect them, are restricted to the federal regions of Belgium, Germany and (to a much lesser extent) Austria. Where the region operates as a level of local government (France, Italy, Denmark and the Netherlands), official responsibility for all international representation and treaty making clearly lies within the authority of the central state.

The formal presence of the European regions on the international stage is strictly limited, but this does not mean that regions do not operate outside their domestic borders. Although formal international links are rarely sanctioned, regions participate in unofficial agreements on a grand scale. These are achieved through what Daintith would characterise as 'dominium' power (Daintith, 1989). They range from vague co-operation agreements to specific arrangements to deal with a variety of issues. To use the word 'treaty' would imply a pact subject to international law and arbitration, which is not the case. Nevertheless, although not always subject to any enforcement procedure, it is in the interests of both parties to abide by the terms imposed. If a party violates an agreement, its ability to conduct such affairs in the future will be damaged.

In practice, of course, the same principles apply in the operation of most international agreements. Few treaties are ever broken, at least blatantly, and the use of international modes of arbitration is limited. There exists, therefore, a network of sub-national agreements beneath international law proper but operating by its rules. As the examples below demonstrate, the issues covered by these links are by no means trivial to the citizen, nor are they always undertaken with the approval of the central state.

The problem for the nation-state in controlling such actions is defining when a region's contacts outside the state constitute 'international relations' in the formal sense. Work done by Wildhaber in 1974, concerning Swiss cantons, uncovered at least 125 agreements still in force between cantons and external bodies. Agreements ranged from 19th century border agreements with France to an agreement of 1970 with German *Länder* concerning environmental protection (Wildhaber, 1974, p 217). In addition the cantons participate in conferences and have permanent contacts with counterparts in Germany and France. These vary from a regional co-ordination conference founded in 1971 to direct negotiations over waste disposal problems and agreements concerning education, border disasters and frontier workers. The final example is significant as it took the EC until

1968 to come up with agreements covering this complex problem (see *inter alia* Council Directive 68/360 and Commission Regulation 1251/70).

Far from being the exception, the multitude of agreements arranged between the countries in this part of Europe are actually the norm. In Italy, for instance, the regions have been specifically authorised to enter into interregional contacts. Most interestingly this led to a regional development group being formed by the Veneto region which included three other Italian regions, four Austrian *Länder*, two Yugoslavian republics (at the time) and one German *Land* (Elazar, 1991, p 131).

The impotence of national governments in stopping these links is emphasised by the Spanish example. Despite Spanish governmental annoyance, both Catalonia and Euskadi established cross-border links and agreements with the French government. Links between the Spanish regions and their European counterparts have also been extensive. However, the Spanish state has been powerless to intervene, as these are not 'international relations' *per se*. When these have crossed into the sphere of international affairs, the Spanish Constitutional Court (for example, in 137/89) has not been afraid to strike them down. Even here, the court has seemed to soften its approach over time, accepting more and more regional activities as being within their spheres of competence (Schmitt, 1994).

Until recently, Italy was the exception to this burgeoning network of informal regional agreements. Although Art 4 of DPR 616/1977 gave the Italian regions the ability to engage in 'promotional activities', the framework established by the state in March 1980 to define this term was extremely restrictive (Agostini and Mattioni, 1992, p 139). This was confirmed by a series of decisions by the Italian Constitutional Court (particularly 179/1987 and 42/1989) which denied regions any formal contacts outside the borders of the national state, with the exception of trans-border co-operation agreements, and strictly defined promotional activities. However, even these exceptions proved problematic, as the 1982 co-operation agreement between Valle d'Aosta and the Franche-Comte region of France was ruled *ultra vires* while the ruling of 1987 denied Italian regions direct contact with the European institutions. Decision 472/1992 marked a significant change in the attitude of the court. Now regions are permitted to operate in all areas of an international character when their content does not affect the external policy of the state. This more flexible approach has led to a significant increase in Italian regional activity outside the state, particularly in relation to the EU.

Although the region has clearly expanded its involvement on the international stage, particularly in an informal manner, we are not even close to a situation of parity between the region and the national level. Nevertheless, the expansion of regions in the European and international arenas has been dramatic. In the late 1970s, only the German *Länder* had limited involvement in this sphere. By the year 2000, the regions of five EU

Member States (Austria, Belgium, Germany, the Portuguese islands and Spain) have at least a limited formal involvement in international affairs. Beyond this, informal agreements have become the norm rather than the exception. The regions have therefore come a long way in the international arena, but what of the European dimension? How effective have regions been in muscling their way into the nation-state club of the EU?

8.3 REGIONAL GOVERNMENT AND THE EUROPEAN UNION

The structure of the European Union does not lend itself to regional participation. Since its birth, the Community has been a nation-state club. The primary legislative body (the Council of Ministers) is entirely organised on national lines, with delegations representing the 15 Member States. The Commissioners are appointed according to nationality, as are the judges of the European Court of Justice. The predominant territorial unit within the EU is unquestionably the Member State, but the region is not totally without representation in the European policy process.

8.3.1 Formal representation

Until 1994, the existence of regions within the formal institutions of the European Union was noticeable only by their absence. Formal regional involvement in the policy process was non-existent, while consultation procedures were limited to exceptional cases and informal contacts. The Maastricht Treaty on European Union introduced significant changes, not least in recognising a formal (if limited) role for non-national representatives in the decision making process of the Union.

The most significant changes are now found in Arts 146 and 198 of the amended Treaty of Rome. Article 146 introduced a small but potentially significant alteration in the definition of the Council of Ministers. The previous incarnation of this Article stated (emphasis added):

> The Council shall consist of representatives of the Member States. *Each government shall delegate to it one of its members.*

This Article ensured that only members of a national government could participate in the Council. Even if a Member State wished to have a regional minister represent the national government within the Council, this was not permitted. The regional tier was thus completely frozen out.

Under Maastricht, this wording was subtly altered. Primarily at the insistence of Belgium, the strict emphasis on national government membership was relaxed. Instead, the national representatives must now be of ministerial rank and authorised to act for the Member State. This does not exclude regional or ministers from acting on behalf of the state (though neither does it specifically include them). The full Article now reads:

> The Council shall consist of a representative of each Member State at ministerial level, authorised to commit the government of that Member State. [Art 146, Treaty of Rome (as amended by the Treaty on European Union).]

As the Belgian Regions and Communities are responsible for international relations in their respective fields of competence, they would not accept their representation at the European level being handled by a federal minister. In addition, no treaty that alters the competencies of Regions and Communities can be agreed by Belgium without their consent. As EU Treaty amendments require unanimity, the Member States had little option but to accept the Belgian proposal if the Maastricht Treaty was to be accepted.

Belgium remains the only state to make formal use of the new Article. To do so, the Belgian delegation to the Council is constructed in accordance with a rather complex agreement. This was drawn up between the various Regions, Communities and the federation under provisions outlined in an agreement concluded in 1994 (Co-operation Agreement of 8 March 1994 on the Representation of the Kingdom of Belgium within the Council of Ministers and the European Union). Where issues of exclusively Regional or Community competence are discussed, the Belgian delegation consists entirely of regional ministers. The ministers of the two largest Regions or Communities alternately head the delegation. In areas where competence is mixed, the Belgian delegation consists of both federal and regional representatives. The tier playing the dominant role heads the delegation while the other members act in an advisory capacity. When a vote is taken, the head of delegation administers all the Belgian votes as a single block (Senelle, 1999).

The operation of Belgian regional ministers within the Council of Ministers is a major change in the EU's perceived status as a nation-state club, but does it have any practical effect? The problem with giving regional access to the Council is that Belgian regional representatives still sit as part of a larger national delegation. Thus, when it comes to voting, the delegation votes on behalf of Belgium. This creates a number of legitimacy problems. First, the regional minister only has a democratic mandate from a region or Community but still represents the entire Member State within the Council. Secondly, as the Belgian votes are still administered as a single block, the position as presented is still a Belgian position, merely one that has been negotiated by regional and national government ministers. Why, then, are regional ministers present in the council?

The first reason appears to be information. By being within the Council negotiations proper, the regions are aware of how both their concerns and the wider discussions are progressing, without relying on the national government as a conduit for such information. The second benefit for Belgium as a whole is one of expertise. As an example, if a question of agricultural policy is discussed in Council, it is necessary for each delegation to have the facts at its disposal. As Belgium has no agriculture minister, it is necessary to use the regional ministries or risk being outmanoeuvred during the discussions. Naivety at the European negotiating table is a significant disadvantage. Finally, their presence in the Council clearly adds to the status and political position of the regional ministers in the Council. If nothing else, it is a visible reminder of the importance of the regional tier in the Belgian federation.

The Belgian regional ministers who participate in the Council of Ministers are not alone, however. An older (but less active) regional presence has been kept by the German *Länder*. Since the 1950s, *Länder* representation has become an intermittent feature of the German delegation to the Council and several associated committees. In addition, a civil servant (*Länderbeobachter*) is employed by the *Länder* to attend all Council sessions (in a non-speaking capacity) and the preparatory meetings of the German delegation. This individual also receives the instructions given to the German EU delegation. These regional 'rights' were obtained through the veto powers of the *Bundesrat*. When passing the constitutional changes necessary for European treaty amendments, the *Länder* have a collective right of veto through their representatives in the *Bundesrat*. Because of this, the federal authorities have been forced to take account of *Länder* demands, although the concessions won by the *Länder* have not always had the intended results.

During the 1950s a number of concessions guaranteeing regional access to European information and the right to comment upon impending European legislation were granted by the *Bund*. These remained informal and at the discretion of the *Bund*, until the introduction of the Single European Act (SEA) gave the *Länder* a real opportunity to put pressure on the federal tier and to demand more formal involvement. The constitutional requirement to pass the Act through the *Bundesrat* allowed the *Länder* to squeeze several important concessions from the federal government. Most notable was an increased right of information, with a new *Bundesrat* committee to examine European Community legislation before giving non-binding *Länder* opinions on issues of concern to them. Crucially, they also won the right for their representative to be a non-speaking member of the German delegation to the Council of Ministers when issues within their competencies were being discussed (Jeffrey, 1994).

Most of these concessions had already been granted on an informal basis, and the agreement of 1987 merely placed them on a formal legal footing. The *Länderbeobachter* (or observer), for example, was actually established through an agreement in 1958. Further regional involvement, formalised during the SEA negotiations, included *Länder* civil servants being part of the German delegation to certain Council of Ministers working groups. These mostly concerned agriculture and regional policy. In the case of environmental protection, the *Länder* representatives won the right to sit as part of the Council delegation itself. Various other informal *Länder* representations on EC committees also became formalised, but only in exceptional circumstances were the regional members permitted to vote, and never on the Council itself (Gerstenlauer, 1995, p 180). Even where they were, they could only express a common *Länder* opinion, rather than reflect any regional differences that might exist.

In practice, the concessions obtained did not have the impact that the *Länder* had hoped for. Although the *Länder* now had a plethora of formal opportunities to express opinions, these remained non-binding. Furthermore, the methods by which these opinions were obtained made the system unworkable. *Länder* opinions were agreed within the existing structure of intergovernmental conferences. The rules of procedure used by these bodies specified unanimity on matters of policy. The chances of all the *Länder* agreeing common responses to detailed European Community policy proposals were slim (Engel, 1992, p 76). In any event, such opinions, decided at a national level between the *Länder*, did not allow individual regions to express their views at the European level. Individual regional autonomy was the loser, even if the German regions now had some collective influence on European policy.

One reason for the problems associated with the procedures introduced after the SEA was that *Länder* influence upon the intergovernmental negotiations had been limited. The German regional tier had only been able to gain concessions from the *Bund*, not the European Community, due to the nature of the EC's treaty amendment procedure. As the SEA had been negotiated under the auspices of the EC Treaty (which it was to amend) these rules applied. In essence, for changes to the EC Treaty to be ratified, all the Member States must agree. This meant that if the *Bundesrat* refused to accept the SEA, the whole project would have collapsed, leaving the Member States to renegotiate from square one. The *Länder* did not want to be seen as wreckers of an Act that they supported, so any resistance had to be qualified and directed solely at gaining concessions from the federal government.

Despite these problems, the SEA episode established a number of important principles. Despite all the difficulties of establishing a *Länder* position, the *Bund* agreed not to deviate from this position unless in the interests of integration or foreign policy. In these cases, the *Länder* were to be informed as to the reasons for the change in negotiating stance. Although such a safeguard is obviously flawed, as many shifts in position could be covered by referring to integration policy, it did establish the principle that the *Länder* were entitled to be heard when the issues under discussion concerned their interests. This was the first recognition of a 'third level' in

EC affairs. Prior to this, only European institutions and the Member States had any involvement in European policy making. Now, for the first time, a group of regions was recognised as having a right of participation, although at this stage it was rather ineffective.

The 1992 Maastricht Treaty on European Union gave the *Länder* another opportunity to flex the constitutional muscles they had discovered in 1987. Once again, any agreement would need the support of the German regions in the *Bundesrat* to be accepted under the Basic Law. This time, the *Länder* were far more organised, and orchestrated a remarkably successful campaign to influence the Treaty during its negotiation. This process was aided by the growth of the European regional tier during the late 1980s and early 1990s. By 1992, the *Länder* had some powerful allies.

In 1987, the heads of government conference of the German *Länder* published the '10 Munich Theses on European Policy'. During the next few years, these became four fundamental and clear demands of the German regions if their support for the forthcoming treaty was to be gained. These were:

(a) the entrenchment of the principle of subsidiarity in the Treaty;

(b) the opening up of the Council of Ministers to ministers from the 'third level' (regions);

(c) the establishment of a regional organisation within the EC;

(d) the introduction of access to the European Court of Justice by 'third level' governments when EU institutions infringed regional rights.

These demands were maintained consistently by all the *Länder*, throughout the entire negotiation process. As Jeffrey notes, this was quite remarkable considering the bitter domestic differences prevalent between the regions at this time (Jeffrey, 1994).

The *Länder* did not restrict their campaign to the domestic political arena as they had in 1987, but lobbied hard in both Brussels and Strasbourg. By creating a pan-European regional lobby, the regions entered the political arena as a truly European phenomenon. Rather than limiting their actions to domestic matters and operating within the context of a national political system, regions were now operating on a European level. This marked a defining moment in the development of the regional tier in the EU.

The most important allies of the *Länder* were the Belgian Regions and Cultural Communities. It was the Belgian delegation that actually introduced the amendment concerning regional participation in the Council of Ministers after the German federation refused to do so (Jeffrey, 1994, p 10).

With the reunification of Germany, the *Länder* were presented with another opportunity to take on the *Bund*. Two commissions (the *Bundesrat* Commission on Constitutional Reform and the Joint Constitutional

Commission of the *Bundestag* and *Bundesrat*) considered the implications of the new united Germany. The *Länder* hijacked these bodies and instead pressed for a 'Europe Article' in the *Grundgesetz* (Basic Law). Again, a united front was maintained, and the ultimately successful campaign led to the introduction of a new Art 23. The new Article, which replaced provisions concerned with the extension of the Basic Law to East Germany, is concerned solely with *Länder* involvement in the EU. Although, as Jeffrey pointed out, the new Europe Article does have symbolic importance as it stresses the unified Germany's commitment to Europe, in practice it emphasised the determination of the western *Länder* to use any means at their disposal to close what they described as the 'open flank'.

The *Länder* actually set out to change Art 24 (concerning international relations) but instead settled for the new Art 23. The change was achieved by a combination of subtle negotiation and blatant threats principally concerning the Maastricht Treaty (which was yet to be ratified). In one single session of the Joint Constitutional Commission, the Bavarian Minister President threatened non-ratification three times (Jeffrey, 1994, p 15). The new Article covers several aspects of relations between the *Länder* and the EU, but the crucial details are in paras 4–6. These state:

4   The *Bundesrat* is to participate in the formation of the will of the Bund in so far as it would have to participate in a corresponding internal measure or in so far as the *Länder* would be internally competent.

5   In so far as in a particular area of exclusive competence of the Bund interests of the *Länder* are affected or in so far as in other respects the Bund has the right to legislate, the federal government is to have regard to the expressed opinion of the *Bundesrat*. If the legislative powers of the *Länder*, the organisation of their authorities or their administrative procedures are affected in a crucial respect, the view of the *Bundesrat* is, to this extent, to be taken into account as the determining factor in the formation of the will of the Bund; at the same time the responsibility of the Bund for all the *Länder* is to be preserved. In matters which can lead to increases in expenditure or reduction in income for the Bund, the consent of the federal government is necessary.

6   Where essentially the exclusive legislative jurisdiction of the *Länder* is affected the exercise of the rights of the Federal Republic of Germany as a Member State of the European Union shall be transferred by the Federation to a representative of the *Länder* designated by the *Bundesrat*. Those rights shall be exercised with the participation of and in agreement with the federal government; in this connection the responsibility of the Federation for the country as a whole shall be maintained. [Art 23, Basic Law.]

The amendments give the *Länder* the collective right to participate in the making of German EU policy and, in particular circumstances, to dictate it. The German Basic Law therefore separates European and international matters, with the former now being removed from the auspices of Art 24 of the Basic Law. Instead, EU affairs are now seen as *sui generis* somewhere between the national and international level. Although this was merely the formal recognition of a political fact, Germany was the first Member State to recognise this explicitly.

8.3.2 Committee of the Regions

The most visible evidence of increased regional involvement in the working of the European Union has been the creation of the Committee of the Regions (CoR). European Community local and regional consultative bodies have been in existence since the Commission established the Consultative Council of Regional and Local Authorities in 1988, under pressure from the European Parliament and the Council of Municipalities and Regions of Europe. Nevertheless, the CoR, established under the Maastricht Treaty, was the first regional institution formally to influence the EU policy process.

Although commonly styled as a regional body, this is a misnomer. Representation is organised on a Member State basis and varies considerably (see Table 8.1). In practice, the involvement of the regional tier in each delegation reflects the relative powers of the regions in each state. The federal and constitutional regions have a high level of representation. The German *Länder*, for example, have taken 21 of the 24 seats allocated to the Federal Republic, with the remaining three being granted to representatives of the municipalities. Belgium allocates all its members on a regional basis. By contrast, England (and until recently the UK as a whole), lacking a regional tier, was represented by local council representatives appointed by the central government. In Scotland, Wales and Northern Ireland, representation (at a level set by the UK Government) is in the hands of the devolved institutions.

Table 8.1: Composition of the Committee of the Regions

Member State	Appointment method	Number
Austria	9 *Länder* representatives Head of local authority association (1) Mayor of Vienna (1) 1 representative of city-states	12
Belgium	7 Flanders Region 5 Walloon Region/French Community Within these allocations, each Region gives up one seat (to give Brussels two representatives) and one seat for half its term (to give the German Community one representative)	12
Denmark	4 *amter* representatives 4 kommuner representatives 1 city *amt* representative Appointees agreed between government and local or regional bodies	9
Finland	1 Åland island region representative 4 local government representatives 4 regional government representatives	9
France	16 regional representatives 4 departmental representatives 4 communal representatives	24
Germany	21 *Länder* representatives (1 per *Land* and 5 by rotation) 3 local government representatives	24
Greece	12 municipality representatives	12
Ireland	7 county and 2 city representatives	9
Italy	13 regional representatives (including all 'special' regions and autonomous provinces: 6 representatives in total) 4 provincial representatives 7 municipal representatives	24
Luxembourg	All local authority representatives	6
Netherlands	5 councillors (4 provinces, 1 municipality) 7 executive representatives (2 provinces, 5 municipalities)	12

Member State	Appointment method	Number
Portugal	2 island region representatives 10 local representatives	12
Spain	17 regional representatives 4 municipal representatives	21
Sweden	7 local and 5 regional representatives	12
UK	England (14): elected councillors appointed by central government on semi-regional basis Scotland (5), Wales (3) and Northern Ireland (2): appointed by assemblies/parliaments	24

NOTE: *These figures represent members only and not their alternates. In a few cases (for example, Belgium), some regional alternates are local representatives.*

Belgium is the only Member State to appoint its entire delegation from the regional tier. This reflects the political power of the Belgian regions in the Treaty's ratification process. All other Member States give a number of seats to local government. The CoR is thus representative of sub-national government in general rather than regions in particular. This has serious repercussions for the operation of the CoR.

The Minister President of Bavaria, with 11 million people in his or her charge, and the power to legislate independently in significant areas, is unlikely to have the same priorities as a councillor from South Yorkshire. The tension between local and regional representation within the committee is evident from the debate on its future. The regions (especially those with greater autonomy) wish to see it develop into a truly regional institution, with a substantive role in the European legislative process, a *Bundesrat* to the European Parliament's *Bundestag*. The local authorities, on the other hand, are content for the consultative role of the committee to continue. In the negotiations before the Amsterdam Treaty, the Minister President of Baden-Württemberg outlined the position of the federal regions clearly:

> The major long term goal remains the further development of the Committee of the Regions into a 'third chamber', alongside the European Parliament and Council of Ministers and with co-decision powers in certain areas. [CoR, 1995.]

The President of Wallonia went further, when discussing the nature of the committee's opinions:

> ... the opinions thus far are advisory. In order to enable the Committee of the Regions to play its rightful role, in the near future I would like to see it given the power of assent in the areas of the environment, energy and land use planning. [CoR, 1995.]

The opinions of these prominent regional leaders were in marked contrast to a Scottish local government representative on the committee, Cllr Charles Gray. He argued that proposals for the reform of the committee:

> ... should reassure the EU bodies that the Committee of the Regions wishes to make constructive proposals and has no desire to seek a legislative role for itself or to compromise the prerogatives of the institutions. [CoR, 1995.]

Such reassurance was unlikely to be found amongst those who read the comments of the Belgian and German regional leaders. Mr Gray's comments should be taken in context, however. He consistently argued that a more conciliatory approach would gain more for the committee than the robust stance taken by some regions. Events subsequent to these comments may have proved him right, but the difference of opinion underlines the clear tensions between a regional tier which views the committee's role as proto-legislative and a local tier which sees it as an advisory institution only.

The appointment of representatives along Member State lines has a further impact on the committee. As the method of appointment is left to the Member States, the committee can become a discussion group for national delegations of local or regional representatives rather than a truly regional debating chamber. The attitude of national delegations varies markedly in each Member State. The representatives of Belgium, Germany and (to a lesser extent) Spain do represent the interests of their individual regions. In countries such as Italy, by contrast, there is much talk of the position of the Italian delegation in their comments. The simplest explanation for this is that in Belgium, Germany, Spain and Austria, each region is individually represented. This is not the case elsewhere (although the Italian 'special' regions are represented). Many delegates are appointed to represent local or regional government in their Member State as a whole, not to represent the interest of their particular constituency. They do not sit as representatives of their own region. This further weakens the committee, even in its advisory role. The committee can reproduce the Council of Ministers but with local representatives.

Even if these problems can be overcome, the CoR representatives remain formally appointed by Member State governments. In most regions this does not present a problem, with the Member State merely approving lists supplied by regional or local tiers (or both). In a minority of cases, however, the centre has introduced its own political opinions into the process and appointed representatives who, although democratically elected, are the choice of the Member State government, not the regional or local tier. The committee is therefore a long way from being the 'European Senate' so desired by those regions who advocate a stronger voice for the third level.

It was expected that the reforms of 1996 would see a significant effort on the part of the regions to reform the CoR. In fact, this did not happen. Even demands to turn the committee into a truly regional body were dropped after significant local lobbying. Although the committee remains weak, the power of some of its constituent regions means that it cannot be ignored completely. The policy of these regions remains to establish a regional institution at the heart of the EU. Dr Stoiber, Minister President of Bavaria, described his view of the committee in the following terms:

> Legislative functions should be exercised by the Council and the European Parliament, supported by the Committee of the Regions. The Committee of the Regions, as the representatives of levels of government close to the individual citizen, should become a fully fledged institution, and in the longer term develop into a purely regional chamber. [CoR, 1995.]

This does not augur well for the local level and is further evidence, if any were needed, that regional power does not necessarily translate into local power. This is not to say that local authorities should not be involved in European Union affairs, but to have the need for local and regional involvement addressed in a single committee is not practical. The diverse nature of the authorities involved at present means that the majority of opinions given by the committee merely amount to saying, 'we agree with proposal x, but there should be more local and regional involvement'. Unless its opinions have substance, the rationale for the committee becomes extremely weak.

What amounts to a 'negotiating position' for the 1996 Intergovernmental Conference was announced by the committee in May 1995. This compromise achieved nearly unanimous support within the committee, with only one against and four abstentions (CoR, 1995a). By concentrating on three areas, the committee hoped to get the majority of their proposals approved in the EC Council, although their proposals were open to negotiation prior to this. The three areas upon which the regions concentrated were:

(a) defining subsidiarity;

(b) access to the European Court of Justice (ECJ);

(c) the structure of the committee itself.

The first proposal concerned defining the subsidiarity principle in Art 5(2) of the EC Treaty to explicitly include regions and local authorities. To police this, the committee demanded a right of audience before the ECJ. This would apply to cases concerning the committee's own powers (rather like the Parliament and European Central Bank at present), issues of subsidiarity, and actions for failure to act by a European institution. This could be achieved by granting the committee institutional status (the preferred option) or by amending specific Articles to allow the committee to instigate legal proceedings. The committee also called for individual regions to be given the right to appeal to the ECJ directly.

The committee further proposed the extension of its mandatory powers of consultation into several new fields including transport, agriculture, environment and research. These powers, which have regional involvement in most Member States, are logical candidates for regional involvement. The most radical proposal concerned the need for the EC Council or Commission to explain any rejection of committee opinions, although the opinions themselves would remain advisory.

With the exception of a significant increase in the committee's advisory role, none of the demands issued by the CoR were met. In fact the stronger regions appear to have lost faith in the committee, at least for the present, and have become rather disillusioned by their fellow regions. If nothing else, this clearly emphasised the committee's lack of teeth when deserted by its most powerful members (Hopkins, 1999).

8.3.3 Informal contacts

Alongside the formal recognition of regional authorities within the European Union policy process there has evolved a parallel network of informal regional influence, of the type explored above in relation to international affairs. The most obvious manifestation of this has been the spate of regional offices established in Brussels to communicate with the institutions of the Union, particularly the Commission.

Keeping tabs on these entities is not easy, but at the last count all 15 German *Länder*, 10 Spanish *autonomías*, all the French *régions* but one (Auvergne), the devolved executives of the UK and several English local authorities, amongst many others, had established a permanent representation in Brussels. In total there were 22 regional offices open by 1992, representing 32 regions, though they now number nearly 100 (Heichlinger, 1999). Many operate joint information bureaux such as the *Association du Grand Sud* (Aquitaine, Corsica, Languedoc-Roussillon, Midi-Pyrénées and Provence-Côte d'Azur) and the *Hanse-Office* (Hamburg, Lower Saxony and Schleswig-Holstein), but whatever the exact method the interest shown by regions in establishing these offices has been immense (Serignan, 1989, p 7). One of the most interesting collaborations is between Picardie and Essex, which was the first office to represent the territorial units of different Member States (Engel, 1992a, p 42). More recent examples include *Centre-Atlantique* which comprises Poitou-Charentes, Centre (both French) and Castilla y León (Spain), and the Tyrol Office (Trentino, Tyrol and Alto Adige). The latter example is particularly interesting as it represents a regional identity that crosses Member State borders.

The role of these offices is somewhat ambiguous. Unlike the permanent representatives of the Member States, regional offices enjoy no formal legal status within the Community. Negotiations and official contacts can occur only between the Commission and Member State representatives. The one exception to this rule is Belgium, where the Flemish, Walloon and Brussels regional representatives (and those of the French and German Communities) are empowered to conduct such negotiations. In practice, the majority of these offices are lobbying organisations, although they do allow regions to remain informed of European developments. This is increasingly important if regions are to influence Commission or Council decisions before they are passed.

The importance of these offices is exaggerated. One *Länder* civil servant working in such an office commented, that 'although they [the Commission] are very polite to us, we can't really do anything'. Nevertheless, even the creation of this minimal presence has not been without controversy. Both the Basque and the Catalan regions have established offices in contravention of the Spanish Government's wishes. Indeed, the Spanish government took legal action to try to prevent their establishment (Cuchillo, 1993). In Germany too the *Bund* has, until recently, refused to recognise the *Länder* offices in Brussels, leaving many of the *Länder* to establish them under private law and out of reach of any constitutional challenge. Even now, the *Bund* will only have the *Länder* observer housed in the offices of the German permanent representation under conditions which the *Länder* will not accept (he or she would have to be under the jurisdiction of the head of the German delegation).

The unease of Member States at regional European offices is puzzling, especially when one considers the practical limitations on these institutions. As Keating points out, money cannot be granted by the Commission to regions directly; all regional aid must pass through the nation-state (Keating, 1986, p 299). With this in mind, Spain's reaction seems to be verging on paranoia. Nevertheless, the number of these offices has continued to grow relentlessly. One assumes, therefore, that the limited role they perform is perceived as worth the expense.

8.4 A EUROPE OF REGIONS?

The importance of international relations to regional systems of government is undeniable. The extent of international co-operation means that domestic affairs can no longer be clearly delineated from international affairs, if this were ever truly possible. If the region is to retain domestic policy independence, the classic horizontal models of federalism, which apportion responsibility for international affairs to the central level, are no longer tenable. Within the Member States of the EU, the issue is further accentuated by the ambiguous nature of European affairs.

The steady flow of legislation emanating from Brussels has a constant and continuing influence on regional autonomy. If the classic horizontal model is applied, and European matters are classed as international, the result will be a serious diminution of regional policy autonomy. Although Community law reigns supreme over both regional and Member State actions, regions are in a far weaker position when it comes to formulating European policy. The European Union continues to be an alliance of Member States and not of their constituent parts. The highest decision making body in the EU remains the Council of Ministers, which represents national interests. The regions, unlike Member States, must implement European legislation over which they have no formal influence.

National governments therefore have the ability to decide policies at a European level in areas from which they would be barred at the domestic level. For this reason, the representation of regions within the European Union decision making process has become an issue of the utmost importance to most European regional regimes.

With the German *Länder* and the Belgian regions in the vanguard, the regional tier has begun to make inroads into the jealously guarded international and European privileges of the Member State. In Belgium, Regional and Community ministers are regular attendees of the Council of Ministers, and the Belgian position cannot be formulated without reference to the regional executives. In Germany, the *Länder* have acquired an important collective role in establishing the German position through the *Bundesrat* as well as a limited presence in the Council. Beyond these regional trailblazers, Spanish *autonomías* and now Italian *regioni* have also secured the right at least to implement European decisions themselves, though formal influence on European institutions may yet be a long way off.

So where in this structure do the devolved institutions of the UK lie? The devolution Acts make two things abundantly clear. First, the devolved units have responsibility for the implementation of European obligations, to the extent that these fall within their spheres of responsibility. Secondly, the formal responsibility for international and European affairs lies exclusively in the hands of Whitehall and Westminster. In all cases, such affairs are reserved. However, in accordance with the government's assurances on these issues, the devolved institutions have been given access to the UK's European decision making process. Relevant ministers representing the devolved institutions will also be permitted to attend the Council of Ministers as part of the UK delegation and, in exceptional cases, to lead it. However, all these measures remain based purely upon Whitehall's largesse through the medium of the Memorandum of Understanding (explored more fully in Chapter 11). Such largesse could be withdrawn.

It is notable that those regions which have been most successful in forcing their way to the European table have been those that enjoy strong constitutional rights within their domestic structures. Åland, the regions of

Belgium and the German *Länder* all negotiated with their national levels from a position of relative strength. Åland had its international status, while the regions in Belgium and Germany retain their powers of veto over changes to the constitution and their legislative authority. Such bargaining chips were crucial in ensuring that the regional tier was represented, however imperfectly, at the European tier. It is on the coat-tails of these regions that others have managed to establish their toehold on the European policy process in the CoR.

Apart from those regions that commanded constitutional weapons to force the Member State to recognise them, regional political strength and the decisions of the constitutional courts in Spain and Italy have also played a part in securing the limited European role for these regions. The devolved institutions of the UK are therefore faced with a problem. Lacking the constitutional clout of their federal counterparts, what is the long term future of their involvement in the UK's European decision making process?

This problem facing the UK's devolved institutions will only arise when their policy preferences deviate from those of the UK Government. When this occurs, the devolved executives may find that the access they have been granted is something of a poisoned chalice. The Memorandum of Understanding comes with the proviso of secrecy. If the UK Government overrules the Scottish executive, it will be faced with either breaking this secrecy (and sacrificing its access to the EU decision making process in the future) or supporting the decision and risking the wrath of its own electorate.

For the time being, then, the devolved institutions can take their place alongside the most influential members of the European third level, but unlike their regional brethren in Belgium and Germany, they do so merely at the whim of the Member State government. This serves to emphasise the point that discussion of a 'Europe of regions' is extremely premature. The presence of regions in various guises at the European level cannot hide the fact that their impact remains, in most cases, relatively limited.

Nevertheless, the emergence of an elected regional tier with significant responsibilities across the continent demands recognition at the European level. Without it, a second democratic deficit will develop, with national governments engaging in policy making at a European level against the wishes of the governments elected to handle such affairs. To do this does not require a 'Europe of regions', but rather a 'Europe with regions'. Until the institutions of the European Union change to allow the regional voices to be heard not as representatives of Member States but as the elected representatives of their regions, the European level will remain an ever-present threat to regional democracy.

CHAPTER 9

PAYING THE PIPER: FINANCING REGIONAL GOVERNMENT

The referendum on Scottish devolution held in 1997 was unusual. In fact, it was two referendums rather than one. The first question asked whether the Scottish electorate supported the creation of a Scottish Parliament, the outline of which was contained in the UK Government's White Paper (Scottish Office, 1997). The second asked whether the Scottish Parliament (assuming the answer to question one was in the affirmative) should be granted the power to raise or lower income tax rates within a 3p band. The revenue raised (or the costs incurred) by such a policy would be reflected in the budget of the Scottish Parliament.

Although in the event, both questions were answered in the affirmative, the campaign that surrounded the Scottish devolution referendum focused primarily on the second of these questions. On one level, the Scottish media and electorate are to be commended. The focus on finance recognised its importance to the successful operation of devolved institutions. Nevertheless, their focus on the tax-raising question alone drew a far too simplistic connection between regional autonomy and financial independence. In fact, as we shall see, regional powers of taxation are notable in Europe mainly by their absence. Their impact is marginal, and they have a minimal effect on regional autonomy. In the Scottish case, the campaigners might have done better to consider the fact that the Scottish budget can be controlled by the UK Government with only minimal reference to either parliament. This is a far more fundamental threat to the successful operation of devolution than the minimal powers of taxation accorded to the parliament.

The relationship between regional funding and devolution is extremely complex and often misunderstood. It is nevertheless crucial to an understanding of how devolved systems actually work. Finance is the essence of modern government and without it little can be achieved. A state may have the power to declare war, but if it has no funds to pay for an army this power is meaningless. Regional governments are no different in their need for secure and adequate finance to function successfully. The crucial difference between most regional governments and their parent states is that the ability to raise such finance is not always in the region's competence.

As with other features of regional autonomy examined in this volume, the legal aspects of regional finance cannot be examined in isolation. Political limitations have a significant impact upon a region's ability to utilise its formal autonomy in financial matters. For example, every Belgian and Spanish region enjoys the power to introduce regional surcharges upon income tax. In practice, political and social pressures make the power to alter this variety of taxation almost a dead letter. To examine regional finance purely in terms of a region's constitutional or statutory powers would give an incomplete and highly misleading picture of the issue.

Figure 9.1: Regional expenditure as a percentage of central government expenditure, including social security (not FRG), 1992

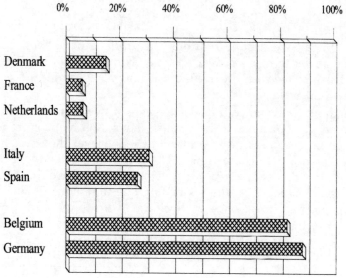

The premise upon which democratic regionalism is based requires regional institutions to have freedom of action to pursue policies independently of other levels and institutions of government. Although the percentages presented in Figure 9.1 give us an impression of the role regional governments have in the governance of their states, they tell us nothing about the extent to which this is independently decided at the regional tier. Although regions may be the institutions that spend the money, this does not necessarily mean that such expenditure is directed by the regional level itself. This requires financial autonomy as well as financial resources. To assess the extent of this autonomy we must break down the regional expenditure figures presented above according to the autonomy of the resources available to the region. For the purposes of this volume, the following broad categories have been used:

(a) independent financial resources;

(b) block funding;

(c) borrowing;

(d) specific grants and mandated expenditure.

'Block funding' describes financial resources which are allocated or set at the national level but which regions spend autonomously within their functional responsibilities. This can include tax receipts raised in an individual region when rates are set nationally. Borrowing is self-explanatory, but the simplicity of the term belies a very complex area of regional autonomy. Restrictions placed upon the region may be far beyond those which constrain the Member State, while economic factors make this resource limited even between regions. The final element is not strictly speaking a variety of autonomous finance at all. Specific grants are allocated by the centre for a specific function or policy area, while mandated expenditure (or 'unfunded mandates' as they are described in the US) is a function which the regional institutions must undertake under central policy decisions, but for which they are not financially compensated. Even in these areas, however, some regional policy preferences can be represented in the delivery of services.

The aim of this methodology is to present an estimate of regional financial autonomy in conjunction with total regional expenditure. The proportion of regional funding raised through independent means gives a picture of the spending autonomy open to the region. This gives us a much greater understanding of the impact of regional finance than raw figures concerning regional expenditure. This analysis, in conjunction with a discussion of the region's constitutional and statutory framework as given above, brings us closer to understanding the true role of regional democracy in the European Union.

9.1 INDEPENDENT REGIONAL FINANCE AND REGIONAL AUTONOMY

The link between the regions' power to raise their own finance and wider concepts of regional autonomy is not as clear as it may first appear. Few regions rely heavily on independent finance, and those that do so (in France and Denmark) play a limited policy role in the Member State. Does this then suggest that regions lack financial autonomy *per se*? There are some interesting points to be noted from the actions of the regions that would suggest that they themselves do not perceive this to be so. Although regions (in common with most governmental institutions) often claim that they are overburdened and underfunded, few actively campaign for an increase in powers of taxation. Instead, regions are more often seen lobbying for a higher level of block funding, specifically through a share in national taxes.

This suggests that regions have something to gain from avoiding over-reliance on independent finance.

Independent finance implies a degree of accountability to the electorate that is, by definition, lacking in all other methods of funding. Regions that lack such accountability are less constrained in their spending than might otherwise be the case. Put bluntly, such regions can play fast and loose with their financial resources in the absence of a taxpaying electorate to control them. The local population may in fact favour a high spending authority as long as they do not foot the bill (Jones, 1978, pp 71–72). This is sometimes termed the 'restaurant bill argument'. If a group of friends have a meal at a restaurant, the collective cost will always be higher when the bill is split equally than if individuals had paid for their meals separately (for more insights into 'Bistromathics', I recommend Douglas Adams' *The Hitchhiker's Guide to the Galaxy*).

Similar reasons have been advanced in the fiscal federalism debate for giving regions taxation powers and thus increasing financial accountability and responsibility (Jones, 1978). If regions are allocated mainstream tax raising powers, they will not only be able to pursue policies independently of the centre but will also be more accountable to the regional electorate. However, if regions were granted such authority, what effect would this have on the national internal market? In particular there is the problem (or advantage) of tax competition. If there are different tax rates in different regions, individuals or companies may choose to move to the more advantageously taxed one, or alternatively to the one where services are of a higher standard (Tiebout, 1972; Oates, 1972). Within the EU, however, the effect of regional taxation on the internal market is minimal, given the limited regional powers of taxation and the reluctance of regional governments to use them.

As Figure 9.2 makes clear, independent regional finance is noticeable mainly by its absence in the EU. Only local government regions, such as those in France and Denmark, rely upon independent finance to any significant extent. In both cases, these regions have a very limited financial role in their respective states (see Figure 9.1). Perhaps most significantly, the constitutional status of these regions is very weak. Nevertheless, these local government regions have some interesting features which need recognition. The Danish *amter* in particular are the only third level to rely substantially upon a regionally set and collected income tax. In 1992, *amter* income tax rates ranged from 8.9% (Ringkjøbing) to 10.4% (Viborg), the average being around 9.6% (Andersen, 1993, p 18). The ability of the *amter* to raise and lower taxes gives them a high degree of formal financial independence.

*Figure 9.2: Independent finance of regions as a
percentage of total regional budgets*

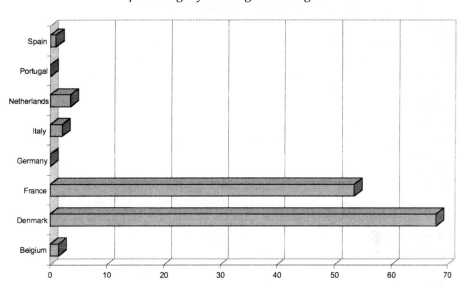

In the late 1980s, the Danish Government pursued a policy of reducing public expenditure and taxation in an effort to limit inflationary pressure on the economy. As part of this policy, agreements were reached with the *amter* to limit their tax rates (Council of Europe, 1993, p 21). On only one occasion (1987) were these restrictions formalised into law. Nevertheless, the central government was in a very strong position in its discussions with the *amter*. National legislation could always be introduced to force them to reduce or maintain their rates. The emphasis, however, remains on negotiation rather than confrontation. It appears that Danish *amter* financial independence may only be acceptable to the Member State when the ultimate power on such matter remains at the national level.

The situation of the French regions is significantly different from that seen in Denmark. French regions rely on a basket of shared taxes with varied responsibilities for tax rates depending on the tax in question. Only one type of finance is entirely the responsibility of the regional tier, a car registration fee (the *carte grise*). All other taxes levied by the regional authorities are subject to some limits set by national legislation. The rates of the taxes in this group can be altered within these limits. Depending on the specific tax, the regions can either change the rate directly or add a surcharge to the national rate. The *carte grise* is a rather arbitrary form of tax paid by the owner of a new car. It is a fixed fee, not dependent on the car's value, although some regions have related it to engine size in an attempt to develop it as a policy tool. Nevertheless, the only clearly identifiable regional tax remains an extremely blunt form of indirect and regressive taxation. As such it cannot be relied upon too heavily. Despite this, it accounted for over 12% of French regional finance in 1993 (see Figure 9.3).

Figure 9.3: French independent revenue
(Les Budgets Primitifs des Régions en 1993)

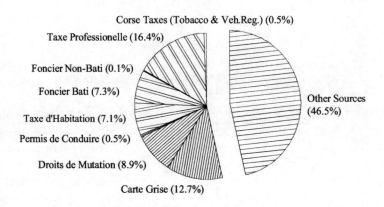

The regions of metropolitan France primarily rely on four taxes, collectively known as the *fiscalité directe*. These comprise the *foncier bati* (property tax), *foncier non bati* (land tax), *taxe professionelle* (business tax) and finally the *taxe d'habitation* (residence tax). These direct taxes are collected by the central state, but their total product is divided between the local authorities dependent on the rates set. As Gilbert points out, the *fiscalité directe* taxes, being divided between different government tiers, lack transparency (Gilbert, 1994). It is not clear to the electorate who is responsible for increases or cuts in taxation.

Each authority may set a rate within a band determined by the central government. Although the strictest limits were abolished in 1986 (curtailing regional tax revenue to a maximum per capita value), the national government has retained the right to limit regional tax rises in the name of limiting the overall tax burden (Gilbert, 1994, p 41). Variations between tax rates can nevertheless be significant. For example in 1993 the land tax varied from 2.61% of rateable value in Rhône-Alpes to 9.98% in Limousin (*Guide Statistique de la Fiscalité Directe Locale*, 1993).

A number of *impôts indirects* (indirect taxes) may also be subject to a regional surcharge (within nationally established limits) which accrues to the regional tier. Formally, the *carte grise* is also an *impôt indirect*, although in this case the national base is zero. Uniform surcharges may be added to the cost of driving licences (permis de conduire) and house sale registrations (*droits de mutations*). The latter increases are limited to 1.6% of house value, although in practice these rates are now at the maximum permitted throughout France (*Les Budgets Primitifs Des Régions en 1993*, p 29).

The limited autonomy afforded to French regions has nevertheless allowed the development of regional tax policies. There is variation between some tax rates across regions, giving at least some indication of regional policy variations, but the most important shift has perhaps been a collective one. Regional policy has seen a significant shift away from reliance on property taxes, which accounted for 61% of regional taxes in 1981, towards car and licence charges, which accounted for 65% of regional income in 1993 (Gilbert, 1994, p 43).

Outside these two examples, regional reliance on independent methods of finance is minimal, and few regional governments have the power to develop such resources significantly. Instead, they have the ability to introduce surcharges on regionally computable sources, including income taxes, and in some cases can develop new taxation in areas not already taxed by the national level. Only the Portuguese regions have no power over regional taxation whatsoever.

In practice, the power to alter income tax has remained theoretical in all but one specific case. The only successful introduction of a surcharge on income tax was achieved by the government of Euskadi (the Basque country) in 1985. This was only a temporary measure, introduced for one year, in the aftermath of severe flooding which affected the region. In 1985 Madrid attempted to introduce a regional surcharge on income tax, but the proposal proved so unpopular that it was withdrawn before implementation (Solé-Vilanova, 1990, p 339). This is an extreme example of the difficulties that surcharged taxes present to regional authorities. Spanish regions will think long and hard before attempting such a move, especially in the wake of Madrid's experiences. Political realities make the use of such tax increases very difficult. The spectre of tax competition has also been raised in Belgium, particularly in Flanders. The Flemish regional government has said that it does not wish to increase the tax burden as 'additional heavy increases could actually impair the competitive position of our companies' (Government of Flanders, undated, p 12). In practice, therefore, the prevailing culture of tax unity within Member States proves more of an obstacle than any legislative constraints.

A similar situation also exists in Spain, where again there are few areas in which the national or local levels do not already 'occupy the field'. Nevertheless, five new regional taxes have been introduced (see Table 9.1).

Table 9.1: Regional taxes in Spain

Regional tax	Autonomías
Bingo	Catalonia, Galicia, Murcia, Cantabria, Valencia, Castilla-La Mancha, Balearic islands
Water civil engineering projects	Catalonia
Petrol	Canary Islands
Hunting	Extremadura
Environment (clean-up levy)	Balearic islands

Article 105(2) of the German Basic Law states that:

> The *Länder* shall have power to legislate on local excise taxes as long and in so far as they are not identical with taxes imposed by federal legislation.

Article 106(2) then goes on to list the taxes which accrue entirely to the *Länder* (property tax, inheritance tax, motor vehicle tax, beer tax and gambling tax), as well as:

> ... such taxes on transactions as do not accrue to the Federation ... or jointly to the Federation and the *Länder* ...

These taxes would appear to be truly independent finance, under the individual authority of each *Land*. In addition, Art 106(2) should give the *Länder* an ability to introduce new taxes in areas not covered by the federation. In practice, as noted above, this general competence is of little value, as few suitable activities remain free from federal taxation. In fact, individual *Länder* do not exercise powers in the field of regional taxation.

From the beginning of the Federal Republic, taxation has been handled almost exclusively at the federal level. This occurred because the *Bund* used its concurrent power under Art 105(2) of the Basic Law to cast its legislative net over the entire catalogue of *Länder* taxes. This was done, perhaps unintentionally, under Art 123(1) of the Basic Law, which adopted the tax structure of the former Reich as a temporary measure. This gave the power to alter all tax rates to the central level (there were no *Länder* under the Reich), thus allowing them to occupy the field almost from day one (Biehl, 1989, p 377). Despite the statements of many distinguished academics to the contrary (Engel, 1993), even the beer tax is uniform throughout the Federal Republic (Federal Ministry of Finance, 1993).

The only regional legislative tax competencies relate to taxes that accrue to local government. With these exceptions, all German taxes are governed by federal law, although in a number of cases the receipts are retained by the *Länder*. This does not entirely exclude the *Länder* from raising finance, as they can increase such taxes and reduce their grants to local government. In practice, as local government is funded primarily by a direct allocation of the federal income tax receipts, this is also of limited use. The only tax differences that exist in Germany today are therefore between local governments. Even here, the *Länder* generally give local authorities the competence to vary the tax themselves. A breakdown of tax responsibilities is given in Table 9.2.

Table 9.2: Regional taxes in Germany

Länder legislative competence	Collective *Länder* involvement
Beverage tax (m)	Beer tax (l)
Church tax (c)	Betting tax (l)
Dog tax (m)	Capital yields tax (f/l)
Entertainment tax (m)	Corporation tax (f/l)
Hunting/fishing tax (m)	Fire protection tax (l)
Licensing tax (m)	Casino levy (l)
	Income tax (f/l/m)
	Inheritance tax (l)
	Motor vehicle tax (l)
	Net worth tax (l)
	Property transfer tax (l)
	Trade tax (m/f/l)
	Turnover tax (f/l)
	Wages tax (f/l/m)

Recipients of tax receipts:

m: municipalities

l: Länder

f: federation

The requirement that the *Bund* must achieve a majority in the second house for legislation concerning taxes accruing to the *Länder* (even in part) ensures continued regional involvement. Nevertheless, this influence does not enhance the financial autonomy of individual regions. Regions are only able to influence taxation when the *Länder* act as a collective entity, diluting the importance of individual *Land* opinions.

Independent regional finance, through the medium of regional taxation, is therefore not the core method of financing European regional government. In fact, those few regions which enjoy significant freedom in this area use such powers sparingly. Income tax, in particular, is rarely altered on a regional basis because of fears relating to tax competition. The only power to vary regional tax rates in the United Kingdom relates to income tax in Scotland (within a 3p band), which does not bode well for independent regional revenue raising in the UK. The most significant feature of regional taxation has been its use as a policy tool, not as a means of raising revenue. The next issue that must be faced is whether the lack of such financial independence significantly impacts upon the ability of the third level to function independently.

9.2 BLOCK FUNDING

The general tendency to focus upon independent sources of regional finance is misplaced. As shown above, few EU regions have any significant powers of taxation, and those that do have rarely exercised them. Clear evidence that this fixation continues to hold true was demonstrated by the focus of the Scottish devolution debate on taxation powers. In fact, Scotland (as well as Wales and Northern Ireland), and most other European regions with significant legislative power, rely primarily upon block funding allocated through national legislation or constitutional provisions. The term 'block funding' is used to cover a multitude of methods. Traditionally, discussions of regional finance have tended to make a distinction between grants from the national level and taxes that accrue to the region. Although this division is of some significance, to focus on it creates a misleading impression. Whether finance comes directly from taxation or indirectly through a national government grant is of limited relevance to the region concerned. Only if the rates of taxation are regionally controlled is there any real distinction. If this is not the case, tax revenues allocated to the regional tier are in fact a very specific form of non-hypothecated or 'block' grant.

Allocations of finance to the regional tier can be divided into two categories. Block funding, including the allocation of tax revenue, is allocated to the region without restriction. It may be used by the institutions of the region as the region sees fit. Specific (or hypothecated) grants are subject to limits imposed by either the national or European levels. The restrictions imposed upon the expenditure of these grants vary considerably. Expenditure may be limited to a specific project or merely to a broad area of policy (for example, transport). The situation is further confused by the existence of nationally established regional obligations and standards, which may demand the use of large amounts of specific and block finance on specific areas to ensure that the national standards are achieved. The whole question of specific grants and mandated expenditure is dealt with below (see section 9.4). For the remainder of this section, we focus on the role of non-hypothecated block funding in funding regional governments.

Block funding is by far the most important method of regional finance utilised across the European Union. It has this distinction because so few regions have the legal capacity to control taxation (or the political will to do so). Block funding is therefore the only significant non-hypothecated source of finance available in the majority of regions. Without significant levels of block funding, the constitutional or statutory autonomy granted to the region would be practically meaningless. The extent to which regions rely upon such finance is therefore a good indication as to their practical ability to utilise their formal autonomy.

The methods of block funding allocation to regions vary significantly between states, but for the purposes of this study we can divide these into four broad groups:

(a) revenue from taxes or portions of taxes ceded to the regions (ceded taxation);

(b) revenue from shares of national tax revenue (shared taxes);

(c) block grants allocated from central government revenue;

(d) equalisation payments received from other regions or central revenue.

In each case, the methods by which the allocation is established are of crucial importance. Resource allocation provisions enshrined in constitutional law, for example, give a much greater security of resources to a region than block grants allocated on a discretionary basis by the central executive.

9.2.1 Ceded taxation

'Ceded taxation' refers to taxes raised from regionally computable resources, which accrue in whole or in part to the region directly. Although most regions rely to some extent upon ceded taxation for at least a portion of their finance, a select number of regions stand out for their high reliance upon this form of funding. Chief amongst these are the German *Länder*, the Belgian regions, the Portuguese island regions and the *forales* regions of Spain. The federal regions in this list are noteworthy for their constitutional right to significant portions of regionally raised revenue.

Article 106 of the German Basic Law outlines the main aspects of *Länder* finance. This gives each *Länder* one-half of all income and business tax revenue raised within its territory. The Belgian regions are in a similar situation, with Arts 175 and 177 of the Belgian Constitution requiring special majority laws to establish the financial regimes of the Regions and Cultural Communities respectively, although German Community finances remain regulated by ordinary statute (Art 176, Belgian Constitution). The financial regimes themselves date primarily from the special finance laws of 1989.

The Belgian special majority laws have established a system whereby Regional finance comes primarily from a share of income tax, or IPP (*Impôt des Personnes Physiques*). The Regional share of IPP was around 41% in 1993, but has increased as greater functions have been devolved. 85% of this allocation is distributed according to where it is raised. The actual allocations are based upon the index-linked cost of service provision at the time that the responsibility was transferred to the regions (primarily in 1989 and 1993). Increases can also occur in tandem with changes in Belgian GDP (Walloon Budget, 1993, pp 50–51; Government of Flanders, undated).

Although constitutional protection for the ceding of particular taxes to the regional tier is found only in federal systems, some regions rely more heavily on this form of taxation than those of Belgium and Germany. The *forales* regions of northern Spain and the island regions of Portugal come into this limited category.

The *forales* system is the modern interpretation of traditional, provincial rights in the Basque speaking area of northern Spain. When these provinces were incorporated into the Castilian Crown, they retained a limited number of financial privileges that they had enjoyed under the suzerainty of Navarre. Under the Franco regime only the province of Navarre itself was given special treatment. The other provinces of Alava, Guipúzcoa and Vizcaya, which together formed the short lived Basque Autonomous Government, were punished for their loyalty to the regional government and its republican sponsors.

Today the four Basque speaking provinces have once again been granted a version of their traditional *forales* rights, which sees all taxation organised on the basis of the provinces (or the Basque 'historic territories'), although the rates remain national. These territories retain a proportion of taxes for the provision of their own services, although most is transferred to the autonomía and then to the central government for the provision of national and regional services. As Navarre is a uniprovincial autonomía, in practice this region both collects and retains its portion of the taxation.

The portion of taxation transferred to the state (the *cupo*) is regulated by a negotiated settlement between the *autonomías* and the Spanish Government. Originally, these negotiations occurred annually, but this proved impractical. Instead, these economic agreements, the *Convenio Económico* in Navarre and the *Concierto Económico* in Euskadi, are now negotiated on a five-yearly basis. There seems general agreement amongst Spanish commentators that the *forales* regions have a distinct advantage over their ordinary counterparts (Sevilla-Segura, 1987, p 289).

The other group of regions that rely primarily on ceded taxation are the Portuguese island regions of the Açores and Madeira. The statutes of both island regions grant all regionally computable tax resources (with the exclusion of VAT) to the regional governments. This accounts for around 40% of regional finances.

With the exception of these examples, ceded taxation plays a peripheral role in the financial mechanisms of other regions. Spanish ordinary regions, for example, receive the revenue from death duties, property transfer taxes, stamp duties and gambling duties, which account for only 10% of regional income. The very limited block funding enjoyed by the Italian regions is also from these sources.

Reliance upon ceded taxes (whether or not the rates are controlled by the regional level) has the advantage of ensuring that a degree of fiscal responsibility is placed upon the region. As the tax base is within its territory, it is in the interests of the region to support it. By giving regions a share of the national tax revenue, the regional government has no incentive to improve the tax base within its own territory. In effect, this is a variation of the 'restaurant bill argument' (see section 9.1 above) which applies to non-independent finance as a whole.

Along with the fiscal accountability that systems of ceded taxation bring to the regional tier are a number of pressures on both individual regions and the system as a whole. Poorer regions with a weaker tax base will be trapped in a 'catch 22' situation. Such regions will be asked to deliver the same services as richer regions from a lower revenue stream. In practice, of course, an underdeveloped or depressed region is likely to require greater expenditure on infrastructure or economic development (lacking as it does the monetary levers such as taxation, currency levels and interest rates). To address the systemic imbalance created by reliance on regional resources, methods of equalisation are used between the constituent regions. This can be achieved through either the allocation of shared taxes or the provision of grants. The first of these is examined below.

9.2.2 Shared taxation and block funding

Regional finance through ceded taxation has the advantage of ensuring a degree of fiscal responsibility at the regional tier. Although most regions are not in a position to alter these tax rates to any significant degree, they benefit from regional revenue, encouraging them to develop this source of revenue and not to spend beyond the region's means.

European systems of regional and federal government rely only partially upon such regionally based finance. Although it satisfies the principles of fiscal federalism, such funding mechanisms benefit financially stronger regions at the expense of their poorer counterparts. The principle of national solidarity is strong enough in the Member States of the European Union to demand a degree of equalisation of resources between richer and poorer regions. The principle of financial solidarity, though a consistently controversial issue in the Member States, is nevertheless an accepted part of European regional and federal systems. This is in sharp contrast to other federations, particularly those of North America.

Fiscal solidarity or equalisation can be achieved through a number of distinct methods. Shared taxation requires the pooling of revenues on a national basis and their allocation according to some form of needs-based criteria. Block grants from the central government are not related to specific tax revenues, but remain allocated on the basis of need. In practice, the distinction between these two methods of regional funding is extremely blurred. Further equalisation can be undertaken through interregional grants or tax sharing as well as the allocation of central funds for specific development projects.

Shared taxation reallocates portions of national tax revenue on the basis of criteria aimed at a fair distribution throughout the Member State. In theory such funding is distinct from central government block grants. Although it may be in the form of a grant from central government, the allocation is based upon national tax revenue, not the spending needs of the region.

The distinction is most clearly demonstrated in the federations of Germany and Belgium, which utilise shared taxation as the first part of the equalisation process. Until 1989, only 15% of the Belgian regional IPP portion (40%) was allocated by regional source, with the other 85% allocated on the basis of need. This benefited the poorer Walloon region. Since 1989, however, fiscal federalism has replaced national solidarity as the key principle of Belgian regional finance, and the situation has been slowly reversed. By the year 2000, only 15% of regional IPP was allocated on the basis of need.

Belgian Cultural Community resources, in contrast with the regions, are funded almost entirely through shared allocation of national revenues. Around 60% of national VAT resources are distributed to the Communities on a broadly per capita basis (45:55 in favour of the Flemish region), with an element of redistribution based upon the number of students in education (Engel, 1993). In effect this gives the French Community a slightly greater share than would otherwise be the case. No other equalisation is undertaken between the Communities. The German Community continues to receive a block grant from the federation, rather than a proportion of the VAT receipts (German Community, 1992). This arrangement is in the process of being reformed, and tax sharing will eventually be the basis of German Community finances.

In Germany, equalisation is achieved to some extent by the allocation of VAT revenue across the *Länder*. This mechanism allocates 35% of VAT receipts to the German regions, according to federal legislation agreed with the *Bundesrat*. Allocation must be in accordance with principles contained in Art 106 of the Basic Law. These include 'the uniformity of living standards in the Federal Republic'. At present, 75% of the regional portion of VAT is allocated on a purely per capita basis while 25% of this amount is used to ensure that at least 92% of the average tax revenue is enjoyed by each *Land*.

The use of VAT to achieve a degree of equalisation allows the formal equalisation method, the *Finanzausgleich*, to operate more smoothly (see section 9.2.3 below).

The use of tax sharing in Germany and Belgium has the advantage of securing guaranteed funding to the regions and a degree of financial equalisation between them. However, the methods of equalisation are rather crude, and based primarily upon the revenue capacity of each region, not upon its particular needs.

In Italy, the shared taxes allocated to the regional tier do incorporate a degree of needs-based criteria, although the allocation is primarily on a per capita basis. A rather crude equalisation mechanism recognises size, the road network and per capita income as relevant factors, and has the effect of giving around 60% of this finance to the southern regions. These funds take on an added significance as they are the only non-hypothecated funding which accrue to the ordinary regions.

On the face of it, shared taxation is also the key principle of the Spanish system of regional funding, although the decision to cede 30% of income tax revenue direct to the regions has significantly increased the fiscal responsibility element. The amount of taxation allocated to each *autonomía* (excluding the *forales* regions of Euskadi and Navarre) is based upon some deceptively complex formulae outlined in the LOFCA (Organic Regional Finance Act), the latest incarnation of which dates from 1988. According to this Act, the 'sharing' rate of each region (S) is defined as follows (Solé-Vilanova, 1990, p 343):

$$S = (N - PC - PF - RR) / TT$$

where:

N = funding needs of region (depending on amount of transferred responsibility as well as per capita income etc)

PC = potential revenue from ceded taxes

PF = potential revenue from fees and charges

RR = responsibility regulator (representing additional or reduced services provided by the region)

TT = total tax receipts of central government (excluding those ceded to regions and contributions to EU)

The tax share is calculated by multiplying the sharing rate (S) by the total taxation (TT), so that the amount of tax sharing (TS) is shown as:

$$TS = S \times TT$$

These mathematical statements obscure the essentially political nature of the grant process. The process is reviewed every five years, but the actual grant awarded to each region hinges on the variable N. The second equation is in a fact a repetition of the first, so:

$$TS = N - PC - PF - RR$$

The potential yields of ceded taxes, regional fees and charges are relatively easy to establish while the responsibility regulator, even if it is an area of controversy, amounts to very little. We are therefore left with N to determine the funding of each *autonomía*. This, according to the LOFCA, must take into account 'population, relative per capita income, relative costs, *needs*, level of services devolved and fiscal effort' (emphasis added). Fiscal effort is of limited relevance, as the regions have very little autonomy in the area of taxation. The other variables may all be quantified with little controversy, but individual regions and the central state do not agree on a formula for quantifying N. Although it recognises the need for equalisation in such a system, tax sharing remains a highly politicised issue, despite the mathematical sheen.

The distinction between shared taxation and block grants is thus less pronounced than is sometimes assumed. The systems of shared taxation examined above have the effect of delivering non-hypothecated funding to regional governments. In theory, they offer a more equal share of regional taxation across the Member State than would be the case if regions relied exclusively upon their own tax bases for funding. In practice, however, such methods of regional finance incorporate a significant degree of needs-based allocation, particularly in the case of Spain. The real difference between tax sharing and block grant allocation is the degree of financial security the former offers for the regional tier, and the extent to which the latter is at the mercy of central state policy.

A crude form of needs-based formula is also evident in the local government regions, although in these cases the formulae are enshrined only in ordinary statute. In Denmark, around 30% of the limited financial resources of the *amter* are gained from this source. Based upon the average per capita income tax for the region, the grant is intended to ensure a degree of equalisation between the *amter*. The French *régions*, although reliant primarily upon independent taxation for their financial resources, also receive a number of grants, most of which are hypothecated, but two of which (accounting for around 10% of French regional funding) are not.

The more important of these two, the *Dotation Générale de Décentralisation*, is intended to make up any financial shortfall between the responsibilities devolved to the regions and the general financial resources which accompany them. Index-linked to VAT, the grant accounts for only around 6% of regional income (Gilbert and Guengant, 1990, p 251). A further grant, reimbursing VAT expended on development projects, completes the block grant allocation to the French regions, although in fact this amounts to a rather regressive form of grant, favouring as it does those regions with the financial resources to indulge in such investment (Prud'Homme, 1990).

Central government grants and tax sharing to create equalisation across the nation-state are therefore the norm amongst European regional systems. The actual mechanisms for delivering such equality of financial resources vary enormously, and reflect the constant tension between the demands of fiscal responsibility and solidarity. There are regions, however, which are granted extra finance through block funding, not as part of a nationwide equalisation process, but as a reflection of the perceived requirements of these regions. It should be noted that these requirements may be as much political as economic.

The autonomous island regions of Portugal, the *Länder* of the former GDR and the devolved governments of the United Kingdom all receive finance specific to their situations and outside any wider equalisation process. In the case of the Açores and Madeira, the national government is committed to the transfer of an 'insularity cost' to the regions, which amounts to 10–15% of regional income. This was allocated on a yearly basis, and thus placed significant control in the hands of the Portuguese Government, but it is now allocated according to a fixed formula, established in statute, providing a greater degree of security to the island regions (author's interviews).

Block grants from central government do not form part of the German system of regional finance. Nevertheless, the accession of the former *Länder* of the GDR to the Federal Republic has led to their use as a method of supplementing the limited financial resources of the eastern *Länder*. Berlin always received such awards under a special financial arrangement, but after unification a special fund was established (the *Deutsche Enheit*) as a temporary measure to provide additional block funding to these regions. Although the DEM115 bn allocated to the fund in the period 1991–94 was provided by a combination of *Bund* and *Länder* resources (59% and 41% respectively), concern was expressed that it offered a significant lever to the *Bund* in its dealings with the former regions of the GDR (Engel and Van Ginderachter, 1993, p 64).

The concern surrounding the use of block grants as a means of influencing or limiting regional autonomy is especially relevant in relation to the scheme of devolution adopted in the UK. With the exception of the marginal taxation powers enjoyed by the Scottish Parliament, the devolved institutions of the UK rely entirely upon block grants distributed by the central government. These grants are set according to needs-based criteria established in 1979 and updated according to the Barnett formula which increases or decreases them in tandem with equivalent changes in expenditure in England. The extent to which such changes are passed on to the devolved institutions depends upon the extent to which a matter is devolved. This complex mechanism therefore delivers a limited, needs-based allocation of resources, but it should not be compared too closely with the German or Spanish examples.

The weakness of the UK system lies in the lack of statutory mechanisms to underpin it. The financial allocations are entirely within the gift of the UK Government as is the formula used to allocate changes to the block grants. There is no requirement that the UK Government should even consult with the devolved institutions or the UK Parliament in any changes it may undertake to the system. Should the political will of the UK and the devolved institutions vary significantly, this may prove a potentially disastrous situation for the devolved authorities. It will take a very restrained UK Government to refrain from pulling on these financial levers if and when the devolved institutions step out of line.

9.2.3 Interregional equalisation

The role of central institutions in providing equalisation can be complemented by direct interregional transfers. In Belgium this is of marginal importance, with a sum originally set at BEF468 per person being transferred between the richest region (in effect Flanders) to the poorest region (Wallonia). The sum is index-linked, and reflects the difference between the tax-based revenue and grant-based revenue for Wallonia when the system was introduced in 1989. No such interregional solidarity mechanism operates between the Communities, as the VAT allocation is designed to ensure equality.

In Germany, the interregional equalisation system or *Finanzausgleich* is fundamental to the financing of the German *Länder*. It is a source of constant friction between the individual *Länder*, and reveals both the advantages of such a system and the political difficulties inherent in operating it. The latest Act, passed in 1988, was unsuccessfully challenged in the constitutional court both by the richer *Länder*, who complained that the settlement was too generous, and by the poorer regions, who argued that it did not sufficiently recognise the duty of equality. In simple terms, the *Finanzausgleich* guarantees all *Länder* at least 95% of the average *Land* tax potential. In theory, the formula for the disbursement of these grants is based upon the needs of each *Land*, though it is actually a revenue equalisation process. The only needs-based criteria included are the costs of major port upkeep (Bremen, Bremerhaven, Hamburg and Emden) and weighting for city-states and urban areas within individual *Länder*.

The 'potential' revenue of each *Land* is calculated as the total tax revenue of the Länder divided proportionately according to the population of each *Land* (weighted at 1.35 per person for the city-states). Prior to 1986, mining, oil and gas royalties were excluded. This obviously favoured those *Länder* with mineral and oil deposits. The constitutional court finally resolved this issue in favour of those regions lacking such mineral wealth (Zimmermann, 1989, p 387). 50% of local government income is also included, calculated along similar lines but weighted according to the size of individual *Gemeinden*. This local government portion is somewhat controversial. Rich *Gemeinden* need less subsidy than their poorer counterparts and, since local government finance is controlled entirely by the *Länder*, using only 50% of local taxes in the calculation of tax potential arguably favours those *Länder* with richer local communities. (The *Bund* wish 60% to be included). This figure for each *Land* is then compared with the national average.

If the total tax potential of a *Land* exceeds 110% of the national average, the entire surplus over the 110% cutoff point is placed in the equalisation fund. 70% of any surplus from 102–110% is also included. A surplus of 102% or under is left untouched. The fund thus established is used to raise the tax potential of poorer *Länder* up to 95% of the national average. Up to 92% of the national average is guaranteed, although a higher figure can be achieved if the financial equalisation fund is sufficient. If the equalisation fund is not enough to cover bringing the poorer *Länder* up to 92% of the national average, then all taxation above the national average can be siphoned off from the richer *Länder*.

The scheme gives the poorer *Länder* guaranteed block funding in addition to their tax base. However, these grants do not show up in the national *Länder* income as they are both paid for and received by regions themselves. The controversy that constantly surrounds this scheme is evidence of the tension between fiscal responsibility and financial equality within the state. Although the central institutions may be under a constitutional (or political) requirement to deliver equality of service across the nation-state, to do so in a transparent manner can be difficult. The experience of the German system gives credence to this claim. It has been a constant source of friction between the *Länder*, and changes to the structure have, without exception, led to challenges in the constitutional court. The latest challenges came in the wake of unification (Renzsch, 1998). The decisions of the court have provided a framework within which the equalisation mechanism can develop but have not established a strict blueprint (I Iingorani, 1997).

The controversial nature of such equalisation methods is further emphasised by the fact that the *Finanzausgleich* is only the final portion of an equalisation process that begins with the allocation of VAT receipts. Without the rather opaque allocation of VAT receipts, the *Finanzausgleich* itself would prove even more difficult to operate, such would be the political pressure placed upon it.

9.2.4 Block finance: conclusions

Given the importance of block finance to the financial autonomy of the regional tier, it is perhaps wise to draw breath at this point and consider the overall picture. As one would expect, given all that has been said above, block funding in all its many forms is the single largest source of finance for most regional governments in the EU. As Figure 9.4 shows, 50–80% of regional income in most Member States comes from this source. With the exception of France and Denmark, this compares with 1–10% from independently raised sources (including borrowing). France and Denmark, in addition to the high level of independent financial resources explored above, rely primarily on non-hypothecated income for the remainder of their expenditure.

Figure 9.4: Block funding in European regions

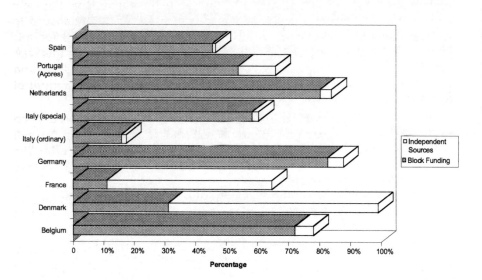

With few exceptions, European regions are spending rather than revenue raising authorities. Their financial autonomy comes from the ability to spend resources, not to generate them. The autonomous financial resources are provided by ceded taxation in some cases, but by far the majority rely upon shared taxation or block grants. The regional reliance on block funding in the regional and federal states of the EU represents a triumph for the arguments of solidarity over those of fiscal federalism. The need to equalise resources within the Member State is deemed more important than the need to ensure regional accountability for resources. Nevertheless, the transfer of a greater proportion of taxes raised in the regions to the Belgian regional tier and its Spanish counterpart is evidence of a shift away from such principles of solidarity and towards a greater emphasis on fiscal responsibility. This trend has been driven by the richer regions. In Spain, it was the Catalans, using their political strength in the *Cortes* to good effect, who influenced the change in Spanish regional finance to include greater reliance on regionally raised taxation rather than nationally allocated funds. Regions with weaker tax bases, both in Spain and elsewhere, are unlikely to find such a trend to their liking. The tensions between regional fiscal responsibility and equality are unlikely to go away.

9.3 BORROWING

Borrowing is a potentially important source of independent revenue, and is particularly important for long term capital investment projects in which the regional authority wishes to invest. Although regions may have the legal freedom to utilise such revenue streams, it would be patently absurd to suggest that a region which relied on deficit funding for 50% of its receipts was more independent than one which only accounted for 10% in this way. For this reason, the following section concentrates more on the legal and practical restrictions for each regional system and less on the amount of borrowing undertaken by the regions.

Broadly speaking, we can divide the restrictions that are placed upon regions' ability to utilise the financial markets into three groups. A small group of regions may undertake such activities freely, or under the supervision of technical institutions. A second group may undertake borrowing, but only within parameters set down by the national government. A third group of regions has no authority to engage in borrowing whatsoever unless specifically authorised by the central authorities.

Once again, the federal regions stand out as having significant autonomy to engage in such actions. The Belgian federal government has no power to limit the borrowing of the regional authorities, but limits on regional borrowing do exist through the Belgian *Conseil Supérieur des Finances* (author's interviews). The 'Financing Needs of Public Authorities' section of this council has the power to limit regional borrowing if the actions of the regional authority could cause harm to the economic and monetary union of Belgium.

Such a decision to limit borrowing can be reached after a referral from the Minister of Finance or through the council itself, acting on its own initiative. In either case, the national Minister of Finance, acting by royal decree, may restrict regional borrowing for a maximum of two years after consulting the cabinet. The members of the Public Authorities section itself are appointed under strict rules that ensure a balance between the parties concerned. Apart from the federal Minister of Finance, who sits as chairman, the members are appointed by the Bank of Belgium and the various regional, Community and federal governments (see Table 9.3). A further member is appointed at the discretion of the Crown. None of the appointees may be members of a legislative chamber, whether regional or national.

Table 9.3: Composition of Conseil Supérieur des Finances (Public Authorities section)

Method of appointment	Number of places
Representative of Ministry of Finance	1
Appointees of the National Bank of Belgium	3
Appointees of the Communities and regions	6

Figure 9.5: Proportion of regional revenue raised through borrowing (Belgian Ministry of Finance, Note de Conjoncture, 1994)

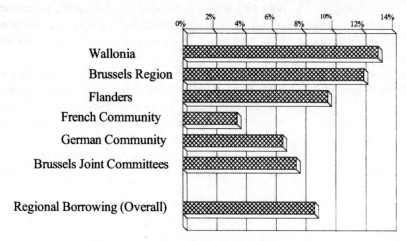

Although the existence of the Public Authorities section means that the regions may have their borrowing restricted, in practice the effect has been minimal. In fact, as can be seen from Figure 9.5, the Regions and Communities have continued to follow the traditions of high deficit spending to which Belgium has become accustomed. The regional section of the *Conseil Supérieur des Finances* has been far from inactive, however. It was this body that developed the convergence plan which was adopted as a result of the Maastricht Treaty and which allowed Belgium to join the European single currency. The findings of the Council, although lacking legislative force, have always been accepted by the authorities concerned (Demeester-De Meyer, 1993, p 13).

The Flemish regional government has established an independent institution (SERV) to monitor its public debt. This advisory body, which comprises the two Flemish employers' organisations and the two major trade unions, is used to establish overall debt restrictions and investment potential in the region. Its advice is not mandatory but has in general been followed by the regional government. In practice, the economic reality reflected by the Flemish SERV system limits regional borrowing more than any constitutional or legislative restrictions.

The reticence on the part of the regional tier in Belgium to indulge in deficit spending is to some extent a result of the debt they inherited from the Belgian unitary state. Unique amongst the regionalised and federal states of the EU, the Belgian regions and Communities have gradually taken on board their portion of the national debt. This was achieved by provisions which required the regional units to undertake significant deficit spending. Until the year 2000 the regional tier was obliged to finance all investment expenditure and 14.3% of operating costs by loans (Government of Flanders, p 10). The federal level, at the same time, was able to reduce its debt responsibilities.

This can be contrasted sharply with the situation in Spain. During the transformation from a unitary to a regional state, Spain did not transfer a portion of the national debt to the autonomías. This created a situation which allowed the *autonomías* to indulge in borrowing with little formal restriction.

The ability of the Spanish central state to limit the borrowing of the regions is rooted in Art 157 of the Spanish Constitution. Section 1(a) gives 'the yield from credit operations' as a valid method of regional finance, while Art 157(2) requires any regulation of these resources to be achieved through an organic law. In some regions, the statute of autonomy confirmed the region's freedom in this field while emphasising the co-operation required in creating any national regulation. Article 45 of the Euskadi statute is provided here as an example of such a provision:

1   The Self-Governing Community of the Basque Country may issue public debt to finance investment expenditure.

2   The size and characteristics of issues shall be established in accordance with the general planning of credit policy, and in co-ordination with the state.

Figure 9.6: Regional borrowing in Spain as a proportion of revenue (Informe Sobre la Financiación de las Comunidades Autonomías en 1986–92)

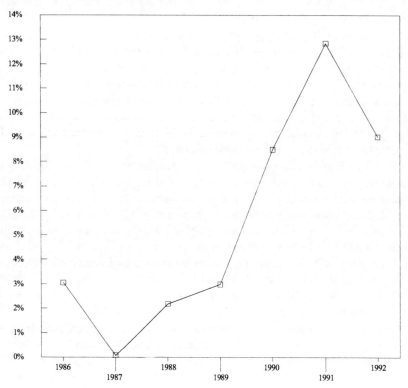

The constitutional restrictions meant that the Spanish Government was unable to alter Ley 38/1988, which regulated regional borrowing. Although this legislation imposed restrictions on the *autonomías*, the practical impact was minimal. Under the legislation, regional borrowing is restricted to capital investment projects while total debt servicing costs cannot exceed 25% of the total regional receipts for the previous year (OECD, 1993, p 71). As the *autonomías* inherited no debt, this allowed them to borrow substantial sums before the 25% limit was reached. Furthermore, the total receipts used for the purpose of assessing this limit included the portion of regional funding which is passed on to the local authorities automatically. The region's financial resources were thus artificially boosted for the purposes of this legislation (OECD, 1993, p 74).

*Figure 9.7: Net regional borrowing in Spain in 1992 (*Informe Sobre la Financiación de las Comunidades Autonomías en 1993)

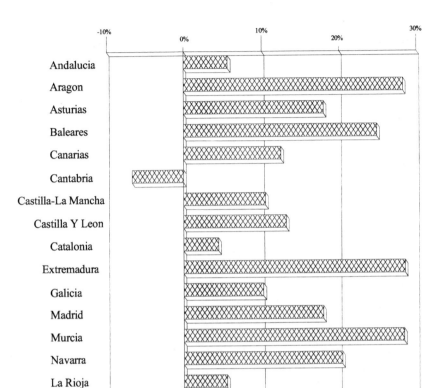

The fact that the regions could spend their loans on capital projects of their own choosing meant that debt was a source of independent finance with fewer political difficulties than raising taxes. The net result of this situation is clear from Figure 9.6. In the years immediately following the granting of autonomy, regional debt increased at a staggering rate, although there were significant regional variations, as shown in Figure 9.7. Cantabria in particular pursued a policy of prestige investment which came at a high price. By 1992, it was persuaded to start paying back its debt, which explains its negative borrowing figure for the 1992 budget.

The Maastricht Treaty, and the resulting need to limit national deficits under the convergence criteria, led to a number of agreements between individual *autonomías* and the central government. Under these, the *autonomías* agreed to reduce their debts by up to 80%, in the case of

Cantabria. The national government in return agreed to devolve further functions and reform the system of regional finance.

Consensus was the key to the Spanish debt restructuring programme. The Council of Fiscal and Financial Policy now meets regularly where previously it had met only once. This institution, comprising the Spanish national and regional Ministers of Finance, scrutinises data produced by regions in relation to their debt management. In return, the national government must present any proposals to alter the rules surrounding regional ceded taxes, including estimates of their effects on regional finances. In the long term it was in the interest of all parties to reach agreement and avoid an internal conflict which could damage Spain's status in the EU.

The German *Länder*, established at the birth of the Federal Republic, were not faced with the debt management problems that faced Spain and Belgium. The *Länder*, like their Belgian federal cousins, are restricted only by the provisions of the Basic Law, as is the *Bund*. Primarily this restricts borrowing to no more than that of capital expenditure (Art 115(1), Basic Law). In practice, creative accounting on the part of both the *Bund* and the *Länder* has limited even this restriction.

The Portuguese autonomous regions also enjoy limited freedom to take out loans on both the domestic and international markets. As in the examples quoted above, the only restriction placed on the regional government is that it may only be used to finance investment. In the Açores this is enshrined in the Statute of Autonomy:

> The region can negotiate internal and external debts, of medium or long term, exclusively for the financing of investment projects. [Art 101, Açores Statute of Autonomy.]

Article 102 of the Açores statute adds an additional requirement that the regional governments gain leave from the national parliament to borrow outside Portugal. Borrowing on the international markets is therefore open to veto by the national authorities. The Portuguese example is noteworthy as the regions may borrow from the Bank of Portugal without interest. Up to the equivalent of 10% of the previous two years' receipts may be borrowed in this manner (Art 101(1), Açores Statute of Autonomy). Investment through borrowing is particularly high in the Açores, accounting for 12% of total expenditure in 1994. Nevertheless, if the national government wished to restrict such actions, a financial incentive would be needed to tempt the regions to comply.

Apart from those regions which are (or were) free to borrow money on the financial markets, a second group operates under restrictions imposed by the state. The restriction on overseas borrowing found in the Portuguese regions is repeated across many other regionalised systems. Italian regions enjoy a surprising freedom to engage in borrowing for capital expenditure domestically. A limited national Deposits and Loans fund offers reduced rates to regional (and local) authorities, but regions may use the commercial sector at normal market rates (Council of Europe, 1993).

Figure 9.8: Regional deficits in Italy 1987–91 (ISTAAT)

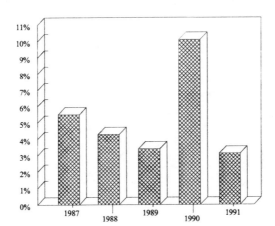

In theory, the Italian regions may also borrow on the foreign markets, with the consent of the national government, but in practice regions do not use this form of finance (Council of Europe, 1992). Borrowing accounts for surprisingly little expenditure in Italy, but this is misleading (see Figure 9.8). The Italian practice of underfunding branches of the state and forcing debt finance means that the true extent of regional deficit is difficult to gauge.

Figure 9.9: French regional borrowing as a proportion of expenditure in 1993
(Les Budgets Primitifs des Régions en 1993)

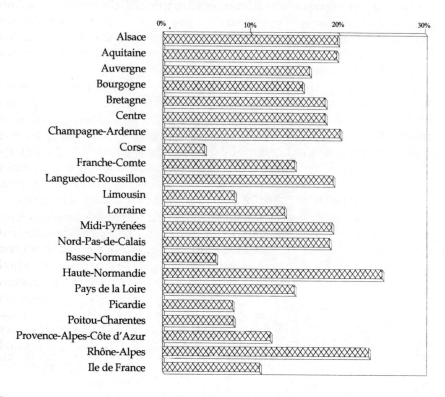

The limits imposed by the French regional 'economic constitution' are relatively lax (Council of Europe, 1992, p 10). The golden rule applies here, as elsewhere, with loans being permitted for capital investments and not running costs (Council of Europe, 1992, p 32). On foreign markets the *régions* may borrow freely under broadly the same conditions imposed on all foreign exchange dealings (Council of Europe, 1992, p 19).

In 1993, over 15% of French regional receipts came from credit operations. Given that one of the regions' remits is to co-ordinate and undertake capital investment, the high level of this figure is understandable. The figure is in itself slightly misleading, however, as the amount of credit financing undertaken varies considerably between individual regions. Figure 9.9 gives a breakdown of the loans taken out by regions in 1993 as a percentage of their total receipts. Despite the homogeneity of politics at the regional level (most regions were under right or centre right control at the time), the policies of the governments vary significantly, particularly in relation to borrowing (Mazey, 1994, p 73).

The final group of regions, in which borrowing is proscribed as a method of regional funding, includes the Danish *amter*. Only when the Ministry of the Interior recognises the existence of 'exceptional' circumstances is this restriction lifted. The *amter* consider this an unreasonable restraint, forcing them to go to the national authorities for any major capital expenditure (for example school building). Deficit finance thus plays virtually no role in the funding of the *amter* (under 1%).

Until recently, this issue was irrelevant. The *amter* had built up significant reserves from their financial surpluses. This excess liquidity became a political issue in the 1980s. These surpluses were eyed with jealousy by the national authorities, which finally insisted that they were to be used to cover general regional expenditure (Bogason, 1987, p 58). By selling the family silver, however, the *amter* were forced to rely subsequently on centrally approved borrowing for major projects which, in the past, would have been at least partially funded from the accumulated reserves.

The discussion above has revealed a situation where most regions have only the 'golden rule' (that borrowing should not exceed investment expenditure) to restrict their domestic borrowing. However, this restriction has more impact on regional governments than on their national counterparts. In a time of recession, current expenditure is likely to increase. In most cases financing such regional expenditure cannot come from tax increases or borrowing. Instead the capital budget must be cut, which must further restrict borrowing. This makes investment and reflation policies very difficult to pursue, and may create a dynamic whereby regional governments are forced to adopt a *laissez faire* approach whatever their political allegiance.

Despite these difficulties, borrowing has become a tempting source of finance for the third level. Figure 9.10 gives a comparison of regional borrowing in selected Member States of the EU. This diagram presents a relatively uniform picture across European regions, with around 5–15% of their expenditure being funded by recourse to borrowing. Regions therefore account for a significant proportion of the national debt in many countries, and thus in Europe as a whole. This has important repercussions for European monetary union, as Member State governments must ensure that their regional governments comply with the deficit restrictions that come as part of the package.

The continued use of borrowing by the regional tier is explained by work undertaken by the OECD in relation to Spain (OECD, 1993). In contrast to the legal and political restrictions which limit the expansion of regional taxation, regions have few curbs on their ability to borrow, at least domestically. Regions may therefore logically turn to borrowing rather than taxation for extra finance.

Figure 9.10: Regional borrowing as a percentage of overall regional budgets in 1992

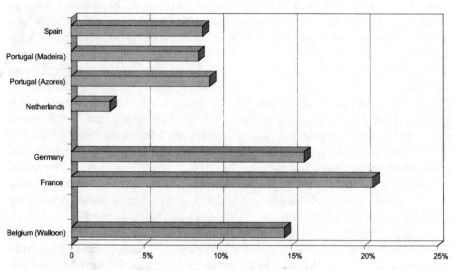

Percentage of Loans in Budget

The markets have been quite happy to lend to the regions. Although regions are a fairly new phenomenon, they represent a relatively safe investment. Some, such as those in Spain, were born without debt. This means they have the ability to borrow extensively before reaching what might be described as saturation point. Starting from zero, the Spanish *autonomías* have been able to continue accumulating debt at a high level in comparison with their revenues. Significantly, this also gave the regions a bargaining counter in their negotiations with the centre. With the Spanish Government increasingly worried about deficit spending the *autonomías* agreed to voluntary deficit controls only in exchange for changes in block funding mechanisms. For regional borrowing to be curtailed, concessions are required on the part of Member States, and additional financial autonomy and responsibility must be granted to the regional tier. This is not necessarily something that all regions will relish.

9.4 SPECIFIC FUNDING

Specific or hypothecated funding describes finance allocated to the regions with conditions attached. At one extreme there are reimbursements for payments given by the regional tier on behalf of the national level. In these cases the region acts as a conduit through which national policies are implemented. These arrangements offer no autonomy to the administering authority as the region merely pays the amount deemed appropriate by national legislation and claims this from the central government. For this reason, they are often excluded from regional accounts. This type of funding is particularly prominent in Germany, where the *Länder* administer all the field services of the Federal Republic with a few exceptions (for example, the Post Office and railways). The *Land* also acts as the agent of the *Bund* where expenditure by the federation in the undertaking (though a *Länder* competence) is over 50%. In the latter case, the *Bund* must obtain approval for such expenditure and its regulation from the *Bundesrat*. Although it passes through *Länder* officers, the social security budget is classified separately in the national accounts (distinct from both levels of the federation). The Portuguese regions also administer significant amounts of national expenditure. These *contas de ordem* account for just over 20% of total Açorian regional revenue (Açores Regional Statistics Service). Although they are included in the regional accounts, unlike the examples listed above, they are classified separately.

Sectoral funds allocated to a specific policy area can offer a degree of flexibility to the region concerned. Examples of this type of funding include the *Dotation Régionale d'Equipement Scolaire* (DRES) in France, and the majority of Italian regional funding. In France these sectoral grants account for a small but significant proportion of regional expenditure (11% in 1992). The DRES is allocated to expenditure on educational infrastructure, but within this remit the région is free to allocate finance according to its own policy priorities. Such funds may be a poisoned chalice, requiring difficult decisions in their allocation. A second sectoral grant is allocated to the regions for vocational education expenditure.

Italian special regions, although in a much stronger position (39% of income is hypothecated), still have restrictions imposed upon them. Unlike their ordinary counterparts, however, the funds may be spent independently within the areas allocated (if autonomy over these areas has been granted under the regional statutes).

With these exceptions, sectoral funds tend to play a limited and generally decreasing role in the financing of regional government. Spain is something of an exception, with around 20% of total regional funding allocated to health and social security matters. This applies only to those *autonomías* which have acquired some competence in this area.

A number of other specific funding resources and obligations influence a region's ability to act within its legal framework. Most important amongst these is the provision of grants as a form of financial equalisation or solidarity mechanism. These 'grants-in-aid' are a common feature of the American federal system. By giving offers of increased financial resources in return for the implementation of a central policy objective, the national authorities hold significant influence over regional policy choices. By such means, the priorities of the region are determined by the national and not the regional level. In other examples, grants-in-aid can only be provided if the regions invest in projects deemed important at the national level.

The classic example of the latter form of specific grants is formalised in the French system of *contrats du plan*. Within this system, national finance is provided to specific projects on the condition that the regional tier finances a portion of the total project. The *contrats du plan* themselves are agreements between regional governments and the national tier to fund projects within the national and regional plans over a specific period of time (usually five years). These funds, though additional to the regional budget, tempt regions to spend a portion of their funds to gain extra expenditure in their region. Once again, the projects will be designed to further regional development but the policy for such development is being influenced, at least in part, by the national level.

Much debate has surrounded the effect of the *contrats du plan* on regional funding. Although the national government may significantly influence the regions through these mechanisms, the extent to which this actually occurs is unclear (Mazey, 1993, p 74). Some authors have argued that it is the regions themselves influencing national expenditure in this area, rather than vice versa (Douence, 1994, p 19).

Although the French *contrats du plan* system has a redistributive effect, it is not an explicitly redistributive mechanism. In contrast, the Spanish regional solidarity system is notable for the significant part played by grants-in-aid distribution, primarily through the Inter-regional Compensation Fund, or FCI. This fund originally invested in projects within disadvantaged regions, though in practice, until 1990, it benefited those regions with the capacity to invest, favouring the wealthier *autonomías*. It is now focused on specific regions defined by national statute each year.

In Germany, the tendency of the *Bund* to use discretionary grants to encourage *Länder* expenditure on federal priorities was identified by Bulmer (Bulmer, 1990). Through reference to the Basic Law's principle of uniform (high) living standards, the *Bund* has been able to influence *Länder* policy by placing restrictions on such grant programmes. These are restricted by Art 104(a) of the Basic Law, which outlines the only mechanisms by which the *Bund* may give specific financial assistance to individual *Länder*. Specific funding is allowed under s 4 of this Article, which allows *Bund* grants to aid 'particularly important investments' by either regional or communal government and to offset economic imbalance within the federation. In all cases, the regulations surrounding such grants must be approved by the *Bundesrat*. The Basic Law ensures that these grants cannot be as used as an explicit political tool, but the criteria set for admissible investment projects can encourage the spending of *Länder* funds on federal priorities.

Such methods have certainly had some effect on *Länder* expenditure, but some argument remains as to their influence. *Länder* reliance on specific grants is peripheral, and has remained steady in cash terms while decreasing slightly in percentage terms. In addition, Klatt has noted that the recession of the late 1980s actually led to a decrease in *Bund* grants and a greater emphasis on the block equalisation scheme (Klatt, 1993). When the grants were reduced, those regions that had previously utilised them clearly suffered.

The final aspect of specific finance to be mentioned is mandated expenditure. This refers to expenditure which the region must undertake, in line with national policy, but for which the regional tier receives no funding. Such unfunded duties limit the policy choices of regions, but the extent to which this is the case is extremely difficult to determine. Nevertheless, it is important to realise that these obligations can have a significant impact on regional autonomy.

9.5 FINANCING DEVOLUTION

The devolved institutions of the UK are funded through a block grant established by formula, not unlike that which applies in Spain. Nevertheless, the UK's system of funding the regional tier is notable for a number of reasons. The calculation of the Scottish, Welsh and Northern Irish block grants is undertaken through the use of the Barnett formula. This formula enjoys no statutory status, and instead operates within the confines of the UK budget process. Introduced in 1978 and used for the funding of the Scottish and Welsh Offices prior to devolution, it increases or reduces funds allocated to the devolved institutions on the basis of equivalent expenditure in England, on a per capita basis. The allocations remain controversial as they favour the peripheral nations over England. Despite popular perception, it is not the formula itself that causes the imbalance but the needs-based expenditure allocations, established in 1978.

Unlike the regional governments of Spain or Belgium, the devolved institutions cannot offset their lack of independent financial resources by the use of borrowing. This remains under the control of the Secretary of State. He or she must give approval for any such deficit on the part of the devolved authorities. Coupled with the lack of independent financial resources, the reliance upon an executive controlled block grant formula appears precarious. It will always lie within the power of Whitehall to reduce allocations without reference to the devolved institutions. Given that the existing formula is itself controversial, in times of conflict or financial hardship the funds of the Scottish, Welsh and Northern Irish blocks may prove very tempting. The block funding of the devolved institutions appears to be only as secure as the UK Government wishes it to be. It will take a truly 'iron chancellor' to resist the temptation to pull the financial levers if the devolved institutions start acting out of turn.

CHAPTER 10

WHAT HAVE THE REGIONS DONE FOR US? FUNCTIONAL AUTONOMY AT THE REGIONAL TIER

Establishing which functions are performed by the various regional tiers of government in the European Union would appear to be a simple task. This appears to have been the belief of some analysts who have produced lists of powers accruing to different regions, in an attempt to give a definitive answer (see for example DETR, 2000). Unfortunately, mere lists of regional responsibilities give us a very misleading picture. Although third level responsibilities may be similar across the EU, the extent to which regions exercise authority within these areas is very different. Aside from the constitutional variations between regions, financial and political limitations can also restrain regional autonomy in the areas assigned to them. Although two regional governments may exercise responsibility over environmental protection, there is a world of difference between the region that can introduce legislation on the issue and one that can only implement national policy.

The task of defining the extent of regional autonomy in particular areas of responsibility is made more difficult by the confusing and conflicting terminology used across regional and federal systems. Similar terms are often used to describe very different functional responsibilities. For example the 'concurrent powers' listed in Art 74 of the German Basic Law are, in practice, federal responsibilities as soon as the federal level occupies the field. By contrast, the term 'concurrent powers' in Spain refers to those that are shared between the tiers of government. This confusion can even occur within Member States. In the UK, the term 'reserved powers' is used in the Scotland Act to describe powers retained by Westminster (s 29, Scotland Act 1998). In the case of Northern Ireland the term refers to powers which are retained by Westminster, but may be transferred at a later date (ss 4 and 6, Northern Ireland Act 1998). These difficulties must all be borne in mind as we attempt to assess the responsibilities of the third level in the European Union.

10.1 COMMON REGIONAL POLICY AREAS

There are noticeable similarities in the functional role of regions across the EU. Although all regions do not operate in the same capacity within these policy areas, seven major areas of policy have significant regional involvement. These are health, education, culture, economic development, planning, transport and police (see Table 10.1).

Table 10.1: Regional functional competencies in the EU

	Health	Culture	Education	Economic planning	Spatial planning	Transport	Police
Austria	x	x	x	x	x	p	x
Belgium	x	x	x	x	x	p	
Denmark	x	x	x		x	p	
Finland			x	x			
France			x	x	x	p	
Germany	x	x	x	x	x	p	x
Italy (ordinary)	x	x		x	x	x	
Italy (special)	x	x	x	x	x	x	x(s)
Netherlands					x	p	
Portugal	x	x	x	x	x	x	
Spain	x	x	x(s)	x	x	x	x(s)
Sweden	x	x	x	x		x	
UK (Scotland)	x	x	x	x	x	x	x
UK (Wales)	x	x	x	x	x	x	
UK (Northern Ireland)	x	x	x	x	x	x	

x: Regional involvement

p: Regional involvement in part of policy area

x(s): Regional involvement (some regions only)

Although slightly misleading (in some countries only a few regions hold the powers mentioned), Table 10.1 gives an impression of the regional input in these policy areas. This provides evidence of an emerging division of authority between national and regional levels. The areas in which regions can exert most formal autonomy are health, education and spatial planning. Some divisions between regions cut across national borders. None of the French, Dutch, Italian 'ordinary' or Spanish Art 143 regions exercise authority in any area to the complete exclusion of the state. On the other hand, the remaining regions represent the significant policy making level in health (with the exception of Germany) and education (with the exception of the Italian 'special' regions). Is this evidence of a 'fast track' group of regions in the EU?

It is clear that within several policy areas, it is no longer correct to describe policies in national terms alone. This obviously has important repercussions for the understanding of policy development within these Member States, but it also has a major bearing on the development of the European Union itself. If regions are undertaking major policy initiatives in areas in which the EU has a legislative role, there are issues of democratic accountability to consider. The 'open flank' of the eastern *Länder* and the Italian regions' difficulties in this area (see Chapter 5) expose how national governments may use the EU to intervene in areas over which they have no mandate. To allow national representatives at the EU to develop policies which in their own countries are largely undertaken by another tier of government undermines representative democracy, and creates a second democratic deficit within the EU. In administrative terms, this is a recipe for disaster, as the officials and politicians with most experience in these areas will be excluded from the discussions. In democratic terms, it denies the 'affirmative' portion of democratic accountability (Harden, 1996).

This brief survey also exposes the fragmentary nature of regional competencies. Control over individual policies tends to be held by several tiers of authority. This limits the policy options open to any particular tier. In transport, for example, regional decisions can rarely be taken beyond a single area of transport policy without entering into co-operation with another tier. This, by definition, means that the region ceases to act autonomously but rather in collaboration. In France, the transport choices open to the regions concern railways (and to a limited extent, buses) alone. Thus the only options open to the regional tier are to spend money on railways or not to spend money on railways. They cannot develop a regional transport policy by transferring money from one sector to another (for example, from railways to roads or vice versa). Such wider strategic plans must be approved by another tier, invariably the central state.

The effect of this fragmentation is that if a region (or indeed any local authority) is given responsibility for a particular mode of transport, they will invariably promote it. For instance, the French regions are unlikely to advocate road expenditure programmes at the expense of the rail network when the repercussions would mean less money for the regions to spend on rail and more for the central government to spend on roads. Thus, if a region wished to improve infrastructure or commuter services and only had authority over road transport, the net result would be a road building programme. An example of how this can be avoided is found in Denmark. The *amter*, although responsible for the majority of road building, halted their programme in favour of cycle provision. The fragmentation of transport, or any other policy, entails the inherent danger of creating a dynamic in favour of one policy option over another, simply because one option is within regional (or local) competence, while another is beyond it. Evidence of this is widespread in the UK. Sheffield's tram system would almost certainly never have happened if local development of bus services had been a policy option available to the local council.

This brief description of regional policy responsibilities, as already mentioned, does not describe the extent to which regional institutions can undertake autonomous policy in these areas. The formal authority of regions varies markedly. It is therefore necessary to examine the varieties of formal responsibility exercised by individual regional institutions to get a more accurate picture of the potential for regional policy diversity in the EU.

10.2 LEGISLATIVE AUTONOMY V ADMINISTRATIVE AUTONOMY

The most obvious constitutional distinction to be drawn between regional governments is between those regions that possess the ability to make primary legislation and those that do not (see Table 10.2). The ability to enact legislation that is supreme within the national territory is the essence of the sovereign nation-state. It therefore follows that those regions that possess such authority within their territories are equally powerful. In practice, as the following discussion shows, the distinction between legislative authority and administrative authority can be less clear at the regional tier than at the national.

The list of regions that can enact legislation in their own right, and without reference to national (primary) legislation, is a short one. Formally it includes only the federations, the Italian special regions, the Åland islands, the Spanish *autonomías* and the Portuguese island regions. In practice, however, the Scottish Parliament and the Northern Irish Assembly can be added to this list. Although the legislative powers of these devolved institutions are formally limited by the devolution legislation (ordinary legislation of the Westminster Parliament), in practice such legislation will have the effect of primary legislation (Burrows, 2000). An additional group of regions has the power to develop secondary legislation within frameworks established by ordinary laws of the national government (Wales and the Italian ordinary regions). One must be careful with both these distinctions, however, as the formal ability of regions to make statutes does not in itself tell us much about their autonomy.

Table 10.2: Legislative regions

Regions with primary legislative powers	Regions with secondary legislative powers
Åland islands	Italy (ordinary regions)
Austria	Wales (UK)
Belgium	
Germany	
Italy (special regions)	
Northern Ireland (UK)	
Scotland (UK)	
Portuguese island regions	
Spain	

The formal existence of a legislative competence should not be taken at face value. Both Austria and Germany, for example, despite having the authority to enact legislation, have very limited fields in which to exercise their competence. The constitution grants the vast majority of legislative authority to the federal level, with few areas of legislation remaining at the regional tier. The formal legislative authority ascribed to the Portuguese islands under Art 227(1) of the Portuguese Constitution also hides a more complex reality. In practice, the Portuguese Constitutional Court has consistently applied Art 6(1) of the Portuguese Constitution, which describes the Portuguese state as 'unitary', to deny regional legislative autonomy (author's interviews). A similar situation is observed in Italy, where the court's interpretation of the organic statutes of the special regions led to their primary legislative powers requiring further approval by national legislation. In practice this converted their primary legislative powers into secondary legislative powers. In many cases, the special regions are still waiting for such transfers.

In addition to these formal limits, a number of informal factors can reduce the effectiveness of regional legislation. As was explored in Chapter 9, the Italian regions (particularly the ordinary regions) suffer from a lack of financial independence that leaves them vulnerable to influence and control by the central state. The ability to enact regional legislation does not negate this weakness. The effect of these various constraints is to diminish the distinction between regional legislative competence and administrative competencies. The legislation of a Member State is limited only by constitutional restrictions, and by limits imposed by the European Union. Regional legislation, by contrast, is often restricted by moveable limitations, in the form of framework laws or other national legislation. This makes them subject to more than the principles laid down in the constitution. Much regional legislation therefore operates within a quasi-administrative framework unheard of at the national level. A region that lacks such legislative authority but enjoys financial autonomy in the exercise of its administrative responsibilities may actually be in a better position to develop distinct policies than its legislative cousin.

Possessing only executive and administrative powers, non-legislative regions rely entirely on the independent management of resources to develop distinct regional policies. This does not deny them the ability to exercise significant autonomy. Although the French regions have no formal legislative power, they still have a significant policy role in the French state. The *région* may lack the ability to make *loi* or *décret*, but this is of less relevance than its financial autonomy.

This is not to suggest that legislation is unimportant, but legislative competence is merely one facet of a region's ability to make individual policy choices for its territory. Such policy autonomy can include the choices open to regions under executive or 'dominium' powers (Daintith, 1989). Daintith describes the phenomenon whereby governments utilise their position in private law to undertake policy, thus avoiding the formalities of legislative provision. Without legislative competence, the region's independence rests on the ability to exercise dominium power and the breadth of 'administrative' autonomy it enjoys. In both cases, financial autonomy is crucial.

In the world of the third level, the distinction between regions that have legislative powers and those that lack them is of limited relevance. What matters is whether regions have policy independence or not.

10.3 GENERAL COMPETENCIES AND SUBSIDIARITY CLAUSES

The methods by which competencies are assigned to the regional tier have a significant impact upon its functional autonomy. Powers can be positively granted to the regional authorities, either by specific constitutional provision or legislative enactment. Alternatively, they can be allocated negatively to the regional tier by reference to a general competence.

A legislative general competence describes the right of a region to enact legislation in any area unless specifically denied it. The specific method of restriction can be the national constitution itself, the regional statute, or national legislation enacted on the basis of these documents (see Table 10.3). General competence is not a form of authority specific only to regional governments. The concept of national sovereignty is the ultimate example of the principle. Theoretically, national governments can make any law within the limits of their constitution, although such sovereignty is increasingly limited by international (and sub-national) obligations. Although additional restrictions do not apply to all regions, regional general competencies are usually much more restrictive than those enjoyed by 'sovereign' states.

Table 10.3: Legislative general competencies in the regions of the EU

Constitutional general competence	Non-constitutional general competence	No general competence
Germany	Scotland	Belgium
Portuguese island regions	Northern Ireland	Italy
		Spain
		Wales

A constitutionally guaranteed general competence is sometimes referred to as a 'subsidiarity clause'. This grants all authority to the lower level of government (the region) unless specifically stated otherwise. Importantly, it gives regions the flexibility to adapt their legislative competencies to changing circumstances without relying on the positive actions of the central state. Germany remains the only EU Member State where such a principle is clearly incorporated into the constitutional text (Arts 30 and 70, Basic Law). This explicitly grants all areas not otherwise assigned in the Basic Law to the *Länder*. The list of powers granted to the *Bund* is found in Art 73 and is surprisingly short. This is misleading, however, as the legislative competencies acquired by the state *de facto* through the 'concurrent' competencies outlined in Art 74 are considerable. In practice, only police, culture and education are absent in their entirety, giving complete autonomy to the *Länder* in these policy areas.

Although the Scotland Act 1998 and the Northern Ireland Act 1998 do not have the constitutional status of the German Basic Law, the method of allocating legislative authority to these regions is not dissimilar to that found in the *Länder*. Scottish legislation cannot cover any subjects in the somewhat eclectic list found in Sched 5 to the Scotland Act 1998. In addition, those UK Acts listed in Sched 4 may not be modified. A similar situation exists in Northern Ireland. In both cases, the restrictions also apply to any legislation which is contrary to European Community law or conflicts with 'convention rights', defined as those recognised by the UK Human Rights Act 1998 (s 29(2), Scotland Act 1998; s 6(2), Northern Ireland Act 1998). In all of these situations, the legislation of the Scottish Parliament or the Northern Ireland Assembly can be struck down as *ultra vires*.

The only other regional units with a *prima facie* constitutionally guaranteed general competence are the Portuguese archipelagos of Madeira and the Açores. The islands are guaranteed the right to address issues 'of specific interest to the regions as are not within the exclusive powers of the organs of supreme authority' (Art 229(1)a, Portuguese Constitution). As the areas of 'specific interest' are defined within the regional statutes themselves, the general competence clause is largely symbolic.

In contrast with the German federation, the Belgian regions enjoy no general competence. A subsidiarity clause was due to be added to the Belgian Constitution in 2000 as part of the final constitutional revision. As yet, this has not happened, but such a clause will transfer the few remaining non-allocated functions to the Regions or Cultural Communities, depending on the content. The extensive nature of the positive allocation of functions under the current Belgian Constitution will make the addition of such a clause of limited relevance in the short term.

The concept of general competence also extends to those regions which lack legislative competencies. The clearest example of this is found in the French regions which, in common with other levels of French local government, possess the power to undertake executive actions which are not within the specific authority of another local authority or executive agency. The allocation of powers to local government in 'blocks' is intended to limit the operation of this general competence. In theory, all powers are allocated to one level of government or another, limiting each tier to its specific block. In practice the ingenuity of the regional tier, and its relative financial autonomy (coupled with the impossibility of dividing functions into clear policy blocks), has led to regional involvement in several policy areas not strictly within the remit intended by the French Government. By using their limited financial resources regional authorities have achieved additional influence on policy within their region, while the bodies on the receiving end of such largesse are unlikely to complain. The Danish *amter* have also utilised their general competence and financial independence to expand into areas such as specialised social services and the arts.

Not all regions have been able to expand the range of competencies assigned to them through the use of a general competence. To discover what impedes this wider exercise of power, it is necessary to examine those regions that lack the formal general competence described above but have still managed to extended their authority. The more independent minded Spanish *autonomías*, such as Catalonia and Euskadi (the Basque country), have been particularly successful in 'pushing the envelope' of their defined autonomy, against the wishes of the central state. The only common link between these Spanish regions and the Danish *amter* is a degree of financial independence. The ability to control a significant portion of their own funds gives regions the ability to use financial means to extend their influence. This is achieved through what Daintith describes as 'dominium' powers (Daintith, 1989). Regional governments, like their national counterparts, can expand their competencies through acting as private individuals, but such actions rely upon financial resources. The same is true of the concept of general competence.

General competencies have a number of advantages for the regional tier. Expansion of regional powers does not require positive action by the national government under such a scheme, and innovative policy initiatives are possible within a region without the positive approval of the national tier. Nevertheless, the existence of a general competence does not in itself guarantee that such innovations are possible. Rather, a combination of financial independence, regional ingenuity and national acquiescence all play their part in the process. For example, if a region wishes to develop and finance a new project, although it lacks the explicit power to do so, the national government may think twice before stepping in and financing the project itself or being seen to disadvantage the region in question. The effect of both administrative and legislative general competencies depends on many factors beyond the purely constitutional.

10.4 VERTICAL AND HORIZONTAL REGIONALISM

The use of general or positive definitions of regional competence examined above describes the powers of the regional tier in terms of where they originate. A general competence will place a degree of default or sovereign power at the regional tier, while positive methods of defining the regional tier in effect devolve powers from the central reservoir to the regional tier. These methods of defining regional competence do not of themselves describe how the areas of policy are delineated. To examine this, we must turn to classic federal theory. Traditional models of federalism divide systems into either vertical (dualist) or horizontal (layer) federations. Dualist systems allocate entire policy areas to specific levels of government. For example, the central government and its agencies might be responsible for all aspects of defence, from decisions over the deployment of armed forces to the payment of individual employees. The region might be responsible for secondary education from curriculum to school buildings. This system has the advantage of clear lines of accountability and responsibility. By allocating distinct blocks of competence to individual tiers of authority, it makes it clear which institution is responsible for the decisions taken in a specific policy area. By this method, 'turf wars' between levels are also reduced and the potential for conflict over responsibilities is kept to a minimum. In practice, such neat divisions of responsibility prove almost impossible. Few areas of public policy can be conveniently divided into neat blocks to be transferred to specific levels of government.

This leads most federal and regional systems to utilise horizontal forms of functional definition. A horizontal system of federalism does not grant specific policy areas to specific levels of government. Instead particular aspects of policy will be given to the most appropriate levels. In the example of education given above, the central authority might have responsibility for minimum standards and ensuring equality of educational provision throughout the territory. The regional tier could have responsibility for specific education policy including curriculum and the provision of teaching staff, while the local level could be assigned administrative responsibilities in relation to the provision of buildings and the funding of the system established by the higher levels.

This horizontal or 'layer cake' division of responsibilities fits well with the principle of subsidiarity (see section 2.2.1). It allows the lowest level of government to manage those aspects of the policy which that level is capable of delivering, while aspects of the policy area which are beyond it can be transferred to a higher level. Such a system brings with it both the potential for greater local accountability and the danger of confused lines of responsibility.

Such classic models do not exist in practice, either in Europe on in other examples of federal or regional government. Elements of horizontal federalism will be present across regional systems. To a lesser extent this is also true of the dualist model. Even in administrative regions (which are by definition horizontal), the attempt to allocate self-defining blocks of administrative responsibility recognises the advantages of the dualist principle.

The result of this conflation of dualist and horizontal methods of functional distribution is what has been termed the 'marble cake' model. This colourful metaphor is used to describe a system where responsibilities between levels of government are mixed and, to some extent, confused. In this model, dualist and horizontal characteristics will exist in tandem in a single regional system. Even then, the distinctions between them may be vague, with clear responsibilities being difficult to establish. There is therefore no benefit in examining federal or regional systems within these traditional definitions. Instead we can examine particular aspects of policy and assess the extent to which they are developed or administered at specific levels. Although the distinction between vertical and horizontal systems will have a role in explaining this, it is only part of a wider picture.

10.4.1 Exclusive regional policies

The policies which exhibit the closest adherence to the classic dualist model are those granted 'exclusively' to the regional tier. Formally, these are the areas in which the regional tier is the only source of policy. Any national involvement will consist of a 'safety net' comprising minimal standards of service, or some co-ordination of regional policies. Understandably, such regional functions are rare, and in practice the dualist nature of these functions is almost impossible to achieve.

The areas of region-only initiative (see Table 10.4) have evolved primarily in the fields of education and culture. Until recently the German *Länder* were the only regions which enjoyed such exclusivity of function. Under the Basic Law, the fields of education, cultural matters (broadly defined) and police are exclusively the responsibility of the *Länder* through their general competence. *Bund* powers in these areas are limited to tightly constrained responsibilities for co-ordination. More recently, the Belgian federation has attempted to construct a dualist system in which significant areas of responsibility are entirely beyond the power of the federal level. In Belgium and Germany both education and cultural matters (including the televisual media) are addressed at the regional level. Beyond these examples, classic examples of dualism are difficult to identify.

Predominantly regional areas of policy can be found elsewhere, however, although not throughout the entire Member State. In a number of high autonomy constitutional regions, for example, education has been devolved to the regional tier. In seven Spanish high and medium level *autonomías* the region has been given sole responsibility for education, although the national government retains a significant involvement through the imposition of national standards to ensure equality of diplomas. This is enough to deny the 'exclusive' tag. In Portugal, too, the islands have the authority under their statutes to develop educational policy, although in practice it follows the Portuguese model. Limitations imposed through the constitutional court's reluctance to accept regional legislation which conflicts with the national legislation makes such autonomy more theoretical than real.

In the UK, the system also reflects a degree of dualist influence, with a number of fields of policy under the exclusive responsibility of the devolved governments in Northern Ireland and Scotland. These include education, health and (in Scotland only) policing. In these examples there is no overarching role for the national tier. This reflects the tradition of deconcentrated administration and separate systems that had developed in the union state prior to devolution.

In areas where a regional language has become a politically sensitive issue, exclusive policy regarding its teaching and use has often been transferred to the region. This is true in the special regions of Italy, some Spanish *autonomías*, the Belgian Communities and Corsica (although at the present time, Corsica lacks legislative power). The notable exceptions are the metropolitan French regions of Occitania and Brittany. Although the non-national languages are taught, it is not the region (or the local levels) which have authority for them.

Outside the legislative regions, it is inappropriate to talk formally of exclusive areas of legislation, although something akin to this has developed in a few examples. Spatial planning in particular is a power that tends to lie at the regional level in most regions of the EU, with the exception of the Netherlands and parts of Scandinavia. In France, the role is undertaken within procedures developed at the national level, but the discretion lies regionally. Limits to regional authority in this area are minimal, and the construction of regional plans is not open to discretionary veto by the national government.

With the exceptions of education and spatial planning it is not easy to recognise any general trends in regional-only policy. Health perhaps falls into this category for the Portuguese islands, six Spanish *autonomías*, Scotland and Wales, but significant national involvement remains. In Belgium significant parts of health policy are handled on a Community basis, but the building and maintenance of hospitals is still organised nationally.

Economic activities are notable by their absence from this list. Although significant responsibility for economic development applies to many regional governments, it is rarely regulated exclusively by the regional tier. Those areas of economic activity that are administered exclusively remain very specific and relatively insignificant. Any importance they have lies in the local or regional context alone. Probably the best example of this is in the Portuguese islands, where the autonomous regions control the use of thermal and hydro energy. Almost all electricity generation on the islands is achieved by these means. The islands' governments are therefore responsible for electricity generation, although this is not explicitly mentioned in the constitutional statute.

Table 10.4: Examples of exclusively regional functions in the EU

	Belgium	Germany	Portugal	Spain
Education	Yes	Yes	Yes	No
Economic intervention	Yes	No	No	No
Health	Within limited areas of policy	No	Yes	No
Police	No	Yes	No	No
Spatial planning	Yes	Yes	Yes	Yes
Transport	No	No	Yes	No

10.5 CONCURRENT AND SHARED POWERS

As the above discussion makes clear, the majority of regional functions are not held exclusively at the regional level. Dualism is the exception in European models of regional government. Instead, a horizontal division of powers is the norm, with some aspects of a specific policy being held at the national level and others addressed regionally. The horizontal analogy may be slightly misleading, however, as it implies a clear distinction between regional and central state responsibilities. In practice, these lines are extremely blurred. For this reason it is more accurate to describe these horizontally divided responsibilities as powers shared or concurrent with other levels, predominantly the national tier.

A 'concurrent' power is one that is formally shared between the regional and the central government. The practical manifestation of this formal position is very different across the regional states of the EU. Concurrent powers in Germany are defined in Art 74 of the Basic Law. This Article lists areas in which the *Länder* are free to exercise exclusive authority until and to the extent that the *Bund* occupies the field. In practice, the legislative aspects of these responsibilities have become federal. The provisions intended to restrict *Bund* intervention in these areas were classed non-justiciable by the constitutional court, and so Art 74 became a list of *Bund* powers from which the *Länder* became gradually excluded (see section 4.2).

Concurrent powers in Spain and Belgium mean something very different. In Spain the term refers to regional responsibilities exercised within nationally established standards. These standards are not without controversy and can be significant limitations, but regions are still able to exercise legislative powers within these frameworks. In Belgium the system does not recognise the existence of concurrent provision, with the exception of taxes, where responsibility is shared (although the federation is clearly the senior partner). Despite this, competencies are not neatly divided. For example, responsibility for parts of the healthcare system (particularly in relation to the provision of hospitals) remains federal despite the Community's 'exclusive' responsibility for health. Concurrence has no formal role in other regional systems, but it clearly exists.

One method of concurrence in the legislative sphere can be achieved through the provision of framework laws (examined specifically below). In this method the central government institutes a legislative framework within which the region can exercise a degree of legislative autonomy. The extent to which such frameworks limit the actions of the regional tier varies considerably. They can provide significant limits upon the action of the region, as in Italy, or merely establish frameworks for technical compatibility, as in Germany. In some examples, such as in the Italian special regions and Wales, they are the basis for regional functional autonomy itself. In these examples, national legislative frameworks must be established before the region can exercise the autonomy within them.

By far the simplest method of dividing policy horizontally is to leave legislation in the hands of the central state, with only executive authority in the hands of the region. Although at first sight this horizontal division of authority puts all policy power in the hands of the central state, it can lead to significant powers accruing to the regional tier. In its extreme form, as practised in Germany and Austria, the central state lacks the ability to implement all but a few specific examples of policy. All field agencies are in the hands of the regional tier. Under the German Basic Law, the *Bund* is strictly limited in the control it can exercise. In addition, the collective power of the *Länder* as exercised through the *Bundesrat* ensures that the regions retain significant administrative leeway in the bulk of legislation approved.

Even in the case of local government regions, central government intervention is limited by practical and political factors. Although the central government could, at any time, introduce legislation to limit the administrative autonomy of the regional tier, it is not in its interests to do so. In practice, a significant degree of discretion over subjects as widely distributed as spatial planning and transport lies within the gift of the administrative regions.

Such horizontal divisions of responsibility can also be achieved on a territorial basis. In these examples (which can be legislative or administrative) the region operates and develops policy within the territory while national aspects are handled by the central state. The classic example of this is the field of transport. Regional infrastructure may remain the responsibility of the region while national routes remain a national responsibility. This division of responsibility occurs in both legislative and administrative systems, and may include a bundle of legislative and administrative powers lying at the regional tier. In common with all these examples, and with the bulk of regional responsibilities, regional policy relies upon co-operation with the central tier.

10.5.1 Framework legislation

Framework legislation, as already mentioned, is the most common method of legislative distribution between the regional and national level. Under systems that employ framework legislation, the regional tier does not exercise exclusive autonomy in any specific area of policy. Instead, all regional actions are restricted by legislative frameworks constructed at the national level (see Table 10.5, p 261). These can be minimal and restricted by constitutional texts to standards of service or compatibility (for example, educational certificates). In practice, these restrictions mean that the policy is effectively left to the regional level, and the system tends towards the dualist model. In contrast, some frameworks can be so restrictive as to deny regions any meaningful policy autonomy. Judicial interpretation of such frameworks, and the extent to which the state is allowed to restrict regional autonomy through them, plays a large role in how tight the restrictions are. In Italy, for example, where the constitutional court has exhibited a centrist bias, the frameworks have tightly constrained regional legislative authority since their inception.

Formally, only the Italian *regioni* and the Welsh Assembly rely entirely upon national framework legislation for their legislative authority, although strictly speaking the Scotland and Northern Ireland Acts also operate in this manner. For the purposes of this discussion, they are excluded as the powers allocated within them are dualist in nature. Even within the two regional structures that formally rely upon framework laws, there are significant constitutional differences. Italian regional legislation, once enacted, is of equal status with that of the central institutions. Welsh Assembly legislation is of a secondary nature. Such constitutional differences are not evident in practice. Article 117 of the Italian Constitution limits regional legislation to being 'within the limits of the fundamental principles established by the laws of the State'. The constitutional courts' interpretation of Art 117 has meant that the regions did not have the right to exercise any of the legislative autonomy outlined in the constitution before the national government defined the relevant framework. Its view of the need for centrally sponsored legislative frameworks was also extended to the special regions. In some cases the framework legislation never arrived, and some special region powers have never been devolved (Zariski, 1987, p 103). Like Wales, the Italian regional tier is entirely reliant on the national parliament's largesse for its legislative authority. Such authority can be reduced by national law at any time.

There is evidence that the German federal system was designed to utilise a similar structure, and it has been suggested that the concurrent list of legislation contained in Art 74 was intended to act as a framework within which the *Länder* could exercise their legislative autonomy (Boase, 1994, p 95). In practice, the German federal system has not developed in this manner. Instead these concurrent powers have become federal in all but a minority of cases, although the *Länder* have recently attempted to claw back some of these powers (see section 4.2.4).

In Spain, the opposite trend has been observed. The Spanish system does not generally recognise the existence of concurrent or shared powers, instead allocating authority along what appear to be broadly dualist lines. Article 148 lists the areas in which the regions will exercise both legislative and executive autonomy. These are fairly clear-cut, but within Art 148 there are a number of areas in which the state can intervene. For example, agriculture is to be exercised within 'general regulations'. In addition, many 'high' and 'medium' regional functions have been developed which go beyond the powers listed in Art 148, particularly in relation to health, education and the police. In these cases, the state has played the role of co-ordinator and has established the frameworks within which regional legislation operates. The Spanish Constitutional Court has consistently recognised a limited role for the centre in establishing frameworks to promote 'general interest' even in areas that were recognised as regional under Art 148. Tourism, for example, was held to be a responsibility which had significant effects upon national economic development, and thus the central government had the authority to develop basic national frameworks.

The legislative importance of the Spanish regional tier can be seen in the raw figures for *autonomía* legislative actions in comparison with those for the central state. In the year 1990, 186 regional laws passed into the statute books, in comparison with only 32 at the national level. If one includes secondary legislation, the numbers are also revealing. In 1990, 3,727 decrees were promulgated at the regional tier, compared with 1,745 at the centre. Although the figures must be discussed with a degree of care, as there are 17 *autonomía* legal systems compared with only one national, it nevertheless represents a clear trend away from detailed legislation being enacted at the national level. Instead, greater emphasis is placed on the region as the focus of legislative activity within frameworks established at the national level (Agranoff and Gallarin, 1997, p 17).

The move towards framework legislation in systems that formally engage in dualist models of legislative division is repeated across other legislative regions. In areas of economic management, in particular, the central government of every regional system retains the right to set framework laws within which the region may develop policy. The extent of autonomy varies substantially, but regional policies are, without exception, significantly restricted. Even in Belgium, where economic development and financial intervention is left to the Regional level, the state still retains control over national monetary and fiscal policy. In practice, this represents a restrictive framework in which the regions can only modify the effects of federal policy through supply side measures. Restrictions on state aids imposed by the EU mean the practical options for the Regions may be quite limited. The failure of the Walloon Region's attempts to follow a different course to that of the federal government gives weight to this argument (Covell, 1986). Further limits are placed on the Region by the constitutional requirement of the internal market. In practice all regions must work within these restraints.

Formally, the German *Bund* may also enact framework laws in a few specific areas, notably in relation to higher education, conservation and land use (Art 75, Basic Law). However, the most significant frameworks arise out of the areas known as the joint tasks, which include economic development, further aspects of higher education, and agriculture.

The variation between different frameworks in different regional systems makes it difficult to assess their impact, and it is difficult to come to any overall conclusion. The legislative frameworks imposed on the regions generally allow a significant degree of flexibility in the implementation of regional policy. In the case of conflict this may be misleading as the region can, in many cases, be controlled by other means.

The requirement in all regional states, regardless of the constitutional situation, that framework legislation must be passed through statute can add a degree of protection. It may not be politically advisable or indeed practical to restrict regional autonomy more than is strictly necessary. The exception to all this is Italy, where the frameworks are universally regarded as being very tight. Whether this is connected with the ability of the national executive to pass framework laws as executive decrees is unclear, but such a power is unlikely to aid the regions' cause. Either way, the strict functional framework, coupled with the lack of financial autonomy discussed above, has had a significant effect on the ability of the regions to function. This is despite the supposed protection granted to them under Art 173 of the Italian Constitution.

From the above discussion it is plausible to suggest that the nature of framework laws depends not on the constitutional status of the region but rather on the existence of a 'culture of decentralisation'. The constitutional limitation on framework legislation in Germany and Belgium gives them an edge in their dealings with the nation-state. If they do not wish to pursue a national policy, the nation-state will have to use more subtle methods than legislation to influence the regional decision.

Table 10.5: Examples of regional responsibilities under national framework laws

	Belgium	Denmark	France	Germany	Italy	Netherlands	Spain
Economic	Minimal	Yes	Yes	Agreed between regional tier	Yes	x	Yes
Education	Minimal	Yes	No	Agreed between regional tier	x	x	Minimal
Health	Minimal	Yes	No	No	Yes	x	Minimal
Spatial planning	No	No	No	No	No	No	No
Transport	No	Yes	No	Yes	Yes	Yes (river)	No

x = no regional responsibilities

10.5.2 Administrative autonomy

Administrative or executive regionalism is a further method of dividing authority within a regional system. By this method a horizontal division is effected along formal constitutional lines (see Table 10.6, p 264). Legislative authority is vested at the central level, with an executive exercising executive authority. If the region only has authority over administrative functions can it have any autonomy?

The German and Austrian federations exhibit the most extreme examples of this form of delineation of responsibilities. In these examples, the regional tier is responsible for almost all executive activities. Lacking the field services to deliver its policies, the federal level relies primarily on the *Länder* to implement them. In both these examples, the *Bund* is barred from developing its own agencies except in specifically defined circumstances (for example to deliver postal services and railways). The lack of national field services means that everything from unemployment to roads must administered regionally.

Under Art 83 of the Basic Law, the German *Länder* implement all federal legislation autonomously, unless specified elsewhere in the Basic Law. By far the majority of executive functions fall into this category. Under Art 84, the *Bund* is severely restricted in its ability to limit such autonomy. Any limits must be approved by the *Bundesrat*, and instructions from the relevant federal ministries are not binding upon the regions concerned. In effect, federal legislation acts as something akin to a framework law, of the type explored above, due to the extensive discretion that remains at the regional tier. In areas where the *Länder* act as the agents of the *Bund*, the restrictions are still limited. Article 85(2) allows the *Bund* both to dictate the institutions used to administer the policy and to implement general administrative rules, but only with the consent of the *Bundesrat*. Although directions from the federal government must be adhered to in these cases, they must be directed at the First Minster of the *Land*, who will use his or her discretion in implementing them. Such directions can only be based upon statute (Art 85, Basic Law). Only if the *Land* fails to obey these directives (which may require *Bundesrat* approval) will the *Bund* intervene, and even then only with the consent of the *Bundesrat*. In practice, this does not occur. Given the limitations placed upon the implementation of federal legislation by the *Land* as agent, the *Länder* have been willing to accept this role in return for the payment of a significant portion of the policy's costs by the *Bund*.

In Austria the position is somewhat different. The Austrian *Länder* lack the constitutionally protected executive autonomy given to their German counterparts. Instead, although most federal legislation is implemented by the Austrian *Länder*, in most cases such implementation is undertaken as the agent of the federation.

Both these forms of federalism nevertheless share a number of similarities. Executive federalism of this type places the executive institutions of the regional tier at the apex of regional autonomy. In both Austria and Germany, this development has been at the expense of the regional legislatures. Designed as legislative bodies, they have needed to adapt to cope with a new role in which their legislative role is minimal. Their role as executive watchdog is not one to which they are entirely suited. This has led to changes in the structure of German *Landtage*, but it is unclear whether such changes are sufficient (Gunlicks, 1998). This executive federalism also demands a high degree of intergovernmental co-operation between the parties. This is particularly true in Germany, where *Bund* attempts to introduce limits on executive autonomy have meant that the majority of Bills require *Bundesrat* approval. Such intergovernmental relations are by their nature inter-executive, and often beyond the scrutiny of both the *Landtage* and the electorate. As such they can pose a threat to accountability, advanced in Chapter 2 as one of the primary reasons for creating a regional democratic tier. This is examined further in the following chapter.

Beyond the executive federations, a horizontal division between legislative and administrative functions appears to be developing in Italy. The Italian Constitution defines a system of regional autonomy based on the division of legislative competencies. Article 117 envisages the development of national framework legislation within which regional legislation will be enacted. Under this model, significant areas of regional legislative autonomy would remain. In practice, the Italian model has drifted towards a far more executive model of federalism of the type seen in Germany and Austria. Most legislation is enacted at the national level, with little room for regional autonomy through legislation. However, the implementation of national policies is increasingly being undertaken at the regional level. The clearest example of this is the abolition of the national departments of tourism and agriculture, with their responsibilities being transferred to the regions by referendum in 1996.

By definition, local government regions can only exercise executive autonomy. However, their lack of legislative authority does not necessarily mean that they do not develop a distinctive regional policy. For instance, the French regions' ability to fund regional rail services may be an executive power, but it is nevertheless a policy one. This area needs further research, and it is difficult to draw clear conclusions as to the extent of the influence of local government regions in the areas where they administer national services. It is clear, however, that the current distinctions are unsuitable. The extent of 'administrative autonomy' given to the German *Länder* provides the potential for significant variation between regions. This does not seem to be the case in Italy but may be so in France. The regional role in the latter varies from policy to policy, but in education, for example, the executive power to organise infrastructure is highly significant. Although further work must be done to recognise the extent to which regional administration gives a regional slant to the implementation of national policy, the fact that it offers significant scope to do so, in some regional systems and in certain policy areas, is beyond dispute.

Table 10.6: Examples of regional administrative responsibilities

	Belg	Den	France	Germ	Italy	Neth	Port	Spain
Economic intervention	No	No	No	Possible	Yes	x	Yes	Yes
Education	No	Yes	Yes	No	No	x	No	No
Health	No	Yes	x	Yes	Yes	x	No	No
Police	Yes (local)	x	x	No	Yes (local)	x	x	No
Transport	No	Yes (roads)	No	Yes (roads)	No	No	No	No

x = no regional responsibilities

10.6 CONCLUSIONS: REGIONAL AUTONOMY AND CO-OPERATIVE FEDERALISM

The brief survey given above confirms what has become apparent from the preceding chapters. Despite appearances to the contrary, the key to decision making in regional systems is co-operation. Whatever method of allocation is used to define the powers of the various tiers of government, few activities can be isolated sufficiently to allow policy making without reference to another tier. Even systems which strive towards such an aim (such as Belgium's) find it impossible to deliver this in practice. This means that the interaction between levels is accorded crucial importance in the autonomy of regional governments.

This interaction comes in many forms. In relation to the functional allocation of authority, it can be through central creation of national frameworks or the establishment of national minimum standards. It can also be through national responsibility for legislative provision with regional responsibility for delivery. Beyond the formal allocation of power, this interaction also includes the provision of financial resources (discussed in Chapter 9) and involvement in international activities (examined in Chapter 8). In all cases, however, the key to these relationships is power.

When the relationship between levels of government is conducted in a way that ensures that all parties are consulted, and the position of all regional governments is taken on board, then the co-operative nature of the system need not undermine regional autonomy. When the regional level is the junior partner, or is ignored entirely, co-operative federalism becomes a euphemism for centralisation. There is a significant role for the law in maintaining which of these outcomes is apparent in individual systems. Institutions which protect the region's autonomy will ensure that the third level's role in the co-operative process is genuine. Where such institutions do not exist, the centre will be in a position to dictate its terms. It is these institutions, and the role they play in regulating intergovernmental relations and dispute resolution, that form the basis of the following two chapters.

CHAPTER 11

THE COUNTERVAILING POWER? REGIONS AND NATIONAL POLICY MAKING

No government exists in isolation. Increasingly, national policies must be conducted in co-operation with neighbours and international partners if they are to be successful. The classic model of the nation-state encounters significant difficulties in adapting to this reality. Its 'sovereign' nature means that granting power to intergovernmental organisations is difficult for both practical and political reasons. The experiences of the Member States of the European Union are clear evidence of this. Although few deny the rationale behind the creation of supranational institutions to govern pan-European activities, the development of the EU has been difficult. The institutions created have evolved without a direct democratic link to the population, leading to the creation of a democratic deficit. Attempts to reduce this deficit through the creation of democratic European institutions have proved politically impossible.

Regional government, in contrast, is not born free. It is a limited institution of governance integrated into a system alongside other limited forms of governance. It comes with intergovernmental relations as standard, and there is no pretence that it can operate independently of other levels of government, particularly its parent state. The acceptance of the need for intergovernmental co-ordination in regional systems leads to the establishment of institutions, agreements and conventions to structure them.

The importance of intergovernmental relations to the operation of a successful regional system is undeniable. The complex interrelationship between European, national, regional and local government is such that without a working system of intergovernmental relations coherent policies would be impossible. Nevertheless, the necessity of intergovernmental relationships to the successful operation of a regional or federal system should not blind us to the fact that they themselves present significant challenges and indeed dangers to the regional systems.

Intergovernmental relations are by their nature executive. Although linkages between the legislative branch of government and other levels of government do exist, the vast majority of such relationships are between executives. This is hardly surprising, as sheer practicality requires representative delegations to engage in such relationships. Any other system would make such a structure unmanageable. When we refer to intergovernmental relationships, we are therefore really talking about inter-executive relationships. These have a significant impact on regional structures, and introduce a number of tensions into the regional system as a whole.

Intergovernmental relations are often also conducted in secret. They are likely to include a degree of political bargaining which those concerned would not wish to become public knowledge. In the case of the United Kingdom, the choice is not left to the participants as concordats stipulate mutual confidentiality of the participants (see for example paras 11 and A1(11), Memorandum of Understanding). This lack of transparency is a problem for the regional (and indeed the national) electorate. If decisions are taken in these intergovernmental forums rather than in the legislative arena, the requirements of open government are not met. The problem is compounded by the nature of regional parliaments. In most cases they are designed as miniature versions of their national counterparts. These bodies are designed to facilitate the discussion and enaction of legislative provisions. In the regional case, the growth of interregional co-operation means that this is no longer the main function of the regional legislative branch. This is particularly the case in Germany, where the legislative role of the *Landtag* was already limited. The increasing role of intergovernmental relations reduces this legislative role even further. The primary role of the regional legislature is now one of holding the executive to account, something for which it is ill suited. This problem is also being experienced at the Member State level in relation to intergovernmental decision making in the European Union. The response of the German *Landtage* has been to alter the state constitutions to reflect this role (Gunlicks, 1998, p 117).

Holding the intergovernmental institutions themselves to account is extremely difficult. They operate in a 'space' between the region and the Member State levels and, as the decisions reached are a compromise between executives, neither the Member State parliament nor the regional legislature will be responsible for decisions taken. Despite this, they may be obliged to follow these decisions.

This leads neatly on to the third challenge that these relationships create for regional structures. At the start of this work, emphasis was placed on the importance of regional autonomy in the study of regional and federal systems. Without autonomy, the rationale for a regional policy making tier is significantly diminished. It is in this area of intergovernmental relationships that the tension between autonomy and co-operation becomes most apparent. Institutions of intergovernmental relations are clearly important for the development of coherent policy, but agreements made by such institutions are by their nature no longer 'regional'. They are examples of regional involvement in national policy making and therefore evidence of the importance of the regional tier, but they are not a reflection of regional autonomy *per se*. If national decisions are being taken by regional executives, they remain national decisions. As such, should they be handled by indirectly elected regional executives rather than through the national legislative process, a process designed for the purpose?

The taking of policy decisions at a level somewhere between the regional and the national has further consequences for the actual decisions themselves. In his work on intergovernmental decision making in the German system, Scharpf identified the existence of a 'joint decision trap' (Scharpf, 1988). Although he focused on the operation of the joint tasks in the German Constitution to expose the difficulties of intergovernmental relations in an EU context, the conclusions he reached are valid far beyond the specific example. One of the problems he identified concerned the quality of decisions reached in an intergovernmental setting, particularly when a qualified majority or unanimity of agreement is required. The decisions taken will reflect the needs of each territory to gain something from the negotiations, leading to decisions that will not deal with the problem in hand. This is particularly true in the joint tasks where, for example, decisions to develop higher education will require that every region is given financial support whether they require it or not. Evidence of this phenomenon is widespread in federal and regional systems across Europe and beyond (for Belgium, see Alen and Ergec, 1998, p 30; for Canada, see Simeon, 2000). It is unclear how our increasingly interconnected world can deal with this most intractable of problems.

Running through the above discussion is a further issue that, although inextricably linked to the question of intergovernmental relations, has yet to be mentioned by name. Before examining institutions that grant regions a limited involvement in national policy making, it is important to realise that such systems are inextricably linked to the resolution of disputes within the federal or regional structure. Intergovernmental institutions always have a role in ensuring technical co-operation and information exchange, but they are only really tested when the parties disagree on fundamental policy decisions. When all sides can agree, the exact methods by which such agreements are reached can be relatively unimportant. Only when the governments are in serious conflict are the institutions (and the system itself) really tested.

The line between intergovernmental relations and dispute resolution is therefore indistinct, and discussing the influence of the regions on national policy separately from dispute resolution is rather disingenuous. Nevertheless, for ease of explanation, the two have been separated here. Chapter 12 focuses more specifically on the question of the resolution of disputes in regional and federal systems, although most of the institutions discussed in the current chapter play some role in this process, either explicitly or through their influence in the political game. Constitutionally regulated conflict is a key component of the regional or federal state. It is therefore worth bearing in mind that the litmus test of intergovernmental structures is whether they will continue to operate successfully when conflict arises; otherwise, claiming that they are effective is like claiming that the Titanic was a very successful ship until it ran into an iceberg.

11.1 REGIONAL SECOND CHAMBERS

Of the 15 Member States of the European Union, only six have upper houses which can be classed as regional. This immediately raises a question: what do we regard as a regional chamber?

11.1.1 Regional chambers without regional representation

The Italian *Senato*, established under the 1948 constitution, was intended to be a further extension of the decentralised Italian state. By representing the regions, it would offer a collective countervailing power to the national government and the lower house. It would also tie the regional tier into the Italian state by being elected on a regional basis (Art 57(1), Italian Constitution).

As with much else in the Italian Constitution, the practical implementation of the Senate proposals did not accord with the spirit expressed at the time of its enactment. The regional implementation legislation was not forthcoming (see section 5.1.1), which left no regional tier to be involved in the election of the Senate. Instead, its 315 members are directly elected, on a supposedly regional basis.

In practice, although each region is allocated a number of senators based upon its population, each region is divided into a number of single member constituencies. The exception to this rule is Valle d'Aosta, whose only senator is elected from a regional constituency. In effect, therefore, the Italian Senate is elected from a national set of constituencies. The only regional element is the use of the region as the basis for the proportional element of the electoral system. Parties that have received less representation within a region than their share of the vote would suggest are allocated regional 'top-up' seats.

The regional elements of the *Senato*, so prominent in the Constitution of 1948, have been all but erased by the legislation that implemented them. The actual worth of the second chamber was further eroded by the government's decision in 1963 to hold elections for both houses of the Italian Parliament on a single day, in an effort to avoid the problems of 'mid-term blues' afflicting the government's presence in the upper house. The overall result is a chamber whose composition closely mirrors that of the lower house. It is hard to envisage a chamber that is so removed in practice from the regional house envisaged by the constitution. Although the chamber has played an important role in the regionalisation process (see section 5.1.1), its role as a regional voice within in the national policy process is nil.

The Dutch Senate is another nominally regional chamber that merits a brief mention. Although the Netherlands tier of regional government in the form of the province plays only a peripheral role in Dutch politics, its role in electing the members of the Dutch upper house is a significant one. Every four years, the *provinciale staten* of each province elects its senators to represent the province in the Senate. The link between the province and the Senate is therefore far greater than in the Italian example. Nevertheless, the weakness of the province in the Dutch system means that these senators represent the province as a whole rather than the provincial institutions. Although this introduces an important check into the Dutch Constitution, this is not as a result of the state's regional structure.

11.1.2 The Spanish *Senado* as a mixed chamber

Another regional second chamber with questionable regional credentials is to be found in the form of the Spanish *Senado*. Although styled as a chamber of territorial representation in the constitution (Art 69(1), Spanish Constitution), this is not borne out in practice. The rationale for this institution in the 1977 constitutional compromise was to give ex-members of the Francoist regime the ability to retain seats in parliament and thus ease the passage to democracy (Colomer, 1999, p 49). This in the event did not occur, at least not in the way expected. Nevertheless, the resulting compromise between an institution of the regional state and a directly elected revision chamber has endured to the present.

By far the majority of senators are directly elected. Each mainland province elects four senators to the *Senado* through elections held, in tandem with those for the chamber of deputies, every four years. Island regions elect senators on an island basis (their provinces having been abolished). The larger islands return three senators, with the smaller islands and archipelagos returning one each. The autonomous cities of Ceuta and Melilla elect two senators each. The 208 directly elected members are complemented by 51 representatives of the *autonomías*. These are elected by the regional parliaments (not the executives) according to procedures established by the region itself. The number of senators allocated to each region is broadly based upon population, although all *autonomías* are guaranteed a senator. For each one million of population they receive another senator (Art 69(5), Spanish Constitution).

The constitution requires that the appointment of the regional senators should 'ensure adequate proportional representation' of the parties within the regional legislature. The constitutional court has been called on to adjudicate exactly what this provision requires. When the Popular Party received a majority of the seats in the Parliament of the Madrid *autonomía* but were kept in opposition by a coalition of the Socialist PSOE and the United Left, they challenged their allocation of only two of the five available senatorial seats. The court ruled that this was 'broadly proportional' and thus an acceptable agreement (Russell, 2000, p 67).

In the majority of cases, regional rules require the regional senators to be members of the regional parliament. In other cases the senators may either be members of the regional parliament or come from outside, although some parties (notably the Basque nationalist PNV) bar dual mandates (Russell, 2000, p 67). Election from outside the regional parliament makes links between the senators and their regional institutions weak. Their links, such as they are, will be through the party, not the region itself. Elections to the regional parliaments can marginally alter the composition of the *Senado* between the four-yearly national elections. This small change was enough in 1995 to swing the majority away from the governing PSOE.

The period 1995–96 was exceptional as it was the only period in which the composition of the *Senado* did not mirror the majority in the chamber of deputies. The electoral system in fact tends to amplify the majority of the governing party, although over-representation of rural areas leads to a slight conservative bias. The Spanish *Senado*, despite the existence of the regional senators, has much in common with the Italian *Senato*. Regional influence through the second chamber is minimal and its role in the regional system is peripheral.

The weakness of the *Senado* can be illustrated by a simple fact; it has never rejected a bill approved in the lower house. Only during the brief period in which its majority did not reflect that of the government did it even delay a bill (Russell, 2000, p 151). Senators, including those appointed by the regions, vote primarily on party lines. This means that bills passed in the *Cortes* find little opposition in the Senate. The only senators to represent their regions effectively are those from the nationalist and regionalist parties, whose position is not reliant on a national party.

In practice this has left the Senate (and senators) with a very low profile and a very limited role in Spanish political life. The regions in particular do not focus their energies on this institution. Instead, *autonomías* whose governments are made up of regionalist or nationalist parties tend to use political strength in the *Cortes* as a method of influencing the central government, while other *autonomías* will operate within the party system (Agranoff and Gallarin, 1997, p 44). The general dissatisfaction with the Senate's performance has led to consistent calls for its reform. These continue to be debated, but given the differences in views between the parties, with the regions wishing for a *Bundesrat* style regional chamber and the national parties favouring direct election, the result of reform, should it happen, may be yet another unsatisfactory compromise.

11.1.3 The federal chambers

A clear distinction can be drawn between the regional chambers of the constitutional regional states examined above and those of the federal states. Although methods of appointment found in the federal chambers vary, their credentials as truly regional chambers is hard to question. Of these federal chambers, the *Bundesrats* of the Austrian and German republics play a far greater role in national policy making than the Belgian Senate. The influence of these institutions extends far beyond their constitutional role and has a huge impact on the federation itself. It is no exaggeration to state that the *Bundesrats* are the key institutions in their respective federal systems. In Germany, the *Bundesrat* is sometimes described as a second government rather than a second chamber. Like all the best satirical comments, this contains a grain of truth.

The German *Bundesrat* (literally 'federal council') has a history which can be traced through the various confederal arrangements that predated the establishment of the German empire in 1870. It has been a feature of German government since unification that the governments of the constituent states should be represented at the central level, although the powers and role of the institution have altered. The Basic Law accepts the principle of *Länder* participation in the federal legislative process in one of its 'eternity' clauses under Art 79(3).

The modern version of the traditional German council of states represents the governments of the 16 *Länder*. Each government has a delegation whose size is loosely based on population. No state has a delegation smaller than three members, and the largest has only six (see section 4.2.5). This reflects fears, prevalent at the time of the Basic Law's enactment, concerning the imbalance created if a single *Länder* (in the past, Prussia) should have an unhealthy influence on the federation as a whole.

The methods of appointment are the clearest indication that the German *Bundesrat* is very different from the Spanish *Senado*. Unlike the Spanish chamber, where even the regional senators are specifically elected individuals, the *Bundesrat* comprises the government ministers of each *Land*. The members of the *Bundesrat* delegation of each *Land* are formally designated. These will be the most senior members of the regional executive. In practice, however, every minister in a *Länder* government will be either a designated member of the *Bundesrat* or an alternate member. This means that the composition of the *Bundesrat* can vary according to the subjects under discussion, with the relevant ministers from each government attending when their portfolios are the subject of the plenary sessions. The composition of the *Bundesrat* means that it is never out of session, rather its composition changes as regional elections bring new governments to power. The *Bundesrat* is truly a chamber of regional executives.

Although it is the members themselves who vote, *Länder* delegations can only deliver their votes in a single block according to the wishes of the *Länder* government. The block is only as large as the number of ministers who are physically in attendance (Art 51(3)). This means that the monthly plenary sessions of the *Bundesrat* bring together ministers from all the *Länder*. Traffic congestion around the small *Bundesrat* building in Bonn on these days is legendary. Although the practice is to hold such meetings on a monthly basis, special sessions can be called at the instigation of two *Länder*.

Although the physical institution of the *Bundesrat* comprises the regional ministers, a large amount of preliminary work occurs prior to each meeting. This is undertaken by civil servants. In addition, the extent of pre-meeting political negotiations makes many of the votes a forgone conclusion. Readers may notice the similarity between the *Bundesrat* and the European Council of Ministers. This is no accident; the latter body is modelled to a significant extent on the *Bundesrat* model.

The German *Bundesrat* acquired a new purpose after the introduction of the Europe Article into the Basic Law in 1994 (Art 23, Basic Law). Through this Article, the *Bundesrat* gained a new role in providing the *Länder* opinion on European Union matters. This is provided by a special committee of the *Bundesrat* which, due to the speed with which EU proposals need to be dealt with, uses simplified procedures (Art 52(3)a, Basic Law).

The legislative role of the *Bundesrat* is such that it has evolved into the cornerstone of the German federal system. This was not always the case, and certainly during its formative years the *Bundesrat* was not envisaged as having the extensive role it does today. The *Bundesrat* is intended to represent the interests of the *Länder* at the *Bund* level. However, it was not intended to have a major legislative role in the federation. The Basic Law confirms this by granting only a suspensory veto to the *Bundesrat* in most subject areas, although all federal legislation must pass through its chamber first. Only in specific areas must *Bundesrat* approval be sought. On the surface, the role of the *Bundesrat* should be minimal. Its approval by a two-thirds majority is required in cases of constitutional change (Art 79(2), Basic Law). When federal legislation limits the administrative autonomy of the *Länder* the consent of the *Bundesrat* is required (Art 84(1), Basic Law). This requirement has meant that whenever the federation has acquired a new power, for example in taxation matters, the *Bundesrat* has ensured that decisions taken under such new authority will require its approval (Blair, 1981, p 93). The power of constitutional assent was also used to great effect during the Maastricht negotiations (see section 8.3.1). Although the constitutional assent requirement has made a significant impact on the German federation, particularly in recent years, it is the requirement of consent for administrative Acts, and the constitutional court's interpretation of this, that has made the *Bundesrat* the powerful force it is today.

The German federation, as explored above, is an executive federation. With a few strongly defended exceptions (principally in culture, local government and the police), legislative authority lies in the hands of the federal level. As a result of this, it was originally envisaged that only a small percentage of federal legislation would require *Länder* consent through the *Bundesrat*. Despite this, successive federal governments pursued a policy of limiting *Länder* administrative freedom in federal statutes. Such limitations always require the assent of the *Länder* in the *Bundesrat*. This practice of setting limits on regional executive autonomy has occurred to the extent that over 50% of federal legislation now requires *Bundesrat* approval, under the procedure out lined in Art 77(2)a of the Basic Law.

The reason for this high figure also reflects decisions of the constitutional court. Questions surrounding the veto powers of the *Bundesrat* arose early in the history of the federal republic, with the *Länder* understandably interpreting Art 84(1) of the Basic Law expansively. This Article requires that 'where the *Länder* implement federal legislation in their own right they shall establish authorities and administrative procedures in so far as federal legislation with *Bundesrat* consent does not provide otherwise'. The constitutional court was faced with a number of challenges from both *Länder* and *Bund* arguing over whether Acts should be classified as requiring *Bundesrat* consent or merely as being open to suspensory veto in the upper house.

Although the constitutional court dealt with this matter several times during the first years of the federal republic, it was not until the late 1950s that it established what became its definitive opinion on the matter. Throughout the period prior to the Prices Act case of 1958, the court had confirmed that in most cases the *Bundesrat* had the power to delay but not veto federal legislation. In most cases, the objections of the second chamber could be overruled by a majority in the *Bundestag* (Art 77(4), Basic Law). Nevertheless, although the court accepted the principle that *Bundesrat* consent was only required in specific cases, it began to recognise a wide range of categories in which this would apply. The court's trend towards accepting a wide interpretation of the veto power of the *Bundesrat* was confirmed by the judgment of 1958.

The case concerned the federal government's attempt to extend the application of the Prices Act 1948 beyond the time limits defined in the Act itself. This Act was a classic example of the type mentioned in Art 84(1) of the Basic Law, whereby the federal law was administered autonomously by the *Länder*. The first decision made by the court on this Act was relatively uncontroversial. The Act's stipulation of the methods by which orders under the Act were to be delivered was a breach of *Länder* administrative autonomy. As such it required the assent of the *Bundesrat*. The court went further, however, and insisted that it was not only the section of the Act that contained these provisions that required *Bundesrat* consent, but the Act as a whole. As a consequence of this, any amendments proposed to the statute (such as its extension) were also subject to *Bundesrat* approval.

The court's view has continued to be based upon this general premise, although a number of other challenges have led to modifications of its general approach. Use of the *Bundesrat* by opposition parties, in particular, to frustrate the majority in the *Bundestag* has led to the curbing of *Bundesrat* veto powers, to exclude from these powers amendments to parts of Acts which fall outside the competence of the *Bundesrat* even if the whole Act itself had originally required *Bundesrat* consent. The court through its judgments has thus recognised the need for a balance between *Bundesrat* consent under the constitution and federal legislative needs (see Blair, 1981, pp 92–113). The fact that *Bundesrat* approval is still required for 50–60% of Acts per year is a clear measure of the significance of the court's opinions to the importance of the chamber (*Bundesrat*, 1992).

The result of this defence of collective *Länder* rights in the federal legislative process has clearly increased the power of the *Bundesrat*. It has also increased the role of the *Länder* executives in the national process. The federal government will consult extensively with *Länder* governments before submitting bills to the *Bundesrat*. The *Bundesrat* thus plays a crucial part not only in giving the regional governments a role in the federal decision making process but also in binding the regional tier into the federal level.

The implications for the German system as a whole are rather more complex, however. The veto powers of the *Bundesrat* arise from the federal government's ever greater involvement in *Länder* affairs. This involvement will by definition restrict individual *Land* autonomy. This is not compensated for by the principle that such legislation requires consent in the *Bundesrat*. The *Bundesrat* operates on a majority system, allowing the voices of individual *Länder* to be ignored. *Bundesrat* power, although important to the federal system, grants increased influence to the political élites of the regions in the national process, but does not necessarily defend the autonomy of regions themselves.

The Austrian *Bundesrat*, in theory, holds a position in the Austrian Constitution that is equivalent to that of its German counterpart. As in Germany, this is a council of states with each *Land* represented. All laws (with the exception of federal budgets and a few other types of specific legislation) are referred to the *Bundesrat* after being approved in the *Nationalrat*. Should the Austrian *Bundesrat* reject a proposal, it is returned to the *Nationalrat*, which can overrule such a rejection in the majority of cases. Only when legislation has the effect of amending *Länder* legislative or executive authority, as outlined in the constitution, is *Bundesrat* consent required (Art 44(3), Austrian Constitution).

Although this looks like a variation on the German *Bundesrat* model, the Austrian federation's very different structure means that its regional chamber has a very different effect. The *Land* delegations are elected by the

Landtage but need not be members of it, although the *Land* governors have a right to attend all sessions as non-voting members, and to speak when issues of concern to their *Länder* are being discussed (Art 36(4), Austrian Constitution). The constitution also stipulates that the delegation must contain representatives from more than one political party (Art 35(1), Austrian Constitution). This delegation does not deliver the block of regional votes as in the German *Bundesrat*. The strength of the Austrian party system means that votes divide on party rather than regional lines.

The competencies of the *Länder* are so proscribed in the constitution that the need for *Bundesrat* consent is minimal. This does not mean that its role is entirely peripheral. Apart from offering a reflective chamber whose opinions, given the political power of the provinces, can be influential, its constitutional role has proved crucial in recent years. During negotiations surrounding Austrian entry into the European Union, the requirement of *Länder* approval in the form of the *Bundesrat* meant that their views had to be taken seriously. The resultant deal for *Länder* involvement in the European Union has been far more favourable towards the Austrian regions than for many other regional governments whose domestic constitutional status is much stronger. Such collective *Länder* power in European Union decision making is not a substitute for the lack of regional autonomy experienced by the Austrian *Länder*, but is evidence of the important 'gatekeeper' role that the *Bundesrat* can play, given specific circumstances (Morass, 1996, p 76).

The Belgian Senate offers a very different model of a regional chamber. As with so much else in Belgium, the composition of the Senate reflects the language divisions that divide most of Belgian society. 40 of the 71 senators are directly elected on the basis of language (15 French, 25 Flemish), with a further 21 being elected from the Community councils (10 French, 10 Flemish, one German). One of the 'special facilities' enjoyed by the *communes* which lie on the linguistic border is the ability to vote for senators from their own language group. The remaining 10 (four French, six Flemish) are co-opted by approval of the other senators. Representation for Brussels is ensured by regulations which state that 7 senators (6 of them French) must reside in the Brussels Region.

The role of the Senate in the Belgian federal state is a contested subject. Although Alen argues that the Senate remains a significant player in law making, both as regards fundamental legislation and in matters affecting the 'federated interests', Fitzmaurice for one sees its role as peripheral (Alen and Ergec, 1998; Fitzmaurice, 1996). It is certainly clear that the role played by the Belgian Senate is very different from that of the German *Bundesrat*. The power of the individual Belgian Communities and Regions is such that a second chamber to represent their interests in federal legislation is less important than in the German example. As legislation of the Belgian Regions and Communities has equality with that of the federal tier, a Senate veto is less crucial. In matters of regional competence such a veto is already present at the regional tier. For the federal government to enact legislation that impinges upon the responsibilities of the regions will, by definition, require their individual consent. The vertical federalism that has been constructed in Belgium excludes the right of the regional tier to be involved in questions that remain the responsibility of the federal tier. The Senate can only delay most bills, and thus acts primarily as a chamber of reflection. The requirement of Senate consent for constitutional amendment, assent to international treaties, co-operation agreements between the composite parts of the Belgian federation and organic laws that define the federal system (as well as all other organic laws) ensures a degree of regional involvement in these decisions. Although Community representatives (note that formally there is no regional representation, but given the dual mandate this is merely a formal pretence) comprise only a minority of the Belgian second chamber, the strength of the linguistic ties is such that the interests of the Communities will be present in these decisions.

The Belgian Senate's other major role is in negotiating conflicts of interest between regional and Community parliaments, but not between executives or in conflicts of competence. This further emphasises its role as a uniting factor in the Belgian federation (Art 143(2), Belgian Constitution). The Senate does not offer a serious countervailing power to the federal government and the house of representatives, but it does not need to. Instead it performs another valuable role in the Belgian system by providing a degree of centripetal force in a thoroughly centrifugal system.

The federal chambers, while performing very different roles, are nevertheless significant players in the federal system. To varying degrees they offer a countervailing power to the national government and the lower house. The extreme example of this is the German *Bundesrat*, which is unlike any other chamber in the European Union. It has evolved into the most important actor in the German federal system. The fact that a body that represents the regions collectively should be the most important institution in the German federal system is instructive. It emphasises both the co-operative nature of the German federation and the collective power of the regional tier. In contrast, Belgium's Senate, with its limited legislative power and its role in the dispute resolution process, emphasises the competitive nature of the Belgian federation. The regions do not need to act collectively to defend their interests; instead, such an institution is required to bind them to the Belgian state.

11.2 REGIONAL CONFERENCES

Regional conferences are institutions by which regional tier representatives, with or without the presence of the central state, conduct intergovernmental relations. These institutions give the regional level a collective voice in the national policy process, although with few of the rights that are accorded to the second chambers discussed above. They allow co-ordination of policy between regional and national levels of government, and between regions themselves. In systems where no regional second chamber exists, or where its impact is limited, these conferences can be the only method by which formal collective intergovernmental relations are conducted. Nevertheless, they are not restricted to systems that lack such regional second chambers. In Germany, Belgium and Austria, regional conferences play an integral part in the co-ordination of regional and central state policy. In the German example, these are crucial to co-ordination of policy in areas of *Länder*-only competence.

11.2.1 Reluctant federalists? Spanish regions and the sectoral conferences

As part of the controversial reforms introduced with the *acuerdos autonómicos* between the main national parties, the Spanish central government introduced a system of sectoral conferences in 1983. Although significant parts of the LOAPA (*Ley Orgánica de Armonización del Proceso Autonómico*; see section 12.1.4) were annulled, the sectoral conferences remained. The purposes of the conferences, as defined in the statute which institutionalises them, are to exchange information, examine problems and propose collective solutions in specific areas of policy (Ley 30/1993). As such they are institutions of co-operative regionalism, and their relationship with individual regional autonomy is complex.

A number of the *autonomías*, particularly those with high autonomy, resented what they saw as interference with their competencies, and have consistently failed to engage with the conference system. Attempts to establish the sectoral conferences were made more difficult by the competitive nature of the Spanish regional system. Unlike the German *Länder*, the Spanish *autonomías* have no tradition of unity. There is no equivalent of the German Conference of the Minister Presidents, and no regional front can be created even on limited issues. Most *autonomías* prefer bilateral links with the central state to a system of interregional conferences. Nevertheless, in certain areas there are signs that the sectoral conference system is beginning to function, at least partially. There are provisions for 24 sectoral conferences and *consejos* (councils), the latter including outside members in addition to the relevant central and regional government ministers. Meetings are formally held twice a year, but in practice the frequency varies markedly (Ley 30/1992). In some cases they rarely meet, while the conferences on agriculture and education, and the Interterritorial Council of the National Health System, meet regularly and frequently (Cendón, 1999, p 159).

Börzel, in her analysis of the sectoral conference system, found only eight of the 23 conferences to be operating with a 'high' degree of effectiveness on domestic issues. This she classed as meeting at least twice a year, dealing with drafts of regional or national legislation in areas of shared competencies, framing joint programmes and addressing funding issues. A further seven conferences were classed as having a 'medium' level of effectiveness, through holding annual meetings and addressing at least one of the issues mentioned above (Börzel, 2000). A further conference established after Börzel's survey (on labour affairs) appears to fall into the highly effective category. Nevertheless, the fact that so many conferences fail to reach even the limited benchmark of medium effectiveness, and that only 15 had any organisations outside the political heads of government in their meetings, suggests that the conference system is still far from being an integral part of the Spanish regional system.

Despite this, Börzel argues that her survey shows a distinct increase in interregional co-operation through the conference system, driven by the needs of European Union membership. The increased Europeanisation of Spanish policy has meant that regions wish to have their voices heard at the European level, particularly as in the majority of cases they themselves will be implementing the legislation. This has driven the *autonomías* into the sectoral conference system despite any fears they might have in relation to their autonomy. The failure of the more independently minded regions to achieve much impact at the European level on their own may also have something to do with the change of heart.

Despite Börzel's positive take on the sectoral conference system, this view is not without controversy. A number of the conferences continue to fail to operate in any meaningful manner, and even more fail to deal effectively with issues outside the European sphere. The blame for this must lie both with those regions that have been lukewarm towards the system and with the national government, which does not wish to discuss policies with the regional tier. The formal bilateral links which have been a feature of Spanish intergovernmental relations continue to play the important role. In addition, it remains the view of many authors that the key institutions in intergovernmental relations in Spain are not those formally created for the purpose, but the all-pervasive political party system (Agranoff and Gallarin, 1997). It is through the largely informal and hidden party links that regions are involved in the national policy process, particularly outside the regions that have strong regionalist or nationalist parties.

In effect, when the regions and the central state need to co-operate on a pan-Spanish basis, they will do so. The sectoral conferences provide the means by which this is achieved. Where it is not in the interests of the *autonomías* or the Spanish Government to operate in this manner, they appear reluctant to do so. European affairs may drive the various competitive elements of the Spanish state together where they perceive a collective front is desirable, but it is far from clear that such collective action will spread beyond the European arena.

11.2.2 Access isn't influence: regional conferences in Italy

Strictly speaking, the Italian system does not have a system of sectoral conferences. Instead it has a number of institutions and procedures which link the regional level to the national policy process. The effectiveness of all these is questionable. Formally, the special regions have the right to participate in the discussions of the national cabinet, but this does not occur. More usefully, individual regions have the right to submit legislation to the national parliament or, collectively, to a national referendum. These powers have been used with some success, but the real influence of the regions upon the national policy process should come from the *Conferenza Permanente Stato-Regioni* (Standing Conference on Relations between the State and the Regions). This body, established in the reforms of 1977, comprises the presidents of the regions, the relevant ministers of the national government and the Prime Minister (or the Minister for Regional Affairs) as chair. Backed by a staff of 60 officials, this is the principal organ of intergovernmental relations established in the Italian regional state (Desideri and Sanantonio, 1997, p 106).

The conference suffers from a number of institutional weaknesses that undermine its formal status. First, its opinions are only advisory, and as the Italian regions are in a weak constitutional position, they do not have the ability of the Belgian or German regions to make themselves heard. Secondly, the conference meets at the behest of the Prime Minister (although meetings must take place every six months) and cannot be called by the regional ministers. It is the central government, too, that sets the agenda. This leaves the regions with guaranteed formal access to the national level but little influence within it.

Regions which lack institutional access to the national level or the provision of a nationally sponsored system of intergovernmental relations, such as those in Italy, are not precluded from establishing such bodies themselves. The Italian Presidents' Conference is the collective voice of the Italian *regioni*. Established in 1980, it holds no formal status within the Italian regional system. Instead it has in effect acted as a powerful lobby group. Although it has had some limited success in abolishing national field agencies through referendum, and has maintained a significant profile for the regions (see section 5.1.1), it is nevertheless no substitute for a *Bundesrat*.

11.2.3 Interregional conferences in the federal systems

Although the three federal systems grant regional governments direct access to the national legislative structure in the form of the regionalised second chamber, sectoral conferences continue to play a pivotal role. Although distinct from the regional involvement in the national legislature, the two structures are not entirely unrelated. The ability of regions to veto national legislation may be a powerful factor in encouraging the federal level to take notice of the decisions of the interregional conferences. Such a luxury is not afforded to the Spanish *autonomías* or the Italian *regioni*.

The key institution in the German system is the Conference of Minister Presidents, held every three or four months. This is the apex of a system of political and administrative conferences that cover the myriad subjects administered or legislated at the *Länder* level. In total around 150 of these institutions existed in 1998 (*Statistisches Bundesamt*, 1998). These conferences discuss matters that fall within *Länder* competence, and should therefore form a distinct structure of intergovernmental relations outside the national framework provided by the *Bundesrat*. In practice, they have increasingly become part of a wider *Dritte Ebene* (third level) system of intergovernmental relations which includes the second chamber.

Specialist *Bundesrat* committees, which generally allow a federal representative to attend, meet regularly to discuss intergovernmental issues. The introduction of the Europe Article (Art 72(2), Basic Law) has meant that *Länder* competencies are increasingly being discussed in the institutions of the *Bundesrat*. The result is a blurring of the formal distinction between the discussion of federal matters by the *Bundesrat* and the discussion of regional matters by the interregional conferences. Inter-*Länder* meetings also have a federal presence in most cases, although this is at the discretion of the *Länder*. Some meetings of these organs remain *Bund*-free zones.

The discussion of *Länder* competencies at the *Bundesrat* level is of constitutional importance. Unlike the *Bundesrat*, these conferences are not established in constitutional law, instead being established through intergovernmental agreement. The decisions of the conferences are reached by consensus and not through majority voting. The transfer of subjects from the conferences to the *Bundesrat* committees leads to the loss of veto for each *Länder*.

The conferences can be the focus for the establishment of interregional state treaties (*Staatsverträge*). These perform an important role in the German system, allowing co-ordination and co-operation in areas of *Länder* responsibility. Rules relating to recognition of university qualifications across Germany were established by such methods, as was Germany's second television channel (ZDF). The result of these trends is a continuing drift away from regional autonomy and towards co-operation. Although this may offer a significant collective countervailing power against the federal level, the clear loser is the principle of regional policy choices and, as a consequence, the *Landtage*.

If the *Bundesrat* is the crucial institution in the operation of the German system of federalism, then the system of intergovernmental conferences is its equivalent in the Belgian federal system. In the highly decentralised Belgian system, these conferences offer a much needed forum for co-operation necessary for the development of successful national policy. As the federal, regional and Community levels possess equal legislative authority, the mode of operation is entirely through consensus. This creates its own problems but does lead to an extreme level of regional impact on the development of federal policy. This is the countervailing power *par excellence*.

The Belgian Constitution (Art 167(4)) and its accompanying special majority laws set down a number of areas in which co-operation agreements must be established, including in relation to international and European Union matters, telecommunications, interregional transport, residence permits and work permits (Polet, 1999). The co-operation agreements established to regulate regional and Community involvement in international agreements and European affairs have been by far the most studied, but the other co-operation agreements and their associated institutions perform an equally important function. The fact that regions and Communities have themselves established co-operation agreements beyond those required is an indication of their utility (Fitzmaurice, 1996, p 160). Each agreement has its own dispute resolution procedures, overseen by the Court of Arbitration itself. Failure to utilise such procedures in the legislative process can lead to the legislation or decree being ruled *ultra vires* (Art 124, Statute of Court of Arbitration; see Fitzmaurice, 1996, p 160).

At the apex of this system of agreements and intergovernmental conferences lies the conciliation committee. This institution acts as a conduit for the exchange of information and, in the final instance, attempts to resolve disputes between the regional, Community and federal tiers. Beneath this committee lie sectoral committees and agreements to ensure that the various federal levels of government are kept informed of each other's actions. The formal separation of powers between the regions, Communities and the federation makes the co-operation mechanisms common in the German federal system less necessary, though it is noticeable that even the limited co-operation agreements and institutions introduced after the reform of 1988 led to criticisms. Most important amongst these was the lack of accountability that these agreements were subject to. The response that most co-operation agreements must be approved by the relevant legislative chamber is only a partial solution, as the decisions reached by the institutions established by such agreements remain outside parliamentary control (Alen and Ergec, 1998, p 30).

11.2.4 Informal and bilateral relations: healthy competition or divide and rule?

The role of informal relations has already been hinted at in the discussion of institutional arrangements given above. In Italy, for example, the Presidents' Conference, although lacking any formal status, has established a prominence in regional affairs due to the limited formal involvement given to the *regioni* in national policy making. In Germany too, the Conference of Minister Presidents has only a semi-formal status, being established by interregional agreement rather than federal law. Informal institutions can clearly make an impact, but to what extent do such relationships give influence to the regional tier?

Almost every Member State of the European Union has an interregional association which co-ordinates regional relations with the central government. In the local government regions these associations are interest groups, not unlike the associations that bind the municipal levels of government. This does not mean they are ineffective or ignored. In Denmark, for example, the association of *amter* councils is formally consulted by the central government on a wide range of issues, and sits on a number of government and parliamentary committees as the representation of the regional tier.

Associations or conferences also play an important part in the federal states mentioned above. Why then do Spain and the United Kingdom lack such collective associations? In the Spanish case the reason lies mainly in the competitive nature of the *autonomías* themselves, but the asymmetrical structure itself clearly plays a part. The same can be said of the United Kingdom. The UK situation will be examined in the conclusion of this chapter, but given the lack of collective arrangements, how do these systems organise intergovernmental relations?

The answer lies in the use of bilateral agreements, particularly in the Spanish system. By 1995, the Spanish Government had agreed 2,500 *convenios* with the 17 *autonomías*. Of these, only 25 were agreed between the central government and more than one region (Börzel, 2000). In addition, a number of *juntas de cooperación* (bilateral commissions) were established to ensure the exchange of information, discussion of joint programmes and settlement of disputes. Notwithstanding the discussion relating to the sectoral conferences above, this bilateral tradition continues to be the norm, particularly between high autonomy regions and the centre. In 1998, for example, Catalonia signed its own agreement on European affairs with the central state (Euskadi, the Basque country, had already done so in 1995). In the eyes of the more regionalist *autonomías* such agreements preserve their autonomy and prevent the problems of the 'joint decision trap' which intergovernmental institutions bring with them.

The bilateral nature of Spanish relations has a significant political element. The minority government of the PSOE in the early 1990s and the Popular Party in 1996 both required the support of regionalist parties to stay in power. The Basque, Catalan and Canary islands regionalist parties themselves (the PNV, the CiU and the CC) were reluctant to join the government itself, given that the basis of their support was pro-autonomy. Instead, they presented a shopping list of demands which were negotiated and implemented through bilateral agreements between the *autonomías* (controlled by the regional parties) and the central state. The political element is not restricted to the high autonomy regions; political parties offer an important route for regional influence on the national tier throughout the Spanish state (Agranoff and Gallarin, 1997, p 37).

Bilateral relations are also a feature of the Italian system. The strong interrelationship between national legislative competence and regional executive competence has lead to the development of programme agreements to co-ordinate policy delivery. It is unclear whether such a system is an example of regional involvement in the policy of the Member State or merely national restriction of already limited regional autonomy. It appears to be something of a two-way process, with the national government relying on regional co-operation to implement its policies. In such circumstances, the financial weakness of the *regioni* must also play a part.

Even in federal systems with far more effective and formalised methods of intergovernmental relations, bilateral relations continue to play a significant role. In Germany, the ability of the *Bundesrat* to veto large sections of the federal government's legislative programme means that it is prudent for the *Bund* to consult with the *Länder* in advance. This it routinely does, giving regions the opportunity to comment upon the proposals and the *Bund* the ability to gauge its chances of success in the second chamber (where the legislation will first be submitted).

The motives of the *Länder* in commenting on this legislation may not be regional, however. It must be remembered that the regional governments are unlikely to be of the same political hue as the *Bund*, and it is rare for the governing coalition to have an absolute majority in the second chamber. This is made more complex by the fact that coalitions at the regional level may be very different from those at the national level. For example, in 2001 an SPD-Green coalition headed the federal government, but in Bremen, Thuringia and Berlin the coalition was SPD-CDU (the principal party of opposition at the national level). The fact that *Länder* elections are held according to their individual timetables means that elections held mid-term often reflect badly upon the governing party. This further raises the likelihood that the *Bundesrat* will favour the opposition parties.

A question then arises. To what extent do the *Bundesrat* and the bilateral contacts that accompany it reflect national politics rather than regional interests? Russell describes the party politics of the German second chamber as 'pervasive' and argues that it is the major driving force behind the *Bundesrat* and its decisions (Russell, 2000, p 86). By extension this could be applied to the informal and bilateral links being discussed here. Is it right to see these merely as political opposition being conducted by other means? There is certainly no doubt that towards the end of the Kohl era the clashes between the *Bundestag* (controlled by the CDU, CSU and FDP coalition partners) and the SPD-dominated *Bundesrat* played itself out along party lines. Does this confirm Russell's thesis?

Closer inspection reveals otherwise. Blair investigated similar suggestions in relation to the *Länder-Bund* disputes that arose from the period 1948–80. He concluded that although these disputes often had a political element, the vast majority were truly disputes about the federal nature of the German state. He pointed out that the opposition, in fact, rarely used all the means at its disposal to defeat the government. Such restraint, he argued, is a crucial part of the German system; should all available methods be used, the state could not function (Blair, 1981, p 69). Nevertheless, party politics and the federal state are closely interwoven. When Chancellor Kohl forgot this towards the end of his career (as Adenauer had done 40 years previously) and attempted to drive his legislation through the federal legislative process without taking account of the *Länder*, who as it happened differed in their political views, the result was predictable. His legislative programme became embroiled in the *Bundesrat* and his failure to compromise played at least some part in his downfall.

Party politics, then, play a part in the intergovernmental relations of the regional system. This is hardly surprising, but the informal control of the party is difficult to gauge. In Germany, it is not enough to overturn the regional aspect of the federal system, while the regional nature of politics in Belgium drives one towards in a similar conclusion. In Spain, the effect is less clear. In those regions where regionalist or nationalist parties dominate, party politics play a role, but as these parties are wedded to the success of their region the impact is transparent. The more opaque examples are found in those regions controlled by the national parties. In these regions, although the influence of the national parties remains strong, it appears that the regional organisation of parties is enough to ensure that a degree of true regionalism remains in the system.

11.3 MUDDLING THROUGH? INTERGOVERNMENTAL RELATIONS IN THE UK

Perhaps it is unsurprising, given the traditions of the British state, that the methods used to structure intergovernmental relations in the United Kingdom are largely informal and bilateral, and lack the clear structural framework seen in most continental European systems. How does this method compare to the examples explored above?

The situation is not unlike that in the early days of the Spanish regional state. With only the more nationalist (and peripheral) regions in existence, bilateral agreements are the easiest, and possibly the only, method of structuring the intergovernmental system. Should the English regions devolve, the desire of the United Kingdom Government to create a degree of uniformity in its relations with the regional tier might increase. It is likely that such a process would be resisted by the 'nations' of the UK, as it was by the high autonomy regions in Spain.

The UK system is not entirely bilateral, however. The unique institution of the British-Irish Council is a clear exception to the bilateral rule, but it is not a fundamental part of the devolved state. Comprising the executives of Ireland, the United Kingdom, Scotland, Wales, Northern Ireland, Jersey, Guernsey and the Isle of Man, this institution was created as a consequence of the Belfast Agreement (Strand 3). Proposed by the Ulster Unionists (in the form of David Trimble) it was intended as a counterbalance to the North-South ministerial councils established under Strand 2, which proved so difficult for the Ulster Unionist Party to accept (Hazell, 2000, p 156). Its genesis was somewhat confused, therefore, but it was noticeable that regionalists and nationalists in Scotland and Wales made much of this new institution, branding it the 'Council of the Isles' and seeing it as an integral part of the wider devolution project. The newly devolved executives in both Scotland and Wales, as well as the executives of the island states, have also warmed to it after initial scepticism, and now embrace it with a degree of enthusiasm.

The enthusiasm of the devolved institutions was not mirrored by those in Whitehall, who have tended to play down its significance. Nevertheless, its importance to the Northern Irish settlement will ensure that it is at least taken seriously by the United Kingdom Government. The institution is merely a forum for discussion between the various governments of the British Islands and Ireland, but as such it represents a distinct break from the past. In fact, it comes as something of a surprise to most outside observers that such an institution did not already exist, given the distinctive nature of the British Islands and the fact that even before devolution five governments existed within them. Only one substantive meeting was held in the first year of the council's operation, although five areas of co-operation have been identified (drugs, social inclusion, environment, transport and the knowledge economy). In each case, a lead administration has been appointed. A further list of future topics was approved in December 1999.

This body is not the only institution to involve the regional tier as a whole in the intergovernmental process. The intergovernmental structure within the UK is capped by the Joint Ministerial Council (JMC). This is the institution through which formal contacts between the regional administrations and the central government in London will be maintained. In practice, the JMC has become a regular feature of the devolved settlement, meeting 12 times in its first year. Hazell sees a political agenda behind the popularity of this body with ministers of the United Kingdom. Gordon Brown in particular has used it as a vehicle to raise his profile in Scotland and to influence the social inclusion agenda he champions beyond England (Hazell, 2000, p 156). The extent to which the JMC is a vehicle for regional influence on national policy is questionable.

Beneath the JMC lies a plethora of sectoral agreements, primarily bilateral, between the government of the United Kingdom and the devolved bodies. All are established on the basis of concordats, or agreements established between the various governments. In practice, the concordats themselves do not appear to be utilised (Canadian High Commission, 2001). The operation of this structure is very much in its infancy and, given that the dominant party is the same in each of the executives, the long term prospects of the system cannot be assessed. Nevertheless, the prevalence of informal agreements may make the position vulnerable.

This brings us to the crux of the issue and links neatly to the subject of the next chapter. The involvement of the regional tier in national policy making is linked inextricably to the issue of dispute resolution. The question that faces the United Kingdom is whether its informal system of concordats will work in a situation where the executives disagree. The question is not so much how the disputes are resolved, but whether the systems created for intergovernmental relations, and by extension dispute resolution, will stand up to these challenges.

CHAPTER 12

DISPUTE RESOLUTION AND
CONSTITUTIONAL ARBITRATION

The fundamental feature that separates regional and federal states from unitary structures is the division of policy responsibility between at least two tiers of government. As demonstrated in Chapter 10, such neat divisions of public authority are very difficult to achieve in practice. Even the most formal systems of divided sovereignty incorporate a high degree of functional overlap. This makes co-operative relationships between the central and regional tiers the norm. The intergovernmental institutions explored in the previous chapter are therefore fundamental to the operation of a successful regional system.

The increasing shift towards co-operative forms of regional and federal government has made the issue of intergovernmental relations the focus of much attention. Nevertheless, the term 'intergovernmental relations' hides a number of complexities which require explanation. Institutions of intergovernmental co-operation can ensure that regions have a role in the creation of national policy and in the development of co-ordinated policy in the state as a whole. The operation of this form of intergovernmental relationship was examined in Chapter 11. The problem is that such institutions do not exist in isolation from the wider political landscape. Regional governments and the central state are political entities, and as such will not always find common cause. A question then arises; what happens when the different levels of government disagree in areas of overlapping interest?

The study of intergovernmental relationships in regional systems is at its core a study of dispute resolution. When all the parties agree, the mechanisms of intergovernmental relations are not challenged. They will work perfectly. The problem arises when such agreement is not forthcoming. It is at this point that the institutions of intergovernmental relations and dispute resolution in the system are put to the test. It is these institutions, which aim to resolve such disputes within the constitutional system, that form the focus of this chapter.

Although many pages of print were used to argue the political advantages and disadvantages of devolution in the UK, rather less time was spent analysing the issue of dispute resolution in the post-unitary structure. In Scotland, the various reports of the Constitutional Convention, although important in establishing the baseline for the devolution settlement, failed to tackle the question of intergovernmental disputes at all. As the convention operated within particular political constraints, it is unsurprising that it avoided the rather negative issue of how the system would operate when things went wrong. Nevertheless, by failing to address the crucial question, the convention appears to have set the trend for ignoring this most fundamental of problems.

The Constitution Unit's report on devolution to Scotland, although examining the issue of disputes, meekly assumed that the final arbiter would necessarily be an existing judicial body, in fact favouring the House of Lords (Leicester, 1996). In practice, this institution was always unlikely to be used, given the constitutional situation. The House of Lords remains a branch of the United Kingdom Parliament and its use would raise the issue of *nemo judex in causa sua* (no one shall judge their own case). Politically this would be difficult to sustain. In the event, the Judicial Committee of the Privy Council was given the dubious privilege of resolving disputes in the UK arising out of the devolved structure (Sched 6, Scotland Act 1998). This institution, although in practice comprising the judges of House of Lords, is not part of the UK Parliament. Nevertheless, whether an existing judicial body, appointed by the national government, is suitable for such a pivotal role in the devolved structure is open to question.

The UK system of devolution will experience disputes and strained relations between the devolved governments and their central counterpart. This has been the experience of every other regionalised state in the EU, and there is no reason to think that the UK's experience will be different. Even in the first years of devolution, when the governing parties are of the same political hue, relations have not always been cordial. Such disputes are an integral part of federal or devolved systems of governance, although this is something that has not yet become accepted in the UK. For such a system to remain stable, the conflicts must be resolved within the constitutional structure.

The following chapter analyses the issue of dispute resolution in the European systems of regional government. Traditionally, mention of dispute resolution causes our thoughts to turn immediately to the judicial branch as the key player in such procedures. This can be misleading. Although the courts are crucial to the resolution of intergovernment disputes, they remain only part of a wider system. It is important to consider the whole system if one is to have a true picture of how disputes are resolved.

The methods used in systems of dispute resolution can be clearly divided into two main groups. What can be loosely termed 'political methods' utilise intergovernmental conferences, second chambers or other varieties of intergovernmental forums to resolve such disputes. Such methods can also utilise national institutions that do not represent regional interests explicitly but rather reflect the wider interests of the state. Often such political attempts at resolution take place within the wider institutions of intergovernmental relations explored in Chapter 11. The key distinguishing feature of these methods is that the resolution mechanisms remain explicitly within the political sphere.

Political methods generally precede recourse to the courts, which comprises the second method of dispute resolution in the regional systems of the European Union. In some cases, the judicial branch will only be involved in the constitutional aspects of dispute resolution, with disputes between the interests of the region and those of the state (or other regions) being handled politically. In practice, this division between the political and the legal is far from clear and often disappears altogether. The interaction between them is a theme of the following discussion.

12.1 THE LEGAL FRAMEWORKS

Invariably the final arbiter in regional systems is judicial. Although the names of the relevant institutions vary (and the title can be politically significant), in practice they can all be described as constitutional courts. Devolution, UK style, has followed this example.

The institution granted the dubious honour of arbitrating over what are euphemistically termed 'devolution issues' under the UK's devolution legislation is the Judicial Committee of the Privy Council. The potential importance of this institution in the development of devolution should not be underestimated. Although all statutes are open to interpretation, constitutional measures are particularly susceptible to dispute. This reflects both the inherent ambiguities that result from dividing power and the controversial nature of such divisions.

It is often easier to avoid such issues than address them in the constitutional legislation (witness the Scotland Act's conspicuous silence on matters of finance and involvement in the European Union). In the interests of passing the legislation, controversial issues may also be left ambiguous. In Spain, the hastily approved regional autonomy granted to Euskadi (the Basque country) and Catalonia proved to have distinct gaps and some contradictions within the legislation (see section 5.3).

These factors may be exacerbated by politicians who wish to exploit such uncertainties for their own ends. This can be particularly true in the early years of a devolved system as the new political actors struggle to assert themselves. In both Germany and Spain, constitutional challenges were a feature of the first years of regional government. The plethora of decisions taken in this period created the fundamental basis upon which the constitutional settlement has developed. The institution that makes these decisions therefore plays a pivotal role in the development of the devolved state.

The role of a constitutional court is far more politically sensitive than that of the ordinary judiciary. Indeed, as the British Lord Chancellor Lord Irving remarked, 'the devolution of governmental power will confer on the British judiciary a wholly new function of a constitutional character' (Irving, 1998). Despite the Lord Chancellor's much quoted opposition to the growth of the political judge, the individuals chosen to administer these new constitutional functions in the United Kingdom will be drawn from the ordinary judiciary. The fact that the judges' new role is supported by statute, 'conferring democratic legitimacy upon this development' (Irving, 1998), cannot hide the fact that democratic legislation will be open to substantive challenge by judges appointed by the central executive.

12.1.1 Some institutional comparisons

In the legislative regions, the arbiter of disputes is, without exception, the final constitutional court or equivalent. Although it is misleading to talk of a 'European' model, the Belgian *Cour d'Arbitrage* and the Spanish *Tribunal Constitucional* exhibit a number of features common to these institutions. To some extent, these characteristics are the result of the influence that the *Bundesverfassungsgericht* or *BVerfG* (the German Constitutional Court) has had on European constitutional thought.

The most striking distinction between these constitutional courts and the UK's institution is the separation of European constitutional tribunals from the ordinary judiciary. This has allowed these courts to develop along lines that are suitable for a constitutional tribunal, although perhaps not for the ordinary courts. The most visible difference between these institutions and traditional courts is the appointment of non-judicial members. In both Spain and Belgium, members appointed from the judiciary form a small minority of the bench.

The Belgian *Cour d'Arbitrage* is perhaps the furthest from the traditional UK court model. Half of the 12 members have no judicial training whatsoever, and qualify for their positions through having previously held democratic mandates in parliament. The remaining six seats are filled with a mixture of legal academics, senior law officers and judges. The peripheral role of the professional judiciary is repeated in Spain. Only three of the 12 Spanish constitutional judges who sat in 1986 were from a judicial background. The remaining nine were appointed from legal academia (although one was a professor of political economy). This practice to some extent follows judicial practice in Western Europe generally, where the appointment of legal academics is the norm. Nevertheless, the extent to which the judiciary is sidelined is greater in the constitutional court than elsewhere.

The separate nature of the constitutional courts is further emphasised by their physical and administrative separation from the ordinary courts and from the other institutions of government. Constitutional courts, without exception, occupy a separate building and are administratively and financially separate from the Ministry of Justice and the ordinary courts. This administrative autonomy serves to underline their independence from the other organs of the state.

12.1.2 Constitutional courts and legitimacy

The fact that a court of the United Kingdom will be empowered to examine the substantive aspects of primary legislation is not, in itself, a negative step. However, it does have serious implications for accountability and democratic legitimacy, none of which have been addressed, or even discussed, in the UK's recent constitutional debate. The failure to examine the wider consequences of bringing the judiciary explicitly into the constitutional and political arena seems based upon the assumption that the Judicial Committee's role will merely be to interpret another statute. Whatever the constitutional position, the devolution legislation will not be perceived as just another statute, and the decisions taken in relation to it will be interpreted in a political context. To ask an ordinary court to undertake this role is not only constitutionally questionable but also politically dangerous.

European approaches recognise the unique nature of a constitutional tribunal, and this is reflected in their separation from the ordinary judiciary. This in itself does not answer the questions of legitimacy that the creation of a superior court raises. However, it does allow these questions to be addressed. The responses can be divided into two types. On the one hand, Belgium has given the *Cour d'Arbitrage* legitimacy by appointing a body which is representative of the major divisions within Belgian society, although with very little democratic accountability. Spain, on the other hand, has followed the German model by appointing constitutional judges for a fixed period and giving the power of appointment to the legislature. The result is a court appointed along political lines with a limited degree of democratic accountability.

The constitutional difficulties were most acute in Belgium where, as in the UK, the concept of parliamentary sovereignty remained a fundamental principle of law. This principle now also applies to the Regional and Cultural Community parliaments. Belgian courts were and, theoretically at least, still are barred from overruling Acts of any of the Belgian parliaments. In addition, the decisions of the Belgian *Conseil d'Etat* and now the *Cour d'Arbitrage* apply only to the case in question. Prior to federalism, Belgian judicial review of public authorities was limited to the procedure and *vires* of secondary legislation. The parliaments remain the only interpreters of Belgian administrative and constitutional law. In common with the UK, however, the Belgian judges had already developed a degree of flexibility in applying these principles.

In 1980, the proposed federalisation of Belgium presented Belgian constitutional theory with a major problem. Although it was accepted that the moves towards devolved government would require some form of institutional arbitration, the form of federalism developed in Belgium posed particular difficulties. As already explored above, the Belgian Constitution has no concept of *Bundesrecht bricht Landesrecht* (federal law overrides regional law). Therefore regional, Community and federal legislation is equally valid within the relevant areas of competence. Should different organs of the federation pass legislation that is contradictory, it is vital for an institution to decide which has encroached on the other's legislative field. Despite the need for such a body, the traditional Belgian reticence towards judicial involvement in political decision making remained. The resulting compromise was the *Cour d'Arbitrage* (Court of Arbitration), created in 1984. The choice of name was symbolic of the idea that this body was not a constitutional court and thus not superior to the democratic organs of the state.

The legitimacy of the court rests upon its representative nature. The inclusion of ex-politicians, representing the different colours of Belgian political opinion, and the significant involvement of regional representatives in the appointment process are the main components of this. The final representative component is the division along linguistic lines. Six of the 12 judges must come from each of the two main language communities of Belgium (French and Dutch). The two Chief Justices (one from each language community) alternate on a yearly basis. The composition of the court therefore recognises the explicitly political nature of the task assigned to it, through the representative nature of its appointments and the inclusion of politicians who are arguably more attuned to the political causes that this institution deals with.

In the event the legislators' fear of 'government by the courts' has proved unfounded and the *Cour d'Arbitrage* has proved a successful institution. By 1988 (four years after its creation), opposition had all but evaporated, and the reforms of that year significantly increased the powers of the court. It is now the guardian of the 'fundamental rights' laid out in the Belgian Constitution (equality, non-discrimination and freedom of education). The court therefore has the explicit power to undertake substantive review of legislation and to strike down any that infringes these principles. The *Cour d'Arbitrage* has interpreted these principles broadly and, to all intents and purposes, is now the constitutional authority of the Belgian state. For Belgium to move from a position where parliamentary sovereignty is a fundamental principle to one where the court is the final arbiter in less that eight years is quite a remarkable achievement.

Although the Belgian compromise created an institution representative of the major divisions within Belgian society, and thus more suited to taking subjective decisions, it is less accountable than most of its European counterparts. When one considers that the primary concern in Belgium was the creation of an undemocratic institution superior to the legislatures, this lack of accountability is rather surprising. It is nevertheless understandable in the context of Belgian society. Given the strong feelings that arise between the constituent regions of Belgium, the regular appointment of *Cour d'Arbitrage* judges could be a point of conflict in a system designed to avoid such constitutional flashpoints. It was therefore preferable to avoid regular elections of the courts. Nevertheless, the system does provide for a degree of political involvement and democratic legitimacy.

The appointment of the Belgian *Cour d'Arbitrage* is in the hands of the Belgian monarch on the advice of the federal government. The choice is limited to those put forward by the Belgian Senate. The membership of this institution represents the parliaments of Belgium's Communities, as well as directly elected members and members co-opted by other senators. The list, which comprises twice the number of judges required, must be approved by a two-thirds majority of the Senate, ensuring that it has the widespread support of the different language and political groupings.

The judges, once appointed, have permanent tenure until the age of 70. The democratic legitimacy of the superior court is thus based on the creation of a representative institution rather than an accountable one. The *Cour d'Arbitrage* remains one of the least democratically accountable of European constitutional courts. Nevertheless, the method of appointment involves a far greater degree of accountability than is utilised in the UK.

The legitimacy of the constitutional courts was something that taxed the framers of both the Spanish and German constitutions, and continues to be a live point of debate in these countries (Limbach, 1996). As in Belgium, the complete separation of the Spanish Constitutional Court and its German counterpart from the ordinary courts allowed a degree of accountability to be introduced into the appointment process. In both these examples, judges are directly appointed by the legislature for a non-renewable fixed term. In Germany, half are appointed by the *Bundestag* and half by the *Bundesrat* (by qualified majorities). The involvement of the upper house ensures that the Länder are involved in the process. The court's legitimacy, however, is founded on accountability rather than its representative nature.

The majority of the Spanish constitutional judges are appointed by the *Cortes* (four by each house, by a 60% majority). The government and the general council of the judiciary also appoint two judges each. The term of appointment is nine years, but a third of the judges are replaced at three-yearly intervals. As in Germany and Belgium, the court's role as arbiter of the regionalised system is recognised by the involvement of the Senate, which includes regional representatives. In practice, despite its claim to be the chamber of territorial representation, the Spanish Senate as presently constituted is not a regional chamber. Only 48 of the 256 members elected in

1993 represented the regions. Although regional representatives are involved in the process, their influence is minimal.

Although membership is open to judges, academics and prosecutors, the Spanish Constitutional Court has been dominated by academics (who comprised nine of the 12 members in 1986). Two of the remaining three constitutional judges are appointed by the judiciary themselves. This preference for academics reflects both the political nature of the court (the academics are generally associated with one political party or another) and the lack of confidence that the population and their representatives still have in the Spanish judiciary (Newton and Donaghy, 1997, p 303).

The resulting courts, in both Germany and Spain, are to some extent representative of the political divisions within the country; more importantly, they are elected. The regular election of constitutional judges gives the court a degree of democratic legitimacy. It should be noted, however, that the election of *Bundesverfassungsgericht* (Federal Constitutional Court) judges has not entirely answered the question of judicial law making, which continues to be a live issue in German legal and political debate. If an elected court raises such objections, it seems inconceivable that an unelected one such as the UK's Judicial Committee will escape such criticism.

12.1.3 The UK's constitutional court?

The decision to leave constitutional arbitration to a judicial body which is, in practice, part of the existing system of ordinary courts fits well with predominant theories of UK constitutional law. The Judicial Committee has performed a similar role before, though more in theory than in practice, during the period of Northern Irish home rule. It was therefore the easiest choice for the job of constitutional arbiter in the new devolved structure. However, although it may be the easiest choice, there has been little or no debate on whether it is the most suitable.

The Judicial Committee dates back to 1833, when it was created to adjudicate on the increasing number of appeals to the Privy Council. Although appeals to the monarch were abolished by the English Parliament in 1640, the crown retained its appellate role in relation to overseas territories. In constitutional terms it is not a court, instead advising the government, which implements its judgments through Orders in Council. Its 'advice' is never ignored.

During the 19th century, the role of the committee expanded considerably, and at its zenith it could claim to be the Court of Appeal of the British Empire. However, this situation was short lived as the court's jurisdiction diminished in tandem with the empire itself. Today, it retains a residual role as the final Court of Appeal of the Channel Islands, the Isle of Man and a handful of dependent territories and ex-colonies. It also retains jurisdiction over a number of other miscellaneous matters including universities, electoral law and appeals from professional bodies.

In theory, the committee comprises a huge membership including the Lord President of the Privy Council (who by convention never sits); the Lord Chancellor; any member of the Privy Council who has held high judicial office in the UK; senior members of some Commonwealth judiciaries (those which still recognise its jurisdiction); and Law Lords and appeal court judges (or equivalent) in Scotland, England and Northern Ireland. In practice, custom restricts its working membership to Law Lords, senior representatives from the Commonwealth, and the occasional senior appeal court judge. This is confirmed by the devolution Acts (s 94(2), Scotland Act 1998) which limit its membership to those members who hold or have held high judicial office in the UK, thus unfortunately excluding judges from Commonwealth jurisdictions which have experience of multi-tier government. Rather surprisingly, the Acts do not appear to exclude retired judges who remain members of the Privy Council.

At present the committee generally comprises five Law Lords, although the quorum is three. The Judicial Committee is therefore the House of Lords' appellate committee by another name. When the Scotland Act decrees that the House of Lords should defer issues of devolutionary importance to the Judicial Committee, unless it feels the individual facts of the case merit a House of Lords decision (Sched 6(32), Scotland Act 1998), it actually requires little more than a change of venue, though custom may also require a change of personnel.

Under devolution, this rather archaic institution has been given the final power to review Acts of the devolved parliaments and assemblies of the UK. This will include the primary legislation that will emanate from Edinburgh and Belfast. The devolution Acts, by defining the authority of the devolved institutions, are the *de facto* regional constitutions of the United Kingdom. They will operate in a way not unlike the regional statutes found in Spain, Italy and Portugal.

On issues of devolution at least, the Judicial Committee will therefore become the UK's constitutional court, if one with a limited remit. Crucially, it will have the power to review the Acts of the devolved legislatures on their substantive aspects.

12.1.4 The significance of constitutional arbitration

During the early years of a regional system, constitutional courts play a disproportionate role in their development. No matter how detailed, the constitutional or legislative structures will always leave significant scope for interpretation. Until these are tested in the cold light of politics, the final shape of the regional state will not be apparent. The fundamental issue that is raised during this period is the extent to which formal legislative or constitutional authority accorded to the region will translate into regional autonomy. In the UK, the devolution settlements have yet to be tested in the courts. Few cases of wider significance have arrived before the Judicial Committee of the Privy Council. Although a number of challenges to devolved legislation have been heard, these have concerned breaches (or alleged breaches) of Convention rights (see section 10.3) and not disputes between the levels of government. Whether such restraint will be maintained when the parties are not of like political mind is debatable.

The Spanish Constitutional Court was flooded with cases during the formative years of the regional system, but the pattern of challenges changed during this period. In 1981, the central state challenged 11 out of the 27 laws passed by Basque and Catalan legislatures, the only *autonomías* established at the times. From this high point, the central state's use of the constitutional court has declined. In 1990, it undertook only 13 challenges of the 186 Autonomous Community laws passed in that year. Only two of these were against high autonomy regions. The reticence of the central state was not matched by the *autonomías*. As cases brought by the central state began to die away in the mid-1980s, regional challenges increased dramatically. In 1985, 13 of the 57 national laws promulgated were challenged by the Basque or Catalan executives alone. Six challenges were made by other *autonomías*. In 1988, the Constitutional Court was kept even busier, with at least 19 of the 44 national laws facing *autonomía* challenge. The activities in this period reflected the jockeying for position by the two tiers of government, with national legislation attempting to impose national frameworks upon the *autonomías*. During this time, the rough edges of the Spanish regional framework were smoothed out by reference to the court. A number of key decisions were reached which have underpinned the Spanish regional system.

Principal amongst these were the cases surrounding the controversial and ultimately unconstitutional *Ley Orgánica de Armonización del Proceso Autonómico* (LOAPA). This organic law, which implemented an agreement between the governing UCD and the opposition PSOE, was introduced in the aftermath of the failed coup of 1981. In the charged atmosphere of the time, the national parties viewed the process of autonomy as a threat to Spanish democracy, since the rapid growth in regional autonomy was used by the plotters as evidence of the collapse of the Spanish state. The LOAPA was duly passed.

The consequences of this law would have fundamentally reduced the autonomy of the Spanish regions. The law envisaged the creation of basic national norms across Spain within which the regions could exercise their autonomy. These would apply across all spheres of regional autonomy, including areas in which the regional statutes granted autonomy to the regional tier. No definition of how extensive these norms were to be was included in the legislation, but if regional legislation were in conflict with them the national legislation would prevail. In effect, the LOAPA would have nullified many of the regional statutes and subjected regional laws to national legislation. Regional autonomy would have been limited to frameworks provided by the national level.

In its decision, the constitutional court ruled that in its fundamentals the LOAPA was unconstitutional. By this decision it set the framework for the future of Spanish regionalism. This was to be a system of legislative regions with full autonomy in those areas granted to them under their statutes. In ruling as it did, the court also exhibited a degree of political awareness. Although it defended the legislative autonomy of the regions, it accepted a number of procedural harmonisation mechanisms. These included the harmonisation of regional elections (in the low autonomy regions) and basic procedural norms in the legislative processes of the *autonomías*. After this and a number of other fundamental decisions of the constitutional courts concerning, among other things, European and international affairs, and *autonomía* attempts to abolish the provincial tier, the system has settled. Although significant autonomy issues still come before the *Tribunal Constitucional*, the amount of legislation now challenged is greatly reduced.

The importance of the constitutional court in establishing the framework of the federal and regional system is repeated in other examples. In Germany, the key decisions came in 1957 (the Concordat case, 6 *BVerfGE* 309), 1961 (the Television case, 12 *BVerfGE* 205) and a series of cases concerning concurrent powers which were confirmed in the 1954 North Rhine-Westphalian Salaries case (4 *BVerfGE* 115). The first of these, the Concordat case, restricted the ability of the federation to use its international affairs competence (Art 73(1), Basic Law) to limit *Länder* competencies, and introduced the concept of *Bundestreue* (federal comity) into the federal system (see section 8.1). It is important to note that the court's interpretation of the relevant provisions in these cases was not a foregone conclusion. Had Art 73(1) been interpreted as including the federal level's right to implement or ensure implementation of international obligations, as is the case in the United States, the powers of the federation would been significantly enhanced at the expense of the regional tier. In addition, the pivotal role now enjoyed by the *Bundesrat* owes much to the Television case (12 *BVerfGE* 205). Again, this was not the only outcome open to the court. Had these cases gone against the *Länder*, the German federation would look very different today.

The same is true of the cases which surrounded the interpretation of concurrent powers and particularly Art 72(2) of the Basic Law. This Article defines the circumstances in which the *Bund* may enact legislation from the list of concurrent powers (Art 74, Basic Law). This was discussed more fully above (see sections 4.2.4 and 10.5.1), but the court interpreted this Article as being a matter of *Bund* discretion, and thus not a matter for judicial interpretation. The court would only review such actions if the *Bund* abused its discretion or went beyond the limits of Art 74 (which the court has generally interpreted strictly). By this decision, the extensive list of concurrent powers in Art 74 became *de facto* responsibilities of the *Bund* as soon as the federation decided that national legislation was required. Over time the *Länder* legislative role in this list has been reduced almost to nil. Once again, the court's interpretation has had a profound effect on the federation. The fact that 40 years later the *Länder* have introduced an amendment to the Basic Law in an attempt to claw back some of these basic powers is evidence of the importance of this decision to the regional tier. Such, attempts will still be dependent on the court's decisions, however. Once again, the pivotal role of the court is clear.

As in Spain, the numbers of regional disputes which have been submitted to the German Constitutional Court have declined over time. Nevertheless, although its impact may be quantitatively less, the court continues to have a significant impact on the federal system. Two recent examples have been the second Television case of 1995 (1 *BVerfGE* 89) and the intermittent challenges to the federal finance arrangements (Hingorani, 1997). Although the Basic Law may give the broad picture, it is the constitutional court that continues to play the key role in defining its practical implications.

The impact of constitutional courts in Italy and Portugal has also been profound. By interpreting the constitutions of both countries in a unitary manner, they have limited the effectiveness of the regional statutes. This has created a very different regional structure from that which is *prima facie* described in the constitutional texts themselves.

The question for students of the UK's fledgling system is how the judicial resolution of intergovernmental disputes will affect the devolution settlement. In most of the examples given above, the courts have been called upon to defend the regional state. There is no reason to suspect that a similar situation will not arise in the UK. The decisions of the Spanish and German courts defended the autonomous system of regional government, often against strong central pressure. By contrast, Italian and Portuguese regions received no such support from the courts. The results in both cases had profound effects on the regional system, far beyond the particular constitutional question. Whether the UK's devolution tribunal will have the will or the ability to defend the devolution settlement remains open to question, but at some point it will be expected to perform this role. If it fails to do so the long term effect on the devolution settlement will be profound.

12.1.5 Will the old dog learn new tricks?

The UK Government's choice of the Judicial Committee as the institutional arbiter of the devolution settlement rests upon the assumption that the committee's role will merely be one of interpreting an ordinary statute. This will not be the case. Whatever the constitutional position, the devolution Acts will be perceived as more than merely ordinary statutes of the Westminster Parliament. The decisions of this institution are likely to be politically charged and its reasoning will be carefully scrutinised. Whatever the constitutional niceties, most cases that reach the Judicial Committee will be disputes between the devolved institutions. This will place the UK's courts in a political spotlight that they are entirely unused to.

Regardless of the strict constitutional position, the committee is and will continue to be the House of Lords by another name. Its exact composition will be decided by the most senior Law Lord and its membership will continue to comprise Law Lords who are themselves appointed exclusively by the UK Government. Although it has been suggested that the committee could sit in Edinburgh, to suggest that this would be anything other than the House of Lords on tour is rather naive. If it looks like an elephant and sounds like an elephant, only those who had never seen one would assert it was anything else.

This presents a potentially serious political problem. There is no pretence that this institution is representative of the political, regional, national or other divisions of the UK, and it will continue to lack any semblance of representation or accountability to the democratic legislature. Given that its role will only be to adjudge Acts of the devolved institutions against their respective devolution Act, the devolved institutions will have no role in choosing their keeper. The idea that an unrepresentative and unelected body should be given the power to overrule a democratic legislature is at best controversial and at worst unconstitutional. The political repercussions of this could be substantial. As a UK institution, the committee will always be open to the accusation that it is representative of the views of the centre. Whatever the truth of this view, it could prove a destabilising factor in the devolution settlement.

12.2 THE POLITICAL CONTEXT

The constitutional aspects of dispute resolution considered above, although crucial to the understanding of devolved and federal systems, mean little when taken out of their political contexts. In this final section we shall examine the effects of court decisions on the wider regional system. It must be remembered that dispute resolution does not sit as a distinct subject on its own. Rather it is part of a wider system of intergovernmental relations, which interact to produce the regional system itself. Dispute resolution, to misquote Chou En-Lai, is a continuation of intergovernmental relations by other means.

The use of political methods to resolve intergovernmental disputes brings with it a number of advantages and difficulties. The clearest advantage for the institutions concerned is that the political actors retain control of the process by keeping such disputes out of the judicial system. This can also be useful in avoiding the overloading of the constitutional adjudication system. It also keeps essentially political disputes in the hands of elected politicians.

In several states (most noticeably the UK and Belgium), there remains strong opposition to giving the judiciary the authority to direct the institutions of government. These traditions remain evident in constitutional settlements that place a heavy emphasis on negotiation in an effort to avoid recourse to a constitutional arbiter. In Germany, although concerns continue to be expressed as to the constitutional court's precise role, it views itself as the guardian of the constitution. This includes the federal principle. Both *Länder* and *Bund* refer disputes to the court, often as part of a wider negotiating strategy. This confirms the acceptance of its status.

The difficulty with political methods of intergovernmental dispute resolution is that they rely on negotiation and consensus politics. Such informal methods therefore require a degree of constitutional trust to be exhibited by both parties in order to operate successfully. Work by Erk and Gagnon has examined the role of what they describe as 'constitutional ambiguity' in the operation of regional and federal systems (Erk and Gagnon, 2000). They define this as a situation where the roles of each level are not strictly defined, leaving the possibility of conflict between levels of government. This, they argue, is a positive aspect in a federal or devolved system, allowing greater flexibility within the system, particularly where interregional tensions remain an issue. This is contrasted with a system where federalism is 'codified'. In the language of public law, Erk and Gagnon are contrasting a system based on convention with one based upon statute.

The problem with such flexible 'ambiguous' structures is that they require some equality of the parties in order to be meaningful. This is often not the case, with the central state having a number of cards that are not held by the regions. Erk and Gagnon argue that for such systems to operate successfully a high degree of 'federal trust' is necessary. This they define as 'reliance on the integrity of one another and an overall commitment to the maintenance of the partnership' (Erk and Gagnon, 2000, p 94). It does not require a common position and consensus. They thus attempt to distinguish their variant of federal trust from the principle of *Bundestreue* (or federal comity) as enforced by the German Constitutional Court, although the argument is not altogether convincing.

Their analysis represents a misunderstanding of the role that constitutions and formal statutory frameworks play in the operation of federal and regional systems. Although the role of formal constitutional rules is important, no constitutional structure can eliminate constitutional ambiguity; even if this were possible, the application of such principles would be heavily influenced by the decisions of the constitutional arbiter.

Nevertheless, there are a number of tempting features in Erk and Gagnon's theory, particularly at its most simplistic level. The evidence clearly supports the assertion that some degree of federal trust is required in systems where intergovernmental relations are based upon convention or informal relations. However, most federal or regional systems rely on conventions and informal agreements to operate successfully. It is therefore more accurate to state that the more a federal or devolved system relies upon constitutional convention for successful intergovernmental relationships, the greater the degree of federal trust required between the parties. The UK's system of intergovernmental relations, which is entirely based upon informal mechanisms, clearly falls at the extreme end of this category.

A second and more fundamental problem lies in the conclusions posited by Erk and Gagnon. They argue that if the parties to a system based upon convention lack mutual trust the system will fail and greater codification will follow. However, does this assertion really get us anywhere? This appears to be a case of stating the obvious. The proof of any federal or devolved structure is its ability to cope with disputes between the parties. When we discuss intergovernmental relations, the key issue is not what happens when the parties agree (though the mechanics of this are nevertheless important) but what happens when the opinions of the participants diverge.

When governments agree, the need for the institutionalisation of relations is minimal. Significant problems only arise when disputes between governments develop. To suggest that a system which incorporates significant constitutional ambiguity requires federal trust to work is like saying that these systems are successful right up until the moment they stop being so. The moment at which a system based upon convention (and by definition, this appears to be all varieties of regional government in the EU) will be tested will be the moment when such federal trust breaks down.

The importance of Erk and Gagnon's work is therefore not in stating that federal trust is required, but highlighting the wider issue of how systems which rely upon federal trust and good faith continue to ensure that such faith is shown by the parties when disputes develop. This is the key to understanding intergovernmental relations in any federal or devolved system. The relationship must continue to operate when the partners are in dispute. How this occurs is based upon a combination of the constitutional power of regions, the decisions of constitutional courts and regional political strength. The way in which these political factors interact with the legal framework surrounding them explains how federal trust is retained in practice.

12.2.1 Dispute resolution and federal trust

The influence of the federal constitutional court on the highly formalised German federal system has been substantial. Nevertheless, to understand its impact fully we must examine it in reference to intergovernmental relations and dispute resolution as a whole. At the apex of intergovernmental relations in Germany is the *Bundesrat*. This constitutionally guaranteed institution of collective regional authority ensures that the regions are represented at the national level. Outside this, inter-*Länder* relations are conducted through the non-statutory intergovernmental ministerial conferences (which include representatives of the *Bund*). Beyond these formal mechanisms the vast majority of relations are carried out through informal and bilateral means. The emphasis is on negotiation and consensus, with most decisions being non-binding unless agreed otherwise.

Despite the differences between the constitutional structures of the UK and Germany, distinct similarities exist in relation to the operation of intergovernmental relations. In particular, the UK's system of concordats emphasises the informal nature of intergovernmental relations. The differences are that beyond the informal agreements there is little in the way of a formal structure. There is certainly no equivalent of a *Bundesrat*. Even the devolution Acts themselves are silent on the matter. What effect will the lack of a formal framework have on the development of these relationships in the UK?

The need for *Bundesrat* approval in all legislation where *Länder* autonomy is restricted (which amounts to over 50% of all legislation) means that co-operation between the *Bund* and *Länder* is vital if the federal government is to successfully deliver its programme. Despite the legislative dominance of the *Bund*, the concerns of the Länder must be considered. The key to ensuring that federal trust is shown by the *Bund* is the constitutional protection that the *Länder* enjoy. The collective power of the *Länder* through the institution of the *Bundesrat* was not guaranteed by the Basic Law. Article 84(1) could have been interpreted restrictively by the constitutional court, allowing most federal legislation to pass without the requirement for *Bundesrat* approval. The fact that it was interpreted broadly along the lines that had been advocated by the *Länder* was due to the Federal Constitutional Court. Through its defence of *Länder* rights, and particularly the development of *Bundestreue*, it has ensured that the *Bund* and each *Land* cannot conduct intergovernmental relations as they wish. Instead, a degree of federal trust must be shown. This 'mutual respect' must also incorporate a degree of loyalty to the federal constitution itself.

The landmark case which set the tone for future *Länder-Bund* relations was set in the controversial *Television* case of 1961 (12 *BVerfGE* 205). The judgment of the court, which went far beyond consideration of the specific issues raised by the case itself, concerned the question of whether the exclusive power of the *Bund* over telecommunications included the establishment of a television station. The judgment incensed the federal government of Konrad Adenauer and, although it may have marked a high point in judicial activism, its impact is still evident in the federal system of today. The judges' view can be summed up in the following paragraph:

> The conduct and style of such negotiations as may become necessary in constitutional practice between the federation and its members and between the *Länder* are also subject to the requirement of *Bundestreue*. [12 *BVerfGE* 205 as quoted in Kommers, 1997.]

The case itself did not require the court to indulge in this type of language. The court felt that the *Bund*, in establishing a second television channel, had clearly overstepped its constitutional competencies as laid out in Art 73(4). Nevertheless, the court also examined the actions of the *Bund* with reference to the policy of negotiating with selected *Länder* (who happened to be of the same political persuasion as the federal government). The court took this opportunity to confirm that the concept of *Bundestreue* applied just as much to the *Bund* as it did to the *Länder* (as established in the *Concordat* case). The *Bund* was therefore obliged to consult all the *Länder* as part of its duty to federal comity.

To some extent the joint tasks have undermined the German court's attempts to monitor intergovernmental decision making. These are a constitutionally defined list of competencies which the *Länder* have agreed to handle at the federal level in co-operation with the *Bund* (Art 91(a) and (b), Basic Law). The legislation covering the operation of these tasks creates a number of committees in which both the *Länder* and the *Bund* are represented. *Bund* dominance of the committees makes individual *Länder* influence limited. Article 91(a) and (b) of the Basic Law, by putting the institutions within a constitutional framework, have placed them beyond the reach of the court. Nevertheless, the court has not stood idly by in this development, and has given signs that it will intervene again if the ideal of federal comity is blatantly disregarded. As ever, the court is conscious of not overstepping its role as constitutional arbiter (Blair, 1981).

The power of the *Länder*, as defined by the constitutional court, and particularly as exercised collectively through the *Bundesrat*, has ensured that their opinions must be considered. It is not enough for the *Bund* merely to pay lip service to the *Länder* in their negotiations, a fact that has further been emphasised by the actions of the constitutional court in its reference to the concept of federal comity. The intergovernmental system may be informal but it is real. The constitutional cards held by the *Länder* collectively, and the defence provided by the constitutional court, have given the regional tier a negotiating platform that on occasion they have been able to use very effectively. The federal trust that is shown by the *Bund* to the *Länder* (and vice versa) was forced upon the *Bund*. Put simply, the *Bund* exhibits a degree of federal trust towards its regional partners because it has to.

The importance of intergovernmental negotiation to the Belgian system is hard to overemphasise. In a federal system where legislation is equally valid whether it originates from the regional or the federal tier, co-operation is the key. This emphasis has led to some major differences between the Belgian system of intergovernmental relations and those established elsewhere. The Belgian system is highly formalised, even to the extent that the establishment of institutions is explicitly mentioned in the constitutional texts. These are grounded in organic laws.

The formal nature of intergovernmental relations in Belgium is driven by the equality of laws. The result is a system headed by a conciliation committee (not unlike the UK's Joint Ministerial Council) comprising the representatives of the governments of all the federal partners. Most discussions take place in the plethora of committees that sit at departmental level and liaise between the relevant federal entities. The key factor here is that agreements must be struck, as no level is capable of overruling another. To some extent the Belgian court of arbitration has also intervened to enforce a degree of federal comity on the partners.

The necessity of 'federal trust' is most clearly shown in the relationship between Belgium and the European Union. The position of the Belgian delegation to the Council of Ministers is agreed between parties before and during negotiations. If no agreement can be reached by the relevant representatives, Belgium abstains. This is a rare occurrence. It is better to have a compromise opinion than none at all. Again, a degree of good faith is forced upon the parties; it does not arise by accident.

The Spanish system of intergovernmental relations has many similarities to the UK system. Unlike Belgian and German regional governments, the Spanish *autonomías* are explicitly constitutionally inferior to the national level. Although they possess a significant level of autonomy under their statutes there is no pretence that they are the equal of the national government. Changes to regional statutes require the support of both houses of the Spanish *Cortes* by absolute majority, but the example of the LOAPA has shown that this can be achieved in matters of autonomy. As in the UK, the greatest protection for the *autonomías* is political. However, such changes to the constitution of Spain would require two-thirds majorities in both houses of the Spanish Parliament, making the political threshold far higher than that needed in the UK. Having said this, the extent of central power in

Spain, particularly in relation to EU matters, is such that negotiations between the parties are not equal.

The sectoral conferences which form the key institutions of intergovernmental relations between the *autonomías* and the central government are established by statute, but agreements reached are by consensus. In practice, the sectoral conferences meet infrequently. The majority of relations between the Spanish Government and the *autonomías* are conducted bilaterally in a system not unlike the UK's use of concordats. Does federal trust exist in this system? Again, the answer is broadly yes. The informal bilateral arrangements generally function, and there is evidence that the sectoral conferences increasingly do so.

However, in contrast to the situation in Germany and Belgium, the Spanish Constitution gives far fewer means to resist the national government's position. There is no *Bundesrat*, and no equality of laws. The negotiating position of the *autonomías* is consequently significantly weaker than that of the Regions or Communities of Belgium and the *Länder* of Germany, so why does the system work? Part of the answer is again clearly found in reference to the constitutional court. The decisions of the *Tribunal Constitucional*, particularly in relation to the LOAPA, have defended the regional space. As in Germany, this has forced the central state to respect the regions' autonomy.

A number of other factors must also be included in the equation, however. The Spanish regions have used political weapons to gain influence. The use of borrowing in the late 1980s to finance expenditure until the central government agreed to a more generous financial settlement was one example of this. The clearest example, however, was the 'kingmaking' power that the regionalist parties (particularly the Catalan CiU and the Basque PNV) enjoyed during much of the 1990s. During this period the regional parties were able to extract significant concessions both for themselves and, by extension, the regional tier as a whole. Once again, the federal trust required to make an informal system work did not emerge by accident. It was forced upon the parties concerned.

Lacking the constitutional bargaining counters that force the *Bund* and the Belgian federal government to take note of the regions in Germany and Belgium, the Spanish *autonomías* have utilised political and financial power to achieve the same ends, with some success. This has been aided by decisions of the constitutional court.

The UK's system of devolution is one built primarily on convention. This in itself is not a problem, but for such a system to work it will require the 'federal trust' evident above. Will this be forthcoming? Federal trust is a concept that does not develop voluntarily. In all the examples discussed above, it has been forced upon the parties concerned. Through a combination of constitutional protection, interventions by the constitutional tribunal and political necessity, the central state has been forced to respect the autonomy of the regional tier. When disputes arise, it takes a very controlled politician not to use the powers available to them to ensure that the policy pursued is the one they favour. When such powers are denied, the temptation is removed.

The informal system of intergovernmental relations coupled with the high level of constitutional convention inherent in the UK's system of devolution will require a significant degree of good faith on all sides to operate successfully. The question is whether there is any method of ensuring that such federal trust will be forthcoming. An informal system of intergovernmental relations cannot exist when one party has the ability to ignore the other's point of view, thus making a negotiated settlement all but pointless. The development of federal trust requires a degree of equality.

In the UK example, the supremacy of Westminster and its domination by the UK Government places all the constitutional cards in the central state's hands. The concordat system is weak, informal and limited, although the possibility of consultation procedures or the giving of reasons may be possible through the concept of legitimate expectation. The result would in all probability be limited to procedural rights, which can prove less than effective within the UK's system of administrative law. The role of the UK judiciary in the devolutionary settlement is such that it will be unlikely to develop into the 'honest broker' that has been seen in Spain and Germany, even should it wish to. The final irony for those who proposed devolution as a defence against the growth of peripheral nationalism in the UK may be that the federal trust necessary to make the informal system of intergovernmental relations work will depend on the threat that these nationalist parties pose. When the stakes are down, the nationalist threat may be the only bargaining chip that the devolved institutions have.

CHAPTER 13

A EUROPE WITH REGIONS?

This volume began by examining the rationales and reasons behind the creation of a regional tier. In this final chapter, we examine the extent to which these aims have been fulfilled and the extent to which the development of the third level has changed the governance of Europe. To begin this assessment we must first establish the true role of the regional tier in the EU today.

13.1 REGIONAL AUTONOMY IN THE EUROPEAN UNION

Part two of this work began by classifying the various types of regional government along traditional 'constitutional' lines. Three clear models emerged. The most constitutionally independent of these were the federations (Austria, Germany and Belgium), followed by the constitutionally guaranteed regions of Italy, Spain and Portugal (and the Åland islands of Finland). Bringing up the rear was a final group of regions lacking constitutional status altogether. This section uses these classifications as the basis for a comparison of regional autonomy. Starting from these legal structures, how extensive is regional independence when the variables of financial and functional autonomy are added to the equation? Do these formal structures reflect a hierarchy of true regional autonomy?

The federal status of Austria, Germany and Belgium has acted as a secure shell within which regional financial and functional autonomy has flourished. These regions remain the most influential within the European Union. Influence is not necessarily autonomy, however, and much of the authority they possess is collective. In Germany, in particular, the *Länder* have significant influence over many policies when they act collectively, but not when they act individually. This will, by definition, reduce the operation of regional policy independence, an effect that is more fully examined below. Despite this tendency to use their freedom to conform, regions in Belgium and Germany in particular have seen the constitutional protection afforded to them translated into a significant degree of potential and actual autonomy.

The inability of the federal level to control Belgian regions through finance or claims of federal comity allows the functional autonomy of the regions to be taken at face value. Belgian Regions and Cultural Communities control policy across a wide range of fields, such as education, health, economic development and agriculture. With the exception of health, these are all handled exclusively by the Region or Community. The lack of a hierarchy of laws forces the different categories of government to negotiate when their competencies clash. Nevertheless, even the highly autonomous Belgian regional structures must act within the macroeconomic framework established by the nation-state. The crisis for the Belgian nation-state may arise when the single currency elevates these decisions to the European arena (even now, some of these functions are already handled supranationally in Benelux).

The involvement of the Belgian regions in international relations is also a major advance for regional authorities in the EU. Until recently, the right to enter into official treaties has been the exclusive preserve of nation-states, with few meaningful exceptions. Even in Austria and Germany, where regional international relations are permitted, such agreements must have the backing of the national government. The ability of the Belgian regions to enter into such negotiations independently makes their status *sui generis*. The involvement of the Communities and Regions in the Council of Ministers, whatever their effectiveness, adds further to this. Despite some limitations, the Belgian regions are clearly the most autonomous in Europe.

Most lay observers would probably identify the German *Länder* as the most powerful independent regions in the European Union. In fact, the 50 years since the federation's inception have seen it move significantly, although not decisively, towards a centralist approach. The German regions have not become irrelevant, however. On the contrary, as Jeffrey has put it, they have in recent years 'fought back' to regain a significant degree of the ground lost to the *Bund* (Jeffrey, 1994). The assessment of Bulmer that 'in terms of both the transfer of constitutional responsibilities and the shift in financial power, West German federalism has been characterised by a process of centralisation' is overly pessimistic (Bulmer, 1990, p 6).

Use of the *Bundesrat* by the *Länder* has been the largest single factor in the defence of regional autonomy. Although the framers of the Basic Law did not envisage the second chamber as having a major legislative function, the role of the *Bundesrat* in this area has developed substantially. The broad interpretation of what comprises *Länder* interests has given the regions the ability to veto a swathe of federal legislation. This need for *Bundesrat* support and therefore regional blessing has given the *Länder* a major influence over the *Bund*, especially in relation to European Union policy. This has forced the *Bund* to listen when the *Länder* have spoken. However, the regional voice is a collective one, not representative of individual regions. The serious drawbacks of this situation are explored below, but it has nevertheless ensured Länder participation in areas which otherwise might have been exclusively managed by the *Bund*. One indicator of this regional participation is manifested in the new encroachment of the *Länder* into the previously exclusive nation-state bastion of international affairs.

Although the official involvement German regions beyond national borders is limited to the EU, and is far less than that of Belgium, the fact that the *Länder* participate at all is a tribute to the success of their 'fight back'.

The weakest link in the autonomy of the German regions is in the functions they are able to undertake. Although the Basic Law gives them a general competence to undertake any power not explicitly granted to the *Bund*, the federation has, through the interpretation of concurrent powers, been given a long list of responsibilities. The regions by contrast retain exclusive competence only for the police, education, local government and culture. Even in these areas, the 'joint tasks' have eaten into their competencies. This removal of functional areas from the *Länder* is the most serious threat to regional autonomy in Germany. To compound this, the remaining areas of *Länder* involvement are increasingly undertaken by *Land* executives on behalf of the regions as a whole. The bypassing of regional parliaments has worrying consequences for both accountability and openness.

Despite these limits, German regional autonomy remains extensive in many areas, notably economic development (where EU funds are distributed by the region) and the traditional areas of culture and education. The *Länder* thus remain formidable independent players in the European arena.

These models of federalism in which a significant degree of state power lies at the regional tier, either individually or collectively, can be contrasted with the situation of Austria. Here the federal façade hides a level of regional government which, although politically significant, is constitutionally weak. The capacity for regions to undertake policy is severely limited by their lack of policy freedom. In this case, the ability of the Austrian *Länder* appears somewhat weaker than that of their non-federal counterparts in Spain. Formal federalism does not, therefore, mean a high degree of policy autonomy.

Outside the federal structures, constitutional status is even less of an indication of regional autonomy. The autonomy of a regional government depends on more than the constitutional safeguards it enjoys. The Italian regions are the best example of this. Despite their constitutional guarantees, Italian regions have consistently suffered at the hands of the government's ability to exercise wide discretionary powers to limit their competencies. This was primarily due to the requirement that secondary legislation be instituted before the regions could be established. This gave central government the opportunity to restrict regional competencies through such frameworks at a later date. The list of regional powers contained in Art 117 of the Italian Constitution is therefore relatively meaningless. Instead of listing the powers the regions exercise it has actually become a vague list of areas in which they may operate. This, in effect, outlines the limits of regional power in Italy, rather than actually defining its extent.

The limited functional autonomy of the Italian *regioni* is compounded by the tight financial control placed upon the regions by the national authorities. With 80–90% of 'ordinary region' resources allocated to specific areas by the central government, the regioni have very limited control over the policy choices still open to them. This is not helped by the discretionary nature of many grants, as failure of a region to undertake the desired national project could result in further financial limitations. In effect this means that the regions can be forced to follow a centrally sponsored policy even where some discretion is formally open to them. In some cases, the limited authority granted to the regions is a poisoned chalice for which the national government wishes to avoid direct responsibility. The Italian health service is a prime example of such a dubious privilege. The national funds granted to the regions are consistently below the level required to fulfil the standards of service laid down by the national level. This shortfall must be made up by regions (as the responsible authorities), not the national level. The legal requirement placed upon Italian regions to deliver such a service further erodes the minimal financial resources they have available to undertake independent policy. The 'special regions' should not be seen in quite the same light as they are much less reliant on national grants in general and specific ones in particular. This makes them less open to financial coercion. However, a combination of corruption, incompetence and obstruction on the part of the national government has to some extent limited the effectiveness even of these regions.

Overall, this may paint too gloomy a picture of the Italian regions' ability to operate independently, but there can be no doubt that the *regioni* operate under conditions hardly conducive to policy autonomy. Financial constraints, a hostile constitutional court and a national government concerned chiefly with retaining as many powers as possible at the highest level have done nothing to aid their development. Indeed, the national government seems to have treated them as an inconvenience rather than a legitimate tier of policy making. Nevertheless, the regions have been instrumental in several policy spheres, notably the environment, and their achievements in the field of economic development, especially in Emilia-Romagna, have been impressive (Leonardi, 1990). Given their limits, the ability of the Italian regions to make any policy impact whatsoever within the Italian political system must be regarded as something of an achievement.

Lack of constitutional protection seems to have done little harm to the regions of France and Denmark. In both cases, the autonomy they enjoy is relatively wide, and they are more able to act as independent policy makers within their limited spheres than some of the Italian *regioni*. The important factor in Denmark and France has been financial stability and the level of financial autonomy they enjoy. Unique amongst European regions, they have control over the bulk of their own resources. Danish *amter* in particular, by controlling tax rates, are able to raise finance without reference to the national level. More importantly, the national level has a limited ability to use financial incentives to influence regional policy (although in France the effect of the *contrats du plan* remains a bone of contention). This, allied with an administrative general competence, has allowed these regions to operate in fields not originally assigned to them and has given them greater flexibility in those which they were allocated. The development of distinctly regional policies in France and Denmark despite the lack of constitutional protection suggests that this protection is far less important than financial independence. It should be remembered, nevertheless, that although the financial resources they possess are relatively free from national interference, the regions spend a very small proportion of the national budget.

Spain, in contrast to Italy, has a constitutionally guaranteed regional system which has prospered. The *autonomías* are the primary legislative tier over a wide range of functional powers in Spain, particularly in the 'high autonomy' regions. Even constitutional restrictions have not proved limiting for the Spanish regions. For example, although international relations remain a nation competence, many have indulged in cross-border affairs despite opposition from the centre. If Spanish regions do have an obvious weakness, it is again in the sphere of finance. Although all *autonomías* have the ability to raise taxes, few have successfully done so on a long term basis. In addition to this, around half the finance received by the *autonomías* is loosely allocated by the national government. This lack of independent financial means has led to a reliance on deficit spending which cannot continue in the long term (indeed it has been reduced recently). The formulaic nature of the block grants gives a limited degree of stability, but finance continues to be a bone of contention between the national and regional tiers. Increasingly, the Spanish system is experiencing a move away from the needs-based system of grants towards reliance upon taxes raised in the region concerned. This has the advantage of providing an element of fiscal responsibility and greater autonomy for those regions with higher GDPs, but 'low autonomy' regions, particularly those with weak economies, may become ever more reliant upon the largesse of the centre. This may not bode well for the long term future of the Spanish regional tier as a whole.

It is clear from the above examples, and the chapters that precede it, that traditional markers such as constitutional status do not in themselves indicate the overall autonomy of a particular regional tier. Although the constitutional status of the region plays an important role, it is not by any means the full story; in fact the financial and functional independence open to the regional tier is of equal significance. The constitutional provisions interact with these other factors to produce the overall system of autonomy. It is unlikely that the Belgian and German regions could operate without the substantial constitutional protection they enjoy. More importantly, the ability of the German *Länder* to defend their autonomy has relied heavily on the constitutional protection they were afforded in 1948 and, perhaps as important, the support of the constitutional court.

Interestingly, no region enjoys high autonomy in both financial and constitutional terms (see Table 13.1). Regions in Belgium, Portugal and Germany have all prospered from significant functional responsibilities but are notably lacking in tax-raising powers or the ability to raise truly regional finance. Those regions without any constitutional status whatsoever (particularly those of France and Denmark) are notable both for their high degree of spending autonomy and for their heavy reliance on 'regional resources', resources which they themselves control. Around 80% of French regional expenditure is available to be spent as the region decides, while there are no restrictions placed on *amter* spending (aside from the maintenance of school and hospital standards). The exception to this rule may be Belgium after the recent round of constitutional reforms.

Why are regions granted either high constitutional status or a high degree of financial independence but never both? If the regional government were given the ability to raise and lower taxes freely, and the ability to do so without even the possibility of national intervention, the unity of the nation-state would be threatened. As the primary source of power, the nation-state must have the ability to enforce at least a measure of solidarity between itself and the regional level. This can only be ensured if finances remain largely a national concern, especially if in constitutional terms the region is given wide-ranging freedoms. To remove both avenues of control would hollow out the state to an unacceptable degree. If and when this occurs, we could truly start talking of a 'Europe of regions'. The fate of Belgium after its latest reforms will be instructive.

Table 13.1: Autonomy of European regions

Member State	Constitutional guarantee	International relations	Financial autonomy	Functional autonomy
Austria	Federal	Some	High	Medium
Belgium	Federal	Full	High	High
Denmark	No	None	Very high	Medium
France	No	Some	Very high	Low
Germany	Federal	Some	High	Medium
Italy (ordinary)	Yes	Some/informal	Low	Low
Italy (special)	Yes	Some/informal	Medium	Medium
Netherlands	Yes	None	Low	Low
Portugal	Yes	Some	High	High
Spain (Art 143)	Yes	Informal/none	Medium	Medium
Spain (Art 151)	Yes	Informal	Medium	High

13.2 COLLECTIVE INFLUENCE OR REGIONAL AUTONOMY?

Although the extent of regional autonomy varies across the EU, the third level is a political reality. The rationale of the region lies in increasing democratic choice and accountability in the field of territorial government, but the rise of regional government within the European Union does not always reflect this rationale. In fact, increasing regional influence has often been coupled with a reduction in regional autonomy. For regional autonomy to exist, individual regions must be able to exercise it. Increasingly, this is not the case. Regional involvement, especially in European affairs but also with reference to national policy, relies on regions working collectively. This trend not only reduces regional autonomy, but questions a region's democratic credentials. When regions work in a collective capacity, it is invariably informal (and secret) and concerns the executive rather than the legislative branch. We therefore see not only a reduction in individual regional policies but also the removal of much decision making from the regional legislative organs. By definition this places a further step between the decision makers and their electorate. The increased power of regional executives is an argument for their direct election. Until recently no regional executives were directly elected, although most Italian regional presidents are now elected by this method, and there are calls for such a system in Austria.

The defence of German regional autonomy has been focused on the *Bundesrat*. However, although this has been very successful in achieving increased *Länder* involvement, especially in European affairs, it has encouraged a collective approach. If the German regions wish to challenge *Bund* decisions, they must agree a common position to challenge the legislation in the federal council. The steady flow of powers away from the *Landtage* has long been documented as a worrying development of increasing co-operative federalism in Germany (Scharpf, 1988). However, the experience of other regional states suggests that this is a more widespread phenomenon, occurring far beyond the borders of Germany.

On European issues, this trend is particularly striking. All regional involvement in the Council of Ministers (with representatives from Germany, Belgium and now Spain) merely means representation of the nation-state's regions as a whole. This again requires a collective decision of the regions within one Member State to be accepted as the 'regional' position. Even in the Committee of the Regions, the regional representatives are, in most cases, delegates of the regional tier in a nation-state. They do not represent their regional electorate.

The problems with the continuation of this trend are twofold. The whole purpose of the democratic region is to allow policy decisions to reflect the preferences of the electorate. If this is not the case, there is no argument for them to be democratically elected. They could just as easily be administrative bodies made accountable to nationally elected representatives. More importantly, one must question whether regional representatives are the right people to make decisions which are in effect national.

When the regional presidents of a Member State meet, they do so as a national, not a regional, body. The decisions that they agree to implement in their regions are no longer examples of regional policy making but become expressions of national sentiment. The only difference is that, unlike those in the national parliament, the representatives agreeing these 'national' decisions are elected indirectly from regional legislatures, not directly by the electorate. The question must be asked whether, if it is deemed necessary to agree a 'national' policy in an area of regional competence, this is not better handled at the national level, which is designed for such decision making.

A further question, examined below, is whether this growth of interregional decision making creates a democratic deficit, rather like that within the EU, whereby the executives through their 'intergovernmental relations' role are excluding the legislatures to the detriment of accountability and democracy. The 'rise of executives' is a common feature of most modern government, and it seems that the regional tier is not immune. In fact it is particularly susceptible, but such alliances and collective activities of regional governments do not necessarily reduce regional autonomy and accountability. These links can be used to create a 'regional front' in order to protect the autonomy of regions to pursue their own policies. Such regional coalitions have been evident in the EU since the early 1990s. As long as they restrict their activities to defending regional autonomy in structural terms, accountability and democracy will not be affected. If, however, policies are decided by such methods, the democratic legitimacy of the region must be reduced.

13.3 THE RISE OF REGIONAL EXECUTIVES

The dominance of the executive level in the activities of European regions is a worrying development for democratic accountability. This trend towards a 'democratic deficit' at the regional level is evident across Europe, but is more marked in some regions than others.

Germany and Italy certainly display a high degree of executive involvement, to the detriment of the legislative branch. In contrast, France and Spain show less indication of following this tendency. Why should they differ? There are four main reasons why this executive dominance has taken hold, and these also explain why the regional level seems to be especially susceptible to it.

First, the nature of the competencies given to the regional tier encourages action by the executive rather than the legislative organs. In Germany and Italy, the vast majority of competencies are classed as administrative. Under this classic definition, the need for legislative involvement is perceived as minimal. However, the definition of what constitutes an 'administrative' duty is vague to say the least. Many 'administrative' tasks handed to regions (see Chapter 10) can give substantial policy autonomy to the devolved tier. The classification of a task as 'administrative' gives the executive the ability to bypass the legislative branch. The decisions taken in the name of 'administration' are presumed unsuitable for open discussion in the directly elected chamber. It is thought appropriate for such measures to be left to the private discussion of the indirectly elected executive body.

The problem is exacerbated by the piecemeal development of the regional tier. As the regions have expanded their tasks through informal means, legislatures have generally been excluded. The reason is that since such competencies are not granted specifically to the region, the executive has not been forced to act through the parliamentary body. Once again, the 'administrative' nature of many of these actions has allowed the avoidance of legislative involvement. One of the most active proponents of this method of regional expansion has been France, yet the French regions do not suffer from so high a degree of executive power as the Germans or the Italians. The reason is found in the French regional structure, which actually excludes the existence of an official regional executive except in the person of the regional president. Although in practice a de facto executive does exist (the bureau), it has no authority of its own and must thus pass even 'administrative' decisions through the regional council. In practice, these will go through sub-committees which can pass the matter on to the plenary if they wish.

The third factor in executive dominance has been the nature of relations between the regions and their own nation-state. The often adversarial nature of these relations has not aided open government. Intergovernmental discussions are often conducted as a political bartering process behind closed doors. This secrecy leaves no opportunity for scrutiny either by the legislature or by the electorate itself.

A final element of executive dominance at the regional tier can be found in the EU. The informal nature of most regional contacts means they are again classed as 'administrative' in nature and therefore beyond the influence of the legislative branch. The minimal 'official' involvement of the regions in the European tier means that the regional executives may operate, in their 'unofficial' capacity, unencumbered by legislative restraints. In the field of international relations, the situation is worse. The lack of full treaty making competence in all but the Belgian Regions and Communities means that the majority of international involvement is achieved through executive competencies and private law, neither of which requires legislative approval.

It seems inevitable, therefore, that regional executive power will play a large role in regional activities. However, this should be limited to the minimum necessary to avoid creating a dangerous democratic deficit at the regional tier and defeating much of the purpose of regional democracy. To achieve this, it must be recognised that regions are not mini nation-states, and thus should not be run along the same lines. The artificial distinction between legislation and administration needs to be examined. If the traditional distinction is applied to regions, then scrutiny of large sections of regional activity will be minimal or non-existent. Structural change is thus required to allow more involvement by the legislative branch.

There needs to be formalisation of these currently unofficial intergovernmental links. This must insist on a high degree of openness, with the proceedings of meetings being available for public inspection. This applies especially in the case of the EU. There must be general acceptance of the region as a partner in the European policy process, and the regions must be given official access to the European level, thus allowing greater accountability in European matters and the chance for individual regional opinions to be heard. Once again, these forums must be open. This would involve a major shift in EU policy, and unfortunately far too many Member State executives enjoy the opaque nature of the European decision making process. Nevertheless, if we accept the need for a democratic regional tier, we must also accept the existence of a high degree of executive power within it. In this way, regional structures can be designed to keep this power to a minimum and ensure that regional executives remain accountable. The core of such structures must be openness, and it is this that is the key to ensuring democratic and accountable government at the regional level.

13.4 REGIONAL AUTONOMY OR RECENTRALISATION?

Chief amongst the rationales for a regional tier of government discussed at the beginning of this volume was the argument for democratic decentralisation. Although the creation of regional levels of democratic governance can lead to the decentralisation of political power, the process of regionalisation is not necessarily a process of decentralisation. Power can be moved upwards to the region and away from local authorities.

This phenomenon of 'recentralisation' has been witnessed in a number of guises in the European Union, but broadly speaking it occurs in two distinct variants. Regional governments can fail to devolve to local government units within their territories. This results in a concentration of power at the regional level, and often a degree of control in excess of that previously imposed by the nation-state. This is possible because the nation-state, despite having a plethora of legal controls to supervise local government, may not use them as effectively as the region. The number of local authorities that a nation-state controls may be huge, and many will be physically remote from the centre. This does not aid central control over local decisions. Such regulation may therefore be less than effective. The French pre-1982 experience was a prime example of theoretical state control being far from totally efficient in practice (see section 6.1.1).

The region, in contrast, is rarely overburdened in its supervisory role and is generally in close physical proximity to its units of local governance. Any interest networks established by local government in the apparatus of the nation-state prior to regionalisation are useless in a new regional order. The influence built up by local government before the arrival of the regions may be one reason for local government's involvement in the second model of recentralisation.

The second strain of recentralisation sees regions bypassed by the central state in favour of the local level. This will often be the case when central and regional governments are of differing political colours. If the local government's views are similar to those of the central government, then direct links are even more likely to result. However, even local governments which do not agree with the policies of the centre may be tempted by promises of extra funds. The catch, of course, is that such grants are either conditional or, at best, voluntary block grants. Either way, financial reliance on the centre and a resultant loss of independence are a likely consequence. Financial control is often a far more successful lever on local government than legal sanctions.

In the federal states there is evidence of a high concentration of power at the regional level through the failure of the respective regional bodies to empower their local levels. The German federal system, as the oldest regional system in the EU, is a good place to start an examination of regional government's influence on local autonomy. At first glance, local government seems well provided for in the Basic Law. Under Art 28(2), the local autonomy of the municipalities is guaranteed, as is the limited autonomy of the counties (Kreis) and municipal associations. Local issues therefore remain with the municipalities under the subsidiarity principle, a right enforceable before the Federal Constitutional Court. Furthermore, the court has interpreted a right to local financial autonomy implicit in Art 28(2) (26 BVerfGE 228). However, despite these guarantees, Länder control of local government is tight.

This is most obviously the case in the structural organisation of local government. Of the three tiers of local governance, only the municipalities are truly autonomous units in every Land. The counties (of which there were approximately 500 in 1992) are generally autonomous political units, but in at least two Länder (Saarland and Rhineland-Pfalz) the head of the executive council is still a Land appointee. In contrast, the districts (Bezirke) are entirely Länder-controlled units of administrative deconcentration. These exist in the six larger western Länder, though the two city-states have no local government at all.

Strict Länder control of local government is further emphasised by the allocation of functional powers to the lower level. The example of North Rhine-Westphalia, where all teachers are appointed from a single office in Düsseldorf, is often cited as an extreme manifestation of this (Paterson and Southern, 1991, p 161). Direct control is also exercised by the Länder over the police, the schools inspectorate, the audit commission and supervision of industry, all through its organ, the district. The district also administers the funding of Land projects in the areas of education, roads and housing, either through local authorities or directly to contractors, thus bypassing the lower democratic layers.

Despite direct Länder control over areas such as police, roads and housing, there exists scope for limited autonomy on the part of the municipalities and Kreis (counties). This is further reduced by their reliance on state and federal funding. Kreis receive a levy from their participating municipalities who are themselves in an extremely weak financial position (Schweitzer et al, 1984, p 131). Although providing most public services, they receive only around 13% of tax revenues, a figure which has fallen from 14% in 1980, with a peak of 14.1% in 1976–77. This compares with around 34.5% for the Länder, a figure which has steadily increased, reaching a peak of 35% in 1978–79. This has led to a reliance on grants from the Land and Bund (totalling 27% of revenue in 1988). Although these grants are partly as a result of the equalisation procedure, the individual Land may decide where the money will be used. All Bund grants must be earmarked for specific projects. This compares unfavourably with the situation in France, where the départements received less than 8% of their revenue from conditional grants (Schmidt, 1990; Mazey, 1993). The situation is worsened by the consistent shortfall (17% in 1988) experienced by the municipalities between expenditure and finance (Schweitzer, 1995, p 185). The gap is filled by communal business profits, assets and, increasingly, loans, leaving most municipalities in serious debt (Council of Europe, 1999).

Subsidiarity in Germany has failed to permeate to local government in the Federal Republic, with power concentrated at the regional tier. This recentralisation at the regional level is complemented by municipalities resorting to federal conditional grants. Is this trend repeated in the newer regional systems, or is the evidence of a concentration of power at regional rather than local level limited to the example of Germany?

Recentralisation has certainly been a process evident in the Belgian moves towards federalism. The main victims in this reorganisation have been the provinces. From 1830 until the reforms of the 1970s the province was the 'regional' unit operating between the communes and the central authorities. These units have suffered a serious reversal of fortunes. From the 1968 policy, which proposed modernisation and transfer of competencies to the provinces, to the 1977 Egmont pact, which proposed their abolition, their fall has been dramatic.

This rapid decline in importance was caused by the fact that the provinces and language regions were seen as competing for the Belgian *meso* level and were thus considered mutually exclusive. The provinces emphatically lost this argument in the late 1960s. This defeat was so complete that Delmartino remarked that 'as an independent policy body, their role is over' (Delmartino, 1993, p 45). The main beneficiaries of the provincial fall from grace have undoubtedly been the Regions and Communities. The role of the province had been to co-ordinate areas such as emergency services, the oversight of communal legality and economic planning. Of these, only the former remains a provincial competence, the other two roles being usurped by the regional authorities, although informal consultation on economic planning does still occur in Flanders.

The provinces have been reduced to a tier of democratic administrative deconcentration. Most remaining functions are of an executive nature, which is reflected in provincial finances. By 1990 almost 46% of the provincial budget was spent on education (a rise of 2% since 1988), an area mandated by the Communities, while a further 10% was spent on administration. In its sources of funding, educational grants again take up a large and steadily increasing proportion (33% by 1990).

There has been, therefore, an upwards shift in policy making within the Belgian system since regionalisation. In both Germany and the fledgling Belgian federation there is clear evidence of a concentration of power at the regional tier. The process of decentralisation at the *meso* level has not extended to local government which, in contrast, has seen a reduction of autonomy and influence, both functionally and financially.

In the cases of Spain and Italy, the trend towards regional recentralisation is somewhat confused by the appearance of a sizeable amount of recentralisation by the central state. In both these systems, resentment between regional and provincial tiers has been a significant area of conflict. In Spain, this is accentuated by the provinces' links with the previous regime, under which they were a means of central control over the local populace, and their indirectly elected nature. Such a dubious past led to attempts at their abolition during the post-fascist reorganisation. This was only narrowly avoided by a right wing alliance in their favour. However, following the regional reforms, only 10 of the 17 regions now contain provinces. The other seven are uniprovincial, with the regional and provincial apparatus being merged.

The retaining of the provinces was by no means the end of the issue. Regional-provincial relations are extremely strained in at least three regions (Cantabria, Catalonia and Valencia). This reached such a peak in Catalonia that the *Generalitat* attempted to abolish the provinces altogether. The *Generalitat* was successful in disbanding the Barcelona City Corporation (Cuchillo, 1993, note 19) but its attempt to abolish the provinces was quashed by the constitutional court in 1980. Nevertheless, the Catalans have persisted in creating a system of 36 *comarcas*. These traditional Catalan local government units deliver regional facilities and deal with the regional government. The provinces, in contrast, are ignored. This extreme example has been repeated elsewhere, with regions dealing directly with the municipalities to the exclusion of the provinces.

The transfer of authority from provinces to regions has encouraged a fresh approach from the provincial governments themselves. Especially in cases where the provincial and central governments are of the same political hue, direct national-provincial links have been established. This has become possible since the 1985 local government Act relaxed restrictions on such contacts. By 1991 this had led to the transfer of a series of central executive functions to the province rather than the region. These functions have included public works, road maintenance and public health schemes. This is state centralisation by the back door, since moneys thus transferred can be allocated to specific projects by the national authorities.

Regional government has not been blameless in this process. The tight nature of its control over local government has caused general resentment amongst local government units towards the region. This is so great that regional governments are often viewed with more distaste than the centre (Cuchillo, 1993, p 24). There are exceptions to this rule. Valencia and Andalusia restrict their *tutelles*, for example, but the most notable exception is Euskadi (the Basque country). Here the provinces have actually taken power from the region. However, this is not an example of *rapprochement*, but rather evidence of the importance of the province (the traditional basis of Basque government) amongst much of the Basque populace. The dispute was so acrimonious that the PNV (the moderate Basque nationalist party) split on the issue, and the president was forced to resign. It has also led to the formation of a 'provinicialist' party in Alava which claims that the province is discriminated against by the regional authority. It gained a number of seats in the regional elections of 1995 and continues to be represented at the regional level.

The conflict between regional and local government is also evident in the Italian system, with the greatest tensions again evident between province and region. This has arisen due partly to ambiguity in the role performed by each tier of government, and partly to the marked reluctance of the regional authorities to devolve power.

When the region was finally born as a political unit in the early 1970s it was seen, according to some commentators, as a 'giant municipality' (Giannini, 1973). This ambiguous role has led to an overcrowding of local government and a resultant clash of competencies. The situation has been worsened by regional reticence in the delegation of power to local authorities, especially the provinces. Regions also introduced the *comprensori* (Michel, 1999, p 218). These bodies had power delegated from the region, and act as co-ordinating bodies for the communes. The similarity to the situation in Catalonia is evident, with the regional governments attempting to bypass the province by creating a new tier, perceived as more favourable to the region. In the event, the *comprensori* were abolished in the 1980s. The weakness of the Italian regional tier meant it was unable to sustain a further level of intermediate government.

This general trend of Italian regional recentralisation is seemingly evident from the public expenditure figures (see Table 13.2). In the 1970s and early 1980s, the regional level enjoyed an increasing share of public expenditure at the expense of all other levels of government, but most notably the lower tiers. These figures do not, however, tell the whole story. There is no doubt that the provincial and communal tiers have been the main losers during this period, but it has been the state and not the region that has gained the most. This is due to the fact that most regional revenue is spent on mandated areas, such as health, over which the region has little if any policy control.

Table 13.2: Division of Italian public expenditure

	State	Regions	Provinces	Communes
1970	70%	3%	5%	23%
1975	64%	12%	4%	21%
1981	64%	19%	2%	14%

As Italian regions have failed to devolve responsibilities, the central government has increasingly bypassed them and dealt directly with the provincial and municipal authorities. The 1977 transfer of functions gave significant powers to local authorities under the principle of 'organically linked' sectors and, in doing so, bypassed the regional tier (Sanantonio, 1987, p 112). This application of subsidiarity gave local control over local issues directly to local authorities. However, such generosity by the central state was accompanied by an increased reliance on state funding by the local authorities. Although legal controls rest with regional government committees, these were really designed for use by a Prefect and are unwieldy in their modern form, especially as the committee itself is overburdened. Instead, control is exercised using financial means. Increasingly this is in the hands of national government.

This reliance on national finance (and therefore potential national control) has been increased by the reluctance of regions to devolve. In looking for ways to increase their responsibilities the provinces, especially, have looked to the centre for support. This trend has allowed the Italian Government to claw back powers lost during decentralisation to a much greater extent than has been the case in Spain. The opportunity for national recentralisation in Italy, in contrast to Spain, would appear to be a consequence of the weakness of the Italian regions in comparison with their Spanish counterparts.

Local government regions have also experienced a degree of regional recentralisation, though to a lesser degree. In Denmark this has generally manifested itself in an increasing reliance on state funding by the municipalities. This is also evidenced by a shift away from block grants and towards specified funding at the municipal level. Block grants to municipalities fell by 50% in the period 1982–85 (DKK3 bn was cut in 1986) in contrast to the modest increase to the *amter*. Nearly 50% of municipality income is in reimbursements from central government for duties carried out on behalf of the state. These functions are mandated (for example, payment of social security) and offer no policy options for the local authority itself. Local taxes account for 35% of the municipal budget, but this compares with a figure of 54% of *amter* budgets. The remainder of the *amter* budget is raised through a state block grant (excluding service charges) which compares with less than 10% of municipal budgets (Bogason, 1987, p 60).

The increased reliance on state funds by the municipal tier is caused by the transfer of certain mandated functions to the lowest level (for example, social security) while policy powers have been granted to the counties (for example, in health service). Although the 1970 reforms have given greater autonomy to lower level governments in the form of the newly democratic counties, there has been a *prima facie* loss of independence by the municipal tier. This has been reflected in the attitudes of those involved in local government. In a 1983 survey, 50% of Danish local government leaders felt that the distance between the citizen and government had increased since the 1970 reforms (Bogason, 1987, p 56).

The most obvious manifestation of this is the reduction in the number of the lowest level territorial units. In Denmark, this has fallen, post-1970, from 1,257 parishes and 85 towns to 275 municipalities. This trend is not unique to Denmark, however, with both Germany (24,300 in 1967 to 8,503 in 1989) and Belgium (2,663 to 589 since 1977) experiencing similar 'rationalisation' of local government.

The most notable exception has been France where, despite the huge number of communes, no rationalisation has occurred. It is also true that France is the only state where the introduction of a new tier of regional government has not reduced the powers of the lower tiers. These two instances are not coincidental. France, with its system of 'notables' (and especially their power in the Senate), has not experienced a significant a loss of powers from communes or *départements* to the *région* or the nation-state. Indeed, the lower tiers have benefited from the decentralisation policy. The downside has, of course, been a weak regional system.

With the exception of France, there has been a *prima facie* shift in power either to regional or national authorities, at the expense of local government. This may be evident through a structural rationalisation, or through a loss of financial or functional autonomy, generally manifesting itself in the form of a *tutelle* over the local government unit.

The above brief analysis refutes any assumption that devolution by definition leads to decentralisation. Regional government can be just as prone to the centralisation of power as can the national tier. The lesson to be drawn from this is that local government still requires strong protection under regionalised systems. Indeed, the closer supervision made possible by the regional tier may mean that the protection of local autonomy must actually be stronger than under a unitary structure.

13.5 A REGIONAL ALTERNATIVE TO THE NATION-STATE?

The initial premise for this work was that the nation-state's record in delivering democratic, peaceful and successful government required reassessment. The mythical nature of its 'organic' legitimacy made it no more 'natural' a method of governance than any other. With this in mind, the development of the region, under the umbrella of the European Union, was posited as an alternative. The non-sovereign region, by replacing the concepts of sovereignty and 'hard borders' with subsidiarity and 'soft borders' could, perhaps, be the vanguard of a new structure of European governance. This section aims to assess whether the region, on consideration of the evidence presented above, reveals itself as an innovative method of governance or merely promises more of the same.

Superficially, the evidence overwhelmingly suggests that regions do not offer a real alternative to the concept of the hard-bordered state. This is immediately obvious from the fact that regions are hard-bordered themselves. They continue the tradition of neat boxes of territory within which all the responsibilities of the territory are handled. Regions do not even cross local government boundaries, never mind national borders. A 'hard-bordered' culture also exists at least within the most powerful regions, which operate as mini nation-states with many of the trappings this implies. Any suggestion that their territorial coverage should be altered would be met with intense resistance. The best example of this is in Germany, where the *Länder*, created less than 50 years ago, have achieved an air of permanence that makes their alteration practically impossible. Even in France, when the democratic *régions* were just 10 years old, plans to reorganise their boundaries met with such opposition that progress proved impossible. A further law, granting more powers to regions that shared competencies with their neighbours in specific areas, proved ineffective. The regions resented national interference in their co-operative arrangements (Mazey, 1994, p 140).

Although first impressions suggest that the region has not radically altered the territorial organisation of power, more subtle changes have emerged. First, although territorial 'soft borders' are uncommon, they are not unknown. Secondly, the development of policy by more than one tier is certainly evidence of a weakening of national sovereignty; if policy is being undertaken at several levels, it can no longer be said to be national. Finally, and perhaps most important for the future, the development of regional government has brought about a significant change in the attitudes of certain regional populations.

The most obvious example of 'soft borders' has, of course, been the Belgian 'experiment' in dividing governance between three specific territorial units, two of which (the regions and the Cultural Communities) have overlapping territorial responsibilities while the third (the federation) has a more traditional, all-encompassing role. Interestingly, much of the territorial novelty of this plan has been lost over time. The Flemish Region and Community are now effectively one body, with distinct borders and a defined territorial limitation on its competencies. Only in Brussels does the Flemish authority continue to encounter 'soft border' ideas.

The two territories where 'soft borders' continue to operate to a substantial degree are Brussels and the German speaking cantons of eastern Belgium. In these cases, the Flemish and French Communities (in the case of Brussels) and the Walloon region (in the case of the German areas) have responsibilities within the territories of other regional units. In the case of Brussels, the Communities handle 'personalised' affairs, while in the

German Community, the Walloon region is the body responsible for economic matters.

The reason for the retreat from the radical territorial innovations as proposed early in the process of Belgian federalisation can be summed up in one word, convenience. Where it has been possible to retain distinct regional 'hard borders' this has been the mode of government. Where such divisions have not been possible (as in the German speaking cantons and Brussels), soft borders have been used as a necessary alternative. Soft- bordered units of governance are not neat or simple. In the territorial sense it has proved simpler to grant 'minority' rights to those Flemish and French who live on the 'wrong side' of the language border than to make governments responsible for cultural activities beyond a distinct territorial area (which would also have been politically unacceptable). Nevertheless, the fact that some areas continue to be governed by overlapping units of governance suggests that this option is at least possible within western democracies.

The chance of regions evolving into soft-bordered entities within nation-states may be limited, but their impact on reducing the emphasis on national borders is potentially significant. In France, for example, the engagement of regions with other regions across the national borders is now actually encouraged by the central government. This development is a practical acceptance of the need to soften national borders within the European Union, while allowing the nation-state to avoid the prickly issue of 'national sovereignty' which would be raised if it indulged in such activities. Even in less autonomous systems such as in Italy, the regions engage in cross-border co-operation agreements with the blessing of the nation-state. Ironically, in Spain, one of the most regionalised states, such encouragement has not been forthcoming. Indeed, the national government has actively tried to limit these links. Nevertheless, agreements between the border Spanish *autonomías*, other regions (especially their French counterparts) and even nation-states are common.

These links are often quite minimal in content, due to the limited competencies granted to some of the regions involved. However, they often cover topics of great importance to the local populations. The Alpine regional conference on economic development, for instance, allows an integrated approach to a problem that does not stop at national borders. Italian, Austrian and Swiss alpine regions have far more in common with each other than with many other territories within their nation-states. Some agreements, perhaps the majority, cover rather mundane issues such as emergency services or airport co-operation, but an independent region (or conceivably a local authority) is in a position to enter into such links far more easily than could a nation-state.

In the cultural sphere, the Basque speaking areas of France and Spain have entered into co-operation agreements in the field of education. This allows the Euskadi government to support Basque speaking institutions in the French Basque territories. In addition, issues concerning the development of the Euskerra language can now be addressed throughout the Euskerra speaking areas, despite the fact that it spans two nation-states. Interestingly, the French Government has acquiesced in this, and it has not led to increased nationalist fervour in French Euskadi. Further links in the field of culture have been established between the Flemish and the Dutch, and between the Belgian German Community, the German border regions and, interestingly, Trento. The list is extensive, but such supranational developments require the regions to possess autonomy in order to control the policy area in question. If regions are to develop soft border policies, they must possess a significant degree of autonomy. It is clear that the EU regions which have engaged in activity of this kind have been those with the autonomy to make such contacts meaningful. Most noticeably, the *Länder*, the Belgian Communities and regions, and the Spanish *autonomías* (also now the Austrian *Länder*) have all been active in this area, and limited interregional organisation has also been evident in France and Italy.

The regional enthusiasm to organise across national boundaries will evidently help address the huge anomalies that result from the nation-state system. Discussions can take place concerning more 'real' economic or cultural areas, unconstrained by the artificial boundaries of the 'nation'. Although these areas will obviously also be limited by regional boundaries, the problems will be fewer than with the nation-state. Most importantly, the agreements will be made between regionally accountable representatives, thus increasing the territorial accountability of such supranational developments.

The most obvious difference seen in the growth of regional governance has been the necessary division of powers it entails. In several areas it is no longer correct to talk only of national policies across Europe. Instead, there are at least three policy levels to consider, the regional, the national and the European. This division of authority is not new; federalism has existed for as long as the nation-state, but it has certainly become more widespread in recent years. Equally, the language of subsidiarity is employed with increasing regularity, and in many countries of the EU the national level is having to justify why it needs power that could equally be resident at the regional (or local) level. One need look only to the wording of the new concurrent powers clause in the German Basic Law for evidence of this.

There can be little doubt that nation-states are no longer the 'sovereign' entities they once were. In most regionalised states, the national level is no longer master in all of its house. In a significant proportion of policy areas, policy cannot be undertaken nationally without at least the consent of the regional tier. *De facto*, this means that the sovereignty of the nation-state has cracked. The region, in turn, has not assumed the failed mantle of a nation-state, because it does not have responsibility for 'all' policies claimed by the nation-state. Furthermore, and this is a very important break from the nation-state dominated past, the regions do not claim such authority.

This leads neatly on to the final, and perhaps most intriguing, result of regionalisation. Although this work is not a sociological study it would be foolish to ignore this final result. In those countries where regionalism has strong roots, the regions invariably do not talk of nationalist aims. Instead, they see greater autonomy within the nation-state and influence within Europe as their goals. This is most noticeable in areas where micro-nationalist sentiments have been strong. In Catalonia and Euskadi, the mainstream nationalist parties no longer talk in terms of independence for their 'homeland', instead describing their goals in the terms outlined above. The success of these parties has been in direct contrast to those espousing a traditionally nationalist position, who have invariably fared badly (Hopkins, 1996).

In Germany, where micro-nationalist sentiment has been all but non-existent, a similar division has been found. The division of powers has been accompanied by a division of identities, with regional, national, local and European identities all existing in tandem. This seems to be as a direct result of the division of powers itself. Far from encouraging micro-nationalism, regionalism (and the division of sovereignty it entails) actually encourages a weakening of the focus on the 'nation' which has plagued Europe for the past two centuries. Interestingly, the inability of certain countries to cope with the concept of European unity has much to do with this concept of national sovereignty. In those areas where regionalism (whether cultural or political) has taken hold, the European Union holds far less fear. Adding another identity to an already multifaceted one is relatively simple. In contrast, where the focus is on one all-purpose 'national' identity, as in England, European identity is perceived as replacing it. The language of those who oppose European integration constantly refer to the 'loss' of identity and sovereignty. The development of regions has shown that sovereignty need not and indeed should not operate in this exclusive and divisive manner. The success of this division of sovereignty, and the accompanying weakening of the 'national' focus of identity, may prove to be the most enduring consequence of the development of regions within the EU.

The region therefore does offer a new approach to government, whether intended or not. This may be due to the non-sovereign nature of the region itself, and the fact that regions are not fixated on the issue of sovereignty which seems to dominate development at the national and European levels. Whatever the reason, the region has certainly increased the use of soft border methods of governance, leading to the addressing of issues in more rational territorial areas. In addition, the division of sovereignty has allowed policy decisions to reflect the differences within national boundaries, consequently weakening the focus on national sovereignty and national identity. This has occurred in those regions which are powerful enough to make a difference in their policy choices, but, as mentioned above, this does not include all regional units currently in existence. To what extent, then, do the effects of the regionalisation process affect the European Union as a whole? Put in simple terms, is the 'Europe of regions' a reality (or even a possibility), or will national borders continue to dominate, restricting regionalism to individual nation-states?

This work began by mentioning the overused prediction that the European Union was developing into a 'Europe of the regions'. In recent years this claim has been ridiculed by a succession of authors. Indeed, some have suggested that nobody even knows what it actually means (Tindale, 1995). This, I feel, is overly harsh. A 'Europe of the regions' envisages a Europe where the dominant domestic tier of government will not be the nation-state. Instead, the region will be dominant beneath a European umbrella. There can be little doubt that this has not happened yet. However, I would contend that there are signs that a major change in the way we govern ourselves is certainly under way.

The fact that democratic regions now exist in 12 of the 15 Member States, in some form, is certainly evidence of the growth of the regional tier. Let us not forget that in 1939 there were no democratic regional governments (with the exception of the weak Dutch provinces) in the countries that now make up the EU. Yet in the 50 years since the end of hostilities, only Greece, Ireland and Luxembourg have been left with no democratic regional level.

The structural building blocks for a regional Europe are therefore almost in place. Functionally, the regions that do exist control wide areas of policy, to a greater or lesser degree. In all cases, these are increasing rather than decreasing. The result will not be a Europe of regions, but in all probability neither the national nor the European tiers will be able to ignore them. The construction of a 'Europe with regions' will be a necessary part of the EU's future development. It is this failure to recognise the changing constitutional landscape of Europe that lies at the heart of the problems of regional government described above. Our systems and structures of government reflect concepts of territorial sovereignty that date back to the 19th century. These concepts no longer apply. It is necessary first to recognise that we live in a Europe with regions and then to build structures that reflect it, both at the national and European levels. Until policy makers and academics realise that the development of soft border policy making has rendered the current institutions of government unworkable, no fundamental progress in this direction will be possible.

13.6 DEVOLUTION AND THE 'THIRD LEVEL'

The UK's unique system of regional government is one that formally grants a significant degree of autonomy to the devolved institutions. It appears, therefore, that the 'third level' has gained a significant trio of members, but the unusual nature of the UK's constitutional settlement makes this assessment open to question.

The legislative powers granted to the Scottish Parliament and Northern Ireland Assembly are among the most extensive held by a regional tier anywhere in Europe. Surpassed only by the Belgian Regions and Communities in their role as the primary source of legislation in their respective territories, the potential for significant policy variation between the devolved periphery and England is already evident. In many cases, this merely continues a tradition of legislative diversity, though now under regional democratic control. There is no reason to suggest that this *prima facie* legislative autonomy will be threatened by judicial interpretation as seen in Italy or Portugal. It may, however, face a threat from other quarters.

Both the Scotland Act (s 28(7)) and the Northern Ireland Act (s 5(6)) explicitly retain law making power to Westminster, though given the prevailing theory of Westminster sovereignty this is perhaps unnecessary. The effect is to give the Westminster Parliament the ability to legislate on any matter regardless of the Scotland and Northern Ireland Acts. This is a situation without parallel amongst legislative regions in the EU. Although the revocation of the devolution Acts themselves will remain politically unacceptable, constraint of devolved autonomy by implied repeal is not inconceivable.

This, in any event, is the traditional view. If this holds true, the legislative autonomy of the devolved institutions will always be open to significant restrictions when Westminster feels the need to impose unity. An alternative view has been posited by Burrows (Burrows, 2000). She suggest that the operation of the Scotland and Northern Ireland Acts will allow for the possibility of legislation of the devolved institutions and Acts of the UK Parliament to apply concurrently. This could result in a degree of legislative 'tennis' as each parliament overrules the other. In such a situation, the Privy Council will be asked to choose which to apply. Burrows argues that the courts in such a situation must choose the Acts of the Scottish Parliament or the Northern Ireland Assembly. It was the intention of the Westminster Parliament to grant legislative autonomy to the devolved institutions and, as in the case of the European Communities Act 1972 (and subsequent amendments), the devolution Acts should apply unless explicitly stated otherwise. Although I have sympathy with this view, it will take a brave court to rule such in a manner which appears to run so contrary to ss 28(7) and 5(6) of the Scotland and Northern Ireland Acts respectively. For those who argue that the central level's respect for the devolved settlement will be enough to ensure such a situation does not arise, it should be recalled that in Spain, Germany and Italy the central authorities have all attempted to use such methods to overrule their regional tiers, with various degrees of success. In any event, such drastic measures on the part of the United Kingdom Government may not be necessary.

The vast majority of government policies rely less upon legislative freedom than on the financial resources necessary to implement them. The autonomy of the German *Länder* and the Italian special regions has not been based upon their limited legislative authority, but rather on their secure financial situation and their freedom to spend their own resources. It is less than clear that such a situation applies in the UK.

The finance of the devolved institutions is only briefly mentioned in the devolution Acts, and leaves the power of financial allocation at the discretion of the central government. Although the system is currently based on the Barnett formula, this is not enshrined in statute, and neither is the spending assessment upon which the blocks are based. Independent sources of finance are limited, with the small income tax powers applicable only to Scotland, although local government finance could offer a further source in Northern Ireland and Scotland. Nevertheless, the control exercised at Whitehall amounts to a financial *tutelle*. It will always be within the power of the UK Government to alter the basis of funding at the UK level without reference even to the UK Parliament. The fact that the financial resources are passed to the Secretaries of State for distribution adds a further level of possible central interference. This individual also controls the actions of the devolved institutions in relation to borrowing. The potential for control of devolved finances by the central government is therefore extensive.

Should the central government in London wish to flex its financial or legislative muscles, it is likely that the court will be called upon to adjudicate. In the regional systems of continental Europe, the constitutional courts have played a crucial role in defending the regional tier. It is difficult to envisage, however, the Judicial Committee and the courts of the United Kingdom performing a similar role. Lacking the constitutional tools given to their European counterparts, could a Television case happen here? Would an equivalent of the LOPCA be overruled? Will the allocation methods of the block grants be subject to judicial review, as has been the case in Germany? If the answer to these questions is no, the courts will be perceived as pro-central. Given the methods of appointment used for the Judicial Committee of the Privy Council, questions are likely to be asked relating to its legitimacy. The higher courts of the UK are likely to be placed in a position that they are ill equipped to deal with.

The courts have only established the frameworks of the continental systems of devolution, and in some cases their influence has been minimal. Most disputes between tiers of government are resolved through negotiation and discussion. Given this, should we worry about the lack of legislative and financial protection afforded to the UK's regional tier? It is worth noting that the higher autonomy regions in particular have, at various times, been placed under pressure to conform by their central tier. Their ability to resist such pressure and to enter into meaningful discussion has been based upon the existence of federal trust. Only in the local government regions of Scandinavia has the culture of decentralisation been enough of itself to ensure regional autonomy. In every other system, federal trust has developed as a consequence of necessity, not as a perceived good in itself.

The UK's regions lack a *Bundesrat* to force the central level to consider the collective regional opinion. Acts of the Scottish Parliament and the Northern Ireland Assembly are open to the concept of *Bundesrecht bricht Landesrecht* (federal law overrides regional law), while Welsh Assembly actions may only take place within the legislative frameworks allocated by Westminster. This deprives the UK's regional governments of the ability to force their way to the negotiating table as the Belgian regions have done. The political system also appears to deny the UK's devolved institutions the pivotal role at the national level that has proved so crucial in the development of Spanish regionalism. Federal trust is not born; it is made. The UK's regional system does not appear to oblige such an attitude on the part of the centre. Only political fears of micro-nationalism seem to stand between regional autonomy and central interference.

The UK's fledgling system of devolution is still in its formative stages. There have been no defining moments, such as those mentioned above, as yet. There has been no equivalent of the Concordat case, and no explicit attempt to limit regional autonomy on the part of the centre. Much of this can be put down to the fact that the governing parties in Scotland and Wales are of the same variety as found in Westminster, although it is noticeable that the presence of the Liberal Democrat Party in the Scottish executive has provided the few disagreements that have already arisen. In Northern Ireland, the key issues for most regional politicians remain parochial, with the most significant clash of competencies to date centring on the flying of flags over public buildings. The disputes that have defined the regional systems of continental Europe have generally occurred when the parties at the regional and central level are not of like mind, and there is no reason to suppose that the situation in the UK will be different. The test of the UK's system of 'make do and mend' will come when the existing political consensus ends, as it surely must. It will be truly tested, however, if and when a party committed to abolishing the union is returned to power in either Scotland or Wales.

The UK is only at the start of what will be a long road to a truly regional system, but as yet it is not clear that those at the UK level have realised the consequences of the direction which they have chosen. As in continental Europe, the UK's policy makers and scholars must realise that devolution has created a new political reality. We may not have a UK of regions, but we clearly have one with regions. The impact of this development upon the governance of this country is profound, particularly as it is unlikely that devolution will remain confined to the glens and valleys of the periphery for long. Some form of English regional devolution seems inevitable, at least in the longer term. The UK, like Europe as a whole, must realise that the nation-state is dead. What we have now is something which may have some similarities to the previous structure, but which clearly lacks that most defining of characteristics, sovereignty. Unless this fact is grasped, there seems little likelihood that the questions of accountability and democracy that this new structure raises will be addressed. One prediction can be made, however; public lawyers are unlikely to face unemployment in the near future.

BIBLIOGRAPHY

Agence Europe, 'The Belgian memorandum on institutional relaunch', annex 1608, 29 March 1990

Agostini, V and Mattioni, A, 'Italy', in Engel, C (ed), *Le Rôle des Régions dans l'Exercise des Compétences Externes des Etats en Europe Occidentale*, 1992, Brussels: TEPSA

Agranoff, R and Gallarin, JAR, 'Towards federal democracy in Spain' (1997) 27 Publius 4

Alen, A and Ergec, R, *Federal Belgium After the Fourth State Reform of 1993*, 2nd edn, 1998, Brussels: Belgian Ministry of Foreign Affairs

Alen, A, *Belgium: Bipolar and Centrifugal Federalism*, 1992, Brussels: Belgian Ministry of Foreign Affairs

Andersen, A, *The Danish Counties*, 1993, Copenhagen: Amtsrådforeningen i Danmark

Aurrecoechea, I, 'The Role of the autonomous communities in the implementation of European Community law in Spain' (1989) 38 ICLQ 1

Baume, R and Bonnet, L, 'From regional to sectoral policies: the contractual relations between the state and the regions in France' (1994) 4(3) Regional Politics and Policy

Beer, WR, *The Unexpected Rebellion: Ethnic Activism in Contemporary France*, 1980, New York: New York UP

Biehl, D, 'A conceptual approach to the reform of German federalism' (1989) 7 Environment and Planning C: Government and Planning

Birch, AJ, 'Minority nationalist movements and theories of political integration' (1978) 30 World Politics

Blair, PM, *Federalism and Judicial Review in West Germany*, 1981, Oxford: Clarendon

Boase, JP, 'Faces of asymmetry: German and Canadian federalism', in de Villiers, B (ed), *Evaluating Federal Systems*, 1994, Dordrecht: Nijhoff, pp 90–110

Bogason, P, 'Denmark', in Page, E and Goldsmith, M (eds), *Central and Local Government Relations*, 1987, London: Sage

Bogdanor, V, 'Devolution: the constitutional aspects', in *Constitutional Reform in the United Kingdom: Practice and Principles*, 1998, Oxford: Hart

Bogdanor, V, *Devolution*, 1979, Oxford: OUP

Bogdanor, V, *Devolution in the United Kingdom*, 1999, Oxford: OUP

Boisvert, PY, 'Regionalism and decentralisation in France, with special reference to Corsica and its special status', unpublished DPhil thesis, 1988, University of Oxford

Börzel, TA, 'From competitive regionalism to co-operative federalism: the Europeanization of the Spanish state of the autonomies' (2000) 30 Publius 2

Breuilly, J, *Nationalism and the State*, 1993, Manchester: Manchester UP

Bulmer, S, *Efficiency, Democracy and West German Federalism: A Critical Analysis*, 1990, Manchester: European Policy Research Unit, University of Manchester

Bulpitt, J, *Territory and Power in the United Kingdom: an Interpretation*, 1983, Manchester: Manchester UP

Bundesrat (ed), The German *Bundesrat*, 2nd edn, 1992, Bonn: *Bundesrat*

Burrows, N, *Devolution*, 2000, London: Sweet & Maxwell

Canadian High Commission, 'Intergovernmental relations in Canada and the UK' (2001) conference proceedings (Chatham House Rules)

Cassese, S and Torchia, L, 'The meso level in Italy', in Sharpe, LJ (ed), *The Rise of Meso Government in Europe*, 1993, London: Sage

Cendón, AB, 'The intermediate level of government in Spain', in Larsson, T, Nomden, K and Petiteville, F (eds), *The Intermediate Level of Government in European States: Complexity Versus Democracy?*, 1999, Maastricht: EIPA, pp 127–74

Clark, RP, 'Euskadi: Basque nationalism in Spain since the civil war', in Foster, CR (ed), *Nations Without a State*, 1980, London: Praeger

Clark, RP, 'Spain's autonomous communities: a case study in ethnic power sharing' (1985) 11(1) European Studies Journal

Colomer, JM, 'The Spanish "state of the autonomies": non-institutional federalism', in Heywood, P (ed), *Politics and Policy in Democratic Spain*, 1999, London: Frank Cass

Committee of the Regions, 'Institutional Reform', 1995a, Brussels: CoR, European Union

Committee of the Regions, press release, April 21 1995b, Brussels: CoR, European Union

Condorelli, L, 'The powers of regions in the field of external relations: The Italian experience', in d'Alcantara, G, Genot, A and Morgan, R (eds), *The Reality of Regionalism in Europe: Its Impact on Political Institutions*, 1986, Leuven: Acco

Conseil Régional Wallon, *Budget des Recettes et des Dépenses de la Région Wallonne pour l'Année Budgétaire 1994*, 1993, Namur

Constitutional Convention, *Scotland's Parliament Scotland's Right*, 1996

Constitutional Convention, *Towards Scotland's Parliament*, 1992

Conzelmann, T, 'Networking and the politics of EU regional policy: lessons from North Rhine-Westphalia, Nord-Pas-de-Calais and North West England' (1995) 5(2) Regional and Federal Studies

Corte-Real, I, 'The regions in Portugal: a challenging theme for citizens, administrators and politicians', in Larsson, T, Nomden, K and Petiteville, F (eds), *The Intermediate Level of Government in European States: Complexity Versus Democracy?*, 1999, Maastricht: EIPA

Council of Europe, 'Allocation of powers to the local and regional levels of government in the member states of the Council of Europe' (1998) 42 Local and Regional Authorities in Europe Study series, Strasbourg

Council of Europe, 'Borrowing by local and regional authorities' (1992) 47 Local and Regional Authorities in Europe Study series, Strasbourg

Council of Europe, 'Structure and operation of local and regional democracy' (1993) National Reports, Strasbourg

Council of Europe, 'The situation of local finance in the Federal Republic of Germany' (1999) (6)3 CPL, Strasbourg

Covell, M, 'Federalization and federalism: Belgium and Canada', in Bakvis, H and Chandler, WM (eds), *Federalism and the Role of the State*, 1987, Toronto: Toronto UP

Covell, M, 'Regionalisation and economic crisis in Belgium: the variable origins of centrifugal and centripetal forces' (1986) 19 (June) Canadian Journal of Political Science

Craig, G, *Germany 1864–1945*, 1981, Oxford: OUP

Cuchillo, M, 'Autonomous communities as the Spanish meso', in Sharpe, LJ (ed), *The Rise of Meso Government in Europe*, 1993, London: Sage

Cullen, R, 'Adaptive federalism in Belgium' (1990) 13(2) University of New South Wales Law Journal

Daiches, D, *Selected Political Writings and Speeches of Andrew Fletcher of Saltoun*, 1979, Edinburgh: Scottish Academic Press

Daintith, T, 'The executive power today: bargaining and economic control', in Jowell, J and Olive, D (eds), *The Changing Constitution*, 1989, Oxford: OUP

Davis, R and Burnham, DJ, 'The role of the federal judiciary in the development of federalism in West Germany and the United States' (1989) 12 (Winter) Boston College International and Comparative Law Review

de Tocqueville, A, *Democracy in America*, 1835 (1945 edn), New York: Vintage Books

Deelen, B, 'Will Belgium survive its constitutional reforms?' (1994) Dutch Crossing

Delmartino, F, 'Belgium: in search of the meso level', in Sharpe, LJ (ed), *The Rise of Meso Government in Europe*, 1993, London: Sage

Demeester-De Meyer, W, *Flanders: A Reliable Financial Partner*, 1993, Brussels: Vlaamse Executive

Dertnig, C and Handstanger, M, 'L'Autriche', in Engel, C (ed), *Le Rôle des Régions dans l'Exercice des Compétences Externes des Etats en Europe Occidentale*, 1992, Brussels: TEPSA

Desideri, L and Sanantonio, V, 'Building a third level in Europe: prospects and difficulties' (1997) 6(2) Regional and Federal Studies 1980

DETR, *Regional Government in England: A Preliminary Review of Literature and Research Findings*, 2000, London: Department of Environment, Transport and the Regions

Donaghy, PJ and Newton, MT, *Spain: A Guide to Political and Economic Institutions*, 1997, Cambridge: CUP

Douence, J-C, 'The evolution of the 1982 regional reforms: an overview' (1994) 4(3) Regional Politics and Policy

Dutch Ministry of Foreign Affairs, *The Kingdom of the Netherlands: Facts and Figures (The Constitution)*, 1980, The Hague

Dyson, K, *The State Tradition in Western Europe*, 1980, Oxford: Martin Robertson

Elander, I and Montin, S, 'Decentralisation and control: central-local government relations in Sweden' (1990) 18(3) Regional Politics and Policy

Elazar, DJ (ed), *Federal Systems of the World*, 1991, London: Longman

Elazar, DJ, 'From statism to federalism: a paradigm shift' (1995) 25 Publius 2

Ellis, PB and Mac a'Ghobainn, S, *The Scottish Insurrection of 1820*, 1989, London: Pluto

Engel C, 'Germany', in *Trends in Regional and Local Government in the European Community*, 1993, Leuven: Acco

Engel, C, 'Allemagne', from Engel, C (ed), *Le Rôle des Régions dans l'Exercice des Compétences Externes des Etats en Europe Occidentale*, 1992, Brussels: TEPSA

Engel, C, 'Rapport général de synthèse', in Engel, C (ed), *Le Rôle des Régions dans l'Exercice des Compétences Externes des Etats en Europe Occidentale*, 1992a, Brussels: TEPSA

Engel, C and Van Ginderachter, J, *Trends in Regional and Local Government in the European Community*, 1993, Leuven: Acco

Erk, C and Gagnon, A-G, 'Constitutional ambiguity and federal trust: codification of federalism in Canada, Spain and Belgium' (2000) 10(1) Regional and Federal Studies

European Commission Committee for the Study of Economic and Monetary Union, 'Report on Economic and Monetary Union in the European Community', 1989, Brussels

European Parliament, 'The powers of regional and local authorities and their role in the European Union', in the Regional Policy series, 1993, Strasbourg: European Parliament Directorate General of Research

Federal Ministry of Finance, *An ABC of Taxes in the Federal Republic of Germany*, 1993, Bonn

Fesler, JW, 'Approaches to the understanding of decentralisation' (1965) 27(4) Journal of Politics

Fitzmaurice, J, 'Reluctant federalism' (1984) 37 (autumn) Parl Aff

Fitzmaurice, J, *Politics in Denmark*, 1981, London: Hurst

Fitzmaurice, J, *The Politics of Belgium: A Unique Federalism*, 1996, London: Hurst

Fortier, DH, 'Brittany: *Breiz Atao*', in Foster, CR (ed), *Nations Without a State*, 1980, London: Praeger

Foster, CD, Jackman, RA and Perlman, M, *Local Government Finance in a Unitary State*, 1980, London: Allen & Unwin

Foster, CR (ed), *Nations Without a State: Ethnic Nationalism in Western Europe*, 1980, London: Praeger

Foster, N, *German Law and Legal System*, 1996, London: Blackstone

Gellner, E, *Nations and Nationalism*, 1983, Oxford: Blackwell

German Community, *Haushalt de Einnahmen und der Ausgaben der Deutschsprachigen Gemeinschaft für das Hauhalsjahr*, 1992, Eupen

German Federal Ministry of Finance, *An ABC of Taxes in the Federal Republic of Germany*, 1993, Bonn

Gerstenlauer, H, 'German *Länder* in the EC', in Jones, B and Keating, M (eds), *The European Union and the Regions*, 1995, Oxford: OUP

Giannini, 'Le regioni: retticia e prospettive' (1973) Nord e Sud

Giarda, P, *Regioni e Federalismo Fiscale*, 1995, Bologna: Società il Mulino

Gilbert, G and Guengant, A, 'France: shifts in local authority finance', in Bennett, RJ (ed), *Territory and Administration in Europe*, 1990, London: Pinter

Gilbert, G, 'The finances of the French regions in retrospect' (1994) 4(3) Regional Politics and Policy

Gildea, R, *Barricades and Borders*, 1987, Oxford: OUP

Gonzalez, P, 'A model of political decentralisation: the Spanish case', MSc thesis, University of Salford 1987 (Pub 38/556)

Government of Flanders, 'Fiscal federalism', undated, Brussels

Guide Statistique de la Fiscalité Directe Locale, 1993, Paris: French Ministry of the Interior

Gunlicks, AB, '*Land* constitutions in Germany' (1998) 28 Publius 4, pp 105–26

Haibach, G and Serong, S, 'Structure and tasks of the *Länder* and the administrative districts within the federal political structure of Germany', in Larsson, T, Nomden, K and Petiteville, F (eds), *The Intermediate Level of Government in European States: Complexity Versus Democracy?*, 1999, Maastricht: EIPA

Hansen, T, 'Meso government in Denmark and Sweden', in Sharpe, LJ (ed), *The Rise of Meso Government in Europe*, 1993, London: Sage

Harden, I, 'Democracy and the European Union', 1996, presented at the Centre for Socio-Legal Studies seminar series

Harden, I, 'Denmark', in 'European Community budgets', discussion paper, University of Sheffield, 1993

Harloff, EM, *The Structure of Local Government in Europe*, 1987, The Hague: IULA

Harris, DJ, *Cases and Materials on International Law*, 3rd edn, 1983, London: Sweet & Maxwell

Hayward, JES, *Governing France: The One and Indivisible Republic*, 1983, London: Weidenfeld & Nicolson

Hazell, R (ed), *The State and The Nations*, 2000, London: Imprint Academic

Hazell, R, *Regional Government in England*, 1996, London: Constitution Unit

Heald, D and Geaughan, N, 'Financing a Scottish Parliament', paper presented at *Beyond Westminster: The Practical Issues*, conference at Parliament Building, Edinburgh, April 1995

Heichlinger, A, *A Regional Representation in Brussels: The Right Idea for Influencing EU Policy Making*, 1999, Brussels: EIPA

Heilbronner, K, 'Subsidiarity as a principle of law', paper presented at *Europäishce Rechtsakademie Trier*, annual conference in Trier, October 1993

Herdegen, M, 'After the TV judgment of the German Constitutional Court: decision making within the EU Council and the German *Länder*' (1995) 32 CMLR

Heywood, P, *The Government and Politics of Spain*, 1995, London: Macmillan

Hine, D, *Governing Italy*, 1993, Oxford: Clarendon

Hingorani, S, 'Territorial justice in the unified Germany: financial equalization, the *Länder* and the Federal Constitutional Court' (1997) 29 Applied Geography, p 4

Hobsbawm, E, *The Age of Revolutions*, 1962, London: Weidenfeld & Nicolson

Hopkins, WJ, 'Regional government in the European Union', in Tindale, S (ed), *The State and the Nations: The Politics of Devolution*, 1996, London: IPPR

Hopkins, WJ, 'The dog that didn't bark: regions and the IGC', in Lazarowicz, M (ed), *New Scotland, New Europe: Scotland and the Expanding European Union*, 1999, Edinburgh: Centre for Scottish Public Policy

Hopkins, WJ, 'The Union of 1707: an historical interpretation of the Anglo-Scottish Union', 1992, unpublished Honours thesis, University of Strathclyde, Glasgow

Irving, D, 'Constitutional change in the United Kingdom', National Heritage lecture, May 1998, US Supreme Court, Washington DC

Ivonen, J (ed), *The Future of the Nation State in Europe*, 1993, Cheltenham: Edward Elgar

Jeffrey, C, 'The *Länder* strike back: structures and procedures of European integration policy making in the German federal system', 1994, FS 94/2, Leicester University: Discussion Papers in Federal Studies

Jones, B and Keating, M (eds), *The European Union and the Regions*, 1995, Oxford: OUP

Jones, GW, 'Central-local government relations: grants, local responsibility and minimum standards', in Butler, D and Halsey, AH (eds), *Policy and Politics*, 1978, London: Macmillan

Keating, M (ed), *Regions in the European Community*, 1986, London: Clarendon

Keating, M and Hainsworth, P, *Decentralisation and Change in Contemporary France*, 1986, Aldershot: Gower

Keating, M and Rhodes, M (eds), 'Is there a regional level of government in England?' (1979) 49 Studies in Public Policy, University of Strathclyde, Glasgow

Keating, M, 'Decentralisation in Mitterand's France' (1983) 61 Public Administration

Keating, M, 'The continental *meso*: regions and the European Community', in Sharpe, LJ (ed), *The Rise of Meso Government in Europe*, 1992, London: Sage

Keating, M, *States and Regional Nationalism*, 1988, Hemel Hempstead: Harvester Wheatsheaf

Keating, M, *The New Regionalism in Western Europe*, 1998, Cheltenham: Edward Elgar

Keldourie, E, *Nationalism*, 1961, London: Hutchinson

Kendle, J, *Federal Britain: A History*, 1997, London: Routledge

King, RL, 'Regional government: the Italian experience' (1987) 5 Environment and Planning C: Government and Policy

Klatt, H, 'German unification and the federal system', in Jeffrey, C and Ronald, S (eds), *Federalism, Unification and European Integration*, London: Frank Cass

Klemmer, P, 'Regional economic policy within the framework of co-operative federalism' (1989) 7 Environment Planning C: Government and Policy

Kliemt, H, 'Subsidiarity as a guiding principle of constitutional design and of constitutional adjudication', paper presented at *Subsidiarity and Democracy*, conference at Manchester University, November 1993

Knecht, RJ, *The French Wars of Religion 1559–1598*, 1991, London: Longman

Kofman, E, 'Regional autonomy and the one and indivisible French Republic' (1985) 3 Environment and Planning C: Government and Policy

Kol, J, 'Subsidiarity: concept and application', paper presented at the 8th Lothian Conference, Egham, December 1993

Kommers, DT, *The Constitutional Jurisprudence of the Federal Republic of Germany*, 2nd edn, 1997, North Carolina: Duke UP

Kortmann, AJM and Bovend'Eert, PPT, *The Kingdom of the Netherlands: An Introduction to Dutch Constitutional Law* 1993, Deventer: Kluwer

Langset, M, 'Intermediate level of public administration and government in Sweden: structure, history and recent developments', in Larsson, T, Nomden, K and Petiteville, F (eds), *The Intermediate Level of Government in European States: Complexity Versus Democracy?*, 1999, Maastricht: EIPA, pp 347–70

Larsson, T, 'The organisation of the intermediate level of government in European states', in Larsson, T, Nomden, K and Petiteville, F (eds), *The Intermediate Level of Government in European States: Complexity Versus Democracy?*, 1999, Maastricht: EIPA, pp 1–20

Lawrence, GRP, *Problem Regions of Europe*, 1973, Milton Keynes: OUP

Le Galès, P, 'Regional economic policies: an alternative to French economic dirigisme?' (1995) 4(3) Regional Politics and Policy

Le Galès, P and John, P, 'Is the grass greener on the other side? What went wrong with French regions, and the implications for England' (1998) 25 Publius 1

Leicester, G, *Scotland's Parliament*, 1996, London: Constitution Unit

Leitner, C and Neuhold, C, 'The intermediate level of government and administration in Austria', in Larsson, T, Nomden, K and Petiteville, F (eds), *The Intermediate Level of Government in European States: Complexity Versus Democracy?*, 1999, Maastricht: EIPA

Leonard, D, 'At last, a federal Belgium', *The Bulletin*, 29 April 1993, Brussels

Leonard, D, 'Dehaene draws new federal map of Belgium', *The Bulletin*, 8 October 1992, Brussels

Leonardi, R and Nanetti, RY (eds), *The Regions and European Integration: The Case of Emilia-Romagna*, 1990, London: Pinter

Leonardi, R, 'Political developments and institutional change in Emilia-Romagna, 1970–1990', in Leonardi, R and Nanetti, RY (eds), *The Regions and European Integration: The Case of Emilia-Romagna*, 1990, London: Pinter

Leonardy, MA, *The German Model of Federalism*, 1994, Centre for Comparative Constitutional Studies, Melbourne: University of Melbourne

Les Budgets Primitifs des Régions en 1993, 1993, Paris: French Ministry of the Interior

Les Finances Régionales, 1986–92, Paris: French Ministry of the Interior

Lewis, JR and Williams, AM, 'Regional autonomy and the European communities: the view from Portugal's Atlantic islands' (1994) 4(2) Regional Politics and Policy

Limbach, J, 'The German Constitutional Court as a source of political power' (1996) 12 HFR, www.humboldt-forum-recht.de

Loughlin, J, *Subnational Democracy in the European Union*, 2001, Oxford: OUP

Mäki-Lohiluoma, K-P, 'Intermediate level of public administration in Finland', in Larsson, T, Nomden, K and Petiteville, F (eds), *The Intermediate Level of Government in European States: Complexity Versus Democracy?*, 1999, Maastricht: EIPA, pp 329–46

Malcolm, N, *Bosnia: A Short History*, 1996, London: Macmillan

Marr, A, *The Battle for Scotland*, 1992, London: Penguin

Mazey, S, 'Developments at the French meso level: modernizing the French state', in Sharpe, LJ (ed), *The Rise of Meso Government in Europe*, 1993, London: Sage

Mazey, S, 'French regions and the European Union' (1994) 4(3) Regional Politics and Policy

Merino-Blanco, E, The Spanish Legal System, 1996, London: Sweet & Maxwell

Michel, F, 'The intermediate level of administration in Italy: from "fragmentation" to "cooperative regionalism"', in Larsson, T et al (eds), *The Intermediate Level of Government in European States: Complexity versus Democracy?*, 1999, Maastricht: EIPA

Mill, JS, *On Liberty*, 1859 (1989 edn), Cambridge: CUP

Mill, JS, *On Representative Government*, 1861 (1931 edn), London: Dent

Minority Rights Group, 'Basques and Catalans' report, 1985, London

Mira, AXL, 'Portugal: the resistance to change in the state model' (1999) 9(2) Regional and Federal Studies

Mitchell, J, *Strategies For Self-Government: The Campaigns for a Scottish Parliament*, 1996, Polygon: Edinburgh

Montserrat, C, 'The autonomous communities as the Spanish meso', in Sharpe, LJ (ed), *The Rise of Meso Government in Europe*, 1993, London: Sage

Morass, M, 'Austria: the case of a federal newcomer in European union politics' (1996) 7(2) Regional and Federal Studies

Morata, F, 'Spanish regions in the EC', in Jones, B and Keating, M (eds), *The European Union and the Regions*, 1995, Oxford: OUP, pp 115–33

Newton, M and Donaghy, PJ, *Spain: A Guide to Political and Economic Institutions*, 1997, Cambridge: CUP

Oates, WE, *The Political Economy of Fiscal Federalism*, 1972, Lexington: Lexington Books

OECD, *Spain*, OECD Economic Surveys 1992–93, 1993, Paris: OECD

Oliveres, AC, 'Financing regional government in Spain: main trends and a comparative perspective' (1987) 5 Environment and Planning C: Government and Policy

Orridge, AW, 'Varieties of nationalism', in Tivey, L (ed), *The Nation State*, 1981, Oxford: Martin Robertson

Osmond, J, 'A constitutional convention by other means: the first year of the National Assembly for Wales', in Hazell, R (ed), *The State and the Nations: The First Year of Devolution in the United Kingdom*, 2000, London: Imprint Academic

Paterson, WE and Southern, D, *Governing Germany*, 1991, Oxford: Blackwell

Pennings, F, 'Is the subsidiarity principle useful to guide the European integration process?' (1993) 2(2) Tilburg Foreign Law Review

Petrella, R, 'Nationalist and regional movements in Western Europe', in Foster, CR (ed), *Nations Without a State*, 1980, London: Praeger

Polet, R, 'Intermediate level in Belgium? The participation of communities and regions in state power', in Larsson, T, Nomden, K and Petiteville, F (eds), *The Intermediate Level of Government in European States: Complexity Versus Democracy?*, 1999, Maastricht: EIPA, pp 21–48

Prud'Homme, R, 'Decentralization of expenditure or taxes: the case of France', in Bennett, RJ (ed), *Decentralisation, Local Government and Markets*, 1990, Oxford: Clarendon

Reed, R, 'Devolution and the judiciary', in *Constitutional Reform in the United Kingdom: Practice and Principles*, 1998, Oxford: Hart, pp 21–32

Renzsch, W, 'Financing German unity: fiscal conflict resolution in a complex federation' (1998) 28 Publius 4, pp 127–46

Rhodes, RAW, 'Regional policy planning and a "Europe of the regions"', in Gillinwater, D and Hart, DA (eds), *The Regional Planning Process*, 1978, Farnborough: Saxon House

Richard, J, *St Louis*, 1992, Cambridge: CUP

Richardson, HN, *Regional Development Policy and Planning in Spain*, 1975, Farnborough: Saxon House

Riker, WH, *Federalism: Origin, Operation, Significance*, 1964, Boston: Little Brown

Rogers, V, 'Devolution and economic development in France' (1998) 26 Policy and Politics 4

Rokkan, S and Urwin, D (eds), *The Politics of Territorial Identity*, 1982, London: Sage

Rosas, A, 'Internal self-determination', in Tomuschat, C (ed), *Modern Law of Self-Determination*, 1993, Dordrecht: Nijhoff

Rousseau, MO, 'France: the bureaucratic state and political reforms', in *Regionalism and Regional Devolution in Comparative Perspective*, 1987, London: Praeger

Rudé, G, *Revolutionary Europe 1783–1815*, 1964, London: Fontana

Russell, M, *Reforming the House of Lords*, 2000, Oxford: OUP

Sanantonio, E, 'Italy', in Goldsmith, M and Page, E (eds), *Central and Local Government Relations*, 1987, London: Sage

Savigear, P, 'Corsica and the French State', in Foster, CR (ed), *Nations Without a State*, 1980, London: Praeger

Scharpf, FW, 'The joint decision trap: lessons from German federalism and European integration' (1988) 6 Public Administration

Schmidt, V, *Democratising France: The Political and Administrative History of Decentralisation*, 1990, Cambridge: CUP

Schmitt, N, 'The foreign policy of Spanish autonomous communities compared to that of the Swiss cantons', in de Villiers, B (ed), *Evaluating Federalism*, 1994, Dordrecht: Nijhoff, pp 362–92

Schweitzer, C-C, Karsten, D, Spencer, R, Cole, RT, Kommers, DP and Nicholls, A, *Politics and Government in the Federal Republic of Germany: Basic Documents*, 1984, Leamington Spa: Berg

Schweitzer, C-C, Karsten, D, Spencer, R, Cole, RT, Kommers, DP and Nicholls, A, *Politics and Government in Germany 1944-1994*, 1995, Oxford: Berghahn

Scottish Office, *Scotland's Parliament*, Cm 3658, 1997, London: HMSO

Scottish Office, *The Structure of Local Government in Scotland: Shaping the New Councils*, 1992, Edinburgh: HMSO

Secretary of State for Scotland, *Scotland in the Union*, 1993, Edinburgh: HMSO

Senelle, R, 'The role of the communities and the regions in the making of Belgian foreign policy' (1999) 5 EPL 4

Serignan, M 'L'évolution des relations entre la CEE et les collectivités territoriaux' (1989) 214–15 (May–June) Après-Demain

Sevilla-Segura, JV, 'Financial aspects of political decentralization in Spain' (1987) 5 Environment and Planning C: Government and Policy

Sharpe, LJ (ed), *The Rise of Meso Government in Europe*, 1993, London: Sage

Sharpe, LJ, 'The European meso: an appraisal', in Sharpe, LJ (ed), *The Rise of Meso Government in Europe*, 1993a, London: Sage

Sharpe, LJ, 'United Kingdom: the disjointed meso', in Sharpe, LJ (ed), *The Rise of Meso Government in Europe*, 1993b, London: Sage

Simeon, R, 'Recent trends in federalism and intergovernmental relations in Canada: lessons for the UK' (2000) April 354 Round Table, p 231

Smith, A, *The Wealth of Nations*, 1812 (1880 edn, reprinted), London: Routledge

Smith, BC, *Decentralisation: The Territorial Dimension of the State*, 1985, London: Allen & Unwin

Solé-Vilanova, J, 'Regional and local finance in Spain: is fiscal responsibility the missing element?', in Bennett, RJ (ed), *Decentralisation, Local Government and Markets*, 1990, Oxford: Clarendon

Spanish Ministry of Public Finance, *Informe Sobre la Financiación de las Comunidades Autonomías*, 1986–92, Madrid

Spicker, P, 'Concepts of subsidiarity in the European Community', paper presented at Subsidiarity and Democracy, conference at Manchester University, November 1993

Spott, F and Wieser, T, *Italy, a Difficult Democracy*, 1986, Cambridge: CUP

State Commission Report 27, 1995, Stockholm: Swedish Official Publications

Statistiches Jahrbuch für die Bundesrepublik Deutschland, 1990, Stuttgart: Metzler-Poeschel Verlag

Sunquist, JL, 'American federalism: evolution, status and prospects' (1987) 19(3) Urban Lawyer

Swan, GS, 'Quasi-federal reforms in Belgium: the 1987 crisis in a constitutional perspective' (1988) 2 (Spring) Journal of International Dispute Resolution

Thomas, P, 'Belgium's north-south divide and the Walloon regional problem' (1990) 76 Applied Geography

Tiebout, CM, 'A pure theory of local expenditures', in Edel and Rothenberg (eds), *Readings in Local Economics*, 1972, New York: Macmillan

Tindale, S, 'Options for English regional government', paper presented at Beyond *Westminster: The Practical Issues*, conference at Parliament Building, Edinburgh, April 1995

Tipton, CL, *Nationalism in the Middle Ages*, 1972, New York: Holt

Tivey, L, 'Introduction', in Tivey, L (ed), *The Nation State*, 1981, Oxford: Martin Robertson

Tomaney, J, 'The Regional Governance of England', in Hazell, R (ed), *The State and the Nations*, 2000, London: Imprint Academic

Toonen, TAJ, 'Dutch provinces and the struggle for the meso', in Sharpe, LJ (ed), *The Rise of Meso Government in Europe*, 1993, London: Sage

Van Ginderachter, J, 'Les compétences internationales des communautés et des régions en Belgique' (1993a) 44(2) Studia Diplomatica

Van Ginderachter, J, 'The Belgian federal model', paper presented at Federalism and Subsidiarity Within the EC, Lothian Foundation Conference, London, 18 December 1993

Vanwelkenhuysen, A, 'Arbitration in conflicts between regions or between a region and the federal or national authorities', in d'Alcantara, G, Genot, A and Morgan, R (eds), *The Reality of Regionalism in Europe: Its impact on Political Institutions*, 1986, Leuven: Acco

Villiers, C, *The Spanish Legal Tradition: An Introduction to the Spanish Law And Legal System*, 1999, Aldershot: Ashgate

Von Hagen, J, 'Monetary union and fiscal union: a perspective from fiscal federalism', in Masson, P and Taylor, M (eds), *The Operation of Currency Unions*, 1992, New York: Academic Press

Wallace, H and Wilke, M, *Subsidiarity: Approaches to Power Sharing in the European Community*, 1990, London: Royal Institute of International Affairs

Watts, RL, 'Contemporary views on federalism', in de Villiers, B (ed), *Evaluating Federalism*, 1994, Dordrecht: Nijhoff

Watts, RL, 'Federalism, regionalism and political integration', in Cameron, D (ed), *Regionalism and Supranationalism*, 1981, Montreal: Institute for Research on Public Policy

Wheare, KC, *Federalism*, 1953, Oxford: OUP

Wildhaber, L, 'External relations of the Swiss cantons' (1974) 12 Canadian Yearbook of International Law

Wolman, H, 'Decentralisation: what is it and why should we care?', in Bennett, RJ (ed), *Decentralisation, Local Government and Markets*, 1990, Oxford: Clarendon

Zariski, R, 'Italy: the distributive state and the consequences of late unification', in Rousseau, MO and Zariski, R (eds), *Regionalism and Regional Devolution*, 1987, London: Praeger

Zimmermann, H, 'Fiscal Equalization between states in West Germany' (1989) 7 Environment and Planning C: Government and Policy